GLOBALISATION AND LABOUR MARKET DYNAMICS

Perspectives, Polemics and Policies

GLOBALISATION AND LABOUR MARKET DYNAMICS

Perspectives, Polemics and Policies

Edited By

Parvesh K. Chopra

Globalisation and Labour Market Dynamics:
Perspectives, Polemics and Policies

First published in 2016 by

Wisdom House Publications Ltd.

Unique House, 1 Dolly Lane, LeedsLS9 7NN, England (United Kingdom)
Tel: +44 (0)113 2420555 Fax: +44 (0) 113 2420963
Email: editor@wisdomhousepublications.co.uk
Internet: www.wisdomhousepublications.co.uk
Simultaneously published in India by

Wisdom House Academic Publishers Pvt. Ltd.

126, Housing Board Colony,
Ambala Cantt. – 133 001, Haryana, India.
Tel: +91 (171) 2821237, 2821299, Fax: +91 (171) 2821282
E-mail: Wisdom_hap@yahoo.co.in
Internet: www.wisdomhousepublications.co.uk

First edition 2016

British library cataloguing in publication data

Chopra, Parvesh K.

Globalisation and Labour Market Dynamics:
Perspectives, Polemics and Policies

ISBN 978-1-84290-250-9 Paperback; ISBN 978-1-84290-251-6 Hardbound

Cover design by Keen Print, Bradford (UK).

Book formatted by www.bookformatting.co.uk

Contents

List of Tables

List of Figures

Also By Parvesh K. Chopra

Measuring Country Risk (2016)

Quality, Excellence and Measurement: A Tribute to Professor Gopal K. Kanji

On Measuring Global Food Crisis: A Multivariate Modelling Approach

Management with Measurement: Can't Measure Can't Manage (with Gopal K. Kanji)

Existing but not Living: Studies in Poverty and Inequality (with B.N. Ghosh)

Poverty as Human Contestability Failure

Globalisation, Human Degradation and Unequal Competition (with B.N. Ghosh)

Political Economy of Rural Poverty Alleviation Measures in India

A Dictionary of Research Methods (with B.N. Ghosh)

Gender and Development (2 Volumes) (with B.N. Ghosh)

A Dictionary of Statistics

A Dictionary of Demography and Human Development (with B.N. Ghosh)

Economics: Basics and Beyond

Logic, Scientific Method and Economic Analysis (1987)

A TRIBUTE TO PROFESSOR B.N. GHOSH (1942 - 2014)

Notes On Contributors

Ahmet Aker is Professor of Economics and Chair, Department of Business Administration, Faculty of Economics and Administrative Science. Cyprus International University. Dr Aker's main skills and expertise are in the areas of international economics and the economy of North Cyprus. Professor Aker has supervised various theses and introduced research and writing projects in his department. He has a long experience of teaching and research, and has published a large number of papers in refereed journals and attended many national and international conferences. Email: aaker@ciu.edu.tr

Amitava Krishna Dutt is Professor of Economics and Political Science in the Department of Political Science, University of Notre Dame, USA, and Distinguished Professor of Economics at FLACSO, Quito, Ecuador. His research focuses on the political economy of development, growth and distribution, and international uneven development. Professor Dutt is the author/editor of several books, including *Growth, Distribution and Uneven Development* (Cambridge University Press, 1990) and *Pathways to Economic Development* (Oxford University Press, 2014) and the author of over 150 articles/papers in edited volumes and journals such as *American Economic Review*, *Cambridge Journal of Economics*, *Journal of Development Economics*, *Journal of Post Keynesian Economics*, *Oxford Economic Papers*, and *World Development*. He is a coeditor of the journal *Metroeconomica*. Email: adutt@nd.edu

B. N. Ghosh was a Visiting Professor of Economics at the Institute of Management and Technology, Punnapra (Kerala), Govt. of Kerala, and also at Sir John Hicks College of Economics and Management, Leeds (UK). Formerly, he was the Director of IMT, Kerala. He has taught in a few universities in India and Malaysia for a long time. He worked in Eastern Mediterranean University, North Cyprus as a Visiting Professor of Economics for many years. He had also a stint as a Visiting Professor at Zhejiang Gongshang University, China. He wrote extensively in refereed professional journals. His research works have been published in India, USA, UK, Canada, Korea, Italy, Malaysia, Singapore, Bangladesh, Netherlands and Philippines. He has written, edited and co-authored a large number of books. His books have been published by, among others, Arnold-Heinemann, Longman, Macmillan, Ashgate (London), Wisdom House (England), Nova Science Publishers (New York), Palgrave-Macmillan and Routledge, London and New York, Oxford University Press and Sage Publications, New Delhi, among others. Upon invitation, Prof. Ghosh delivered special lectures/attended international conferences in Malaysia, Florence, England, Tunisia, Iran, India and China, among other countries. He has undertaken short-term consultancies for various organizations including the, UGC, UNDP and the Govt. of

Malaysia. He was Chief Editor of *Journal of Human Development*. Professor Ghosh was the recipient of the Emerald Award (UK) for the year 2006.

Dany Lang is Associate Professor (maître de conferences) in economics at the Université of Paris 13, Sorbonne Paris Cité and coordinator of the task group "International macroeconomics and Post-Keynesian analyses" of the CEPN (Center of Economics of Paris North, National Center for Scientific Research). He works mainly on Post-Keynesian economics, including growth, income distribution, unemployment issues and path-dependence and the importance of time in economics. He is the author of *Hysteresis in Unemployment: Time, Unemployment, and Economic Dynamics* (VDM Verlag, 2009) and of various papers published in journals such as *Journal of Post-Keynesian Economics*, *Review of Political Economy*, *International Journal of Political Economy*, *Intervention*, and *International Review of Applied Economics*. Email: dany.lang.p13@gmail.com

Fatma Güven-Lisaniler is Associate Professor of Economics in the Department of Economics of Eastern Mediterranean University, Famagusta, North Cyprus. She got her Ph.D in Economics (1994) from University of Istanbul, Turkey. She is the Chair of Center for Women's Studies of the University. She has a book, *Assessing the Status of Women: A Step Towards Equality*, (2004) on gender equality in the labor market and education in North Cyprus. She has publications in academic journals and chapters in books on Cyprus problem, migrant workers, and gender equality in the labor market. She was involved in various domestic and international researches. Current researches are "Analysis of the Labour Market of North Cyprus" and "Assessment of Unregistered Economy in North Cyprus". Dr. Güven-Lisaniler is also Editor of international refereed journal *Kadın/Woman 2000, Journal for Women's Studies*. Email: fatma.guven@emu.edu.tr

Jacqueline Liza Fernandez is a Senior Lecturer at School of Social Sciences, Universiti Sains Malaysia, 11800 Penang, Malaysia. Dr. Fernandez earned her B.Sc., M.Sc. in the field of Social Sciences from Universiti Sains Malaysia and obtained her PhD (Economics) from the University of Malaya. Dr. Fernandez's main research interests include international and comparative labour, human resources, labour economics, labour supply, gender and labour in Malaysia. Dr Fernandez supervises postgraduate research in the field of labour economics and gender-related issues. She has written several conference papers and published articles in the area of gender and work. Email: fjacq@usm.my

Jacques Hersh is Professor Emeritus at the Research Center on Development and International Relations, Aalborg University, Denmark. Born in Paris and after receiving accreditation from the City College of New York, the University of Vienna, and the University of Copenhagen, Dr Hersh became a Professor in Development Theory and International Relations at Aalborg University. Professor Hersh wrote extensively on a variety of subjects including the system of capitalist development, Soviet-Third World relations, the US's role in the rise of East Asia, human rights, globalisation, neo-liberalism, among others. Correspondence and contact details: Fibigerstraede 3, 9220 Aalborg, Denmark; Tel: +45 9940 8404; Fax: +45 9815 5346. Email: jac.ellen@gmail.com

Jay Drydyk is Professor of Philosophy at Carleton University in Canada. Dr Drydyk was elected a Fellow of the *Human Development and Capability Association*, and Past President of the *International Development Ethics Association*. Professor Drydyk is interested in how human rights, justice, and democracy can be understood from global and cross-cultural perspectives. His major works include *Global Justice, Global Democracy: Prospects for a New Internationalism* (1997), *Global Ethics, Capabilities, and Human Rights; Displacement by Development: Ethics, Rights, and Responsibilities* (Cambridge, 2011); *Theorizing Justice: Critical Insights and Future Directions* (2016), among others. His work on the values of development ethics and on disempowering processes arises from two projects on development-induced displacement, one funded by CIDA and Shastri Indo-Canadian Institute, and another on empowerment funded by the Social Sciences and Humanities Research Council of Canada. Dr Drydyk is author of numerous journal publications on ethics and development, the capabilities approach, social and global justice, human rights, and global ethics. Dr Drydyk won a Carleton University Teaching Achievement Award in 2002. Email: jay-drydyk@carleton.ca

Johannes Dragsbaek Schmidt is Associate Professor, The Faculty of Social Sciences, Department of Political Science, Aalborg University, Denmark. Dr Schmidt is also associated with associated organisations namely Global Refugee Studies and Global Development Studies. He has published books and research papers in the areas such as work and labour market, business economics and trade, sociology and social conditions, politics and administration including globalisation, international politics and economy, human rights and terrorism. His research works have been published invarious journals including *Canadian Journal of development Studies*, *ASEAS*, *Copenhagen Journal of Asian Studies*, *Globalisations*, *Global Peace*, *Journ*al *of Human Development*, *Journal of Development Studies*, *Ny Verden, Nordjyske Stiftstidende*, among others. His main publishers include Adonis & Abbey, Ashgate, Curzon Press, Edward Elgar, Gyan Publishings, Longman, Palgrave Macmillan, Nova Science Publishers (New York), Palgrave-Macmillan, Routledge, Springer, Serials Publications, among others. Email: jds@dps.aau.dk

Myron J. Frankman, Professor of Economics, McGill University 855 Sherbrooke St. West, Montreal, Quebec, Canada H3A 2T7 and Senior Research Fellow, Centre for International Sustainable Development Law, Canada. Dr Frankman retired from McGrill University in 2010 where he taught development economics and was the founding Director of the International Development Studies program from its creation in 1992 until 2008. The research interests of Dr Frankman include economic development, employment and poverty, global federalism and taxation, among others. Professor Frankman's early writings are on economic policy in the Andean countries. His current concern with world institutional change consistent with a sustainable and just global order is explored in his latest book, *World Democratic Federalism: Peace and Justice Invisible* (London: Palgrave Macmillan, 2004). Email: myron.frankman @mcfill.ca

Nancy Doubleday is a Professor, Department of Philosophy and holds the HOPE Chair in Peace and Health at McMaster University, Canada. Dr Doubleday holds an LLB from Osgoode Hall, PhD from Queen's University, Canada and is a member of the Law Society of Canada. She joined the Department of Philosophy and the *Centre for Peace Studies* at McMaster University in 2009. Professor Doubleday is a biologist and lawyer with extensive national and international experience in Arctic issues, health, environment, justice, human rights, and environmental science related to policy and governance. Dr Doubleday works in resilience and adaptive co-management; particularly with integration and mobilization of knowledge to promote peace and health. Currently Professor Doubleday chairs the *Cold Region Environments Commission of the International Geographical Union* and has just completed a major International Polar Year research project addressing human experience of impacts of a changing tree line to better understand change and adaptive capacity in social-ecological systems. Email: doublen@mcmaster.ca

Ozay Mehmet is a Distinguished Research Professor and Professor Emeritus, International Affairs, Carleton University, Ottawa, Canada. He has specialized in economic development with special reference to Asian Tigers. Since retirement he has taught economics and during 2008-2010 served as Dean of the Faculty of Business and Economics, Eastern Mediterranean University, North Cyprus. He has over 25 books and monographs and over 100 scholarly articles on global economic issues, including international migration and labor market dynamics. He has consulted extensively for such bodies as the World Bank, Asian Development Bank, UNDP, WHO, ILO, CIDA, etc. Most recently, he has shifted his research interests to Turkish political economy, writing on Turkey-EU relations and the Cyprus Problem. He has also started writing historical novels about Cyprus, including UZUN ALI, ANGELINA'S TREASURE. Email: mehmet5010@rogers.com

Padmaja D. Namboodiri took her masters, M.Phil, Ph.D from the University of Kerala, India. She joined the department of Economics of Sanatana Dharma College in 1985 and has been teaching at the graduate and post graduate levels. Her area of research is growth economics and her PhD is on *The Constraints on Growth of the Kerala State*. Dr Namboodiri is a regular faculty member for the refresher courses conducted by the Academic College of UGC, University of Kerala. She has presented papers in international, national and regional seminars. Her recent publications include, *The Economy of Kerala: Yesterday, Today and Tomorrow* (2009). Email: drpadmajadn@gmail.com

Parthiban S. Gopal is a Senior Lecturer, Development Planning and Management, School of Social Sciences, Universiti Sains Malaysia, 11800 Penang, Malaysia. Dr Gopal's main research interests include poverty issues (urban and rural), development economics, human capital development, Indian studies, among others. Email: parthi@usm.my

Parvesh K. Chopra is Director of *International Centre for Development and Performance Management* at Sir John Hicks College of Economics and Management, Leeds, England. He received his education in India and England, taught Economics at various levels and published singly or jointly various research papers and 18 books. His major recent publications include: *Measuring Country Risk*, *Quality, Excellence and Measurement*, *Poverty as Human Contestability Failure*, *A Dictionary of Research Methods*, *Management with Measurement: Can't Measure Can't Manage* (Co-author), *Development Macroeconomics, Global Issues and Human Development* (ed.), *On Measuring Global Food Crisis: A Multivariate Modelling Approach.* Dr Chopra's research has ranged over a number of areas including human contestability, country risk, poverty and inequality, emotional intelligence, gender and development, environmental health, corporate social responsibility, performance management, development macroeconomics, management, health economics, quality and excellence, human development, statistical measurement, work stress, among others. Dr Chopra is the Winner of "*Economia Internazionale Prize*" with Professor Gopal Kanji for their paper, "On Measuring Country Risk" published and selected by Jury of the Prize as the best scientific paper published in *Economia Internazionale/International Economics* (Italy) for the year 2010. Dr Chopra is working on a research project, *On Measuring Globalisation: A New Systems Modelling Approach.* Email: drparveshchopra@gmail.com

Raj Kumar Sen is a (Retired) Director of Centre for Studies on Environment and Sustainable Development and Professor and Head, Department of Economics, Rabindra Bharati University, Kolkata, India and currently Chairman, International Institute of Development Studies (IIDS). He received UGC (Post Doctoral) Career Award (1984-87). Professor Sen was the founder Director, Tagore-Ikeda International Center on Global Citizenship (TIICGC). He authored many books/articles and also edited journals/books. He travelled many countries on academic invitations. Dr Sen is one of the founders of IIDS and BEA (Bengal Economic Association) and was President, Indian Economic Association, India. Email: rk_sen25@rediffmail.com

Sébastien Charles is Associate Professor in Economics at the University of Paris, France. He has a Master in History of Economic Thought from ENS (Ecole Normale Supérieure) and University of Paris and received his PhD in Economics from the University of Paris. His research focuses on heterodox macroeconomics, Minskyan models, Post-Keynesian models of growth and distribution and shareholders' impact on macroeconomic stability. He has published several articles in the *Cambridge Journal of Economics*, the *Journal of Post-Keynesian Economics*, *Louvain Economic Review*, *Papers on Political Economy*, the *Review of Political Economy*, *Economie Appliquée* and the *International Journal of Development Issues.* Email: sebcharles92@yahoo.fr

Shankaran Nambiar is Head of the Policy Studies Division and Senior Research Fellow at the Malaysian Institute of Economic Research (MIER), Kuala Lumpur, Malaysia. Earlier he held teaching and administrative positions in private educational institutions. His areas of research are mainly in trade policy, development and institutional economics. Dr Nambiar has been a consultant to the Ministries of International Trade and Industry; Finance; and, Domestic Trade and Consumer Affairs, in Malaysia. He has also been consulted for UNESCAP, UNDP, ILO, ADBI and the ASEAN Secretariat. In addition, Dr Nambiar has been a resource person for various capacity-building programmes in Central and Southeast Asia. Dr Nambiar is author of various publications including, *Sen's Capability Approach and Institutions (2010)* and *The Malaysian Economy: Rethinking Policies and Purposes* (2014). Email: nambiar@mier.org.my

Somnath Hazra is a Post Doctoral Fellow (Climate Economics), Jadavpur University, India and Unit Head (Forestry and Biodiversity), CTRAN Consulting, Bhubaneswar, Orissa, India. Dr Hazra is a young Environmental Researcher and has a PhD in Forest Economics with 14 years of reaserch experience. His main areas of research are environmental economics, forest economics, climate change, poverty, and energy. The recent publications of Dr Hazra include, *Globalisation and Environmental Governance with Reference to India* (2011), *Global Warming and Indian Economy* (2011), *Environmental Problems and Challenges: Recent Issues and Opportunities* (2013), among others. Email: somu.durg@gmail.com

Sule Lokmanoglu Aker is currently an Associate Professor at the Department of Business Administration, Eastern Mediterranean University, North Cyprus, North Cyprus. Formerly, Dr Aker was also the Chairperson of the same department. She has supervised various theses and introduced research and writing projects in her classes. Dr Aker has written extensively in the areas of international economics and the economy of North Cyprus. She has a long experience of teaching and research, and has published a large number of papers in refereed journals and attended many national and international conferences. Email: sule.aker@emu.edu.tr

Prefatory Note

Heraclitus, a pre-Socratic Greek Philosopher, rightly said, "Everything changes and nothing remains still, you cannot step in the same river twice", because it is always flowing. Change is inexorable and constant. It is rightly said, "If you don't create change, change will create you: Things will not stay the same". The same is true for not so feeble phenomenon of *globalisation* as it is persistently in a flux. The intensity, severity and the basic nature of globalisation have been undergoing changes at an incredibly fast pace. These changes are taking place in *spatial* (trade, political representation, communication and cultural exchange), *temporal* (increased speed of travel, transactions, political change, resource depletion and social mobility) and *cognitive* (neo-liberal economics, human rights and democratic principles) constituents of globalisation. Ever since its existence in terms of economic, political and cultural exchanges between national economies, globalisation and its diverse drivers, channels and processes have never ceased to influence our lives in a rapidly integrating and unifying 'one world'. With the collapse of communism and development of new technologies such as jet planes, computers and satellite communications up to 1980s, the business activities and international migration started to spread and then intensified across the globe. The subsequent privatization, deregulation, liberation of domestic markets, and further opening of the borders resulted in international trade openness and its escalation integrated the global markets for goods, services and finance significantly. Changes in institutions and policy regimes at the international and national levels facilitated the growth of multinational corporations, global brands (Microsoft, Sony, McDonalds, and so on), and increasing capital mobility that acted as a further stimulus to the growth of globalisation. Additional developments and progress in technology, transport and communications increased the tempo of globalisation and, consequently, global economy has become 'global village', an advanced stage in sociopolitical and economic evolution of mankind that started with clans, tribes, empires, and probably will end up in the planetary super state.

The nature and intensity of globalisation further changed due to increase in global migration and circular migration, foreign direct investment, dissemination of scientific and technical knowledge, off-shoring, out-sourcing, global consumerism, global medical tourism, and increase in the number of global organisations (e.g., the United Nations, The World Bank, International Monetary Fund, WHO, World Trade Organisation, G20, etc.) with their policies influencing the entire world. The profound insights into the contemporary research on globalisation highlight diverse critical interconnected transformations that are taking place around the globe. However, tremendous remunerations of globalised world have come to some but not to others. Even though the nation-state has been on the retreat over the last few decades, undermining its authority due to birth and growth of European Union, deregulation, liberalization, privatization, lower taxes on the rich, growing power of multinational corporations, and so on, globalisation does not pose any serious threat to the nation-state or the welfare-state as evident from an increase in the number of the members of the United Nations from 154 to 193 between 1980 and 2016.

Furthermore, the new era of twenty-first century witnessed an unprecedented rise in the cross-border *flow intensity* of goods, services, finance, individuals, ideas, data, communications, transportations, culture, media, and so on. Our global economy further changed from a interconnected one to an increasingly *hyperconnected and knowledge-intensive world* mainly due to the spread and use of internet across the world and continuous advancements in digitally smart technologies such as Twitter, Facebook, Whatsapp, cloud computing, Linkedin, researchgate, smartphones, 4G, wireless networks, Skype, snapshot, and so on. The expanding network of diverse global flows has produced five major changes that are of great consequence. First, there is a remarkable emergence and growth in *micro-multinationals* via online platforms such as Ebay, Gumtree, Amazon, mobile phone apps like UBER, hungry house, and the like, enabling sole entrepreneurs and/or smallest companies sourcing or selling goods, services, and ideas across borders, Second, the developing and emerging economies, including India, China, Brazil, South Africa, Mexico, Russia, Indonesia and others are rapidly catching-up and integrating more deeply into the world economy. Third, the nature of cross-border flows is changing. A decade ago outsourcing of labour-intensive tasks and commodity-intensive flows, like oil, finished goods, from developing countries with lower labour and/or material costs, is rapidly being replaced by knowledge-intensive goods and activities with high R&D component or utilize highly skilled labour such as high tech products (semiconductors and computers), pharmaceuticals, automobiles, medicines, and business services (such as accounting, law, call centers, architectural, marketing, and engineering).

Fourth, digital technologies are now briskly contributing to the overall productivity and quality of goods and services. They are transforming the production, distribution and operations of physical goods (e.g., online tracking goods shipments) and rapidly replacing the cross-border flows of physical goods and work by the low-costs online and digital flows such as e-books, digital music, computer games, news, entertainment, and streaming movies. Fifth, the network of global flows is contributing significantly to the rising prosperity and living standards of the global economy making it possible for almost all the countries and their citizens to participate via digital technologies. Rising incomes in rapidly developing economies are creating new centers of consumer demand, global production, and commodities trade as well as sending more people across borders for business and leisure.

Above and beyond the major economic opportunities of participating in various global flows of our present world, the benefits of this new face of globalisation have not spread evenly among all types of economies, regions, cities, businesses or individuals, particularly for low-income countries that may be marginalized. The increased competition from low-wage countries are destroying jobs in richer nations and there is a 'race to the bottom' as countries tend to reduce taxes, wages, welfare incentives and environmental controls to be more competitive and attractive to foreign investments, at enormous socio-economic and environmental costs. The concerns regarding the negative consequences of globalisation relate to the whole range of issues, including undermining national sovereignty, financial market instability, rise in structural unemployment, poverty, inequality, global economic dependency, public debt crisis, severe economic cycles, environmental degradation, global taxation problems, insecurity and terrorism, changes in many other fields of human interactions such as health, culture, food habits, and so on.

The speedily growing global physical and virtual interconnectedness have also produced many good and bad consequences for labour market dynamics across the globe. A serious concern is that globalisation has deteriorated the labour market outcomes such as employment insecurity, declining real wages, discrimination, job transfers and so on. Labour market is a system in relentless change. The measurement over time of changes, movements and flows in activity status of individuals, i.e., the activity status of individuals (employed, self-employed, unemployed, underemployment, and inactive affected by hiring, separation and establishment and closure of self-employed activities), changes in earnings of individuals over time, and changes in jobs situations (entrepreneurial job-creating and job-destroying activities) falls under the umbrella of labour market dynamics. However, the issues of labour market dynamics have not yet been adequately addressed in research studies on the impact of globalisation in the developing countries as much as could be expected.

The basic purpose of this volume is to deal with the dynamics behind the labour market outcomes in both developed and developing economies in the perspective of globalisation. In interpreting and evaluating theoretical and empirical linkages between globalisation and labour market dynamics, the book focuses on the following three critical dimensions:

- To present the right perspective
- To concentrate on the polemical issues, if there be any, and
- To analyze the policy alternatives/ implications of the study.

The chapters selected in the present volume deal with important correlates of labour market dynamics, e.g., employment flexibility, trade and wages, employment-unemployment, inequalities, flexicurity, migration, privatization, sectoral growth, labour market discrimination, multivariate causal pathways model and so forth. The prophylactic regimen includes, *inter alia,* an upward harmonization process, global justice and a new but a more humanistic world order based on unconditional love, compromise and cooperation. All these are well-analyzed in the present volume.

I started to edit this volume with Professor B.N. Ghosh, who sadly and untimely passed away on 4th of August 2014. I dedicate this work to him for his true and tireless hard work and unquestioned dedication to invaluable theoretical and empirical research throughout his life. He was a real scholar and he made several original contributions in diverse areas of Economics. He will be sadly missed by family, friends and colleagues across the globe.

The contributors of the volume are well-known, gifted and dedicated international scholars. I am grateful to them for their patience and also for complying with my request to write for this volume in spite of their very hectic schedule of teaching and research assignments.

I have incurred heavy intellectual indebtedness for this small volume. Many of my friends and colleagues in India and abroad have created useful positive externalities for giving gravitas to this volume. Since their individual names are too numerous to be mentioned here, I simply take the poetic excuse by saying that unheard melodies should taste sweeter. However, I must mention but one name of Professor Ozay Mehmet, Senior Fellow, Modern Turkish Studies and Distinguished Research Professor of Carleton University (Canada), who posted far apart, has always remained an inspiration for me; and with his suggestions and efforts, I have been able to get some really valuable contributors from Canada. Indeed, he deserves my "big thank you". I am highly indebted to Emeritus Professor Malcolm Sawyer, Leeds University Business School, The University of Leeds, Leeds, UK who always helped me his analytical advise, constructive comments and valuable support ever since I completed my second PhD under his supervision back in 2002. I am grateful to Professor Pritam Singh, Department of Accounting, Finance and Economics, Oxford Brookes University, UK, who taught me *Marxian Political Economy* at Panjab University, Chandigarh (India) nearly three decades ago. He remains a great source of inspiration and human contestability expansion for me. I would like to take this opportunity to express my sincere gratitude to Professor Kanti V. Mardia, Senior Research Professor, The University of Leeds, Visiting Professor in Oxford University, and is a Fellow of Kellogg College Oxford, for his encouragements and suggestions. I have been immensely benefitted from the numerous discussions and analytics advise from my uncle Professor Hans R. Chopra, an expert in information management and library performance excellence, Department of Library and Information Sciences, Panjab University, Chandigarh, India.

However, I am aware that all the lapses that remain in a volume of this genre are always the unconditional liability of the editor.

Editor
Leeds, United Kingdom
15th of August, 2016

Introduction

A Synoptic View of a Globalised Labour Market

Parvesh K. Chopra

Global economy is speedily rising all around us driven by the opening of borders, internet-related technological advancements, developments in global transportation networks, neo-liberal international and national policies, reduced costs of making cross-border transactions and exchanges, and increased mobility of manpower and capital. Globalisation, albeit not a recent phenomenon, may be conceived as a wide-ranging process (or set of processes) of diverse networks and flows giving rise to growing cross-border integration, interconnectedness, interrelationship, and interdependence between different actors and numerous economic and non-economic variables in a global economy. Globalisation, in short, can be defined as the widening, intensifying, speeding up, and growing of world-wide interconnectedness. This conceptualization of globalisation highlights its five main elements. First, globalisation involves the expansion of economic and non-economic activities across borders. It is much broader than internationalization (i.e., opening business activities in more than one country). Second, globalisation results in *core changes* in economic, social, political, cultural, environmental, security, technological and other spheres. Third, the *nature of globalisation* is changing from simply connected to increasingly hyper-connected. Fourth, the opening of international borders between countries is making cross border flows fast and, ergo, *national boundaries* are becoming less important. Fifth, *interdependence* means that welfare of one country depends upon another's or a group of others, and vice versa and they are connected in such a way that if something happens to one, all will be affected.

Globalisation is also fabricating an evolving set of consequences for global economy - some good, some bad and some inadvertent. The international streams of people, goods, services and capital are contributing to a greater extent towards an increasing complexity, competitiveness and contestability pressures on all nation-states and allowing multinational corporations to greater exploitation of economies of scale. Globalisation has led these countries towards social, economic and political disclosures and hence keeping them competitive in the product, labour and financial markets. This is the genesis of the phenomenon of *country contestability* – a blend of global attractiveness and competitiveness with humanistic order of a country (Delgado et al., 2012; Chopra, 2015).

The broader linkages between the drivers of globalisation and labour market dynamics vary across and within, economies, sectors, occupations and activities. Pathways analysis reveals five main causal pathways connecting the elements of globalisation and labour market dynamics. The first pathway evaluates the causal links between the movements and flows of goods via global trade and production networks and labour market dynamics. The second channel causally connects international migration and circular migration of manpower to labour market adjustments. The third pathway establishes causality and mechanisms between international financial capital flows (financial globalisation) and labour market outcomes. The fourth pathway casually ties labour market with the global trade in tasks, activities and services via information and communication technology-enabled world-wide outsourcing and offshoring. The fifth pathway illustrates how hyper-connected knowledge-intensive global economy is affecting labour market dynamics (Wladawsky-Berger, 2014). Such a path analysis allows us to understand the magnitude of causal links and relationships and the nature of processes involved. However, the underlying profound complexity of the entire set of processes and linkages suggests that we are still in the infancy of our attempts to develop apposite theoretical scaffolding for analyzing, interpreting and evaluating the empirical research on multiple issues involved.

Be that it may, the various widely referred key theoretical frameworks developed by major developers (trade and labour economists) of neoclassical and modern international trade theory linking globalisation and labour markets include the general structure of general equilibrium trade models (Meade, 1952; Johnson, 1959; Jones, 1965), the Stolper-Samuelson theorem[i] (1941), Heckscher-Ohlin-Samuelson model of 1949 (Matusz, 1985)[ii], imputed output approach (1997)[iii], Jones and Scheinkman analysis (1977), Chipman's generalization of Stolper-Samuelson theorem (1969) and many other generalizations (Ethier, 1984) such as factor-content methodology (Borjas, Freeman and Katz, 1992); Deardorff and Staiger factor-content analysis (Sacks and Shatz, 1994); adjusted factor-content analysis (Wood, 1994); Borjas, Freeman and Katz (1992); Baldwin and Cain analysis (2000); computational general equilibrium models determining the economic implications of openness to foreign markets and regional integration (Shoven and Whalley, 1974; Miller and Spencer, 1977; Krugman, 2000); and so on. The so called 'new trade theory' argues that, alongside the gains from trade due to the conventional comparative advantage, by enlarging markets, international trade raises competition and allows greater exploitation of economies of scale (Krugman, 1979; Helpman, 1981; Ethier, 1982).

The growing pace of economic globalisation has created more migrant workers than ever before. Even though international migration has come to attract a great deal of attention during the recent decades of globalisation, the expansion is far behind in comparison to flows of large amounts of commodities and capital (Lucas, 2008). There are substantial contributions in literature studying theoretical and empirical casual connections between immigration and labour market outcomes. There are three broad methodologies for studying the empirical link between immigration and labour markets: structural econometric analyses; reduced form regression analyses; and natural experiments (Greenway and Nelson, 2001). Some empirical studies found no labour market effects of immigration on employment, participation, unemployment and wages of the resident population (Card, 2000; Butcher, 1998; Reimers, 1998; Dustmann, et. al., 2005). However, immigration quality has been a major theme of Borjas' work (See, Borjas, 1999). The deteriorating quality of immigrants has far reaching implications for labour market outcomes of natives. On the other hand, many studies have found the negative effects of immigration on the reduction in wages and increase in unemployment (Bojras, Freeman and Katz, 1992; Altonji and Card, 1991; Ruhs, 2015). Moreover, the *sense of mobility* strongly varies across countries (Ward-Warmedinger and Macchiarelli, 2013).

The correlations between financial globalisation (foreign direct investment in particular) and labour market outcomes have been evaluated by developing theoretical and empirical research frameworks such as real capital arbitrage models (Hymer, 1960; Ruffin, 1984), market power/industrial organisation models, firm-specific models (Dunning, 1981), partial equilibrium models (Carmichael 1992; Bughin and Vannini, 1995; Zhao, 1998), and general equilibrium models (Helpman, 1984; Markusen, 1984; Ethier, 1986; Brainard, 1993; Brecher and Choudhri, 1996; Ernst and Escudero, 2008). However, the labour market impact of inward foreign direct investment increases earnings dispersion, the use of relatively more skilled labour in the domestic firms and technology spillovers occur from foreign to domestic firms (Driffield and Taylor, 2000). The relationship between FDI inflows and employment generation depends upon the nature of investment and the sector in which it is made, i.e., capital-intensive or labour/employment-intensive.

The rapidity of global integration over the last two decades suggests that structural changes in the impact of globalisation on labour market dynamics may also have taken place. Globalisation is associated with rising living standards but its benefits are not shared automatically by all workers. It has given rise to the labour market inequalities marked by widening gaps in wages and unemployment rates due to increased demand for skilled (relative to unskilled) labour relative to supply. As a result, there is a rapidly rising skill-premium by comparing skill-intensive products with unskilled-intensive products (Lawrence and Slaughter, 1993). Empirical evidence, country-level panel data studies and cross-sectoral studies of skill intensity, productivity and employment provide more support to the falling barriers to international transactions (globalisation hypothesis) in relation to the skill-based technological change, loosely defined to include factoral and sectoral biases in production methods, product innovation and shifts in the composition of final demand, (technology hypothesis) as an explanation for these inequalities (Wood, 1998). Moreover, globalisation or technical change may be acting singly or together in a complicated way producing changes in the *nature* of labour market inequalities in terms of fall in demand for unskilled workers, wage inequality among skilled workers, inter-country wage inequalities as well as inequalities within countries. Globalisation appears to have deepened inequalities in the international distribution of income. However, the link between globalisation and inequality is not very obvious as there is a need to test this relationship comprehensively with the help of a causal model. Literature review reveals only the explanatory variable follows a considerable long term trend to income inequality is the durable goods trade deficit as a percentage of GDP (Borjas and Ramey, 1994). Furthermore, global meltdown since 2007 led to the dependence on state for the salvation of the market. Globalisation and liberalization produced many negative consequences such as tsunami of scams and massive corruption due to liberalization, flight of domestic money to foreign banks, growing food insecurity in the world since 2007, technological revolution and falling elasticity of employment leading to jobless growth, degeneration of entrepreneur based competitive market into corporate led oligopolies and suboptimal allocation of resources leading to perverse forms of growth, and growth of service sectors and neglecting the real sectors.

From above adumbrated discussion, there is no denying the fact that voluminous literature has been produced on the goods and bads of globalisation. However, the present volume is based on both theoretical and empirical analyses of the effects of drivers of globalisation on labour market dynamics in different countries. The focus of this book is on the perspectives, polemics and policies of labour market in the light of globalisation, through a series of studies empirically linking different issues with globalisation and labour market outcomes. In this respect, the book addresses a number of issues that have hitherto been unobserved in most of the debates about globalisation and labour market. Labourers in general and poor labourers in particular, have remained in all ages and in all countries most unfortunate and unhappy lesser mortals. Workers as a class deserve more of distributive justice so that they are not denied the fruits of development and growth. In this context, chapter by B.N. Ghosh (chapter one) analyses some of the issues that pertain to the labour market dynamics in a globalized world in general, and in the context of India, in particular. The analysis focuses on a number of labour market perspectives, polemics and policies. In the concluding section of this chapter, a few policy issues have been highlighted.

A call for greater employment flexibility is a major aspect of neoliberal policy reforms in the era of globalisation. The rising employment flexibility and its impact on labour market dynamics are highly debated issues in contemporary countries (Muffels, 2014). The flexibilisation of labour markets has led to various negative socio-economic side-effects such as a growth in the proportion of workers in various atypical employment relationships (temporary or part time jobs), rising in-work poverty, and so on. In this milieu, Amitava Krishna Dutt, Sebastein Charles and Dany Lang (chapter two) argue that an alternative approach to economic analysis and the labor market may well give rise to different policy conclusions. To make this point, this chapter makes some general comments about neoclassical economics, stressing its relative neglect of the role of uncertainty, power and institutions and their interaction. It then develops a simple macroeconomic model that takes seriously these important factors neglected in mainstream economics to consider an alternative perspective and to examine the implications of increasing employment flexibility.

The Holocene epoch (which began almost 12,000 years ago after the last major ice age) is over now and we all live in Anthropocene age (the human age) since human beings have permanently changed the planet. Undeniably we are *ad infinitum* having a full planet-scale impact on environment in terms of air and ocean pollution, changes in atmosphere and mass extinctions of plants and animal species, among other enduring impacts (Chopra and Kanji, 2011; Hamilton, 2015). Keeping in view that we are altering the planet at an unprecedented pace in a way that is already measurable and even noticeable to untrained observers, Myron J. Frankman (chapter three) examines the phenomena of globalisation and inequality in the age of Anthropocene. Nevertheless, the long reigning paradigm in economics sums up production and income distribution as little more than the outcome of a simple relation of capital and labor. Levels of complexity have been added to the theoretical edifice, but, like a giant inverted pyramid, the aptness of policy recommendations cannot withstand the slightest whisper of wind. The realities of increasingly interconnected human activity have given rise, inter alia, to writings suggesting that the world is an optimum currency areas and also recent calls for national social protection floors for all. Add to the current context the continuing displacement of labor by robotics and unknowable effects as the Anthropocene age advances and the need for a radical review and vast shift in the nature of the conversation about "Labour Force Dynamics" appears to urgent.

The forces of globalisation of labour and capital are threats, not just to those most exposed to their operations, but to the complex systems that compose our commons, Earth, and to our collective sense of place and options for survival. There are many more "reasons" that can be presented here as to why this is the case, but to give a few suggestions: the issues are too complex; authorities are lax; power is not deployed for the good of all; winning is still possible when others lose; people are apathetic; or blame may be attached to various actors. Considering this, Nancy Doubleday (chapter four) examines the nexus among globalised labour, ecology and peace in the Anthropocene. Peace is not an endpoint, rather a continually changing process of engagement. It is dynamic, ebbing and flowing as conditions and understandings change. Conditions favouring peace are created by commitments to reasonableness, consideration, mutual support, equity, fairness, justice, respect, and sustainability, *inter alia.* We are all participants in the creative process, co-creating conditions for one another and for future generations, favouring peace - or not. In this sense, we can enrich our understanding of the properties necessary to produce peace just as seminal work in the social determinants of health has informed health disciplines and practices in international policy, and when we locate it, peace is found at the nexus of equitable systems of protections for labour, for sustainable social-cultural-ecological systems, and economic frameworks designed to secure rather than exploit.

Globalisation has expanded a class of inequalities that might be called 'transnational', meaning (a) that they are global as well as local, and (b) a country's place in cross-border transactions or relationships undermines its ability to reduce them without the aid of international cooperation. Some labour inequalities caused by globalisation are transnational in this sense (Beer and Boswell, 2001). Keeping this in view, Jay Drydyk (chapter five) presents a model of public reason that (other things being equal) would identify these inequalities as unjust and call for their elimination over time, through 'upward harmonization'. In contrast, he shows that, while nationalist models of deliberation like that of John Rawls can avoid these conclusions, they do so at the cost of embracing double standards for justice. The global workforce is marked by inequalities that are both local and global. Not only wages but working conditions and labour standards can be highly varied both within state borders and across them. That much is obvious, but what is not so obvious is that some of these inequalities are particularly tenacious because of economic activity that crosses borders. *Jay Drydyk* asserts that transactions cross borders, but workers cannot, and various workforce inequalities can therefore be difficult to remove. What is ever more interesting is that there is a large family of inequalities that are similar in two respects: (a) being both global and local and (b) being tenacious due to cross-border activity of some kind. He calls these *transnational inequalities,* and in this chapter he explores the question of what global public reason should conclude about them. Are they inequalities that matter? Are they unjust? Jay argues that, facing such transnational inequalities, nationalist approaches like that of John Rawls are particularly unhelpful, creating double standards for justice. A comparative approach like the one proposed by Amartya Sen gives better guidance, and what such an approach calls for, generally speaking, is an upward harmonization of standards.

Gobalization has been an integral part of capitalist development since its very beginning. 'The accumulation of capital has always been a profoundly geographical and spatial affair. Without the possibilities inherent in geographical expansion, spatial reorganization, and uneven geographical development, capitalism would long ago have ceased to function as a political-economic system' (Harvey 2000: 20, 24-5). This means that it can be interpreted as the empowerment of capital relative to labour and the intensification of social relations so that local happenings are shaped by events occurring many miles away, and vice versa. Harvey reminds us that capitalism is under the impulsion to accelerate turnover-time, to speed up the circulation of capital and consequently to revolutionize the time horizon of development. Secondly, capitalism is under the impulsion to eliminate all spatial barriers, to 'annihilate space through time' as Marx put it, but it can only do so through the production of fixed space. Coupled with the deregulation of finance, and the twin information revolution cum monopolization of media power, and finally the reduction of cost and time of moving commodities and people or 'overcoming space', as Harvey note, have altogether created immense contractions. According to these tendencies wider spaces for private profit maximization strategies are created and thus exploited by economic actors on a world-wide scale. It is now possible to avoid the expensive time-consuming regulations belonging to the shield of social protection which traditionally guarantees human and/or socio-economic security (Ghosh, 2006).

The Industrial Revolution caused a centuries-long shift in power to the West and thus giving birth to the coloniality of power. Eurocentrism posits European values, culture and system as normal and superior to the rest of the world, therefore, helping to produce and justify Europe's dominance within the global capitalist world system (Hobson, 2012). Ergo, coloniality of power continues to affect non-European continents in quite different ways. Furthermore, Eurocentric capitalism has now become the principal source of instability and inequality in the world. Keeping this in view, Ozay Mehmet (chapter six) analyses the labour-capital conflict from a perspective of Eurocentric capitalism and advocates a new humanistic world order. Organized in four parts, the II part of this chapter focuses on the weakest link of Eurocentric capitalism, i.e. the increasing disconnect between the capital market and the labor market. Capital is now driven by speculation, delinked from the real economy of production, employment and earnings. The labor mobility is blocked and unable to serve as a mechanism of social justice. The systemic failure has assumed global proportions. In part III a Race-to-the-Bottom global market is formulated to account for systemic failure of capitalism. In the spirit of positivism, part IV outlines transition to a Humanistic World Order, using the global public good paradigm in the case of international taxation and autonomous sustainable development.

Unemployment is a highly complex problem. The robust linkage between unemployment and social benefits has produced multiple outcomes across countries (Dixon, 1999). Over and above unemployment, there has been a substantial and disproportionate growth in *atypical employment* like part-time, temporary, fixed-term, or self-employed, in different parts of the world that provides less security, carrier prospects, training chances for workers as well as disqualifies them from social benefits (Fleetwood, 2001). As a result of growing flexibility of employment due to globalisation, technological change, migration and other factors, the idea of *flexibility* was introduced in the Netherlands and Denmark during the 1990s to promote a better security of atypically employed. Flexicurity is an integrated strategy of labour market flexibility (easiness in hiring and firing workers), social security of workers (income protection of unemployed) and active labour market policies (job search assistance, labour market training, etc.) (Wilthagen, 2001). However, the crucial question that arises is that: what has happened to the Dutch/Danish phenomenon of flexicurity in a dynamic economy since it was first introduced? The answer to this question has been explored by a profound analytical study by Johannes Dragsbaek Schmidt and Jacques Hersh (chapter seven) by revisiting Danish flexicurity by investigating how the protracted multi-layered crisis has affected the Danish model in the past decades and focuses on the policy options and institutional responses in the attempt of adjusting the economy to the demands of neoliberalism and globalisation while moderating and/or managing the impact on social and labor market conditions. More specifically, it offers an analysis of the collective agreements, income support, and wage negotiations and specifically on the strength/weaknesses of organized labor as a collective partner in the workings of the corporatist model. The first part questions the mainstream explanations of the crisis and strategies offered as a way out of the crisis. It also introduces the conceptual framework embedded in the "social structure of accumulation" for understanding the essence of the crisis and rather than its symptoms. The second section is devoted to a reconstruction of the historical background behind the shift from the corporatist welfare state (the so-called Danish model) to the corporatist competition state leading up to the crises of the private sector in the United States and Europe. The third part proposes a brief re-reading of the restructuring of the Danish welfare state while the fourth part offers an analysis of the impact of the crises on the labor market regulation model of flexicurity in Denmark. The fifth section discusses the options and limits of the Left under the current crisis while the last part presents some concluding remarks.

The process of globalisation and its forces such as trade liberalisation, capital mobility, global migration, foreign direct investment, offshoring, skill-based technical change, and so on, have been deteriorating labour market performances. As a result, communities, individuals and social groups have been experiencing diverse labour market experiences. Some people in an area have been immensely benefited from globalisation while others have been marginalised or excluded. Therefore, globalisation has been witnessed as an uneven world market development. It has been negatively contributing to the drop in mobility of low quality manpower, rise in unemployment rates, fall in real wages, social exclusion, wage inequalities, discursive localisation of poverty in low-income as well as high-income economies, and the like (Stiglitz, 2002 and 2006). What is, nevertheless, controversial is the *nature and degree of relationship* between different elements comprising globalisation and labour market outcomes. Considering the widely divergent claims made in the literature on globalisation and labour market dynamics, there is a call for apposite theoretical framework that enables a systematic and scientific evaluation of empirical work on the problem in hand. Therefore, Parvesh K. Chopra (chapter eight) proposes a new theoretical scaffolding of *causality* and *mechanisms* among the elements of globalisation and labour market outcomes. It is comprehensible that labour market performances are heterogeneous among different countries. It, for the first time, introduces and constructs a robust, structural and multivariate causal pathways model to understand and analyse the dynamics behind labour market outcomes in a global economy. It contributes to this domain of research by building and proposing a multivariate framework that reveals how the key labour market aggregates/outcomes are statistically related to various internal and external shocks, failures and interventions in a global economy.

One facet of globalisation permits multinational corporations to seek economies with the elements that are most advantageous to their investments. At one end of the favoured spectrum are those countries that offer low-cost labour; at the other end of the spectrum, MNCs prefer economies where there is an abundant supply of skilled labour that can produce technologically intensive, high value-added goods. Malaysia is a small, open economy and consequently its growth is export-driven (Nambiar, 2014). In this framework, it is necessary for Malaysia, given its limited domestic market, to be sensitive to the global environment. Shankaran Nambiar (chapter nine) seeks to argue that the labour market is trying to respond to its external and domestic constraints. On the domestic front there is concern regarding a situation of skill shortage. This is further compounded by the fact that Malaysia no longer enjoys the benefits of a cheap low-skilled labour force. In response to these challenges, migrant labour has become a predominant way to address the shortage of labour. Nevertheless, migrant labour poses its own difficulties, including the possibility of being trapped in a low human capital situation. This goes against the government intention of transforming Malaysia into a knowledge-based developed economy.

Stiglitz believes that globalisation has the potential to improve the lives of most of the world's citizens and specialization will bring higher real incomes but in reality there is very little scope for developing countries. Stiglitz also recognizes that unemployment is a regular feature of a capitalist economy, and that its solution cannot be left to the market. According to Paul Krugman, free trade is part of an economist's creed. Some mainstream economists believe that free trade provides a free lunch. However, results in the last two decades show that a) there has been less than expected growth rate of the world under globalisation, b) truncated or partial globalisation in the true sense leading to problems of labour intensive developing countries like India, c) global meltdown since 2007 and dependence on state for the salvation of the market, d) growing food insecurity in the world since 2007, e) tsunami of scams and massive corruption due to liberalization, f) flight of domestic money to foreign banks, g) increase in the global inequality in the last two decades in an accelerated rate, h) technological revolution and falling elasticity of employment leading to jobless growth, i) degeneration of entrepreneur based competitive market into corporate led oligopolies and suboptimal allocation of resources leading to perverse forms of growth, j) growth of service sectors only neglecting the real sectors and for India leading to pre reform growth scenarios and similar other situations. Hence, the future world development paradigm should be: 1) definition of proper role of State and Market, 2) implementation of full-fledged globalisation with human face, 3) State guided but free market based development pattern for inclusive growth, and 4) better governance with corruption within tolerable limits.

Let us now have a look at the impact of globalisation on two giant Asian countries, India and China. The integration of these economies into the global economy has substantially boosted global labour supply with their significant reserves of underemployed labour. Raj Kumar Sen and Somnath Hazra (chapter ten) assert that there were a number of reasons for the initiation of LPG based economic reforms since the last decade of the last century in India and other developing economies. These are: 1) failure of USSR as a socialist economy, 2) slow rate of growth in developing economies like India under socialistic pattern of society, 3) rampant corruption in public sector due to politicization 4) expected high rate of growth under market based development paradigm, 5) efficiency of public sector dominated development and removal of poverty, 6) acceleration of global growth rate under globalisation, 7) theory of convergence leading to decrease in inequality among countries, and 8) a surge in employment through high growth, optimum allocation of resources and increased competition and similar other factors. The authors conclude that India and China have experienced the period of jobless growth as the employment situation has worsened in the era of globalisation. Both countries have also witnessed a positive relationship between inequality and globalisation. Recently, China has declared corruption as the number one problem in that country.

Sule L. Aker and Ahmet Aker (chapter eleven) assert that the two major targets of macro economic policy has long been the achievement of a satisfactory rate of economic growth and the maintainence of a sustainable level of employment. The two, however, have rarely moved toghether. On the contrary, it is very rare that economic growth and employment show any degree of parallelism. The old classical credo that "employment rises with economic growth" is no longer valid for a large number of countries where unemployment remains a persisitent problem despite the fact that the country in question experiences impressive paces of economic growth. This has led many scholarss and researchers to look for ways to explain the dilemma of why unemployment persists in the face of relatively rapid economic growth. A major question is whether golbalization may be a significant factor. Does economic growth and globalisation affect employment and unemployment in ways that have so far not been discovered? Turkey is a country that has recently been experiencing a continuous pace of economic growth. Traditionally, economic growth and high levels of employment have gone hand in hand in Turkey. In the present analysis, however, which has been conducted at a sectoral level, the findings indicate that there is indeed a positive relationship between the growth and expansion of exports and employment. This is probably because Turkey's exports are mainly labour intensive products. If so, the liberalization of world trade has indeed helped Turkey both to export more and increase employment in the export sector at the same time. Another finding of this study is that FDI has an employment destroying effect because there is a positive relationship between the size of FDI and unemployment. From this it may be fair to conclude that globalisation in the form of inflows of FDI in Turkey has had a negative impact on employment. Another finding of this study is that investments in capital and technology do substitute for labour and have an adverse effect on employment. So the study finds that globalisation have helped employment in the export sector, but globalisation increasing FDI in Turkey increased unemployment.

The impact of globalisation on brain drain is momentous. Ergo, brain drain has become a major policy challenge for countries undergoing globalisation (Krings, 2011). Keeping this in view, Jacqueline Liza Fernandez and Parthiban Gopal (chapter twelve) emphasize that Malaysia aspires to become a high income nation in the near future. One of the requirements to achieve this goal is to increase the stock of skilled human capital. However, due to globalisation and the increased mobility of labour, Malaysia has to compete for talent in the international labour market. Against this backdrop, brain drain - or the cross-border migration of talent - poses a specific challenge. Clearly the brain drain is by no means unique to Malaysia, but how critical is it then? What is the magnitude of Malaysia's diaspora - the worldwide dispersion overseas of men and women born in Malaysia? How many among them are skilled and can be considered as part of the brain drain? These are the questions that this chapter will attempt to address. Out of a population of 27 million, there are an estimated 1.5 million Malaysians living abroad. Many of these Malaysians are skilled workers who emigrated to Singapore and Organisation for Economic Co-operation and Development (OECD) countries such as Australia, UK, and USA. Hence, brain drain is a serious challenge to Malaysia's transformation ambitions. Besides, brain drain and the loss of talent are symptoms of underlying issues that need proper scrutiny. For Malaysia to meet the requirements of its new growth model, it will need to develop, attract and retain talent. If indeed there has been and continues to be an exodus of talent as the data suggests, the brain drain could well be a major stumbling block in Malaysia's journey towards transforming itself into a high income nation by the year 2020. To curb brain drain, there needs to be collective action of the public and private sectors. Structural reforms are needed to address the problem as Malaysia strives to achieve its goals and maintain its competitiveness in an increasingly globalised world economy. This chapter discusses the extent and intensity of brain drain in Malaysia. Next, it unravels the factors that contribute to Malaysia's brain drain problem. The final part of the chapter examines the policies that have been outlined to counter the loss of skilled workers.

The connection among migration, globalisation and gender underlines the growing feminization of migration flows. Considering this, Padmaja Namboodiri (chapter thirteen) asserts that historically migration had been the domain of men, but in 2005, for the first time the number of female migrants equaled that of men. According to IOM 2008, there are more than 200 million migrants around the world today, and almost 50% are females. The increase in female migration has several explanations, among them trans-globalisation of economies which have opened up jobs in service sectors. There is an inflow of skilled and unskilled female migrants from India, Latin America, South East Asia, and Eastern Europe to Europe, America and Gulf countries as teachers, nurses, domestic servants, assistants in hospitality sector etc. Today there is an interesting asymmetry in migration policies pursued by different countries. The developed countries want skilled immigrants and are changing their immigration policies from to bias them away from unskilled to skilled migrants. The under developed and developing countries on the other hand, want their unskilled citizens to migrate and they are not clear in their attitude towards skilled citizens. As a result the supply of unskilled migrants exceeds demand in rich countries and this leads to illegal migration where as in case of skilled, demand exceeds supply in the developed countries and the poor economies face the problem of brain drain. In this background this chapter attempts to analyse the dynamics of female migration over the years in the international labour market, their socio-economic profiles, their status in the labour markets, extent of illegal migration and how far the immigration policies of different economies are gender sensitive.

Over the last four decades, policies of privatization have been promoted and implemented internationally. Sadly these policies tend to ignore labour issues. Fatma Guven (chapter fourteen) analyses the employment impact analysis of privatization of Cyprus Turkish Airlines and Cyprus Turkish Petroleum. Although privatization began in 1977 in North Cyprus, despite its significance, labour has been one of the least addressed issues in privatization practices until 2012. One important element of this research is an analysis of the impact of privatization on the privatized public enterprises' (PE) employees. The increased rate of privatisation in North Cyprus in the past two years has yielded a need for this kind of study to get the employment impact of privatization. The privatisation of PEs often involves the changes in the hiring, firing and working conditions of their employees. The impact can be positive or negative, depending on the economy, labor market conditions and situation of each case and the subjective viewpoint of each worker. This chapter is an attempt to study the employment impacts of privatization in North Cyprus with a gender perspective. The starting point is an overview of the economy and labour market of North Cyprus. Overview followed by an outline of the privatization practices and the impacts on employment in two case studies; Cyprus Turkish Airlines and Cyprus Turkish Petroleum. To reveal the human resource aspect interviews with male and female workers in case studies are used.

References

Altonji, J.G. and Card, D. (1991). "The effects of immigration on the labor market outcomes of less-skilled natives", In: Abowd, J.M. and Freeman, R.B. (eds.), *Immigration, Trade and the Labor Market*, The University of Chicago Press.

Baldwin, R. (2000). "Inferring relative factor price changes from quantitative data", In: Blomstrom, M. and Goldberg, L. (eds.), *Topics in Empirical International Economics: A Festschrift in Honour of Bob Lipsey*, Chicago: University of Chicago Press/NBER.

Beer, L. and Boswell, T. (2001). "The effects of globalisation on inequality: A cross-country analysis", Halle Institute Occasional Paper, www.citeseerx.ist.psu.edu

Borjas, G., Freeman, R. and Katz, L. (1992). "On the labour market effects of immigration and trade", In: Borjas, G. and Freeman, R. (eds.), *Immigration and the Workforce*, Chicago: University of Chicago Press, NBER, 213-244.

Borjas, G.J. and Ramey, V.A. (1994). "Time-Series evidence on the sources of trends in wage inequality", *The American Economic Review*, 84, 10-16.

Brainard, S. L. (1993). "A simple theory of multinational corporations and trade with a trade-off between proximity and concentration", NBER Working Paper, 4269.

Brecher, R. and Choudhri, E. (1996). "Liberalising multinational investment: The Stopler-Samuelson question revisited", In: Feenstra, R., Grossman, G. and Irwin, D. (eds.), *The Political Economy of Trade Policy*, Cambridge: MIT, 77-88.

Bourguignon, F (2015). *The Globalisation of Inequality*, Princeton University Press.

Bughin, J. and Vannini, S. (1995). "Strategic direct investment under unionised oligopoly", *International Journal of Industrial Organisation*, 13(1), 127-145.

Butcher, K. (1998). "An investigation of the effect of immigration on the labor-market outcomes of African Americans", In: Hamermesh, D. and Bean, F. (eds.), *Help or Hindrance? The Economic Implications of Immigration for African Americans*. New York: Rullell Sage Foundation, 149-181.

Card, D. (2001). "Immigrant inflows, native outflows, and the local labour market impacts of higher immigration", *Journal of Labour Economics*, 19, 22-64.

Carmichael, F. (1992). "Multinational enterprise and strikes: Theory and evidence", *Scottish Journal of Political Economy*, 39(1), 360-368.

Chipman, J. (1969). "Factor price equalisation and the Stolper-Samuelson theorem", *International Economic Review*, 10(3), 399-406.

Chopra, Parvesh K. and Kanji, Gopal K. (2011). "Environmental health: Assessing risks to society", *Total Quality Management & Business Excellence*, 22 (4), 461-489.

Chopra, Parvesh K. (2015). "Country risk: A theoretical and empirical analysis with special reference to Northern African economies", *Economia Internazionale/International Economics*, 68(1), 81-137.

Delgado, M., C. Ketels, M.E. Porter and S. Stern (2012). "The determinants of national competitiveness", *The National Bureau of Economic Research*, NBER Working paper No. 18249, July.

Dixon, John E. (1999). *Social Security in Global Perspective*, Praeger Publishers.

Driffield, N. and Taylor, K. (2000). "FDI and the labour market: A review of the evidence and policy implications", *Oxford Review of Economic Policy*, 16 (3), 90-103.

Dunning, J. (1981). *International Production and the Multinational Enterprise*, London: Allen and Unwin.

Dustmann, C., Fabbri, F. and Preston, I. (2005). "The impact of immigration on the UK labour market", Centre for research and Analysis of Migration, Discussion Paper Series, CDP No 01/05, www.eprints.ucl.ac.uk.

Ernst, E. and Escudero, V. (2008). "The effects of financial globalisation on global imbalances, employment and inequality", *International Labour Organisation Working Paper 191*, 10 June, www.ilo.org.

Either, W. (1982). "The general role of factor intensity in the theorems of international trade", *Economics Letters*, 10, 337-342.

Ethier, W. (1984). "Higher dimensional issues in trade theory", In: Caves, R., Jones, R. and Kenem, P. (Eds.), *Handbook of International Economics*-V.I., Amsterdam:North-Holland, 91-184.

Fleetwood, S. (2001). "Conceptualising unemployment in a periodof atypical employment:A critical realist perspective", *Review of Social Economy*, 59(1), 45-69.

Ghosh, B.N. (2006). *Globalisation and Third World*, Palgrave – Macmillan: London and NewYork.

Greenaway, D. and Nelson, D. (2001). "Globalisation and labour markets: Literature review and synthesis", Research Paper 2001/29, The University of Nottingham.

Hamilton, C. (2015). "Human destiny in the Anthropocene", In: Hamilton, C., Bonneuil, C. and Gemenne, F. (eds.), *The Anthropocene and the Global Environmental Crisis: Rethinking Modernity in a New Epoch*, London: Routlegde, pp. 32-43.

Helpman, E. (1981). "An exploration in the theory of exchange-rate regimes", Scholarly Articles 3445091, Harvard University Department of Economics.

Helpman, E. (1981). "International trade in the presence of product differentiation, economics of scale and monopolistic competition: A Chamberlin-Heckscher-Ohlin approach", Journal *of International Economics*, 11(3), 305-340.

Helpman, E. (1984). "A simple theory of international trade with multinational corporations", *Journal of Political Economy*, 92(3), 451-471.

Hobson, J. (2012). *The Eurocentric Conception of World Politics: Western International Theory, 1760-2010*, New York: Cambridge University Press.

Hymer, S. (1960). *The International Operations of National Firms: A Study of Direct Foreign Investment*, Cambridge: MIT Press.

Johnson, H. G. (1959). "International trade, income distribution and the offer curve", *Manchester School*, 27, 241-260.

Jones, Ronald W. (1965). "The structure of simple general equilibrium models", *The Journal of Political Economy*, LXXIII (6), 557-572.

Jones, Ronald W. and Scheinkman, Jose A. (1977). "The relevance of the two sector production model in trade theory", *Journal of Political Economy*, 85 (5), 909-935.

Krings, B.J. (ed.) (2011). *Brain Drain or Brain Gain?: Changes of Work in Knowledge-based Societies*, Berlin: Sigma.

Krugman, Paul (1979). "Increasing returns, monopolistic competition, and international trade", *Journal of International Economics*, 9(4), 469-479.

Krugman, Paul (2000). "Technology, trade and factor prices", *Journal of International Economics*, 50-(1), 51-71.

Lloyd, P. and A. Schweinberger (1997). "Conflict generating product price changes: The imputed output approach", *European Economic Review*, 41 (8), 1569–87.

Lucas, R.E.B. (2008). *International Labour Migration in a Globalizing Economy*, Washington: Carnegie Endowment for International Peace. www.ciaonet.org.

Markusen, J. (1984). "Multinationals, multi-plant economics and the gains from trade", *Journal of International Economics*, 16(3/4), 205-226.

Matusz, S.J. (1985). "The Heckscher-Ohlin-Samuelson model with implicit contracts", *The Quarterly Journal of Economics*, 100(4), 1313-1329.

Meade, J. E. (1952). *A Geometry of International Trade*, London: Macmillan.

Miller, M. H. and Spencer, J. E. (1977). "The static economic effects of the U.K. joining the EEC: A general equilibrium approach", *Review of Economic Studies*, 44, 71-93.

Muffels, R.J.A. (ed.) (2014). *Flexibility and Employment Security in Europe*, Cheltenham, UK: Edward Elgar Publishing.

Nambiar, S. (2014). *The Malaysian Economy: Rethinking Politics and Purposes*, Kuala Lumpur: Strategic Information and Research Development Centre.

Reimers, C. (1998). "Unskilled immigration and changes in the wage distribution of black, Mexican-American, and Non-Hispanic white make dropouts", In: Hamermesh, D. and Bean, F. (eds.), *Help or Hindrence? The economic Implications of Immigration for African Americans*, New York: Rullell Sage Foundations, 107-148.

Ruffin, R. (1984). "International factor movements", In: Jones, R. and Kenen, P. (eds.), *Handbook of International Economics- Vol. 1*, Amsterdam: North Holland, 237-288.

Ruhs, M. (2015). "The labour market effects of immigration", 22nd May, *migrationobservatory.ox.co.uk.*

Sachs, J. and Shatz, H. (1994). "Trade and jobs in U.S. manufacturing", *Brookings Papers on Economic Activity*, 1, 1-69.

Samuelson, Paul A. (1949). "International factor-price equalisation once again", *Economic Journal,* 59 (234), 181–197.

Shoven, J. B. and Whalley, J. (1974). "On the computation of competitive equilibrium on international markets with tariffs", *Journal of International Economics*, 4, 341-354.

Stolper, W.F. and Samuelson, Paul A. (1941). "Protection and real wages", *Review of Economic Studies*, 9 (1), 58-73.

Ward-Warmedinger, M. and Macchiarelli, C. (2013). *Transitions in Labour Market Status in the European Union*, LSE 'Europe in Question' Discussion Paper Series, November, LEQS Paper No. 69/2013.

Wilthagen, T. (2001). "'Flexicurity': the emergence of a new paradigm in labour market and employment regulation?, The Dutch background and experiences". Paper presented at the 13th Annual Meeting of the Society for the Advancement of Socio-Economics (SASE), University of Amsterdam, June 28-July 1.

Wladawsky-Berger, I. (2014). "The changing nature of globalisation in our hyperconnected, knowledge-intensive economy", *The Wall Street Journal*, June 20. www.blogs.wsj.com.

Wood, A. (1998). "Globalisation and the rise in labour market inequalities", *The Economic Journal*, 108 (450), 1463-1482.

Zhao, L. (1998). "The impact of foreign direct investment on wages and employment", *Oxford Economic Papers*, 50(2), 284-301.

Chapter One

Globalisation and Labour Market Dynamics: Some Obiter Dicta

B.N. Ghosh

Introduction

Leo Tolstoy's celebrated novel, *Anna Karenina*, opens with the genial statement: "Happy families are all alike; every unhappy family is unhappy in its own way". It is indeed so. Labourers in general and poor labourers in particular, have remained in all ages and in all countries most unfortunate and unhappy lesser mortals. Persons believing in destiny will blame the workers for their bad *karma*. Whatever may be the reason for their sad plight, there is no denying the fact that in a democratic state based on the ideals of socialistic pattern of society, they have the right to live a meaningful life with justice, equality, and equal opportunities as others. The problems of labour must be dealt with fairness and justice.

Philosophers believe that there are three things worthwhile in this universe and none of them can be defined in a compelling way. These things are: beauty, truth and justice. Most of the labourers being *proletariats*, need justice and fairness. Sometimes justice is defined as fairness. However, it is indeed very problematic to define fairness. There are indeed many unfair complications attached to the question of fairness. For instance, what is a fair wage? What should be the number of working hours for labourers per day? Should wage be equal to the ability of labour, or the need of the worker? Should the workers get high wage or low wage? Is a high level of minimum wage good or bad? Is there any relation between the wage rate and the employment level? There are many such questions which do not admit of unique answers. There are indeed many theories of justice (see Sen, 2009).

Be that as it may, poor workers should deserve our special attention. Thus, John Rawls in his difference principle points out that all basic goods should be equally distributed, but if some inequality is permitted, it should be in favour of the poor (see Ghosh, 2012). Workers as a class deserve more of distributive justice so that they are not denied the fruits of development and growth. In the present chapter, an analysis will be made on some of the issues that pertain to the labour market dynamics in a globalized world in general, and in the context of India, in particular. The analysis will focus on some labour market perspectives, polemics and policies.

Globalisation and Labour: Some Polemical Issues

The proponents of globalisation have assured that labour is immensely benefitted by it in the sense that it will increase wages and employment, reduce overall inequality and enhance the mobility of labour. However, country evidence suggests that whereas the mobility of capital has immensely increased, the mobility of labour, in particular the low quality manpower (LQM) has gone down. The developed nations do not permit this manpower to enter their countries.

Falling Wages and Expanding Multinationals

In the United States, 'real wages are below their level of 1973'. Estimates from 2001 showed that one-third of all US workers are identified as contingent workers and this appears to be a conservative estimate (Parker 2002, p.109). Conventional fixed-term employment, in manufacturing and services, is being swiftly replaced by part-time, low paid, non-unionized labour. Unionized labour in manufacturing fell from 42 per cent in 1950 to less than 14 per cent in 1994. The intention of employers has been to eliminate unions, cut labour costs, gain greater control over the labour process and increase their profits, as was done in earlier phases of industrial capitalism.

Since the 1980s, labour markets in the US have been characterized by falling wages and growing inequalities (Schmidt, 2006). Paul Krugman observes that in 2013, in the United States, the real wage was substantially lower than what it was the 1960s and meanwhile labour productivity has doubled (New York Times News Service, quoted in the Hindu, February 19, 2013, p.9). Europe has been cast in a high structural long-term unemployment, for both the lowest deciles of the labour market (Cuyvers and Rayp, 2001). These trends have emerged as a result of the transfer of production and manufacturing to low-wage countries. The proportionate decline in the US manufacturing work-force has had dramatic impacts for the de-industrialization of the US war economy and increasing unemployment in the goods producing and manufacturing sectors. The 'lucky' laid-off workers have been able to obtain employment in the low-paid service sector which increased, relative to the total labour force, from 66.7 per cent in 1970 to 80.5 per cent in 2000 (Berberoglu, 2003, p. 101).

What we are witnessing is jobless growth in the North, that is, economic growth rates with growing unemployment. With the predominance of financial capital and a permanent stage of surplus production the manufacturing sector cannot find new outlets for its production. 'Only minute fractions of all industrial jobs were generated within the TNC manufacturing sector, a job sector that is being rapidly degutted. Over the past decade, the world's top 500 corporations shed over 400,000 workers yearly. There are no signs of a turning point as any casual perusal of the financial press would confirm. Job extremism continues to move in concert with TNC expansion' (Clairmont, 1996, p. 45).

One of the disquieting polemical issues concerns with the escalating income inequality in every type of country. Available evidence from many countries both developed and developing suggests that globalisation has most adversely affected the market. Unemployment has been rising, real wages are plummeting and income inequalities are escalating. While the issues relating to wages and employment will be discussed later in this section, the available data in almost every country shows that globalisation has been associated with increase income inequality. It is interesting to note that income inequality in hard-core capitalist countries has substantially increased (Table 1.1).

Table 1.1 Growing Income Inequality in Capitalist Countries

Country	Gini Coefficient Mid-1980s	Gini Coefficient Late 2000s
USA	0.34	0.38
UK	0.32	0.35
Italy	0.31	0.34
Australia	0.31	0.34
New Zealand	0.27	0.32
Japan	0.30	0.33
Canada	0.28	0.33
Germany	0.25	0.30
Netherlands	0.27	0.30
Luxembourg	0.25	0.29
Finland	0.21	0.27
Sweden	0.20	0.27
Czech Republic	0.23	0.26
Norway	0.22	0.25
Denmark	0.22	0.25
France	0.30	0.30

Source: OECD Database on Household Income Distribution and Poverty (2011), Paris. www.oecd.org/social/ministerial

Note: Out of 16 developed countries, only in France, income inequality has remained unchanged. In all other cases, income inequality has increased. In cases of Turkey and Greece (not shown in the Table), income inequality has decreased a bit, but these are not, truly speaking, hard-core capitalist economies.

It seems that the European model of social capitalism increasingly is converging with the American model of market fundamentalism. Proponents of the neo-liberal discourse claim that in the long run the benefits of globalisation will eventually trickle down but unfortunately in the long run we are all dead, as Keynes said. If we look at the contemporary Indian scenario on wages, a few important facts cannot escape our attention.

Some Contemporary Facts and Issues

- In spite of a lot of hue and cry, National minimum wage for workers in the country has not yet been determined. In some states, attempts have been made to determine MW, but it is not based on any study of wage-productivity nexus. It seems that there is no minimum wage policy in India.

- Wages for ordinary labour are declining in the organised sector but those of white-collar and high quality manpower (HQM) are constantly increasing with better pay and perks.

- In many occupations which are dominated by competition due to the existence of unemployed labour, wages are declining. This is specially the case about contract labourers.

- The decline in wages in many private industries is due to a significant increase in capital/labour ratio, or what Marx calls the rising organic composition of capital. It is found by a study that (as reported in Datt and Sundharam, 2012, p.752) one unit rise in K/L per worker, leads to 0.053 unit fall in wages.

- The same empirical study comes to the conclusion that labour productivity growth has a positive impact on the wage rate in India. One unit growth in labour productivity leads to 0.15 rise in wage per worker. This is an encouraging piece of empirical finding for the growth of wage rates in India. The National Commission on Labour (2002) also made the similar recommendation that the workers in India have to be interested in the growth of productivity to ensure higher wage rate. One of the reasons for declining wages in the private sector is the decline in labour productivity or its stagnancy.

- Economic theory propounds that as the wage rate falls, there is a tendency for labour employment to expand, particular in the situation of less-than full employment. However, unfortunately, this is not happening in India. In the private sector, perhaps more and more capital-intensive method of production is being introduced. PSUs already suffer from the problem of surplus labour.

- The private sector firms, especially the MNCs working in India, practise the policy of race to the bottom. This means that they reduce the wages of unskilled manual workers, and give them the option either to accept lower wages or get fired, and their work is got done (outsourcing) from the unorganised sector at a much cheaper rate. This practice has substantially reduced the wages of low grade factory workers in India. These classes of workers are also not strongly protected by trade unions. As a matter of fact, trade unions are becoming weaker and weaker in the organised sector in India (see, Ghosh, 2013, Ch. 23).

- In many cases, the fixation of wages in India is not based on market forces of demand and supply, or by equating the marginal productivity of the worker, but simply by the whims of the employer or by the conventions of the institution. But this often goes against the interest of the worker in any industry. The bargaining power of the employer is much stronger. In some cases, the labourer is asked to sign a paper where higher wage is shown to have been paid but in actual practice, he is paid less. This is especially the case in many union-less organizations.

- The national wage policy in India has not considered agricultural wage policy; it has not been able to evolve any principles by which wage anomalies for the same types of jobs are removed; it has not fixed any wage rate for casual labourers and has not fixed any wage rate for different types of employment schemes now in force in India. Over-all, it is an incomplete policy.

Employment Scenario in India: Pattern, Problems and Policy

The national employment scenario of India reveals the regional uneven pattern of employment creation in India. Some of the states are having more unemployment than others. For instance, unemployment rates in Kerala, Bihar and Orissa are extremely high, and therefore, employment creation is palpably low. Overall, India has an unemployment problem 9 per cent of the labour force, apart from underemployment and disguised unemployment. This is much higher than the natural rate of unemployment which may be about 3 per cent in India. Another associated problem in India is that the rate of growth of labour force is generally higher than that of population (labour force growth rate 2.85 overtakes the population growth rate of 1.70). If one compares the sectoral pattern, it is found that the public sector in India is creating about 70 per cent of all employment. However, the *employment elasticity* of the public sector being low (in some cases minus), further growth in employment will be difficult for this sector. In the Indian economy, for both private and public sectors, employment elasticity in the post-reform period has significantly gone down (Upender, 2011). Output elasticity of employment measures the change in employment as a result of a change in output. The elasticity value was 0.84 in the pre-reform days and it declined to 0.11 in post-reform period. Moreover, the public sector is gradually trying to be more market oriented rather than philanthropic. Some of the sick and loss-making public sector units are also being privatized. It seems that the target of the Task Force to generate 10 million jobs in India is unattainable on a regular basis. The prospect of private sector in the growth of employment is rather bleak. There are many reasons to expect such a situation, of which the following are important:

- The capital intensity (capital/labour ratio) is rather high in the private sector, and it cannot be expected that it will come down, rather there is the possibility that it will go up. In such a case, employment generation per unit of capital will be still lower.

- The private sector in India has been downsizing since long to reduce the labour cost. It is getting the temporary work done through outsourcing and by engaging contract labourers.

- One of the reasons for reducing labour employment is to save the enterprise from the corrosive impact of trade unionism which is mostly political, and is concerned more with strikes and protests and less with labour welfare, labour education and industrial peace.

- Every wage increase through trade unionism is retaliated by downsizing, shutdown and willful lockout. Unionism is a dirty word for the private sector in LDCs, because it is more vindictive, radical and reactionary. In such a case, the private sector resorts to more capital-intensive method of production.

- In fact, labour is less productive in India, and compared to the wages paid; the net value added is much low and the production is never just in time. So the production plant is made fully automatic. It is a well-known fact that when the capital-labour ratio goes up, labour becomes more productive and the need to have an expanding labour force automatically vanishes away.

- Most of the big private industries and the corporate bodies are trying to practice what is known as *labour flexibility* by which they can any time shed out the unnecessary labour. This may be soft name for '*hiring and firing*' practised by MNCs in many countries. The Government of India has tacitly permitted this labour flexibility clause.

- It is found from experience that during the period of neoliberal globalisation as India has been experiencing, a scarcity of high quality manpower (HQM) occurs and proliferation of low quality of manpower takes place. This is what is happening in India (see Ghosh and Ghosh, 2013). Whereas India is experiencing the shortage of HQM in research, education, soft ware industries and so forth, we have an abundance of plebian manpower. People from this category join trade unions as a cover to carry on anti-social activities and their real productive value is sometimes negative. It is hard for them to get permanent employment.

- The question of employability in this context is a serious issue in India. India has a plenty of labour but a shortage of employable labour. All labourers are not employable. Some labourers do possess hard-skill but not soft skill. Soft skills make one proficient in dealing with people, management and society. I have explained elsewhere the qualities of soft skills which make persons employable (see Ghosh, 2012a). So, all these will not be discussed here.

In the backdrop of what is adumbrated earlier, it is easy to appreciate the basic thrust of the employment policy in India, although the focus does not remain the same throughout the Plan period. A large percentage of the unemployed people being low-educated and even illiterate, it is impossible to absorb them in modern high-tech industries being developed by the private sector. For the educated and high quality manpower (HQM), employment does not seem to be much of a problem. Employment problem is mainly encountered by medium level professionals and uneducated masses. The expansion of education and skill will indeed be very helpful to prepare a large part of the unemployed masses to take up small and odd jobs with low skills. People with even low-level technical skills never suffer from chronic unemployment in a developed or developing country. However, the employment policy does not make any provision to teach low level technical skill to *aam aadmi* (common people). When the prospect of absorbing a large number of people in the agricultural sector is becoming limited, technical skill and education should be the only way out. In fact, the share of employment in agriculture has come down from 61 per cent in the 1990s to around 50 per cent in recent years but its contribution to GDP is nearly 16 per cent. It is expected that a rapid rate development will make the sector still slimmer.

There was a time when the public sector was the citadel of surplus manpower. The policy of the government was to create more of underemployment than of open unemployment. This was obvious for the success in election politics. However, things have changed now with the introduction of economic reforms. The labour market is becoming extremely competitive. So, the government policy tried to create more jobs for the masses in sectors and industries which are more labour-intensive and not human-capital intensive. These areas are transport and communication, agriculture, construction and trade. Thus, the Ninth Five Year Plan put more emphasis on the development of agriculture by all means. It was thought that the promotion of agro-based industries, horticulture, small scale and cottage industries and so forth will create enough employment opportunities. The emphasis on the consumer goods sector was a correct policy direction as it creates substantial employment opportunities. But agriculture has its limitations. Non-agricultural jobs, not necessarily in the organised sector, can be increased to a considerable extent in India.

As pointed out by A.K. Sen and others, not much importance is given to the education and health sectors for the generation of sustainable employment generation in India. There are many ad hoc schemes introduced as safety nets to provide short-term income and employment generations. The Jawahra Rozger Yojana (JRY) is one such temporary scheme.

The employment guarantee scheme (EGS) could not take off very far, although it provides an important palliative for the unemployed people. There are many anomalies in such ad hoc schemes. The income from such temporary employment is not the same in all states. It needs to be uniform as far as possible.

The government at the Centre is subsidizing about 90 per cent of the cost of additional employment in the states. However, state administration does not seem to be very serious or competent to create jobs on sustainable basis. Another related important issue is that due to corruption, the money spent on employment creation does not fully reach the beneficiaries. The emphasis on job creation is lop-sided, and sometimes money is being spent without studying much of the impact, focus and the priority sectors. Our growth process is not employment friendly and is creating jobless growth, which is a very prominent in western capitalist economies. Unless this is checked, India will have a high quantitative growth rate with a lot of poverty and widening income inequalities.

The labourers that cannot be absorbed in the agricultural sector must try their luck in the unorganized sector and informal sectors. The government has been giving emphasis on the growth of the informal sector, but the efforts are not sustainable or continuous. The services sector has made substantial improvement in the creation of employment. It is now accommodating more than 28 per cent of the labour force. But as the experience of developed countries shows, unless the sector is made more capital-intensive, productivity is likely to fall. The experience of DCs also shows that the services sector is developed after the development of agricultural and industrial sectors; in India, it is developed prior to the development of the industrial sector. A large part of the services sector in India is the abode of lowly productive jobs. This may increase employment but with much less value-added. Our services sector is doing well only because of a few selected high valued industries like communication, software development and so forth. The private sector-led model of growth that India is steering through, does not offer much hope for employment maximization, and is giving indirect incentive for the informalisation of the labour market. Globalisation has been associated with more and more informalisation of the formal sector. More than ninety per cent of labour employment in India is in the informal sectors (Jacob, 2007).

On the other hand, the organised sector's share in employment is gradually plummeting. Hence, it is better to expand the informal sector as widely as possible by making a link with the private sector for outsourcing and contracting out. In view of the poor cargo effect of the organised private and public sectors to salvage the unemployed people, any sector that can use labour-intensive method of production and distribution should bear the brunt of future employment creations in India. The whole idea of the employment policy is to create gainful employment and not just employment. The basic purpose of the policy is to create a decent livelihood for every worker. In fact, the right to employment should be a fundamental human right to be enforced by laws. But our employment policy is silent on this issue.

Be that as it may, an important development in the employment scenario that has been taking place in India is the *casualisation* and *proletarianisation of labour* (Ghosh,1992, 9 June). This trend is visible because some of the marginal agricultural farmers who find agricultural occupation as un-remunerative come to towns and become casual labourers, without any asset or property. Some of the casual labourers become contract labourers without having any backing from the trade unions. This trend may continue in India for quite some time to come, as the private sector is not much interested in bearing the long-term cost of permanent labour. The casual labourers are mostly underemployed; but it seems that some amount of underemployment is better than open unemployment in the present situation of labour market flux. The bottom line is that our Plans are not job-oriented, but growth-oriented and the trickle-down effect that is expected to help the social sector in generating employment and income has not evidently happened. What is really needed is a paradigm shift in favour of the social sector even by reducing to some extent the quantitative growth rate, and a suitable trade-off between economic growth and employment creation needs to be found out to save the people. Can trade unions provide any help?

Paradigm Shift in Trade Unionism in India: The Post-Liberalization Scenario

The impact of globalisation is visible in the area of trade union movement in recent years. A number of research studies in India have focused on the emerging trend of Indian trade union movement especially after the period of liberalization in 1991. A few papers published in *Indian Journal of Labour Economics* in 2006 (vol.49. #4) have dwelt on the emerging trend in trade unionism and industrial relations in India in the post-liberalization period. The paper by Kuriakose Mamkoottam (2006) focuses on the emerging trend in the trade union movement. K.R Shyam Sunder (2006) also concentrates on trade union and new challenges in India. Mamkoottam's study shows that in the 21st century, there is going to be a paradigm shift in the trade union movement, and the attitude towards to confrontation and conflicts between labour and management will be replaced by cooperation and collaboration. Shyam Sunder explains the growth of trade unionism in India as the product of the colonial period, however, the movement picked up strength and dynamism after India's Independence. The liberalization-privatization-globalisation (LPG) model of growth that India adopted since 1991 has gradually changed the whole focus of trade unionism in India in several ways, of which the following are critically important (see also Datt and Sundharam, 2012):

First, the government was very sympathetic towards workers and trade unions before the introduction of the LPG model of development. It always promoted the interests of the working class. In the post-liberalisation period, the government is very keen to promote the private sector and capitalist enterprises. This sector wants labour market reforms and does not accept many of the demands and labour market traditions.

Second, the private sector in India is very powerful now and does not have to dance with the tune of the government. It wants the real value-added, and the determination of wages is not done through trade union's demand but by productivity of workers. If the productivity is low, the wage has to be low. Allocative efficiency demands that the wage level must be equal to the marginal productivity of workers. Private-sector led capitalist method of development is not a charitable process. Earlier, wages were not linked with labour productivity in a rigorous way, but after liberalisation, every wage increase needs economic justification and not the fiat or fear of the government, and the trade union is redundant and helpless.

Third, in the post-liberalisation period, the importance of trade unions has tremendously declined. If the private enterprise that it is more cost conscious wants to get the work done from outside, it will be outsourcing the work from the unorganized sector, or it can hire contract workers for a short-period. Thus, it is quite possible that the enterprise will shed out a part of the regular work force. And all these will make the trade union like the Samson with his lock shorn. Trade unions will be weaker and weaker under the LPG model.

Fourth, in order to increase the quantum of profit, the private sector has been adopting a number of policy options including closure of factories for a long period, downsizing the labour force, use of contract labour and so forth to reduce the labour cost in the name of labour market flexibility, and the permission to use such actions of labour flexibility has been granted by the government. Obviously, the importance and the need for trade unions have considerably reduced now.

Fifth, the government sector has also started the process of reduction in labour employment through shedding out of surplus labour, voluntary retirement schemes and so on, and the privatized industries have already reduced the redundant labour force in industries. Trade unions are helpless and silent spectators.

Sixth, since strikes and protests by labourers are disrupting the normal lives of citizens and creating an increasing amount of troubles for the public, many states including West Bengal, Haryana, Uttar Pradesh and Tamil Nadu, and so forth have started ruthless actions on the strikers. Not only the states, common citizens are quite against the strikes in organizations which are supplying essential services like hospitals and communications and the like. Interestingly, the judiciary has also condemned strikes by observing that "employees have no fundamental rights to go on strike". In many new cases, it has reversed its earlier stance. All this shows that one of the every fundamental weapons of trade unionism was put back into the sheath, and to that extent, its pristine position was seriously blighted.

Seventh, the growth of independent industry unions, as in banks, financial institutions, hospitals, and the like, is attracting the attention of the society in a more respectable way. The skilled workers in many organizations do not join any unions but have their own associations to look after their professional development. All these have trivialized the importance of politically affiliated unions. The affiliated unions are wading through rough waters of rivalry, conflicts and confrontations.

What transpires from the aforesaid discussion is that Indian trade unions are sailing though the turbulent waters and the wind is blowing from the other direction. The private sector is now working in collusion with the government sector and their policies are to protect capital more and labour less. Trade unions are now spreading their wings to reach the unorganised sector. Perhaps the days of militant trade unionism are over for good. The unions must now take a stand for compromise and cooperation, and not conflict and confrontation. Does all these need labour market reforms?

Labour Market Reforms

It is found by many experts abroad that Indian labour laws are archaic, rigid and most restrictive in the world, and this is one of the reasons of slow growth of the Indian manufacturing sector (see *The Economist*, February, 2007, p.16). Since it is an important issue in the whole system of industrial relations and development of the country, let us give it a close look.

India has a very complex array of labour laws such that they encourage more of litigations and less of practical solutions of industrial disputes (Sharma, 2006). The issue of labour market reform has become very prominent after the introduction of economic reform in India in 1991. The argument that is often put forward is that economic reform cannot be fully successful unless it accompanies labour market reform. This is so because, without such a reform, the capitalist method of production and marketisation philosophy cannot go hand in hand, and economic efficiency cannot be attained. What should be trajectory of labour market reform (LMR)? The following are the fundamental constituents of LMR, as proposed by experts:

* LMR should give more and more power to the non-capitalist firms to determine wages on the basis of demand and supply, or on productivity. The wage must be based on market principle without any fear or favour. The market should determine the value of labour power.

* The employing firm which is based on the principle of profit maximization, must have the power of hiring and firing as followed in other capitalist economies (also in China).

* Only productive labourers who can contribute to value-added should be retained in the job.

* Labour cost has to be the minimum. Hence, there will be outsourcing and contracting out.

* Rigid laws which have been unnecessarily working for the laboring class without any economic justification will have to be repealed or amended.

* The power of the trade unions must be diluted substantially as they interfere with the functioning of the productive system through erratic strikes, lockouts, protests and so forth. All these hamper production.

* Government protection to trade unions must go off, and instead, the protection should be in favour of the capitalist method of production, its philosophy and functionings.

* State intervention in the matter of labour disputes, or any other matter of that nature will be unwanted. It will be a completely free market principle.

It is indeed very difficult for an Indian firm that employs more than a hundred workers to fire workers without the permission of the central government. The government at the center is not able to change labour laws without the support of the communist party of India. The rainbow coalition at the center has to heavily rely on the CPI(M) support. In theory, it is always possible to have a flexible situation regarding labour market problems. However, in practice, the rules of the central government are tacitly followed. The regional trade unions always support such laws as are favorable to them. If the Indian manufacturing sector is to really grow, what is first needed is to introduce suitable labour market reforms as soon as possible. The private sector in India wants such reforms very urgently in order to be internationally competitive (Ghosh, 2009, p. 22) .

Labour Market Reform: Progress, Problems and Prospects

Although the Government of India has not passed any legislation, it has had a tacit understanding and approval of labour market reform being very slowly introduced by the private sector in India.

- Labour flexibility in the form of shedding out of unnecessary labour has already been started in the industrial sector. Now in both public and private sectors, labour employment has appreciably come down (see Ghosh, 2013, ch. 24). The size of the labour force has changed by nearly 7 per cent for the regular workforce. Many industries have introduced voluntary retirement schemes.

- The protection from the central government that the labour sector used to get earlier is being gradually discontinued. Now the capitalist sector is getting more protection from the government sector. However the trade unions still have the same mindset and want to enjoy the same paternalistic protectionism.

- The Fifth Pay Commission (1994) recommended an increase of 30% wage hike to labourers but at the same time ordered a downsizing by 30 per cent too.

- The fact that the archaic labour laws should change during the period of rapid economic growth for a country wedded to the philosophy of LPG model, has been accepted by all rational economists and political economists. However, in a country like India, democracy has its own cost in terms if delay and dissension. However, it is expected that before long, labour market reform will be introduced in India.

- Some of the boisterous trade unions are already tamed by the private sector. Their aggressiveness and nuisance value are reduced now. A plethora of reform has been done in the area of trade unionism in India. In 2006, 2.3 million mandays were lost and in 2010, the figure came down to 1.8 million (Govt. of India, 2011-12, p.212). The number of strikes has also considerably reduced all over India except in Kerala, West Bengal and Tamil Nadu.

- The Supreme Court of India has given the verdict that the right to strike and all other disruptive activities is not the fundamental right of any trade union. It means that the judiciary is also against the militant trade union activities.

- It is heartening to note that collective bargaining has been decentralized in many industries, and the number of strikes and disputes due to the failure of collective bargaining has considerably reduced.

- Politicalisation of union activities in a number of private industries has been banned. Employers now are encouraging internal unionism for labour welfare, training and skill development; outside influence of unions is kept at bay.

- LMR is essential in view of the fact that almost every day, more than a million mandays are lost in India because of poor work culture, irresponsibility and unethical work practices. This must be prevented to make the industrial sector more competitive and efficient.

- There is a lurking fear that the introduction of LMR will destroy at least some 5 million jobs in the organised sector. This will be a huge problem to tackle. The government will have to come forward with a strong safety measure that will prevent the fall of the labour force to the poverty trap (safety net). If this is not done, the poverty rate will further go up.

It is clear from the aforesaid discussion that LMR has already started in India and labourers' militancy now is being replaced by employers' militancy. As a matter of fact, it is correctly said that, "labour today has lost its teeth".

The Report on the National Commission on Labour: Is it Pro-Labour?

The Report of the Second National Commission on Labour (NCL) is based on the fact that globalisation and liberalisation as processes cannot be wished away. Hence, the report observes that labour had to adjust itself to changes at all costs, methods and places of production, on employment and the skills necessary to retain employability; and mobility and the responses that were necessary to acquire and retain economic efficiency and international competitiveness (see *Frontline*, 2002 for details). However, the Commission thinks that trade unionisation is at low ebb and, therefore, collective bargaining should be encouraged.

The report almost guarantees unfettered right to close establishments that employ up to 300 workers. Currently, according the Industrial Disputes Act, establishments employing up to 100 people should secure prior permission from the government concerned before resorting to closures. The report suggests that in the case of closure of establishments employing more than 300 workers, the employer shall apply for permission to the appropriate government 90 days before the closure and also serve a copy of the application to the recognised negotiating agent. If the government does not respond within 60 days of receipt of such an application, permission will be deemed to have been granted.

A distinction is drawn between core and non-core activities. Contract labour, recommends the Commission, shall not be engaged in core production or services or activities. However, to meet sporadic seasonal demand, the employer may engage temporary labour for such activities. In essence, it legitimizes the use of contract labour even in core activities. The Commission states categorically that in view of the fast-changing economic situation and changes in technology and management, the number of posts in an organisation cannot be fixed permanently. The report said: "Organisations must have the flexibility to adjust the number of this workforce based on economic efficiency." It is clear that the basic approach of the report is to wean trade unions from adopting confrontationist tactics.

The general tenor of the report is against labour strikes. It recommends the much-abhorred system of strike in the case of essential services such as water supply, medical services, sanitation, electricity and transport in the event of an unsettled dispute between employer and employee. Strikes, as a rule, can be called only by the recognized negotiating agent, that too only with the support of 51 per cent of the workers in a strike ballot. The formation of unions will also be difficult as the Commission has recommended that only a union that has at least 10 per cent of employees in a unit as its members would have the right to represent the workers in various forums.

The NCL report admits that employment generation had actually fallen since the 1980s despite the growth in the economy. It also notes that around the same period employers began to outsource production work from the unorganised sector.

Assessing the impact of globalisation, the report says that the industrial sector has been affected during the last few years and the slowdown and loss of production and employment have resulted in a lower demand of consumer goods which, in turn, has led to a general leveling of all productive activities.

The final report has been unduly kind to employers and the owners of industries. The emphasis is on arbitration and mediation in industrial relations. In sum, industrial peace, and not unrest, has been over-emphasised. Trade unions have been urged to reflect on the current situation and not to create conditions that would alienate public sympathy. The report frowns upon the kind of industrial action that has taken place so far and is critical of the "increasing tendency on the part of the trade unions to get together in ad hoc struggle committees to launch struggles or to support a struggle one of them has launched".

Concluding Observations: Towards Some Policy Options

In this concluding section, a few policy issues will be highlighted. All said, it must be accepted that labour market reform has started in India and perhaps it is necessary to do away with archaic labour laws. But a strict application of LMR will make many labourers redundant. It is estimated that about five million jobs will be knocked by LMR. The introduction of casualisation and labour market flexibility will, in all probability, increase the quantum of labour unemployment. There must be some provisions for the maintenance of these workers at a reasonably humanistic level, and these labourers need legal protection against exploitation. In view of the absence of a minimum wage policy (MWP), it should be imperative to introduce a productivity-linked wage policy. A national wage policy is indeed the crying need of the day.

In the process of globalisation, the ordinary manual labourers are the worst sufferers. The wage gap between skilled and unskilled workers should be minimized as far as reasonable. The employment policy must incorporate various measures encouraging on the job-training and skill formation for the low level workers. Trade union movement must be geared for better collective bargaining and maximization of labour welfare. Perhaps the days of militant unionism are over in India. Trade unions should work in cooperation with the management and not take up the policy of confrontation. Workers' protests and strikes that paralyze essential services and utilities should be legally banned. Before changing the gear for further quantitative economic growth, India's labour policy should concentrate on labourers' education, skill development and health status. In the longer run, such a policy should prove beneficial for both labour and capital and also should go a long way in developing a better and a more sustainable stage of industrial relations in a country like India.

References

Clairmont, F.F. (1996). *The Rise and Fall of Economic Liberalism: The Making of the Economic Gulag*, Southbound and Third World Network, Penang, Malaysia.

Datt, R. and Sundhharam, K.P.M (2012). *Indian Economy*, S. Chand and Company, New Delhi.

Frontline, Vol. 19, Issue 16. August 3-16, 2002.

Ghosh, B.N. (1992). "Proletarianisation of Indian labour: Some evidence", *Mainstream*, 9 June.

Ghosh, B.N. (2009). *A Tale of Two Economies: Development Dynamics of India and China*, Nova Science Publications, New York.

Ghosh, B.N. (2012). *Business Ethics and Corporate Governance*, Tata McGraw Hill, Delhi.

Ghosh, B.N. (2012a) (ed.). *Skill Management for Personality Development*, Tata McGraw Hill, Delhi.

Ghosh, B.N. and Ghosh, R. (2013). *Human Capital Migration: A Study of Typology and Impact,* New Academic Publishers, Delhi.

Government of India (1969). *Report of the National Commission on Labour,* Government Press, New Delhi.

Government of India (2012). *Economic Survey* (2011-12), Oxford University Press, New Delhi.

Jacob, Tony (2007), "The unorganised sector in India", *https: docs.google.com*

Mamkoottam, Kuriakose (2006), "Emerging trend in the trade union movement", *Indian Journal of Labour Economics*, 49, 4.

Schmidt, J.D. (2006). “Flexicurity, casualization and informalization of global labour markets” In: B.N. Ghosh and Halil Guven (eds.), *Globalisation and the Third World,* Palgrave-Macmillan, London and New York.

Sen, A.K. (2009). *The Idea of Justice*, Penguin Books, New York.

Sharma, Alakh Nath (2006). “Flexibility, employment and labour market reforms in India”,*Economic and Political Weekly*, May 27.

Shyam Sunder (2006). “Trade unions and the new challenges”, *Indian Journal of Labour Economics*, 49, 4.

The Economist (2007). “Briefing Indian Economy”, 3 February.

Upender, M. (2011). “Differential output elasticities of employment during post-reform period in the Indian economy”, *Singapore Economic Review*, 56, 2.

Chapter Two

Globalisation, Economic Analysis and Employment Flexibility

Amitava Krishna Dutt, Sebastien Charles and Dany Lang

Introduction

The global economy and the economies of almost all countries have experienced major changes in the last several decades, of which three are particularly striking. First, globalisation, especially as reflected by the increasing interdependence on countries involving international trade and international capital movements, has been proceeding apace. Second, the state has been on the retreat in most countries, due to deregulation, liberalization, privatization and lower taxes on the rich. Third, income inequality has been increasing in many countries.[iv] Arguably, the three trends are causally related. Although the increase in interaction between countries through international trade and capital flows has resulted partly from improvements in transport and communications technology, it is largely the result of changes in government policies involving trade and capital account liberalization, which are aspects of the rolling back of the state. Globalisation is also seen as strengthening the case for the retreat of the state, with the argument that in a globalizing world state intervention is ineffective and even counterproductive because it makes countries less efficient and internationally uncompetitive and because it scares away foreign capital and pushes local capital to flow out of the country. All this results in competitive liberalization, involving what is called a "race to the bottom". Both globalisation and the rolling back of the state have an adverse effect in income inequality and the vulnerability of low income people. On the one hand, globalisation implies increasing competition in trade and the mobility of capital without an increase in the mobility of labor, especially of low-skilled labor. On the other hand, the rolling back of the state, reflected in deregulation and reductions in taxes on upper income groups and government expenditure, particularly "social" spending.[v] Fiscal austerity in the wake of financial crises (resulting amongst others from unstable hot money flows) has reinforced the latter trend. Austerity policies also worsen inequality by increasing consumer debt and transferring income from the debtors (often poor or middle classes households) to the rich as interest payments. Increasing inequality, and the consequent increase in the political influence of the rich who want greater "economic freedom", implies that the state adopts more market-friendly policies, which further rolls back the state and promotes globalisation.[vi]

Thus, market-friendly policies that roll back the state have been adopted for a variety of reasons, including the increase in the power of those who favor such policies and globalisation. However, the nature of mainstream economic analysis has, arguably, also had a major role in this dynamic. Keynes (1936), in concluding *The General Theory* emphasized the role of academic economists in influencing the direction of economic policy with the words:

> [T]he ideas of economists and political philosophers, both when they are right and when they are wrong, are more powerful than is commonly understood. Indeed the world is ruled by little else. Practical men, who believe themselves to be quite exempt from any intellectual influences, are usually the slaves of some defunct economist. Madmen in authority, who hear voices in the air, are distilling their frenzy from some academic scribbler of a few years back. I am sure that the power of vested interests is vastly exaggerated compared with the gradual encroachment of ideas ... [S]oon or late, it is ideas, not vested interests, which are dangerous for good or evil.

Although he may have underestimated the importance of "the power of vested interests", his emphasis on the "academic scribbler of a few years back" seems to be right on the mark. This is especially so if we take into account the interactions between academic economics and vested interests. The power of vested interests influences the ideas of academic economists directly when they serve a consultants and hired guns, and indirectly – and perhaps more pervasively –because of the reward structure in the academy in terms of research funding, publications, tenure and promotion. Moreover, academic ideas – because of their diffusion through educational institutions and the media – also increase the power of vested interests by dominating knowledge and persuading others of the efficacy of policies that are often against their own interests and the common good.

The purpose of this paper is to examine one aspect of this general argument, that is, the call for increased employment flexibility, a central aspect of proposed policies of neoliberal "structural" reforms widely argued to be necessary for improving economic performance, especially generating output and employment growth.

For a while now it has been claimed that the alleged lack of labor market flexibility, including employment flexibility, in Europe has contributed to the disease called "eurosclerosis" (Giersch, 1985). In this view, "generous unemployment benefits, restrictions on hiring and firing, and restrained wage competition have led to rigid, "eurosclerotic" ... economies, which could not cope with the big shocks of the 1970's" (Bentilola and Bertola, 1990). Policymakers in Europe have argued in favor of greater employment flexibility since the beginning of the 1980s, as reflected in the various OECD annual reports, but these calls have intensified since the onset of the so-called "debt crisis" in 2009.[vii] These issues have been discussed not only in the context of high income countries, but also for less-developed countries such as India (see Dutt, 2006). It has been argued that the market-friendly reforms in India have not had their full positive effects because labor markets have remained inflexible (see Bhagwati and Panagariya, 2012).[viii] In European countries, similar views have also been provided and the governments have undertaken major reforms. In France for example, the law on labor relations passed in April 2013 will make increase internal and external flexibility dramatically[ix]. Amongst others, employers will be able to fire easily, without risking any judicial proceedings.

This paper argues that the support for employment flexibility comes from the mainstream or neoclassical view of the labor market, and that the adoption of an alternative approach to economic analysis may well give rise to a different policy conclusion. To make this point, the rest of the paper proceeds as follows. Section 2 makes some general critical comments about mainstream or neoclassical economics focusing on what crucial issues about the real world it leaves out or addresses insufficiently and inadequately, and the implications of this for policy regarding employment flexibility. Attention is given especially to the role of uncertainty, power and institutions. Section 3 develops a simple model that takes seriously these important factors neglected in mainstream economics to consider an alternative perspective and to examine the implications of increasing employment flexibility.

Employment Flexibility and Economic Analysis

Labor market flexibility has a number of different dimensions. The kind of flexibility we focus on in this paper is what has been referred to as *external numerical flexibility*. For the sake of brevity, we will refer to as employment flexibility. An increase in this kind of flexibility seeks to allow firms to fire and hire employees more easily (that is, by decreasing the time of notice, as well as the costs of hiring and firing, for example severance pay, should be decreased), removing the requirement that firms seek the permission of the government to reduce employment by a large amount, and to relax the laws and regulations on temporary work or fixed-term contracts.[x]As a consequence of employment protection legislation (EPL), labor cannot be adjusted freely (because of costs of labor firing due to severance pay requirements, giving advance notice, or seeking the permission of the government).

Proponents of employment flexibility argue that EPL reduces the demand for labor. This happens because firms have a reduced incentive to hire workers who they will find difficult to fire in case they need to, so they substitute capital for labor and adopt labor-saving technological change. The lower level and growth of labor demand and employment, they argue, has the effect of reducing wages. Moreover, they argue that such employment restrictions reduce profitability (by making it necessary to continue employing workers no longer required and by reducing the productivity of workers who do not fear the threat of being fired), and, therefore, reduce investment and the growth of output in the economy. Furthermore, they argue that employment inflexibility hinders structural change needed for the transition to an innovation-based economy (see Saint-Paul, 2000). Thus, not only do government restrictions on firing workers (and the closing of firms which implying large-scale firing of workers) result in poor economic performance in terms of efficiency, profitability, investment, technological change and growth, but it also hurts those it intends to help, by reducing the growth of employment and wages.

Discussions of the effects of EPL sometimes focus on the dual labor market approach which sees labor markets as separated into a "primary" and a "secondary" sector. Related to the idea of the dual economy in less-developed countries (see Lewis, 1954) and to the work on Doeringer and Piore (1971) on internal labor markets within firms in advanced capitalist countries, the approach distinguishes between employees in the *primary sector* who have rather stable jobs, relatively high pay and status, good working conditions and opportunities for promotion through a developed internal labor market on the one hand, and employees in the *secondary sector* who have poorer working conditions and salaries, little job security and virtually no promotion or training opportunities. For less-developed countries, a similar distinction is made between the formal and informal sectors (see Tokman, 2008) where workers in the formal sector can either have characteristics of primary sector workers (having long term employment) or those of secondary sector workers (who are often casual workers with short tenure) and the informal sector in which all workers have the characteristics of secondary sector workers. In some less-developed countries like India, formal workers comprise less than ten percent of the total labor force.

It is sometimes argued by EPL critics that since such legislation generally applies to, or applies more stringently to, workers in the primary sector, it induces firms to hire more casual workers with short employment tenure. Thus, employment legislation results in the informalization of labor, worsening the conditions of workers in general. It is further argued that the protection given to labor in the organized sector amounts to pampering a labor aristocracy at the expense of the unemployed and those employed in the unorganized sector or as casual workers, who do not have such protection. The fact that secondary-sector jobs tend to be filled by women, ethnic minorities and people from poor backgrounds has led some of proponents of the EPL reforms to argue that more flexibility would reduce inequality and promote fairness.

The argument in favor of increasing employment flexibility and in weakening EPL is often made in terms of the neoclassical approach to labor markets.[xi] In this approach, EPL creates a distortion in the economy, resulting in an inefficient outcome. The actual outcome will be a lower level of employment and its growth: profit maximizing firms will take into account the fact that if they hire more workers, they will be costly to fire (which firms will want to do if there are negative expected or actual future shocks) because of EPL, so that the incentive to hire new workers will be reduced. Moreover, there may be an effect on the productivity of workers who, because they are difficult to fire, will not work as hard as they would if they could be fired more easily. If there is EPL which requires firms to pay some minimum wages and benefits to more regular workers, but not casual workers (or workers hired by firms with whom they subcontract), then firms will respond to laws about firing by replacing regular workers by casual workers and outsourcing to subcontractors who may use casual labor. Moreover, in matching models *a la* Saint-Paul (2000), the lack of external numerical flexibility is a major explanatory factor of the higher unemployment rates for women, the low-skilled, the young and the senior workers.

One issue that is neglected in the simple neoclassical analysis of labor markets discussed so far is the fact that even without laws which restrict firing, there is a considerable degree of labor hoarding by firms which takes the form of holding on to labor when they face declines in the demand for their products. This phenomena, however, is not difficult to reconcile with the neoclassical optimizing approach without distortions if one takes into account the hiring and training costs of workers required to augment the firm-specific skills of workers (see Oi, 1962). In the presence of these costs, profit maximizing firms may not reduce their workforce by much when there is a fall in the demand for their product because the costs they would save by doing so may be less than the costs of hiring and training new workers when they need to expand their workforce when there is a rise in demand. Taking this into account does not negate the neoclassical view of employment legislation, however, since such legislation, if it is binding, creates additional restrictions to what firms can do in terms of how much excess labor they will carry (see also Bentolila and Bertola, 1990).

This neoclassical approach can be accused for having a number of shortcomings. Most relevant for our purposes is its neglect or inadequate analysis of three major features of real economies, that is, uncertainty, power and institutions.[xii] Regarding uncertainty, it can be argued that many, if not most, important economic (and other) decisions that have implications for the future are made in an uncertain environment. Following Keynes (1937), we need to distinguish between risky situations, in which objective probabilities can be assigned and uncertain situations in which it is not possible to do so. Neoclassical economics, with its insistence on using optimization as a basis for analysis, assumes away uncertainty in this sense and confines itself to certain or at most risky situations, in which optimization can be equated to "rationality". In situations of uncertainty decision-makers: form expectations about the future with varying degree of confidence; follow various conventional patterns of behavior, attempt to maintain liquidity in an attempt to postpone decisions which are difficult to reverse; and make various types of arrangements attempting to reduce the uncertainty they face. Economic analysis needs to take into account these kinds of behavior, which are context depending, rather than binding itself in the optimizing straightjacket (even if it does so with modifications of one sort or another).

Regarding power, despite the fundamental role it arguably plays in the economy and society, has been introduced only sporadically in neoclassical economics in the analysis of market power under imperfect competition and in game theoretic models of intentional behavior and is usually defined as the ability of some individuals (or groups) to take actions or make decisions which make others act in ways that is against their interests and which they would not have otherwise done.[xiii] The optimizing axiomatic approach, however, is limited in scope, both because it confines attention to conscious and intentional actions in the context of relations between the dominator and the dominated, and because it does not provide, and arguably does not lend itself to, an analysis of the complex and multiple sources power. Other approaches, more closely related to the analysis of Marx and institutionalist economists, which do not start from the individual optimizing agent provide a richer perspective, for instance by invoking the notion of structural power, which is distinguished from relational power that is exercised in the interaction between two or more individuals or groups, and which, while taking into account intentional actions by people and groups to influence the structures within which society operates, recognize that these structural outcomes may be unintended or unconscious (see, for instance, Strange, 1988 and Guzzini, 1993).

Institutions, sometimes defined loosely as the "rules of the game", can be defined to include: more or less codified constitutions, laws and regulations; collections of shared norms and habits which garner wide acceptance; and formal and informal organizations such as government bureaucracies, firms, markets and families (Hodgson, 2006). The "new" institutionalist economists, following the contributions of Coase, North and Williamson, have introduced institutions into neoclassical economic analysis, reversing its long neglect of them. Although some "new" institutionalist economists do point out that the actions of individuals in society may not lead to efficiency-improving institutional changes, they generally take the view that it is possible to identify good institutions – such those that secure private property rights and increase market flexibility – which reduce transactions costs and promote the efficient operation of free markets and capitalist societies, and recommend their adoption. This approach is problematic for various reasons. Firstly, its concept of transactions costs, which can refer to virtually all aspects of the economy ignored in the theoretically constructed smoothly-functioning market, is arguably too vague to allow the proper identification of specific real-world institutions. Secondly, the goal of efficiency is problematic to define if preferences are endogenous (as North, 1994, allows) and need not be the only, or even the most important, goal for society (since it ignores other goals such as fairness, functionings and capabilities and reducing vulnerability), and because the analysis of institutional change involving the optimizing approach focuses on some issues, like those emphasized in Olson's (1965) theory of collective action, and does not take into account unintentional and unconscious forces which affect institutional changes involving all three of its dimensions.

Taking uncertainty, power and institutions seriously has implications regarding employment flexibility that are very different from those that emerge from the neoclassical approach. In general terms, as emphasized by Keynes and some Keynesians, most notably the post-Keynesians, the existence of uncertainty implies that aggregate demand in the economy, especially investment demand, depends on expectations, and may not be high enough to fully employ all workers who seek employment. Moreover, there may be no free market adjustments – through reductions in wage, the price level and the interest rate – that take the economy to a situation of full employment or some natural rate (or non-acceleration inflation rate) of unemployment. Money wage and price deflation, rather than increasing aggregate demand and employment, may well reduce them, for instance, by redistributing income from debtors to creditors, reducing cash inflows of firms and – if wages fall more than prices – redistributing income from wages to profits (see Dutt and Amadeo, 1990, for details). A reduction in the interest rate is unlikely to increase borrowing and spending business and consumer confidence are low in an uncertain situation. Wages and prices may become rigid as workers and firms try to reduce uncertainty with long-term wage agreements and pricing strategies, and due to social norms about fairness that affect money wages and relative wages. Great wage flexibility can, in fact, increase uncertainty, reduce aggregate demand and increase liquidity preference, which will increase employment rather than reducing it.

The implication of all this for long-term labor arrangements is as follows. First, in situations of unemployment, reductions in aggregate demand which reduce output can lead to sharper contractions if workers are fired when they are not needed for current production, because of a decline in wages and consumption demand from those who lose their jobs, than if they are retained because they are employed under long-term arrangements.

Second, concerning employment decisions, neoclassical economists have mostly focused on the costs of hiring and firing for explaining labor hoarding, not taking into account social norms regarding fairness, and uncertainty. Uncertainty regarding future demand conditions when hiring and firing costs are significant can induce firms to hire more long-term labor. Some ideas that have been discussed in explanations of wage rigidity – for instance, the idea of gift exchange (see Akerlof, 1982) – apply to long-term labor arrangements as well. Long-term employment agreements are provided to workers who return the gift of greater loyalty. This, as well as greater familiarity with firm-specific employment, can imply higher productivity growth with long-term labor arrangements than short-term ones, something that can induce firms to prefer long-term labor even at a higher wage. Fairness can dictate that workers are not fired, due to no fault of their own, whenever times are bad and workers are not needed, and violations of fairness norms can reduce morale and productivity. A counter-argument suggests that short-term workers are more likely to work harder because they fear the threat of immediate dismissal, or the hope of being hired long term, but it is not obvious which effect is in fact stronger overall. In any case, labor markets are best seen as institutions in which social norms have a major influence, rather than as markets in which anonymous buyers and sellers make transactions.[xiv]

Third, the existence of uncertainty implies not only that firms may hire labor with long term contracts, but also that they may not know the precise amount of labor to employ under long-term contracts at any point in time. Moreover, although they may realize the positive monetary consequences to them of hiring with long-term contracts, they may underestimate the less tangible benefits of lower recruiting costs and productivity benefits and pay more attention to the more certain cost-facing measures due to firing workers not necessary for current production. It is therefore quite likely that employers will follow some norms about how much long-term labor to hire which is likely to be less than what may be warranted by productivity gains and other benefits. It follows that the amount of long-term labor they will hire will increase when they are required by government regulations to hire them, changing the hiring norms they follow. Moreover, these regulations are likely to benefit them at the firm level, but also at the aggregate level since aggregate demand can be kept buoyant by regulations that prevent large and swift declines in employment which is not something that they would take into account in their decentralized decision making.[xv]

Finally, the relative power of workers and employers can affect both the amount of long-term labor hired by firms and the pressures the two sides bring on the state to change employment policy. While employment stability is of direct concern to workers because it provides them security and reduces their vulnerability to macroeconomic changes, employers can be expected to generally prefer having more freedom to make employment decisions. Thus, greater power for employers is likely to reduce the amount of long-term labor. Moreover, increased power for employers leads to greater influence on the state to increase employment flexibility. The balance of power between workers and employers can be affected by many factors, including the degree of slackness in labor markets, the political orientation of the government, the international mobility of capital, and the financial resources available to each group. Moreover, power also depends on the public's beliefs on how the economy actually works, which can unintentionally or, in some cases intentionally, be influenced by the dominant ideas taught in classrooms and available in academic journals and reflected in the popular media. On the last issue, the dominance of the neoclassical approach can be expected to increase the power of those who favor greater employment flexibility.

Employment Flexibility, Growth and Distribution

Our discussion in the previous section showed that taking into account important aspects of real economies, such as uncertainty, power and institutions is likely to have implications of employment protection legislation that are very different from those which emerge from the neoclassical approach. In this section, we will develop a simple model of growth and distribution to formalize these possibilities. To do so, we draw on what have been called post-Keynesian and Kaleckian (PKK) models which attempt incorporate these issues into the analysis using macroeconomic relations rather than individual optimizing behavior.

We use a simple framework that assumes that the economy produces a single good which can be both consumed and invested with two basic factors of production, labor and non-depreciating capital (the latter being physically the same as the good produce) with fixed coefficients of production which show the maximum amounts that can be produced with each input.[xvi] We assume that the economy has two classes, workers who work for wages and consume their entire income and capitalists who own the capital and firms and receive profits of which they save a constant fraction. Firms hold on to all the capital they own and always maintain excess capital. We abstract from financial considerations and government fiscal activity. Finally, the economy is a closed one and has no economic relations with the rest of the world. Most of these assumptions, made for simplicity, are fairly standard in the simpler PKK models of growth and distribution, and can be modified to incorporate additional elements into the model. We will later comment on the implications of modifying these assumption, especially that about the closed economy. Our final assumption, and this is the new feature of the model, is that there are two kinds of workers, those with long-term labor contracts who cannot be fired instantly even if they are not needed for production, and those without such contracts who can be hired and fired at will.

The equations of the model are as follows. Total income is distributed among the two kinds of workers and profits according to

$$PY = W_l L_l + W_s L_s + rPK \qquad (1)$$

where P is the price of the good, Y is real income and output, W_l is the money wage for workers of type i, where the subscript l denotes long-term labor and s denotes short term labor, L_i is the amount of labor employed of type i, r is the rate of profit defined as a ratio of total profits divided by the value of capital at replacement cost, and K is the real stock of capital.

The major difference between long-term and short-term labor is that in the short run, at a point in time, the amount of long-term labor, L_l, is fixed, whereas the amount of short-term labor, L_s can be freely altered and even be driven to zero. We assume that the amount of labor required per unit of output for each type of labor is given by b_i, and that the long-term labor is no less productive than short-term labor, so that $b_l \leq b_s$. The assumption that long-term labor is more productive can be defended on the grounds that they have more firm-specific knowledge compared to short-term workers, have more motivation because they feel more secure and because, as we shall see below, have higher wages. It is possible, as noted in the previous section, that short-term workers may work harder because they are more concerned about losing their jobs, but we assume that the effects discussed earlier are not dominated by this effect, given that even long-term workers are not guaranteed jobs, and can be fired after the passage of time. As we shall see later, this productivity advantage is not important for our results. We are assuming, for simplicity, that apart from this productivity differential, long- and short-term workers are perfect substitutes in production. We denote the maximum output than can be produced by long-term workers as

$$Y_l = \frac{L_l}{b_l} \qquad (2)$$

and $L_s = 0$. If actual output, $Y \leq Y_l$, actual employment will be given by L_l.

If $Y > Y_l$, we have

$$L_s = b_s(Y - Y_l), \qquad (3)$$

which, using equation (2) implies

$$L_s = b_s\left(Y - \frac{L_l}{b_l}\right), \qquad (4)$$

Money wages for both kinds of workers are fixed, and we assume that long-term workers are paid a higher wage, and the long-term wage premium, $\sigma>1$, is given by

$$\sigma = \frac{W_l}{W_s}. \qquad (5)$$

We will also assume that

$$\sigma \geq \frac{b_s}{b_l} \qquad (6)$$

that is, the wage premium is no less than the productivity differential between long-term and short-term workers. In a world with uncertainty and social norms, firms are still assumed to work with long-term workers although from a strict short-run cost-minimization perspective it would seem that short-term workers are more profitable.

In terms of pricing, we assume that firms set their price as a fixed markup on unit long-term labor costs assuming that long-term labor will be fully utilized, so that

$$P = (1 + z)b_l W_l, \qquad (7)$$

where z is the fixed markup set by firms, which depends on the degree of monopoly à la Kalecki (1971). We assume that long-term labor is used as a basis of the price because they consist of the bulk of labor, and short-term labor is used, if at all, as a way of producing what cannot be produced with long-term labor.[xvii] Thus, short-term labor's contribution to unit costs is ignored by firms in setting the price of the product. It is being assumed that $b_l W_l$ is used as a basis of pricing rather than actual average costs when the firm holds excess long-term labor because average costs are not constant but depend on actual output, which goes against the Kaleckian notion of the price being fixed by labor cost and independent of output. As noted earlier, firms are always assumed to hold excess capital and are never constrained by available capital.

Savings is given by

$$S = srK \quad (8)$$

where S is real saving and s the fixed saving rate of capitalists out of profit income. Real consumption is, obviously, given by

$$C = Y - S \quad (9)$$

Regarding the dynamics of long-term labor, L_l, we will assume that the rate of growth of long-term labor, l_l, is equal to the rate of growth of the stock of capital minus the rate of growth of the productivity of long-term labor, so that we have

$$l_l = g - \hat{b}_l \quad (10)$$

If we define , $\lambda = \frac{\frac{L_l}{b_l}}{K}$ we have

$$\hat{\lambda} = l_l - \hat{b}_l - g \quad (11)$$

so that equation (10) implies that λ becomes a constant. In this simple formulation we assume that the extent of employment flexibility is measured by the level of λ, which is taken to be exogenous. One way of interpreting this is to assume that firms are required by the government to maintain a given long-term labor to capital ratio, and choose to hold no more of it. Of course, as discussed in the previous sections, firms may have good reasons to employ long-term labor to encourage loyalty, to reduce the costs of hiring and firing and to speed up technological change. These factors can, therefore, also have a role in determining the size of λ. However, it is likely that firms will not hire enough long-term labor left to their own devices because they may know that there are benefits of hiring long-term workers, but may not do enough of it because they feel that they reduce their flexibility. Thus, government regulations are likely to increase λ, that is, the propensity of firms to employ long-term labor.

We assume that firms make investment plans based on expected profitability, the buoyancy of aggregate demand, and the importance of long-term labor. More specifically, and as is assumed in some PKK models, we take planned investment to depend on the rate of capacity utilization and the rate of profit (see Dutt, 1984 and Rowthorn, 1981). We also take into account the fact that investment is affected by λ. Since λ is taken to be a measure of employment flexibility, it is possible that an increase in employment flexibility or a fall in λ will have a positive effect on hiring long term labor which implies a rise in g. Thus, a rise in λ, or a fall in employment flexibility, can be assumed to reduce g. However, a rise in λ can also be taken to imply an increase in productivity growth, since it can be assumed that long-term labor increases the knowledge base of the firm and increases productivity growth by increasing the motivation of workers to increase productivity at a higher rate, which in turn increases the investment, given a positive relation between technological change and investment (see, for instance, Storm and Naastepad, 2012). This contribution of long-term labor to productivity growth can provide an explanation of why firms may wish to hire long-term labor which is less flexible in terms of hiring and firing than short-term labor, at a possibly higher cost. The contribution of a higher rate of technological change on investment is a standard feature of a number of PKK models, including those in Rowthorn (1981), Dutt (1990) and Storm and Naastepad (2012). We therefore assume that

$$g = \gamma_0 + \gamma_r r + \gamma_u u + \gamma_\lambda \lambda \,, \qquad (12)$$

The sign of γ_λ can be positive or negative depending on whether the positive technological change effect or the negative disincentive effect of employment rigidity is dominant while γ_r and γ_u are positive.

We will assume that labor productivity growth caused by a higher level of λ increases the productivity of both long-term and short-term labor, and that the wage of each type of labor increases proportionately with productivity growth. Thus, σ and bl are constant over time. This implies, from equations (5) and (7), that changes in λ leave z and σ, that is, the markup and the long-term wage premium, unchanged.

Finally, we assume, as in standard PKK models that the goods market clears through variations in capacity utilization. Goods market equilibrium requires that

$$Y = C + I \,. \qquad (13)$$

Using equation (9) this implies that in short-run equilibrium the standard saving-investment equality holds so that

$$\frac{S}{K} = \frac{I}{K}. \qquad (14)$$

Using equations (8), (12) and (14), we obtain

$$(s - \gamma_r)r - \gamma_u u = \gamma_0 + \gamma_\lambda \lambda \qquad (15)$$

The rate of profit will depend on whether only long-term labor is used or both long-term and short-term labor is used.

In the former case, in which, $Y \leq, \frac{L_l}{b_l}$ the rate of profit is given, using equations (1), (2), (5) and (7), by

$$r = u - \frac{\lambda}{1 + z} \qquad (16)$$

where $u = Y/K$ is a measure of the rate of capacity utilization. In the latter case, when both types of labor are used, we have $Y \leq \frac{L_l}{b_l}$, and the rate of profit is given, using equations (1) through (5) and (7), by

$$r = \left(1 - \frac{b_s}{(1 + z)b_l\sigma}\right)u - \frac{\lambda}{(1 + z)}\left(1 - \frac{b_s}{b_l\sigma}\right). \qquad (17)$$

In the case in which only long-term labor is used, so that $u \leq \lambda$, substituting from equation (16) in equation (15) we obtain

$$u = \frac{\gamma_0 + \left(\frac{s - \gamma_r}{1 + z} + \gamma_\lambda\right)\lambda}{s - \gamma_r - \gamma_u}. \qquad (18)$$

Substituting into the investment or saving function this implies that the rate of capital accumulation (and output growth, since u is a constant) is given by

$$g = s\,\frac{\gamma_0 + \left(\frac{\gamma_u}{1 + z} + \gamma_\lambda\right)\lambda}{s - \gamma_r - \gamma_u}. \qquad (19)$$

In the second case, with both kinds of labor, so that $u > \lambda$, substituting from (17) into equation (15) we get

$$u = \frac{\gamma_0 + \left(\frac{s - \gamma_r}{1 + z}\left(1 - \frac{b_s}{\sigma b_l}\right) + \gamma_\lambda\right)\lambda}{(s - \gamma_r)\left(1 - \frac{1}{(1 + z)}\frac{b_s}{\sigma b_l}\right) - \gamma_u}. \qquad (20)$$

The rates of growth of capital and output are given by

$$g = s\,\frac{[(\gamma]_0 + \gamma_\lambda \lambda)\left(1 - \frac{b_s}{(1+z)b_l\sigma}\right) + \frac{\gamma_u}{1+z}\left(1 - \frac{b_s}{\sigma b_l}\right)\lambda}{(s - \gamma_r)\left(1 - \frac{1}{(1+z)}\frac{b_s}{\sigma b_l}\right) - \gamma_u} \quad . \qquad (21)$$

The model and its four equations (18) through (21) have the following properties. First, since λ is exogenously given and all the other symbols in the right-hand side of equations (18) through (21) are parameters (which therefore do not change over time), the values of *u* shown in equations (18) and (20) clear the goods markets and those of *g* in equations (19) and (21) show the rate of growth of output and capital consistent with those values and implied rates of profit. In other words, they are equilibrium values of the rates of capacity utilization and growth which do not change over time due to endogenous changes in some state variables.

Second, since we have assumed that output and the rate of capacity utilization adjust to clear the goods market, the stability of equilibrium requires that the response of saving to the rate of capacity utilization is greater than the responsiveness of investment. This requires that the denominators of the right-hand sides of equations (18) and (20) are positive. In the case in which only long-term labor is used, the stability condition is $s - \gamma_r > \gamma_u$, while in the case in which both kinds of labor are used it is .

$$(s - \gamma_r)\left(1 - \frac{1}{(1+z)}\frac{b_s}{\sigma b_l}\right) > \gamma_u$$

Since we have assumed that the inequality given by (6) is satisfied, $\frac{1}{(1+z)}\frac{b_s}{\sigma b_l} < 1$

if $s > \gamma_r$, which we assume, the first stability condition is more easily satisfied than the second condition: if the second is satisfied the first is necessarily satisfied, but the first may be satisfied without the second being satisfied. Thus, the stability of equilibrium is more likely to be satisfied if only long-term labor is used than if both are used. The reason for this is as follows. When only long-term labor is employed, an increase in capacity utilization results in an increase in output and profits without any increase in wage costs, since all labor costs are fixed, so that all of the increase in output results in an increase in profits. When both types of labor are employed, an increase in output requires an increase in the employment of short-term labor, which reduces the increase in profits. Thus, in the second case the increase in investment due to an increase in capacity utilization is larger in comparison to the effects on an implied increase in profits which affects saving and investment, than in the first case.

Third, we examine the effect of an increase in λ on *u* and *g*, assuming that the stability conditions in both cases are satisfied. The effects of a rise in λ on capacity utilization and the rate of growth are seen to be affected by the sign of γ_λ, that is, the effect of λ on investment. Recall that the sign of this depends on whether the positive effect of λ on labor productivity growth, and through it, on investment, is stronger or weaker than the negative disincentive effect of employment rigidity on the rates of long-term labor and capital accumulation (which, in the model, are assumed to be equal). If $\gamma_\lambda>0$, it follows from equations (18) through (21) that an increase in λ increases *u* and in *g* in both cases. In the case in which only long-term labor is used, an increase in λ increases aggregate demand by increasing wage income at the expense of profits, since there is saving out of profits but not out of wages. Therefore, the overall effect of an increase in λ on *u* and *g* is positive even if γ_λ is negligible, and may even be positive if γ_λ is slightly negative. In the case in which both kinds of labor are used, if the condition given in (6) is satisfied as a strict inequality, a rise in λ increases *u* and *g* by increasing aggregate demand since long-term labor, which generates a higher level of income than short-term labor, substitutes for short-term labor. Thus, the overall effect on *u* and *g* can be positive even with γ_λ slightly negative. If (6) is satisfied as an equality, and there is no positive effect on labor income by substituting from short-term labor to long-term labor, and the only effect of an increase in λ is through the effect on investment.

If we assume that $\gamma_\lambda>0$ but small, the relation between λ and *u* can be shown in Figure 2.1. The bold line shows the relation. The line is seen to be steeper in case I, in which $\lambda \geq u$ and only long-term labor is used, than in case II where both types of labor are used, since, comparing the two slopes we find that

$$\frac{\left(\frac{s-\gamma_r}{1+z}+\gamma_\lambda\right)}{s-\gamma_r-\gamma_u} > \frac{\left(\frac{s-\gamma_r}{1+z}\left(1-\frac{b_s}{\sigma b_l}\right)+\gamma_\lambda\right)}{(s-\gamma_r)\left(1-\frac{1}{(1+z)}\frac{b_s}{\sigma b_l}\right)-\gamma_u}$$

The two segments of the line meet on the 45^0 line at the value

$$u=\frac{\gamma_0}{(s-\gamma_r)\frac{z}{1+z}-\gamma_u-\gamma_\lambda}$$

as shown in Figure 2.1. Since λ is exogenously given we can find the value of *u* from the bold lines in the figure, as well as the case in which the economy finds itself. The relation between *g* and λ can be shown in an analogous manner.

Figure 2.1 Effects of an increase in λ on *u*

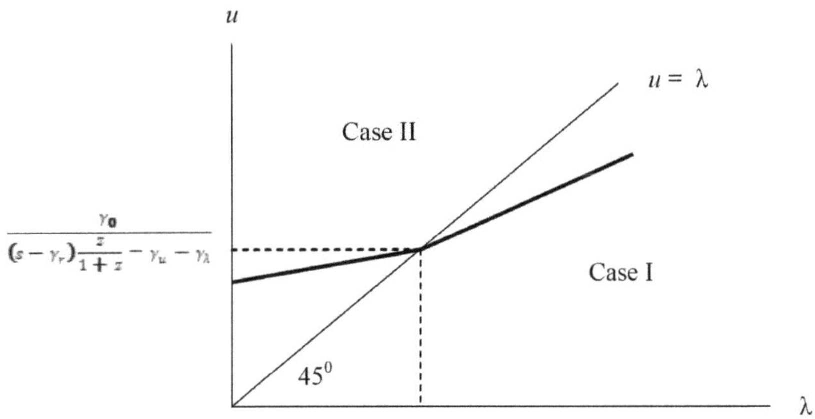

Fourth, the effects of the shifts in the parameters of the model other than λ can be seen in terms of a shift in the bold u schedule. For instance, an increase in z, the markup rate charged by firms shifts the point of intersection of the u line and the 45^0 line downwards, and reduces the slope of both segments of the line. Given our assumptions, the effect is to reduce u at all levels of λ. The increase in the markup rate redistributes income from workers of both kinds to profit recipients who have a higher propensity to save, which reduces consumption demand and aggregate demand, reducing capacity utilization.[xviii] To examine the effect on g, we need to consider separately the two cases. For case I, it follows from an inspection of equation (19) that an increase in z reduces g. For case II, when both types of workers are in use, equation (21) shows that

$$\frac{dg}{dz} = -s\gamma_u \frac{\left[\left(1 - \frac{b_s}{\sigma b_l}\right)(s - \gamma_r - \gamma_u)\lambda + \frac{(\gamma_0 + \gamma_\lambda \lambda) b_s}{\sigma b_l}\right]}{\left[(s - \gamma_r)\left(1 - \frac{1}{(1+z)}\frac{b_s}{\sigma b_l}\right) - \gamma_u\right]^2 (1+z)^2}$$

which, given our assumptions, is seen to be negative if $\gamma_\lambda \geq 0$ or if $\gamma_\lambda < 0$ but small in absolute value. In both cases, an increase in the markup shifts income from workers to capitalists, increases consumption and aggregate demand, capacity utilization, and investment, despite the positive effect the markup has on the rate of profit, as shown in equation (17).

We can summarize the effects on an increase in employment flexibility by examining the various effects at work. A high level of employment flexibility, by implying a low level of λ, has a number of consequences on the performance of the economy.

First, as we saw, a low level of λ results in the greater likelihood of goods market instability. If the economy is subjected to shocks there may be a tendency for greater instability and variability rather than stable adjustment. This result is due to the fact that when aggregate demand changes, variations in employment are likely to be greater when there is more labor market flexibility which is likely to imply greater variations in profits and output. Long-term labor is adjusted slowly over time, while short-term labor is freely adjustable. It should be noted that the slow adjustment of long-term labor implies, when aggregate demand declines, not only that there is a lower decline in employment, but also that, as a result, since there is a consequent lower decline in aggregate demand, there is a lower need to reduce employment.

Second, a lower level of use of long-term labor can have a negative level effect on aggregate demand if the long-term wage premium exceeds the productivity gap between long-term and short-term labor. The wage premium may be due to norms, and may be reinforced by the fact that long-term workers result in higher levels of productivity growth.

Third, a lower level of long-term labor can have a negative effect on the rate of technological change in long-term workers are more loyal to the firm and are more involved in bringing about and accepting productivity increases, and result in the accumulation of firm-specific knowledge. This can provide a boost to investment spending.

Fourth, a lower level of long-term labor use can be seen by firms as reducing the flexibility of labor and reducing costs, and this can spur investment, other things constant. We have included these effects into our model by making λ affect the profit rate and by allowing the possibility of a negative effect of λ on investment.

Fifth, a higher level of employment flexibility implies that the bargaining power of all workers is likely to fall, long-term workers because they are more susceptible to dismissal, and short-term workers because it reduces solidarity between workers of different types, and because layoffs of long-term workers can increase the ranks of the short-term labor force – or what can be called the reserve army – and this can exert downward pressure on all wages. We can examine the consequences of this by allowing z to increase, raising the profit share. There is a fair amount of empirical evidence which supports this conclusion. We have already examined the consequences of an increase in z and shown that it is, in addition to shifting the income distribution away from workers, growth retarding.

Finally, changes in employment flexibility can also be expected to have an effect on σ the long-term labor wage premium, which can be examined in terms of our model. If greater employment flexibility reduces the wage premium by reducing the bargaining power of long-term workers more than it does that of short-term workers, σ will fall. The examination of the implications of this, resulting changes in the relative productivity of the two kinds of workers, and possible feedback effects on λ which can be endogenized, is left for future work.

Conclusions

This chapter has examined the desirability of increasing employment flexibility in the economy by weakening employment protection legislation. While proposals for increasing employment flexibility are not new, the frequency and urgency with which they are made both in high-income and low-income countries has grown in recent years, in an increasingly globalized world and in the context of a major economic crisis.

The argument in favor of greater employment flexibility has usually been made in terms of a neoclassical approach to the analysis of the economy in general and the labor market in particular. This chapter has argued that the standard neoclassical approach overlooks many important aspects of real-world economies, including uncertainty, power and institutions and once one takes into account these features, the argument in favor of increasing employment flexibility need not hold up. To illustrate this we have developed a simple model of growth and income distribution along post-Keynesian/Kaleckian lines with two types of labor – short- and long-term labor - to show how increases in employment flexibility can reduce the rate of growth of the economy and worsen the distribution of income and thereby have an adverse effect on economic performance.

We should emphasize that our analysis does not imply that reducing restrictions on the firing of workers is necessarily bad for economic performance. Three remarks should be made in this regard. First, even our model does not unequivocally imply that greater employment flexibility is bad for the economy. We find that the effect of greater employment flexibility on the rate of growth depends on the relative strength of two different effects of greater employment flexibility on investment. The positive effect of flexibility is that it allows firms to be less concerned about being stuck with workers they do not need when they expand their employment. The negative effect goes through the diminished productivity growth due to having fewer committed and long-term workers. If the first effect is, in fact, stronger and sufficiently so, the effect of greater employment flexibility may be to increase growth. Second, our results have been obtained using a simple model with a number of specific assumptions. For instance, we have made the aggregate demand regime what has been referred to in the literature as wage-led rather than profit-led by virtue of the assumption that investment depends on the rate of profit and the rate of capacity utilization. If, instead, investment were taken to depend on the rate of capacity utilization and the profit share, as in Bhaduri and Marglin (1990), it is possible for a higher wage share to reduce the rate of growth. The reason is that a shift in income distribution away from profits reduces investment directly and possibly offsets and overcomes the positive capacity utilization effect due to the increase in consumption demand. However, since our model does take into account the possible negative effect on an increase in λ on investment, it does not ignore the negative effect of λ on profits. More importantly, we have assumed that the economy is a closed one, which may seem surprising for a chapter which has the word 'globalisation' in its title. To consider an open economy we need to take into account exports, imports and international capital flows, including foreign direct investment. Net exports, which can contribute to economic growth both by increasing aggregate demand and by avoiding external imbalances, depends on the real exchange rate and on the quality of goods produced for exports. While it has been argued that weakening EPL reduces labor costs and the price of domestic goods, thereby increasing international competitiveness, our analysis suggests that this fails to take into account the productivity-raising effects of long-term labor. The latter not only increases the real exchange rate but also improves product quality, which has a positive effect on exports, especially for high-income and semi-industrialized countries, for which export competitiveness is likely to depend more on quality than on price competitiveness. It has also been argued that EPL discourages foreign direct investment inflows. However, it has been found that it also discourages outflows, the consequences of which have to be netted against those of inflow especially for high-income countries (see Dewit, Görg and Montagna, 2009). The positive growth effects of FDI inflows in low-income countries, moreover, are unclear, with growth leading to FDI rather than the reverse in many of them (see Duttray et al, 2008) and in cases where FDI has important positive development impacts, the efficacy of special zones in which job security can be traded off against higher wages can be examined. About financial capital flows, empirical evidence suggests that international financial markets do react to changes in government policies but, especially for high-income countries, the degree of freedom of governments that governments have to pursue policies of their choice, in particular, regarding labor laws, is high (see Mosley, 2003). Low-income countries, in any case, need to be careful about such hot money flows and can benefit from capital controls and other policies which discourage them.

These comments imply that theoretically the case against EPL is not as strong as the neoclassical approach suggests and, if one takes into account issues such as uncertainty, power and institutions, and their consequences for norm-based behavior, the role of aggregate demand, and the interaction between growth and income distribution, there are many reasons why weakening EPL is likely to result in undesirable consequences.

Is it possible that empirical work can decide whether increased employment flexibility has positive or negative consequences? There are many empirical studies on this issue for high-income and low-income countries. For high-income countries, OECD (2007) concludes that rigid labor markets and stringent EPL are a major cause of slow productivity growth. However, Howell et al (2007) and Strorm and Naastepad (2010) present evidence to show that increasing labor market flexibility, including weakening EPL, will have the result of slowing down productivity and economic growth. For low income countries, Besley and Burgess (2004) find that pro-worker labor legislation reduces output, employment, investment and productivity in organized manufacturing in India (across states), while Dutta Ray (2004) finds that job security legislation in India did not reduce employment growth.[xix] The empirical evidence showing that there would be a positive effect of increased flexibility on the labor market is clearly inconclusive. Freeman (2005, 130) concludes that "there are two reasons for inconclusive debate over the claim that labour institutions impair aggregate performance. The first reason is that many adherents to the claim hold strong priors that labour markets operate nearly perfectly in the absence of institutions and let their priors dictate their modeling choices and interpretation of empirical results. The second reason is that the cross-country aggregate data at issue is weak, too weak to decisively reject strong prior views or to convince those with weaker priors."

This chapter will have served its purpose if it can make our priors less partial to the mainstream neoclassical approach.

References

Akerlof, George A. (1982). "Labor contracts as partial gift exchange", *Quarterly Journal of Economics*, 97(4), 543-569.

Atkinson, Anthony and Piketty, Thomas. (2006). *Top Incomes over the Twentieth Century*. Oxford: Oxford University Press.

Atkinson J. (1984). "Flexibility, uncertainty and manpower management", IMS Report No 89,

Brighton: Institute of Manpower Studies.

Bentolila, Samuel and Giuseppe Bertola (1990). "Firing costs and labour demand: How bad is Eurosclerosis?" *Review of Economic Studies*, 57 (3), 381-402.

Besley, Timothy and Burgess, Robin (2004). "Can labour regulation hinder economic performance? Evidence from India", *Quarterly Journal of Economics*, February, 91-134.

Bhaduri, Amit and Marglin, Stephen A. (1990). "Unemployment and the real wage: the economic basis of contesting political ideologies", *Cambridge Journal of Economics*, 14(4), 375-93.

Bhagwati, Jagdish and Panagariya, Arvind (2001). *India's Tryst with Destiny. Debunking Myths that Undermine Progress and Addressing New Challenges*, London and New York: Harper Collins.

Bhattacharjea, Aditya (2006). “Labour market regulation and industrial performance in India”, *Indian Journal of Labour Economics*, 49(2), 211-32.

Dewit, Gerda, Holger Gorg and Catia Monagna (2009). “Should I stay or should I go? Foreign direct investment, employment protection and domestic anchorage”, *Review of World Economy*, 145(1), 93-110.

Doeringer, Peter B., Piore, Michael J., (1971). *Internal Labor Markets and Manpower Analysis*, Lexington, MA: D.C. Heath and Company.

Dutt, Amitava Krishna (1984). “Stagnation, income distribution and monopoly power”, *Cambridge Journal of Economics*, 8(1), 25-40.

Dutt, Amitava Krishna (1990). *Growth, Distribution and Uneven Development*, Cambridge, UK: Cambridge University Press.

Dutt, Amitava Krishna (2006).”Labour, liberalisation and aggregate demand”, *Indian Journal of Labour Economics*, 49(1), January-March, 13-28.

Dutt, Amitava Krishna (2014). “Dimensions of pluralism in economics”, *Review of Political Economy*, 26(4), 479-94

Dutt, Amitava Krishna (2015). “Uncertainty, power, institutions and crisis: Implications for economic analysis and the future of capitalism”, *Review of Keynesian* Economics, 3(1), 9-28.

Dutt, Amitava Krishna and Edward Amadeo (1990). *Keynes's Third Alternative? The Neo-Ricardian Keynesians and the Post Keynesians*, Aldershot: Edward Elgar.

Dutt, Amitava Krishna, Sebastien Charles and Dany Lang (2011). “Long-term labor contracts, growth and distribution”, unpublished, University of Notre Dame, University of Paris 8, University of Paris, 13.

Dutt, Amitava Krishna, Sebastien Charles and Dany Lang (2014). “Could more flexibility of labor markets help to resume growth? Lessons of an amended Kaleckian model”, in L. Mamica and P. Tridico, eds., *Economic Policy and Financial Crisis*, London: Routledge.

Dutta Roy, Sudipta (2004). “Employment dynamics in Indian industry: Adjustment lags and the impact of job security regulations”, *Journal of Development Economics,* 73(1), 233-56.

Duttray, Mousumi, Amitava K. Dutt and Kajal Mukhopadhyay (2008). “Foreign direct investment and economic growth in less developed countries: An empirical study of causality and mechanisms”, *Applied Economics*, 40, 1927–1939.

Freeman, R. (2005) 'Labour market institutions without blinders: The debate over flexibility and labour market performance', *International Economic Journal*, 19(2), 129– 145.

Hodgson, Geoff (2006). "What are institutions?" *Journal of Economic Issues*, 40(1), 1-25.

Galbraith, James (2002). "A perfect crime: Inequality in the age of globalisation", *Daedalus*, 131(1), 11-25.

Giersch, Herbert (1985). "Eurosclerosis." Kiel Discussion Paper No. 112, Institut fur Weltwirtschaft, Universitat Kiel.

Government of India (2013). *Economic Survey, 2012-13*, New Delhi: Ministry of Finance, Government of India.

Guzzini, Stefano (1993). "Structural power: The limits of neorealist power analysis", *International Organization*, 47(3), 443-78.

Howell, David R., Dean Baker, Andrew Glyn and John Schmidt (2007). "Are protective labor market institutions really at the root of unemployment? A critical perspective of the statistical evidence", *Capitalism and Society*, 2(1), 1-71.

Kalecki, Michael (1971). *Selected Essays on the Dynamics of the Capitalist Economy*, Cambridge, UK: Cambridge University Press.

Keynes, John Maynard (1936). *The general theory of employment, interest and money*, London: Macmillan.

Lewis, W. Arthur (1954). "Economic development with unlimited supplies of labour", *Manchester School*, 22, 139-191.

Milanovic, Branko (2010). *The Have and the Have-nots: A Brief and Idiosyncratic History of Global inequality*, New York: Basic Books.

Mosley, Layna (2003). *Global Capital Markets and National Governments*, Cambridge, UK: Cambridge University Press.

North, Douglass C. (1994). "Economic performance through time", *American Economic Review*, 84 (3), 359-68.

OECD (2007). "More jobs but less productive? The impact of labour market policies on productivity", in *OECD employment outlook2006*, chapter 7, Paris: Organization for Economic Cooperation and Development.

Oi, Walter Y. (1962). "Labor as a quasi-fixed factor", *Journal of Political Economy*, 70(6), 538-55.

Olson, Mancur (1965). *The Logic of Collective Action,* Cambridge, Mass: Harvard University Press.

Rowthorn, Robert E. (1981). "Demand, real wages and economic growth", *Thames Papers in Political Economy*, Autumn, 1–39.

Saint-Paul, Gilles (2000). *The political economy of labour market institutions*. Oxford: Oxford University Press.

Solow, Robert M (1990).*The Labor Market as a Social Institution.* Oxford: Blackwell.

Stiglitz, Joseph E. (2012). *The Price of Inequality*, New York: Norton.

Storm, Servaas and Naastepad, C. W. M. (2012). *Macroeconomics Beyond the NAIRU*, Cambridge, Mass: Harvard University Press.

Strange, Susan (1988). *States and Markets: An Introduction to International Political Economy*, Oxford, UK: Basil Blackwell.

Tokman, Victor E. (2008). "The informal sector", In: A. K. Dutt and J. Ros, (eds.), *International Handbook of Development Economics,* Vol. 1, Edward Elgar.

Chapter Three

Globalisation and Inequality in the Anthropocene

Myron J. Frankman

'Don't tell us about theory. Economic theory has led us to social failure. Simply look around you'. - Jeff Madrick (2011)

Capital and labour were once useful categories. Their centrality and the meanings of the terms were reasonably clear in the early days of industrialization in Europe and North America. With the formalization of these concepts in the then fledging study of economics and with changing opportunities for investment and employment a gap between theory and reality began to widen perceptibly. Nonetheless, the longest reigning paradigm in economics sums up production and income distribution as little more than the outcome of a simple relation of capital and labour.

The world has changed and so has economics, but not for the better. That we have not had a paradigm shift in economics is consistent with the hard sociology of knowledge hypothesis. That perspective, developed by Steve Fuller (2003), contends that those who benefit from the practical consequences of a theory, are tireless in their efforts to sustain the life of that theory. Vested interests find it quite profitable to generously support theory with a strong 'free enterprise' bias which bears handsome financial rewards to them. If one can cloak a theory with a mantle of complexity, its staying power can be extended for as long as possible, if not indefinitely. In the 1960s Joan Robinson spoke of economics as having run off to hide in the thickets of algebra. That was just a way station: today no element of mathematical complexity is missing from the fully-trained economist's tool chest. Levels of complexity have been added to the theoretical edifice, but, like a giant inverted pyramid, the aptness of policy recommendations so derived cannot withstand the slightest whisper of wind.

Comparative Advantage: A Flagship for Obfuscation

In the July-August 2011 issue of *Foreign Affairs*: Michael Spence, co-recipient of the Nobel Prize in Economics in 2001, observed that the economic structure of developing countries "changed in response to the forces of comparative advantage" and that in certain sectors the "U.S. economy continues to have a comparative advantage." 'Comparative advantage' as either an explanation or as a guide to policy is consistently invoked as an immutable principle.

Why continue to assign explanatory power to a concept that springs from an early 19th illustration by David Ricardo about why Portugal would gain from importing cloth from England in exchange for Portuguese wine even though Portugal is in Ricardo's example the lower cost producer of both goods? The holding power of the theory of comparative advantage owes much to parsimony, to formalization, to repetition and to familiarity. It no doubt owes far more to its considerable serviceability in sweeping aside arguments for restrictions to access to export markets. The power of interests to invoke the Panglossian benefits of opening markets when it is convenient for them cannot be overestimated.

A careful comparison of reality with the assumptions incorporated in the theory of comparative advantage quickly leads to the conclusion these are two distinct non-intersecting sets. I shall not pretend to give a full account of the shortcomings of the theory. Suffice it to say that the theoretical demonstration of comparative advantage, commonly referred to as the 'Noah's Ark Model', features two homogeneous tradable goods, two countries and two homogeneous factors of production (commonly labour and capital). Prices of both goods and both factors are fully flexible. The model is timeless and reversible and all changes occur instantaneously. Both countries produce both goods before and after trade. To focus on 'labour', it is worth noting that here as elsewhere labour has no age, no gender, no ethnicity and no physiological needs. In short: no humanity. Thorstein Veblen summed up well economic man (labour) in 1898:

> "The hedonistic conception of man is that of a lightning calculator of pleasures and pains who oscillates like a homogeneous globule of desire of happiness under the impulse of stimuli that shift him about the area, but leave him intact. He has neither antecedent nor consequent. He is an isolated definitive human datum, in stable equilibrium except for the buffets of the impinging forces that displace him in one direction or another. Self-imposed in elemental space, he spins symmetrically about his own spiritual axis until the parallelogram of forces bears down upon him, whereupon he follows the line of the resultant. When the force of the impact is spent, he comes to rest, a self-contained globule of desire as before. Spiritually, the hedonistic man is not a prime mover. He is not the seat of a process of living, except in the sense that he is subject to a series of permutations enforced upon him by circumstances external and alien to him".

Nor is there a spatial dimension to either of the countries in the two-country comparative advantage model. Hence, what Gunnar Myrdal (1957) spoke of as the backwash effects which prejudice poor regions and poor countries and benefit those gainers who are distant is not a possibility of the model. Forgotten is the admonition of Paul Samuelson (1949) following his theoretical demonstration of the possibility of the absolute equalisation of factor prices: "In the face of these hard facts [i.e., reality] it would be rash to consider the existing distribution of population to be optimal in any sense, or to regard free trade as a panacea for the present geographical inequalities."

An Optimum Policy Area

In the middle of the 19th century, long before one could possibly have thought of the world being a single integrated market, John Stuart Mill spoke of the eventual adoption a single world currency. He wrote in his *Principles of Political Economy*:

> "So much of barbarism, however, still remains in the transactions of the most civilized nations that almost all independent countries choose to assert their nationality by having to their own inconvenience and that of their neighbours, a peculiar currency of their own".

Today we have the theory to support the case for a single world currency, but national sovereignty still stands in the way. The citation for the 1999 Nobel Prize in Economics awarded to Robert Mundell spoke of "his analysis of optimum currency areas," which are regions characterized by integrated factor and product markets. According to Mundell (1961), unified markets would benefit from having a single currency. Using Mundell's concept, Ronald McKinnon (1963) referred to the world as being an optimum currency area and Charles Kindleberger (1967) spoke more broadly of optimum policy areas.

The continued existence of many different currencies in a relatively unregulated environment has been associated with the hyper-mobility of financial transactions. As early as 1972 James Tobin proposed a tax on currency transactions in order, as he put it, to throw sand in the wheels of international finance. Despite considerable enthusiasm from different quarters for some version of what is now referred to as a Tobin Tax, the closest we have come to the implementation of a form of his proposal are current initiatives in the Euro area to implement a financial transactions tax. Since Tobin first proposed his tax, many proponents have focused on the apparent significant revenue raising nature of the Tobin Tax, rather than the purpose he intended for it of reducing market volatility by diminishing the volume of speculative transactions. Indeed, were his tax to serve as a deterrent to speculative currency transactions, resulting revenues would be minimal. This would appear to have been what he anticipated as he devoted very few words to the size or the use of transaction tax revenues.

For Tobin (1994), the exchange transactions tax was a second best solution. His first best preference was for a world currency, consistent with writing on the logic of the world as an optimum currency area:

> "A permanent single currency, as among the 50 states of the American union, would escape all this turbulence. The United States example shows that a

> currency union works to great advantage when sustained not only by centralized monetary authorities but also by other common institutions. In the absence of such institutions, an irrevocably unique world currency is many decades off'.

In a world that is increasingly interconnected, where financial flows truly know no bounds, where ideas freely flow (with the possible exception of North Korea), where trade in goods is largely free of impediments, and most nations try to achieve a cost advantage, the absence of either world level policy and/or generalized policy harmonization leaves the people of the world to be pawns of what Veblen called the Vested Interests. The burden of maintaining the pretense of sovereignty in the context of a generalized race to the bottom falls heavily on the common people. The response to the possibility of jobs and production moving offshore is often to cut taxes, cut wages, and/or divert public funds to subsidies to the firms that have one foot out of the door. These rear guard actions are misguided *sauve qui peut* responses to a global collective action challenge.

The countries of Western Europe reeling from the effects of two major wars on their territories and the Great Depression in little more than three decades slowly took steps to replace enmity with cooperation. Throughout the process, there have been limits to what nominally sovereign countries were willing to cede to a supranational entity. The resistance of the member countries to cede significant revenue raising powers to a central authority made for a fair weather union, as has been clearly demonstrated during the current global financial crisis.

In considering what might be an appropriate budget for the central authority for a united Europe a Study Group chaired by Sir Donald MacDougall reported in 1977 to the Commission of the European Communities on the role of public finance in European integration. Timothy Bainbridge provided a succinct summary:

> "When the report was written, total spending by the Community institutions was about 0.7 per cent of the Community's gross domestic product (GDP). 'Pre-federal integration' meant raising the latter figure to between 2 and 2.5 per cent. A 'small' Community public sector was reckoned to be from 5 to 7 per cent, and a 'large' something approaching 25 per cent of GDP".

On this calculation, the European Union is still well short even of the 'pre-federal' stage: in 2000, total union expenditure was estimated at about 1.08 per cent of the Union's GDP.

Without a sizable central budget and a commitment to increasing policy coordination as integration of the European Community progressed, a race to the bottom took place within Europe, as shown most notably by a growing divergence in corporate profit tax rates, with the Irish rate having been reduced to 12.5% while rates in Belgium, France, Germany and Italy, for example, are above 30%. Textbook discussions of

integration insist that higher levels of economic and political integration require higher degrees of coordination, particularly for the case of the adoption of a common currency. The insights of Tobin, McKinnon and others have been swept aside by the influence of the powerful and by the delusions of safeguarding national sovereignty.

Income Distribution: Kuznets Reversed

For much of the history of economics, income distribution was a non-issue. The relevant distribution was the functional distribution: the shares of a firm's product received by capital and labour. Historically this was a microeconomic concept, not a macroeconomic one. Basic questions on the relation of capital, labour and (functional) income distribution in neoclassical microeconomics were settled matters. In the mythical world of free markets, where all that is relevant is assumed away, everything fell neatly into place. Homogeneous capital and homogeneous labour were each compensated according to its contribution to marginal revenue, which, in turn, established the functional distribution. And that basically was all there was to that. Any deviation from that outcome resulted from market imperfections (such as were caused by meddlesome governments or obstreperous groupings of workers). Policy was clear: eliminate the imperfections. Indeed, in the absence of national income accounting until the 1930s, the personal or household income distribution was not even a meaningful consideration.

Concentrations of income and wealth are nothing new, but the magnitude and the ease of accumulating and the acceptance of enduring inequality is new. Our current circumstances of growing inequality represent the fulfillment of a utopian vision turned dystopian: accumulation of wealth was expected to bring with it a comparable increase in the wealth of the community through productive investment. The rhetoric denied the extent to which entire societies could fall under the thrall of destabilizing inequalities of income and power.

This is not the first time that income has become concentrated and not the first time that responses have been crafted. Leveling arrangements have been common in many societies: the potlatch, elaborate marriage celebrations, financing the building of churches or mosques. Where individuals were slow to share with the community, estate taxes and steeply progressive income taxes were enacted. All have served to varying degrees as unifying devices, as have social welfare programs, free public schooling and even universal military service. Fear of the hungry masses played a role in establishing early welfare programmes. Better to share a carefully measured portion of one's gains, however gotten, than risk it all in a violent upheaval. That restraint is scarcely to be found today.

When discussion turns to the household distribution, the most famous proposition is the inverted U pattern hypothesized by Simon Kuznets (1955), who was one of the pioneers in helping to shape the national income accounts. Kuznets advanced the notion in a most tentative way that changes over time in the Gini coefficient would likely sketch an inverted U pattern. Indeed, this has been corroborated for the immediate post-World War 2 decades. Reaction to the hardships of the years of the Great Depression and the War brought the widespread growth of the welfare state and a consensus favoring active governments.

Greed, slowly at first, but then accelerating, turned the inverted U income distribution pattern into something akin to a wave motion as Gini coefficients increased in the latter decades of the 20th century after declining in most of the industrial countries in the decades which immediately followed the end of the Second World War. As Thomas Piketty and Emmanuel Saez wrote in 2003: "Today, the Kuznets curve is widely held to have doubled back on itself, especially in the United States." At the time, they were of the opinion that "a new industrial revolution has taken place, thereby leading to increasing inequality, and inequality will decline again at some point, as more and more workers benefit from the innovations." More recently they have each pointed to the role of offshoring production, tax havens, reduced inheritance taxes and inflated remunerations to corporate executives as playing key roles in increasing inequality yet further.

Governments everywhere were prompted by their financial and business elites to preserve competitiveness by reducing tax rates. Rather than behave like several self-interested oligopolists who recognize the importance of not breaking ranks, governments have engaged in a race to the bottom by cutting tax rates and bases. Among the effects of inevitably reduced government revenues are the eroding of welfare programmes, social solidarity and political integrity. The growth of prison populations, impoverishment of working classes and weakening of the ability of governments to provide stimuli have also resulted. On the other side of the coin of inequality are gated communities and the vertiginous growth of the private security industry. All of these things have been happening in the extreme in the United States.

Income distribution data are probably the least reliable statistics at our disposal, particularly with respect to high incomes. Nonetheless, even a substantial underestimate conveys a picture of growth of income inequality since the beginning of the 1980s. The multiple adverse effects of the escape from taxation have triggered serious research to build databases on the weakest link in national data: on the nature and extent of inequality at the top of the distribution. Path breaking work has been done, much of which is summarized in "The World Top Incomes Database." (http://topincomes.g-mond.parisschoolofeconomics.eu). Table 3.1 illustrates clearly that the concentration at the top of the income distribution in the United States in 2006 was the highest since the 1920s. Not shown in Table 3.1 are the figures for total income share including capital gains. In 2006 these were: top 1%, 22.8%; top 0.01%, 5.5%.

With more open access to data and with the posing of different questions we have a clearer idea of the worldwide skewing of income and wealth distributions to favor the top of the distribution. Recent data have provided an indication of the extreme concentration of income and wealth at the top in both country distributions and the world distribution. Branko Milanovic (2002) was one of the first to estimate world distribution by household, rather than by country. He came up with some of the highest measures of income distribution that have been seen: a Gini of 66% for 1993 when using purchasing power parity adjusted data and 80.5% when using unadjusted data. No matter how great estimates of concentration of income and wealth at the top of the income distribution may be, they are likely to all be underestimates owing to the role of tax avoidance and evasion. Household surveys, which Milanovic relied upon, are notoriously unreliable for those at the top who are unlikely to be among those surveyed. However, as the authors of the World Top Income Database observed "Like all economic data, they measure with error the 'true' variable in which we are interested."

Table 3.1 United States, Top Income Shares

Year	Top 1%	Top 0.01%	Year	Top 1%	Top 0.01%
1916	18.6	4.4	1966	8.4	0.6
1926	18.0	2.5	1976	7.9	0.6
1936	17.6	2.2	1986	9.1	1.0
1946	11.1	0.9	1996	14.1	2.0
1956	9.1	0.7	2006	18.1	3.3

Note: Estimates exclude capital gains; fractiles are defined by total income excluding capital gains.
Source: Alvaredo, F., Atkinson, A., Piketty. T and Saez. E. The World Top Incomes Database, http://topincomes.g-mond.parisschoolofeconomics.eu [Viewed May 1, 2013].

Disaggregated data can be startlingly instructive in a context of major inequality of income and opportunity. For example, during the very modest economic recovery in the United States from 2009 to 2011, aggregate data show that average real income per family grew by 1.7 percent. An examination by Saez (2013) of how that increase was distributed showed: "Top 1% incomes grew by 11.2% while bottom 99% incomes shrunk by 0.4%."

Does inequality as reflected in extreme wealth matter? Let me count the ways: extreme wealth compromises political democracy, destroys societal restraints, compromises public truth, compromises individual honesty, compromises community and solidarity, compromises livelihood, compromises domestic tranquility, compromises quality, and compromises sustainability. Harvey Kempf (2007), following the century-old formulation of Veblen (1899), sees the profligate consumption patterns of the rich contributing mightily to the destruction of the planet as their usages spread through the global income pyramid. Each endeavors to emulate the consumption pattern of those with incomes above their own. This spreads to all worldwide on a reduced scale as one moves down the income pyramid. The rich provide the model and others emulate.

From Job Benefits to Social Protection Floor

> "workers aren't bushels of wheat . . . they're human beings"
> Paul Krugman, Feb 18, 2013

During the age of industrialization, the focus of attention was on jobs in industry. We tracked the growth in the numbers of those employed, their remuneration, their hours and working conditions. We divided the world into industrialized countries and developing countries, with industrial employment as the hallmark of success. Since the 1970s that has changed markedly: while industrial value added may be the largest contributor to gross output, the number of those employed in production fell relative to those carrying out administrative tasks within firms known for their production of tangible items. More recently, all employment in industry has declined: both production line and front office functions.

The success of opening trade has been inversely proportional to the declining employment in industries where jobs have moved overseas. In the case of the US, the first round of migration of employment from antiquated factories and unionized workers to new factories with cutting edge technologies and effort saving workplace layout and non-unionized workers was from the northeast and mid-west to the south and west. Countries whose outdated factories were destroyed during the Second World War were able to recapture a competitive advantage by rebuilding modern, efficient factories. In the same period, US firms recovered competitive advantage by abandoning 'rust belt' facilities and simultaneously escaping from unions and from higher taxes. As the initial moves weakened the sense of place loyalty and local citizenship, the eventual shift to offshore production carried no qualms of abandoning a constituency.

The change has given rise to books whose very titles tell the story, such as Jeremy Rifkin's 1995 *The End of Work: The Decline of the Global Labor Force and the Dawn of the Post-Market Era* and Guy Standing's 2011 *The Precariat: The New Dangerous Class.* Many of the skills of yesterday's craftsmen are now embedded in chips that provide the guidance for production. Policy discussions tenaciously cling to a dream about renewed growth of industrial employment, but decline of the industrial labour force is like the decline of the agricultural work which preceded it. The sitting of new production is now a question of where in the world it should be. We are no longer in a world of steamships and cable transfers of information. In the meantime, jobs in service activities have mushroomed everywhere in the world. Yet even there, continuous new developments of information technology are eliminating jobs. Conditions in 'services' can range from extremely penury and insecurity to well-remunerated jobs requiring high cognitive abilities.

The realities of increasingly interconnected human activity have given rise, *inter alia,* to writings calling for national social protection floors for all. As both jobs and job-related benefits have been disappearing, a countervailing discourse has been occurring. The Universal Declaration of Human Rights which was endorsed by the United Nations General Assembly (1948) is increasingly being invoked on behalf of those who have not realized its promise. The latest development in this long march which has included in 1966 the International Covenant on Economic, Social and Cultural Rights and the International Covenant on Civil and Political Rights is a 2011 Report of the Social Protection Floor Advisory Group convened by the ILO with the collaboration of the WHO and chaired by Michelle Bachelet (who has since been re-elected President of Chile in December 2013). Their report *Social Protection Floor for a Fair and Inclusive Globalisation* essentially affirms that social support provided by the state is a right. This a critical affirmation in a world in which benefit derived from work is not widely available or even adequate. Add to the current context the continuing displacement of labour by robotics and unknowable effects as the Anthropocene Age advances and the need for a radical review and vast shift in the nature of the conversation about "Labour Force Dynamics" appears urgent. The Bachelet Group report aimed to fill the gap. The Report calls for each nation to devise a set of policies which would constitute a social protection floor. In particular, the Report urges the G-20 countries to set the example by strengthening and extending their existing sets of social protection floor policies.

The strength of the Group's report is that it obtained the consensus from the United Nations System Chief Executives Board for Coordination (CEB). The CEB has 29 members: the Secretary-General, who serves as Chair, and the heads of 28 UN member organizations, including the World Bank and the International Monetary Fund. Input from an IMF team, in particular, judged that most developing countries would be able to self finance social protection floors, except for a few who would still need development aid for that purpose. In the second decade of the new millennium, when people increasingly recognise that we now live in a world which is interconnected in almost every imaginable sense, the time has come for world level initiatives that aim at convergence rather than competition.

The promise of automation and robotics is nothing less than the emancipation of each and every one of us to be truly human: that is to give full expression to our empathic selves, to be exposed to possibilities which we may pursue as our inclinations dictate. The shift should be from labour market policy to a human fulfillment strategy to support in all the fullest expression of our humanity. Shaping true world citizens with rights and obligations that span national boundaries is one of the key challenges of our times.

Citizens of the World, Unite!

"Democracy and capitalism have both been hacked" -- Al Gore (2013)

Gore's diagnosis that the institutions of governance that offer the promise of equal opportunity and protection of the rights of all have been compromised is certainly not unique to our time. Adam Smith probably said it best in the *Wealth of Nations* when he spoke about "the monopoly which our manufacturers have obtained against us":

> "This monopoly has so much increased the number of some particular tribes of them that, like an overgrown standing army, they have become formidable to the government, and upon many occasions intimidate the legislature. The Member of Parliament who supports every proposal for strengthening this monopoly is sure to acquire not only the reputation of understanding trade, but great popularity and influence with an order of men whose numbers and wealth render them of great importance. If he opposes them, on the contrary, and still more if he has authority enough to be able to thwart them, neither the most acknowledged probity, nor the highest rank, nor the greatest public services can protect him from the most infamous abuse and detraction, from personal insults, nor sometimes from real danger, arising from the insolent outrage of furious and disappointed monopolists". (Smith, 1776, Book IV, Chapter 2)

By comparison, Marx and Engels (1847) in the *Manifesto of the Communist Party*, summed up the state of the polity and society in more sweeping terms:

> "The bourgeoisie has at last, since the establishment of Modern Industry and of the world market, conquered for itself, in the modern representative State, exclusive political sway. The executive of the modern state is but a committee for managing the common affairs of the whole bourgeoisie".

And:

> "The bourgeoisie, wherever it has got the upper hand, has put an end to all . . . idyllic relations . . . and has reduced the family relation to a mere money relation."

Karl Polanyi observed almost one century later in his *The Great Transformation*:

> ". . . a self-adjusting market . . . could not exist for any length of time without annihilating the human and natural substance of society; it would have physically destroyed man and transformed his surroundings into a wilderness".

It is time to recognize that not only do we have a single world 'market', we have as well a single world ecosystem. There are, of course, local idiosyncrasies, but our circumstances cry out for mutually reinforcing responses that narrow the differences between jurisdictions in cases where significant spillover effects exist.

The quest for human rights must name and shame, must speak out loudly. Labour is a subset of our common humanity and quest for well-being. In the extension of rights as in scientific principles, parsimony should be a basic principle. Arrangements should be shaped that provide a maximum of freedom, that enhance life chances, that in a real sense leave none behind by recognizing and accommodating human diversity. We all have a place on this planet and all have an entitlement, insofar as no one is a self-made person. We are all products of our environments, of our socialization, of the panoply of our experiences. The path for all should lead to the full expression of our humanity and a right to acquire competence.

The 21st Century must be about the federated citizen, in his/her multiple associations in his/her immediate entourage(s), to the neighborhood through the many levels of the global hierarchy, to the level of world citizen with portable rights, some immutable and some reflecting the values of a particular jurisdiction or organization, consistent with the issue specific, ever shifting, principle of subsidiarity.

Revolution in the South / Discourse Change

"The Development Revolution from the Global South" is the subtitle of a work which describes the spread of cash transfer programmes in developing countries. The 2013 *Human Development Report* of the United Nations Development Program bears the subtitle *The Rise of the South.* For at least one decade we have heard prominence being given to the BRICS: Brazil, Russia, India, China and South Africa. And from another perspective, the OECD has added to its ranks South Korea (1996), Mexico (1994) and Chile (2010). We may well be in the midst of a change of the global hegemon. The United States emerged from the Second World War clearly as the dominant economy in the world. Remnants of British dominion over global finance and territory still remained, but the shift was indisputable. Joseph Schumpeter (1950) pinpointed the sclerosis of institutions and spoke of creative destruction. The federal government of the United States has reached a point which has charitably been described as gridlock, thanks in part to a Constitution which, whatever its strengths, was fashioned for the late 18th century. Ironically, numerous worthy practices, which have been resisted in the United States itself, have been successfully implanted in the global South. When the good intentions of a hegemon can not be translated into a consistent set of actions, a shift of influence on the global scene can be seen to be emerging.

It is in the Global South where responses to the challenge of the Anthropocene are occurring. Christiana Figueres, the head of the United Nations Framework Convention on Climate Change (UNFCCC) has argued that the countries of the world must make haste on their own, without waiting for global agreement: "Nothing is going to be agreed internationally until enough is legislated for domestically,"[xx] And it is indeed some of the southern countries that are proceeding to do so. The UNDP's *Human Development Report 2013: The Rise of the South: Human Progress in a Diverse World* makes the point specifically about the new dynamics in the 'South':

> "The rise of the South demonstrates that the world has become more diffuse and cross-connected. One consequence is that rather than looking to the North for inspiration, developing countries are looking to their peers in the South for appropriate development models. Here, rather than seeing a sterile menu of ideological options, they can examine what has worked, under what circumstances, and choose the most appropriate tools" (p. 119).

The Anthropocene: The Human Age

> "Real power lies in today being able to will common global laws rather than in asserting individual national sovereignty"
>
> Benjamin Barber (2003)

While the suggestion that the Holocene Epoch (which extended over almost 12,000 years) is over and that we now live in the Anthropocene appears to have first been suggested by Paul Crutzen near the start of the current millennium, *The Economist* and *National Geographic* magazines both played a role in introducing the term into common usage. The former did so with a June 2011 account accompanied by an illustrated cover announcing "Welcome to the Anthropocene". The latter in a March 2011 article "Enter The Anthropocene -- Age of Man" written by Elizabeth Kolbert, the author of a 2014 book *The Sixth Extinction: An Unnatural History*. Simply put, we are altering the planet at an unprecedented pace in a way that is already measurable and even noticeable to untrained observers.

Worse yet, natural processes have long lead times. Were we to abruptly stop the use of fossil fuels tomorrow, we might be able only to slow somewhat the pace of change, but not the direction. Unpredictable extreme weather events are already occurring. At the 15th Conference of the Parties to the United Nations Framework Convention on Climate Change in Copenhagen in December 2009, some observers were chanting 1.5°, survive; 2.0°, genocide; 2.5°, suicide. An NGO formed by Bill McKibben is simply called 350.org, said to be the maximum parts per million (ppm) level of atmospheric CO_2 consistent with maintaining our planet habitable. He and his followers, including leading atmospheric scientist James Hansen, insist that no further CO_2 should be discharged into the atmosphere. Yet we first crossed the 400ppm threshold in May 2013.

Each day seems to bring evidence that scientific projections of the time likely for the occurrence of adverse consequences have to revised downward. Martin Parry, Co-Chair of the Fourth Assessment Report of the Intergovernmental Panel on Climate

Change remarked that this is no longer about future generations: "Now it's not only your daughter who is at risk, it's probably you as well."[xxi] In the apparent hope of sounding an alarm, a recent report published by the World Bank bears the title *Turn Down the Heat: Why a 4°C Warmer World Must be Avoided.*

Community engagement and restraining excess are two sides of the coin of our very survival in the Anthropocene. The overwhelming scientific consensus has not yet been able to unite the world in undertaking concerted, coordinated, comprehensive responses. That is the supreme challenge for us all. A future where growth is predominantly non-material and where innate human needs are nurtured may well be the only path to sustainable development which addresses the social, the environmental and much transformed 'economic' ends.

References

Alvaredo, F., Atkinson, A., Piketty. T and Saez. E. (2013). *The World Top Incomes Database*, http://topincomes.g-mond.parisschoolofeconomics.eu/ .

Bainbridge, T (2002). *The Penguin Companion to European Union*, 3rd ed. London: Penguin.

Barber, B. (2003). *Fear's Empire: War, Terrorism, and Democracy*, New York: W.W. Norton & Co.

Fuller, S. (2003). *Kuhn vs. Popper: The Struggle for the Soul of Science*, New York: Columbia University Press.

Gore, A. (2013). *The Future: Six Drivers of Global Change*, New York: Random House.

Hanlon, J., Barrientos, A. and Hulme, D. (2010). *Just Give Money to the Poor: The Development Revolution from the Global South*, Sterling, Va.: Kumarian Press.

Kempf, H. (2007). *Comment les riches détruisent la planète*, Paris: Edition du Seuil.

Kindleberger, C. (1967). "The Politics of International Money and World Language," *Princeton Essays in International Finance, No. 61.*

Kolbert, Elizabeth (2014). *The Sixth Extinction: An Unnatural History.* New York: Henry Holt and Company.

Krugman, P. (2013). "Raise that wage", *New York Times* (Feb. 17).

Kuznets, S. (1955). "Economic growth and income inequality", *American Economic Review*, 45(1): 1–28.

Madrick, J. (2011). *Age of Greed: The Triumph of Finance and the Decline of America, 1970 to the Present,* New York : Alfred A. Knopf.

Marx, K. and Engels, F. (1848). *Manifesto of the Communist Party* http://www.marxists.org/archive/marx/works/1848/communist-manifesto/.

McKinnon, R. (1963). "Optimum currency areas", *American Economic Review,* 53(4), 717-25.

Milanovic, B. (2002). "True world income distribution, 1988 and 1993: First calculations based on household surveys alone", *The Economic Journal,* 112(46), 51-92.

Mill, J. S. (1865). *Principles of Political Economy*, 5th London ed., New York: D Appleton and Co.

Mundell, R. (1961). "A theory of optimum currency areas", *American Economic Review*, 51(4), 657-65.

Myrdal, G. (1957). *Rich Lands and Poor: The Road to World Prosperity*, New York: Harper.

Piketty, T. (2014). *Capital in the Twenty-First Century*, Cambridge, MA: The Belknap Press of Harvard University Press.

Piketty, T. and Saez, E. (2003). "Income inequality in the United States", *Quarterly Journal of Economics,* 113 (1), 1-39.

Polanyi, K. (1944). *The Great Transformation: The Political and Economic Origins of Our Time*, Boston: Beacon Press.

Ricardo, D. (1817). *On the Principles of Political Economy and Taxation,* London: John Murray.

Rifkin, J. (1995). *The End of Work: The Decline of the Global Labor Force and the Dawn of the Post-market Era,* New York: G.P. Putnam's Sons.

Robinson, J. (1963). *Economic Philosophy*, Chicago: Aldine Publishing.

Saez, E. (2013). "Striking it richer: the evolution of top incomes in the United States (Updated with 2011 estimates)". http://elsa.berkeley.edu/~saez/saez-UStopincomes-2011.pdf.

Samuelson, P. (1949). "International factor-price equalisation once again", *Economic Journal*, 59 (234), 181-97.

Smith, A. (1776). *An Inquiry into the Nature and Causes of the Wealth of Nations*. http://www.econlib.org/library/Smith/smWN.html.

Schumpeter, J. (1950). *Capitalism, Socialism, and Democracy*, New York: Harper.

Social Protection Floor Advisory Group. (2011). *Social Protection Floor for a Fair and Inclusive Globalisation*, Geneva: ILO & WHO, http://www.ilo.org/global/publications/books/WCMS_165750/lang--en/index.htm.

Spence, M. (2011). "The impact of globalisation on income and employment: the downside of integrating markets", *Foreign Affairs*, 90 (4), 28-41.

Standing, G. (2011). *The Precariat: the New Dangerous Class*, London: Bloomsbury Academic.

Tobin, J. (1994). "A tax on international currency transactions," United Nations Development Programme, *Human Development Report 1994*, p. 70.

United Nations Development Programme (2013). *Human Development Report 2013. The Rise of the South: Human Progress in a Diverse World.*

Veblen, T. (1898). "Why is Economics not an evolutionary science?", *Quarterly Journal of Economics*, 12 (4), 373-397.

Veblen, T. (1899). *The Theory of the Leisure Class: An Economic Study of Institutions,* New York: B.W. Huebsch.

World Bank. (2013). *Turn Down the Heat: Why a 4°C Warmer World Must be Avoided.* http://climatechange.worldbank.org/content/climate-change-report-warns-dramatically-warmer-world-century.

Chapter Four

Globalized Labour, Ecology and Peace: Understanding the Nexus in the Anthropocene

Nancy C. Doubleday

Introduction

The evils of globalized exploitation and violence are not in dispute. The predatory behaviour of economic forces with respect to human beings and to nature is familiar. What is new is the emergence of gathering forces asserting that the impacts of exploitation, violence and predatory economic systems are much more pervasive than expected and that it is not only the lives of the immediate victims that are directly compromised. Rather there is a growing advocacy for the view that these impacts also steer us away from sharing benefits and increasing social capital through trust-building, reducing our collective adaptive capacities, and diminishing our hopes for peace. While an economic assault may harm some explicitly, it may also cause others to be negatively affected in the future. Seeing winners and losers as part of usual economic life is not new, but questioning the acceptability of current distributions of costs and benefits is. One case in point is the efforts to challenge the conventions associated with acceptance of gross national product as a proper measure of development (U.N. General Assembly, A/67/697, 2013).

Other contributions to the debate about social justice and the nexus with labour include sketching ways of seeing health and well-being as shared social goods, as a form of "commons'. Another is to relate impacts of globalized labour to parallels with environmental threat and damage, seeking to understand common elements and to find effective counter measures. Here we look to common elements in the threats to trust-building, to development and to peace, in order to learn from the intersection of a range of large forces. Then we examine a case study requiring integration of social-cultural-ecological systems for purposes of management, and draw out some understandings of the consequences at the nexus of globalisation, labour, and ecology.

Framing

Globalisation is understood here as a process of increasing interconnectedness fostered by accelerating communications and the emergence of global systems of banking, trade, legal arrangements and diverse forms of cooperation amongst areas of the world previously separated to varying degrees by geography, culture, language, politics and numerous other distinctions. Older forms such as colonization can be understood as functioning through the exploitation of difference and its conversion to operational forms of distinguished differences, which are then used to justify the inequitable exercise of power. Examples include construction and adoption of a consuming gaze capable of "othering", such as the viewing of the "subaltern" as in "Orientalism" (Said, 1978) or as the "justification for slavery" (Campbell, 2006, p.10) as enabling, destructive, global-scale, practices. Similarly potent, yet of a much darker shade, is the emergence of the denial of identity of "the new racism, or raceless racism," across institutional scales, and most disturbingly, as Susan Searls Giroux reveals, within the academy itself (Searls Giroux, 2010, p. 6). More disturbing than a consuming eye, is that of the wilfully blind.

Labour is understood here a form of embodied property, rendered as a tradable commodity that is created by conversion of life energies, knowledge and experience, into units formed of commodified complexes of time-work-product-service. Labour possesses agency to varying degrees: the Gibson-Graham (2010) analysis of economic agency of individuals and community groups, presents a strong case for what Bandura (1997) and his colleagues have identified as "self-efficacy", also understandable as capacity for adaptation, resilience and self-governance, rooted in the individual and strongly ecological in its perception of community relations. The capacity of labour to self-organize, to form representative groups such as unions or to participate in movements remains a highly significant indicator of the success of the struggles of labour to secure livelihood rights and provisions. Increasingly under siege, as the globalisation of labour flows as well as capital movement change the geopolitical power relations, undercutting the unions, and facilitating the off-shoring, and out-sourcing, of skilled work in a race to the bottom.

Ecology is understood as a system of knowledge of the life-creating and life-sustaining biosphere, and its productive and evolutionary potential, with all of its component parts including myriad minutiae and its large slow systems, and its emergent systems properties, such as evolution, but not restricted to it, as well as a referent for the system of life itself. Land health refers to the symbiosis of humans and landscapes in caring and respectful relation (Leopold, 1949, 1966). Ecohealth refers to the dynamic potential of such landscapes seen through a resilience lens (Berkes et al., 2012).

Peace is understood here as a process of becoming, of development, and of attaining a state of co-existence, that reduces our collective dependency on inequitable, violent and exploitive relations in social, cultural, economic and environmental domains. Galtung (1969) offers a way into the understanding of peace as an absence of violence, but one also requiring an understanding of violence as complex and multidimensional, and extending well beyond physical and interpersonal violent acts. It can be experienced by individuals as determining the quality of life, and of access to opportunities and prospects for human flourishing or happiness, and is, arguably, also a property of sustainable complex systems. Entwined with health and well-being, peace may also arguably be interconnected with happiness. Indeed as the World Happiness Report in 2012 describes the Happiness Index, there appear to be many potential synergies between the factors contributing to happiness, to health and well-being, and to peace:

> "The Happiness Index is based on four pillars and was developed from 33 cluster indicators with 124 variables, categorized under nine domains. In each domain, the objective indicators were given higher weights, and subjective and self reported indicators were given lower weights. The four pillars include good governance, sustainable socioeconomic development, cultural preservation and environmental conservation. The issues under consideration within the nine domains are: psychological well-being; health; education; literacy; educational qualifications; knowledge; values; culture; time use; good governance; community vitality; ecological diversity and resilience; and living standards" (U.N. General Assembly, A/67/697, 2013, p.5).

Having just expanded the field of enquiry to fully encompass human endeavour and nature, we need to find a way to identify key actors and to follow key features, to preserve and to investigate the process of exploring, co-creating and developing agency. The question, then is how can we envision the interplay when globalized labour, and ecological foundations of global systems encounter, and further how can we learn to understand and to engage with these large forces, not to the narrow benefit of a successful few on the basis of exploitative relations, but rather to the benefit of all, in terms of health and well-being as understood in the broadest terms of social, cultural and ecological determinants, that is to say, in the direction of creating conditions for peace, in support of human flourishing, intergenerational equity and ecological viability?

First, we could agree that peace is more than the mere absence of the violent conflict that we call war, just as: "Health is a state of complete physical, mental and social well-being and not merely the absence of disease or infirmity. (WHO, 1946). Recognition that health requires so much more than the absence of disease has resulted in far reaching assessments of broad social, economic and environmental factors such as social justice, fairness, autonomy and control (see, for example, Marmot et al., 1991; Townshend,1988; Helliwell et al., 2012). We now have the methodologies to make comparisons across the globe and to critically assess the quality of life resulting from regional and international strategies for economic growth, management of labour flows, and protection of human rights and the environment. For example, in January 2012 the United Nations issued the evidence-based World Happiness Report (Helliwell, Layard and Sachs, 2012). Here we see a convergence of economic indicators, health and well-being and the subjective reports of happiness, supported by data:

> "...we proposed that happiness data and research should underpin the design and attainment of the four pillars of sustainable development: ending extreme poverty, environmental sustainability, social inclusion, and good governance. The happiness consequences of ending poverty, building social inclusion and achieving good government have been well documented by the data and research in Chapters 2 and 3" (Helliwell, Layard and Sachs, 2012. p.96).

It is proposed here that this convergence also constitutes peace as understood in the dynamic sense of this chapter, located at the nexus of the interaction of globalized labour and ecology where sustainability and intergenerational equity as well as social justice, fairness and equity are prioritized. Revulsion with wholesale commercial trade in human beings has contributed to an ideological repudiation of slavery by national governments as well as international organizations. However, slavery can be seen to be persistent in practice: arguably some forms of exploitative employment in some places can be seen to constitute a form of economic slavery. Such exploitative practices are found with troubling frequency. Whereas the transatlantic slave trade is understood as extending from the time of Columbus to the abolitionist movement of the 1800s and is reported to have involved some 15 million African victims (Campbell, 2006, p. 1), the propagation of forms of economic dependency, in some instances arguably, tantamount to slavery, can now be seen to have metamorphosed into a globalized phenomenon, driven by "the process of economic restructuring imposed by international creditors on developing countries since the beginning of the 1980s" (Chossudovsky, 1998, p. 15). More recent events accelerating the fractionation of wealth within even western democracies presumed to be relatively stable, have drawn the attention of international protest movements, such as "Occupy". Impacts occur in localized situations as well as in the global. Evidence of trends in wealth concentration and economic abuses of workers points to the widespread impact of globalized economic policies now, and the potential for impacting billions of people worldwide, in the future.

The slow development of theories of human rights, and of forms of democratic government, are also emergent system properties. These ideological forces in turn can be understood as influencing and being influenced by political and legal theory, values and practice. Similar advances have been made in conceptualizing environment and its relation to sustaining health and well being in individuals and societies. From Aldo Leopold's work on wolves and wilderness forward, we have acquired deeper and more intricate ideas about biotic potential and its relation to health of man and land (Berkes et al., 2012). We inhabit complex systems and we influence them through action and inaction.

These systems have multimodal drivers - some slow, some fast, some local or micro in focus and others long, slow and planetary or interplanetary in scope. We have an instrumental understanding that has allowed us to operationalize systems of control and exploitation, in some instances very efficiently. In other areas we lack competence, are inefficiency and struggle, often resorting to force, moving away from, rather than toward, conditions from which peace may emerge.

These areas include our capacities to share, to implement values promoting individual freedoms while restraining selfish and destructive acts, and to think of our planet beyond self-interest. Arguably we are also suffering from deficiencies in our abilities to conceive of inclusive, generous relations that are also capable of facilitating sustainable, nurturing forms of human security. To move past these limits into a zone of values where priority can be assigned to realizing respectful consensus that favour evolutionary prospects for peace, health, sustainability, and ultimately for individual and collective survival, requires effort to critically and creatively articulate compassionate values based on openness and understanding.

The strands of social justice and equity serve as warp and weft for the weaving of the living fabric of social and economic life on the loom of ecological possibility. Within this frame, choices are continually made, metaphorical and actual, each altering the integrity and strength of the cloth, social and ecological, as a whole. Pieces are cut, joined, shaped. All of this activity can be understood as "labour". It is also an expression of relationships, economic and ecological, as well as those both social and legal. It is the relationships that concern us here, and the implications that these relationships hold for our commons and for future generations.

If we think of stages of transformation of human-nature in historical perspective, the first remove is that of enclosing actual commons. Examples include colonization movements and wars of empire amongst nations, as well as intertribal conflicts at local scales. As a standard practice, human societies and groups were abstracted from landscapes, coerced into forced labour, and/or killed. This first moment of conversion of human-nature complexes renders vulnerable humans into forms of property, in whole, as slaves' bodies, to be owned by others outright, or in part, as their capacity for labour, to be sold separately. It is important to note that in the great diversity of the human experience, slavery did not always require war or colonization in order to precipitate enslavement. Status and lack thereof, including capacities for the binding of humans in servitude, have been assigned in a host of arrangements in most societies at different times.

Similarly, this enclosure of human-nature to create property and its subsequent division into bundles of rights, ranging from rights of ownership outright, to rights to exploitation of its parts, enables conversion of place to space. This extraction of people from place, and the subsequent commodification of peoples as "labour", and of places as "property" allows for their inter-convertibility, understood here as the second moment of conversion of human-nature complexes, and produces capital. The white space in between these moments is the unspoken loss: the loss of human-scale connection through time to living landscape and to natural productivity, on one hand; and the loss of human social and cultural connectivity to life-time and to social and cultural autonomy, on the other. The counter current is composed of exploitation, injustice and unfairness. The prospect is conflict.

Seeing the world whole, as one consisting of many lives, lived together in a biosphere that is also itself alive apparently runs counter to the more familiar narratives of labour, property, and capital. These narratives compose many of our accounts of the globalized world and also support many of the models by which we both theorize it, and seek to change it. Is there any point in stepping aside briefly from these dominant narrative framings? Here it is gently suggested that there may indeed be value in exploring altered perspectives on these relationships. Below we examine a comparative case study of adaptive co-management in regions of Northern Canada where this extractive process of dividing people from landscape, and from their labour, has not yet been entirely complete.

Re-Framing

Beginning with the recognition that ecological understanding means many lives lived within a living landscape, social-cultural-ecological systems thinking offers one alterative starting point in conceiving of relations and connections. Folke and Berkes have made this point very effectively (1998). To develop an appreciation of human impacts on systems-change dynamics, we can look at examples from forest industry histories (e.g. R. And V. Routley, 1974), dynamic coastal environments (e.g. Ommers, 2007), or adaptive co-management (e.g. Berkes, 1986; and Doubleday, 1986, and below).

The case study that follows presents adaptive co-management (ACM) in both narrow and expansive terms: narrowly as a particular, specified form of natural resource management, and more expansively as a hybrid of formalized power structures and informal grounded and epistemic complexes of knowledge and rights. As such, it is argued, ACM offers a paradigm for future forms of co-evolving, adaptive governance, a potential contributor to happiness and eventually peace.

We have begun to appreciate that evolution, in the sense of gradual change along a continuum, can apply to human development at the scale of the individual (Kegan and Lahey, 2009). Arguably we also accept the evolution of institutions and other forms of social organizations. In the context of culture, some disciplinary perspectives are contingent upon acceptance of culture as evolving. Here we are attempting to look at evolving, integrated systems under the rubric of "adaptive co-management", as applied to an emergent world, to the realization of potentials for peace and health and well-being ("the greater good"), and in particular, to governance of this future world. No small task, yet one that is clearly worthy of effort.

Adaptive Co-Management (ACM) is an amalgam of "adaptive management" and "co-management" (Armitage et al., 2007). Adaptive management began in ecology when science moved from description to empirical intervention in landscapes and ecosystems, where some efforts focused on effects on species, and others on systems themselves. Early examples of these ecologically framed experiments include long-term programs of research, such as those of David Schindler and colleagues at ELA in northwestern Ontario, and Herbert Bormann and Gene Likens, at Hubbard Brook in New Hampshire. Essentially adaptive management experiments would manipulate environments and note the results, feeding new information about responses into new rounds of experimentation. Co-management on the other hand resulted from efforts to create fairer, more inclusive forms of management of natural resources, especially renewable resources, during the process of negotiation of comprehensive land claims in Northern Canada. Here, outstanding Aboriginal rights to lands and resources were perceived to constitute a barrier to northern development by governments and industries, making the settlement of these claims a political imperative during the twenty years between 1970 and 1990. Early examples include the James Bay and Northern Quebec Agreement (JBNQA) of 1975 (Berkes, 1986), which resulted from Hydro Quebec's desires to develop northern rivers for hydro electric power; and the Inuvialuit Final Agreement of 1984, which was driven by government and industry interests in northern oil and gas exploration and development (Doubleday, 1986).

Adaptive Co-Management or ACM, then, can be understood to be a hybrid of the adaptive management school of experimental manipulation of large ecological systems and of the negotiated processes of co-management design and practice, resulting from attempts at reconciling competing interests, expressed politically, economically, culturally and ecologically, in lands and resources. This is the "narrow" sense in which ACM is usually thought about.

A Comparative Case Study:

Comprehensive Land Claims and Co-management

(a) James Bay and Northern Quebec Agreement, 1975

As pointed out by Fikret Berkes in 1986, Cree and Inuit negotiated and signed this agreement under duress: the massive hydro-electric development was proceeding and both Indigenous groups were struggling to retain their rights to access to resources. Also as emphasized by Berkes, these groups ceded only undefined land rights in exchange for specific rights to lands, resources and compensation: this was not a total surrender of all Aboriginal rights. In addition to the recognition of specific rights related to livelihood, Cree and Inuit also gained rights of participation in fishery and wildlife co-management structures:

> "The co-management provisions of these agreements are quite detailed, and provide for a level of user group participation in resource decision-making which is simply unparalleled in Canada and rarely achieved elsewhere" (Berkes, 1986, p. 190).

The negotiation process created a framework for participation of Cree and Inuit in decision-making concerning fisheries and wildlife resources. However, implementation of the framework and harmonization with pre-existing regulatory regimes and with competing users and conflicting practices left much to be resolved, following the land claims settlement. One of the key co-management bodies established was the Co-ordinating Committee. Berkes gives a number of examples involving the Co-ordinating Committee, making the point that cultural differences between the norms of Indigenous knowledge and practices of Cree and Inuit, and those of "white man's" institutions, including science and European governance, were disadvantageous to implementation of Cree and Inuit rights under the land claim, including rights to participation.

(b) Inuvialuit Final Agreement, 1985

Signed by the parties in 1984, and then legislated and signed into law in 1985, the Inuvialuit Final Agreement (IFA) is the contract by which Inuvialuit extinguished their aboriginal rights to lands and resources and ceded these undefined rights in exchange for specific rights to lands and resources, as well as compensation and participation in decision-making (Doubleday, 1986). The IFA created a number of co-management bodies, with provisions for Inuvialuit participation. There are separate co-management bodies for fish and for wildlife: the Fisheries Joint Management Committee (FJMC) deals with harvesting and conservation of species falling under the responsibility of the Fisheries Minister, including whales; and the Inuvialuit Game Council (IGC) decides issues in connection with terrestrial organisms. Both bodies address conservation, allocation and access issues.

As in the case of the JBNQA, if the goals of the IFA are to be achieved, attention to implementation is critical. Signing an agreement is only the beginning,

Shared Elements

Both of these agreements and their co-management provisions are rooted in the existence of the distinctive identities of the Cree and Inuit and Inuvialuit as peoples and, very directly, in their rights to lands and resources and to autonomy, which act to shape their distinctive identities and by so doing, act to maintain their right to recognition and to justice. This conception of identity in relation to autonomy and related rights, has been examined elsewhere (Doubleday 2005), and is raised here only briefly, to draw attention to its role and significance. Without identity and autonomy, landclaims would be difficult to maintain. In co-management, the polarity introduced by identity and autonomy constitutes one end of the "co-management bridge" as constructed through landclaims.

As Berkes (1986) points out, the construction of the co-management bridge is largely of western design, a major disadvantage for Indigenous Peoples seeking to participate. Berkes also points out the qualitative differences between Western science and Indigenous Knowledge, particularly in relation to wildlife management that may make co-management more difficult. One solution is to emphasize knowledge sharing and co-creation, in order to create greater mutual understanding and respect, and to put co-management on a more equitable footing as regards evidence to be taken up by co-management bodies and upon which their decisions are to be based. This linkage between knowledge creation from combining western science and knowledge of the land based on experience, with management decision-making capable of considering these different ways of knowing as well as the differences in interests that accompany them, requires a learning organization. Diduck et al., (2005) have written about double-loop social learning in the context of northern resource co-management under the Nunavut Wildlife Management Board, as a property of resilient (adaptive) systems. In this study, Diduck et al., (271) identify as key processes of double-loop social learning, relevant to co-management, the following features: "detecting the mismatch between intention and outcome"; "investigating the source"; "developing alternatives to avoid future mismatches"; identifying conflicts over competing visions or goals"' "resolving that conflict"; "implementing the preferred alternative"; "evaluating the results"; "modifying practice and theory" and "embedding the modified practice and theory in social memory".

Here we see a generalizable schematic of social learning that maps readily onto research and management practices. It is this social learning component that lends the paradigm of co-management a dynamic aspect that also makes co-management adaptive, as well as relevant to the larger issues of governance beyond its customary application within landclaims. Earlier efforts to address the issues of differences in ways of knowing included co-operative research methodologies in which the process of research as knowledge production was structured so as to bring hunters and scientists into extended collaborative contact. Recently this approach has been revisited in the context of sharing non-local or Western perspectives of landscape in relation to the extended experience of local Indigenous peoples (Grimwood et al., 2012).

If we step back from an assumption about congruence of intention and outcome, and go outside the charmed circle created by formalized co-management arrangements, we find the possibility of competing and perhaps conflicting intentions located farther up the chain of action learning. This is the realm of the yet-to be negotiated difference or conflict, and it is here that we may be able to find some useful insights based on the potential for co-management as part of a negotiated process for realizing higher-order shared values. By this I mean values constituting social goods such as justice, equity, fairness, peace, health and well-being. Implicitly these values must be shared if they are to be achieved by any one party, just as co-management requires inter-party collaboration. How might this work?

Games theorists have long considered this problem and its related expressions (e.g. Axelrod, 1984), but often with a win/lose paradigm in mind. By this I mean that the objects of the competing/conflicting intentions have been understood as "winning". Implicitly, in this construction, as in chess, winning comes at the cost of imposing a loss, or a draw. Opponents of nuclear war have argued that should nuclear weapons be used, climatic and other consequences would mean that there would be no winner (e.g. Crutzen, et al., 1982). Even a regional nuclear conflict has been held to have global consequences (e.g. Mills et al., 2008). How then is it even possible to construct categories of winners and losers in a conflict of this magnitude? Clearly such an imaginary distorts the range of the possible: no one wins when the Earth becomes uninhabitable.

To carefully focus in on complex cross scale systems change briefly, we need an appreciation of change through time and across space. Examples of meticulous attention to detail can be found in the work of ecologists and others who study living systems (e.g. Aldo Leopold, 1949), or in the results of the medical researchers who link health and quality of life to social determinants (e.g. Marmot, 1991; Townsend et al., 1988). Similarly, references to an inverse correlation of the deep despair of suicide to degrees of autonomy and cultural continuity are appearing in interdisciplinary literature, (e.g. Chandler and Lalonde, 2008).

If we can work out the inappropriateness of the zero sum game device in this extreme example of nuclear war, what of our capacity to address the slow catastrophes in a similar spirit? By slow catastrophes, I am referring to those large scale systemic changes that may be imperceptible to the solitary observer or to an individual in his or her life time, yet when occurring cumulatively over time, constitute a potentially radical transformation of social, cultural, ecological conditions. One top of mind example of such systemic change is climate change. However, voices of concerned scientists are increasingly emphatic in pointing to evidence that climate change is no longer a slow catastrophe, in the sense of requiring more than one (human) generation in order to have perceptible consequences, and rather is likely to have decided observable impacts in a human half-life. Yet we continue collectively to fail to appreciate the other slow catastrophes in the making that result in part from a failure of our collective intentions. The role of communications, both in response and in anticipation, where slow catastrophes are emerging, is a critical element (Goldstein, 2009.) Just as Diduck et al., (2005) pointed to the need for social analysis and learning where a mismatch of intentions and outcomes occurs in co-management, so we are in need of a form of social learning that can be scaled up. Why is it possible to comprehend the possibility of social learning in one case and not in the other? Simple answers can only be approximate and are likely to contain large errors, but it is not unreasonable to assume that negotiation of a co-management regime creates a forum for participation, analysis and for further negotiation in relation to shared aims. Such prospects are a basis for hope for the future and for resolution of differences and conflicts without resorting to violence. So, what if we scaled up co-management as a first step to creating conditions for scaling up social learning?

Previously, I proposed that greater inclusion, achieved by "making a bigger tent" using co-management, could contribute to social justice and peaceful resolution of differences by providing a form of scalable governance (Doubleday, 2010). Here I would like to press this idea further, continuing the analogy with formal co-management as developed under land claims in Northern Canada. Expanding "land claims" as assertion of a membership in a commons, the argument unfolds in this way:

1. common interests, in the form of identity and rights, constitute the core of a claimant group's land claim;

2. the land claim is a claim with respect to a bundle of rights, individual and collective, to those shared "goods" that constitute human security, and that human security is itself a commons;

3. the land claim is good against those whose interests constitute a threat to the security of the claimants;

4. the land claim provides standing for participation of the claimants in co-management arrangements;

5. co-management arrangements constitute a form of participatory governance, based on sharing of decision-making processes and powers with other interests; and

6. in doing so, they maintain the integrity of the land and its people as an integrated social-cultural-ecological system, and as members of a commons.

To scale up to intractable issues as an illustration, we could begin, in the language of Picard (2003) and others, with "threats" or with "cares". However, when the issue approaches some outer limits, as in the case of nuclear war, and becomes one of mutually assured destruction, the difference between the two categories of concern arguably diminishes. However, interestingly, in the case of slow catastrophic change, such as climate change in the period between 1750 and 1900, or perhaps the failure of the global economic system to deliver equitable treatment to all nations regardless of size, or the failure of regulators to effectively police the investment banks in the United States between 1990 and 2010, we seem unable to come to the realization that we share the "cares" and "threats" collectively, as well as sharing the fallout from failing to negotiate their resolution successfully.

The tragedies of dying for work occur everywhere, constituting shared cares, but are more frequent in lesser developed regions, What is not seen is that the forces of globalisation of labour and capital are threats, not just to those most exposed to their operations, but to the complex systems that compose our commons, Earth, and to our collective sense of place and options for survival.

There are many more "reasons" that can be presented here as to why this is the case, but to give a few suggestions: the issues are too complex; authorities are lax; power is not deployed for the good of all; winning is still possible when others lose; people are apathetic; or blame may be attached to various actors. While these circumstances may contribute to our sense of impotence, none possess absolute explanatory capacity. What then is needed if we are to engage with slow change to avert perceived catastrophe?

Returning the analogy with land claims, can we learn:

1) to see our common interests in security, meaning social-cultural-ecological security, as a ground for identity and rights?

2) to understand that we collectively hold the rights to this security?

3) that our claims to social-cultural-ecological security are good against all who threaten it?

4) that our claims are the basis for our participation in governance?

5) that as in co-management, where difference is negotiated and decision-making powers are shared, we need an inclusive evolving form of adaptive governance?

In natural resource conflicts, the roots of disputes often involve claims and counter claims for resource development rights. Inadequate provision for inclusion of competing and conflicting claims ensures failed negotiation of disputes. Failure to understand the epistemological differences between claimants and to address them further exacerbates tensions. This realization in the 1980s and 1990s led to the use of co-management models in land claims agreements to design regimes for user participation in government-directed wildlife management. In turn co-management, called for cooperative research in order to found equitable cooperation in resource management.

However, given the transformation of flows of power, materials, ecosystems and peoples over time, in social-cultural-ecological spaces, and the global changes evident in past and present, the assumptions of goals and objectives for management must be responsive both to changes in the environment or context as well as to changing needs expressed in social and cultural terms. In short, management as a process governing decision-making must acquire the capacity to learn.

Development forms that promote violence, whether direct or systemic in its effects, must be challenged. Violence constitutes threats: to peace, health and well-being, justice, livelihood, including labour rights, and life itself. The violence that often accompanies conflict over natural resource development is evidence of conflict and also threatens immediate human needs for security, peace and good governance. It cannot be fully addressed in a static formalization of co-management: it requires embedded action learning systems in order to become adaptive. To be successful in the longer term under conditions of conflict and disruption, co-management needs to develop an adaptive capacity, or to become resilient: hence the term "adaptive co-management". Here, "success" is interpreted as understanding that human needs for identity rest in security and that human security encompasses the needs of humans for fair value for their labour and also the opportunity to work, as well as the needs of healthy ecosystems for autonomy in their own ecological and evolutionary development. Envisioning the synergy of human security and eco-health as expressions of good governance is a corollary of an adaptive co-management paradigm.

Peace is not an endpoint, rather a continually changing process of engagement. Peace is dynamic, ebbing and flowing as conditions and understandings change. Conditions favouring peace are created by commitments to reasonableness, consideration, mutual support, equity, fairness, justice, respect, and sustainability, *inter alia.* We are all participants in the creative process, co-creating conditions for one another and for future generations, favouring peace - or not. In this sense, we can enrich our understanding of the properties necessary to produce peace just as seminal work in the social determinants of health has informed health disciplines and practices in international policy, and when we locate it, peace is found at the nexus of equitable systems of protections for labour, for sustainable social-cultural-ecological systems, and economic frameworks designed to secure rather than exploit.

Postscripts

Heightened by the intensity of the push of globalisation coupled with access to diverse communications sources, the "white space" darkens and shapes come into focus: perhaps this shirt produced 18 cents (Canadian) for a Bangladeshi woman, and $9.81 for the value chain it moved through? Perhaps this woman was one of those forced back into an unsafe building and who subsequently died when the building collapsed? What value, then, her labour? Her life?

Finally, according to John Helliwell et al., and the World Happiness Report (p. 96):

> "The environmental debate could be importantly recast by changing the fundamental objectives from economic growth to building and sustaining the quality of lives, as assessed by those whose lives they are. This will depend

crucially on the human capacity for cooperation that we have documented. The assumption that individuals are only interested in their own material standards of life has made the possibilities for preserving the environment seem unrealistic to many observers. But such pessimism is misplaced. On the contrary, people gain in happiness by working together for a higher purpose. There can be no higher purpose than promoting the Earth's environmental balance, the well-being of future generations, and the survival and thriving of other species as well. Sustainability is an instrumental goal, because without it, our health and prosperity are bound to collapse. But environmental sustainability is also an end goal: we care about nature, we care about other species, and we care about future generations. Building a wider sense of common identity among all peoples, with each other, with other species, and with the future of a threatened planet, will not be easy. But it is the only possible way forward for human thriving and even survival."

To this, we might add:

"...and for peace as well."

References

Armitage, D., F. Berkes and N. Doubleday (2007). "Introduction: Moving beyond co-management". In: D. Armitage, F. Berkes and N. Doubleday (eds.), *Adaptive Co-Management*, University of British Columbia Press, Vancouver, 1-15.

Axelrod, R.M. (1984). *The Evolution of Cooperation.* New York: Basic Books.

Bandura, Albert (1997). *Self-efficacy: The Exercise of Control.* New York: W. H. Freeman.

Berkes, F. (1986). "Co-Management and the James Bay Agreement", In: E. Pinkerton (ed.), *Co-operative Management of Local Fisheries: New Directions for Improved Management and Community Development*. UBC Press: Vancouver.

Berkes, F. and C. Folke (eds.) (1998). *Linking Social and Ecological Systems. Management Practices and Social Mechanisms for Building Resilience*. Cambridge, UK: Cambridge University Press.

Berkes, F., Nancy C. Doubleday, and Graeme S. Cumming (2012), "Aldo Leopold's land health from a resilience point of view: Self-renewal capacity of social–ecological systems". *EcoHealth*, 9, 278–287, DOI: 10.1007/s10393-012-0796-0.

Campbell, J. T. (2006). *Middle Passages: African American Journeys to Africa, 1787-2005*, New York: The Penguin Press,

Chandler, M. J. and Lalonde, C. E. (2008). "Cultural continuity as a protective factor against suicide in first nations youth", *Horizons --A Special Issue on Aboriginal Youth, Hope or Heartbreak: Aboriginal Youth and Canada's Future*, 10(1), 68-72.

Crutzen, Paul J. Birks, John W. (1982). "The atmosphere after a nuclear war: Twilight at noon", *Ambio*, 11 (2–3), 114.

Diduck, A., N. Bankes, D. Clark, and D. Armitage (2005). "Unpacking social learning in social-ecological systems: Case studies of polar bear and narwhal". In: F. Berkes, R. Huebert, H. Fast, M. Manseau and A. Diduck, (eds.), *Breaking Ice: Renewable Resource and Ocean Management in the Canadian North*, University of Calgary Press, Calgary, 269-290.

Diduck, A., J. Sinclair, G. Hostetler, and P. Fitzpatrick (2012). "Transformative learning theory, public involvement, and natural resource and environmental management", *Journal of Environmental Planning and Management*, 55(10), 1311-1330. DOI: 10.1080/09640568.2011.645.

Doubleday, N.C. (1986). "Co-Management provisions of the Inuvialuit final agreement", In: E. Pinkerton (ed.), *Co-operative Management of Local Fisheries: New Directions for Improved Management and Community Development*. Vancouver: UBC Press.

Doubleday, N.C. (2003). "The nexus of identity, Inuit autonomy and arctic sustainability: learning from Nunavut, community and culture." *British Journal of Canadian Studies*, Special Issue on Environment, Community, Resources, 16(2): 297-308.

Doubleday, N.C. (2010). "Justice and governance: A role for adaptive co-management" in: B.N. Ghosh, (ed.), *Global Governance, Labour Market Dynamics and Social Change*. Leeds: Wisdom House.

Galtung, J. (1971). "A structural theory of imperialism" *The Journal of Peace Research*, 8 (2), 81-117.

Galtung, J. (1969). "Violence, Peace, and Peace Research". *Journal of Peace Research*, 6(3), 167-191 Sage Publications, Ltd. Article Stable URL: http://www.jstor.org/stable/422690.

Galtung, J. (1980). "A structural theory of imperialism" Ten Years Later Millennium, *Journal of International Studies*, 9 (3), 181-196.

Gibson-Graham, J.K. and Gerda Roelvink, (2010). "An economic ethics for the Anthropocene. The point is to change it", In: N.Castree, M. Wright, W. Larner, N. Heynen, and P. Chatterton, (eds.), *Geographies of Hope and Survival in an Age of Crisis. London: Wiley-Blackwell. Antipode, 41(s1): 320-346.*

Goldstein, B. (2009). "Resilience to surprises through communicative planning", *Ecology and Society,* 14(2):33. [online] URL: http://www.ecologyandsociety.org/vol14/iss2/art33/

Grimwood, B. S. R., Doubleday, N. C., Laidler, G. J., Donaldson, S. G., and Blangy, S., (2012). " Engaged acclimatization: Towards responsible community-based research in Nunavut", *The Canadian Geographer*, 56(2), 211-230. Article first published online: 12 Apr. 2012.

Gunderson, L.H. and C.S. Holling (eds.) (2002). *Panarchy. Understanding Transformations in Human and Natural Systems.* Island Press, Washington DC.

Helliwell, J., R. Layard and J. Sachs, (eds.) (2012). *World Happiness Report*, Earth Institute, Columbia University, New York.

Kegan, R. and L.Laskow Lahey, (2009). *Immunity to Change*. Harvard Business School Publishing Corporation: Boston

Leopold, A. (1949 and 1966). *A Sand County Almanac with Essays on Conservation from Round River*. New York: Random House

Marmot, M. G.; Davey Smith, G.; Stansfield, S.; et al., (1991). "Health inequalities among British civil servants: The Whitehall II study". *Lancet*, 337 (8754), 1387–1393. doi:10.1016/0140-6736(91)93068-K. PMID 1674771.

Marmot, M. G. (2004). *The Status Syndrome: How Social Standing Affects Our Health and Longevity* (1st American ed.), New York, N.Y.: Times Books/Henry Holt.

Mills, Michael J., Owen B. Toon, Richard P. Turco, Douglas E. Kinnison, and Rolando R. Garcia (2008). "Massive global ozone loss predicted following regional nuclear conflict". *Proceedings of National Academy Sciences*, U.S.A. 105(14), 5307–12.

Ommer, R. (2007). *Coasts under Stress. Restructuring and Social-Ecological Health.* McGill-Queen's University Press, Montreal and Kingston.

Picard, C. A. (2003). "Learning about learning: The value of "insight", *Conflict Resolution Quarterly*, 20, 477–484. doi: 10.1002/crq.41.

Routley, R. and V. (1974). "The fight for the forest: the takeover of Australian forests for pines, wood chips, and intensive forestry", *Research School of Social Sciences*, Australian National University, Canberra.

Searls Giroux, S. (2010). *Between Race and Reason: Violence, Intellectual Responsibility, and the University to Come*, Stanford University Press,

Townsend, P., P. Phillimore and A. Beattie, (1988). *Health and Deprivation: Inequality and the North.* Croom Helm: London

United Nations (2013). *Happiness: Towards a Holistic Approach to Development.* Note by the Secretary-General. January 16.

World Health Organization (1948). Preamble to the Constitution of the World Health Organization as adopted by the International Health Conference, New York, 19-22 June, 1946; signed on 22 July 1946 by the representatives of 61 States (Official Records of the World Health Organization, no. 2, p. 100) and entered into force on 7 April 1948.

Chapter Five

Transnational Inequalities, Public Reason, and Global Justice

Jay Drydyk

Introduction

The global workforce is marked by inequalities that are both local and global. Not only wages but working conditions and labour standards can be highly varied both within state borders and across them. That much is obvious, but what is not so obvious is that some of these inequalities are particularly tenacious because of economic activity that crosses borders. In short: transactions cross borders, but workers cannot, and various workforce inequalities can therefore be difficult to remove. What is ever more interesting is that there is a large family of inequalities that are similar in two respects: (a) being both global and local and (b) being tenacious due to cross-border activity of some kind. I call these *transnational inequalities,* and in this chapter, I explore the question of what global public reason should conclude about them. Are they inequalities that matter? Are they unjust? I will argue that, facing such transnational inequalities, nationalist approaches like that of John Rawls are particularly unhelpful, creating double standards for justice. A comparative approach like the one proposed by Amartya Sen gives better guidance, and what such an approach calls for, generally speaking, is an upward harmonization of standards.

Transnational Inequalities

Many of the inequalities that contemporary theory of justice must address can be called 'transnational' in two senses. First, they are global as well as local inequalities. Second, and perhaps most significantly, it is because of international or transnational activities that these inequalities are tenacious. In other words, a country's place in cross-border transactions and relationships will challenge or undermine that country's ability to remove or eliminate those inequalities.

(a) Local and global. There are several ways in which an inequality can be global as well as local. (i) The most obvious is that instances of the same kind of inequality can be found in more than one country: thus, a particular gap between rich and poor can

be found in several countries, and 'global' here would mean 'found in various parts of the world'. (ii) In addition, the inequality may be greater or more pervasive in some countries than others, and 'global inequality' here means 'inequality between people in one place and people in another place'. For instance, in every country there is the following local inequality: some people can read, and others cannot. The corresponding global inequality is this: in some countries the rate of literacy is higher than in others. The fact that some people live longer than others is a local inequality, and so is the fact that life expectancy is higher for some social groups than for others. The fact that life expectancy is higher in other countries makes the inequality global. (iii) Notice also that some global inequalities can be 'internalized' locally: even if the average life expectancy is higher in Northern countries, there will still be social groups within the South that enjoy the same life expectancy, much higher than the averages for their country or for people in Southern countries overall. Some of the same social inequalities that can be found between North and South can also be found within Southern societies. Indeed, the idea that there is a bit of the North everywhere in the South is no longer a hotly contested thesis of dependency theory; it is now a commonplace.

(b) Cross-border tenacity. I have the following sort of tenacity in mind. (i) because of cross-border activities or relationships, (ii) a state embarked on a project of reducing some particular inequalities will face a path of steepening resistance. That is, the economic and political consequences of beginning the project reduce its capacity as a state, first, to complete the project and, second, to prevent the resurgence of previously-suppressed inequalities. Arguably, if a state in a developing country began to address inequalities in working conditions by introducing and enforcing labour law at international standards, and if it attempted, moreover, to do so single-handedly in a world with mobile capital and globalized production, the resulting capital flight would undermine – both politically and fiscally – not only the state's capacity to persevere in improving working conditions, but also its capacity to remove other local and global inequalities such as inequalities in health and education. Similarly, to cite a Northern example, if Canada had attempted to carry forward proposals of two decades ago to develop a national system of publicly funded daycare, the response by international financial markets might have fiscally and politically undermined not only the daycare project but the Canadian state's ability to sustain its extensive public health care system as well.

Cross-border activities and relationships often create this path of steep resistance in the case of inequalities that are costly and lucrative. By calling an inequality 'costly' I mean that the national government where it occurs lacks sufficient resources of its own to eliminate or reduce such an inequality quickly. In some countries, the literacy rate represents a costly inequality, although in most countries it does not. By calling a type of equality 'lucrative', I mean that preserving or promoting that inequality locally is one way in which a country can increase its national wealth or income.

The following are striking examples of transnational inequality.

Forced labour. As Mehmet, Mendes and Sinding (1999) have shown contemporary forced labour reflects a morally objectionable type of restructuring in the labor market, entailing hidden and illegal transactions in a global underground economy. This underground economy includes illegal trafficking in human beings as commodity, money laundering, drugs and sex trade and prostitution rings, controlled by unscrupulous middlemen motivated purely by quick monetary return. The global underground economy represents what effectively amounts to a new slave trade. It is the clearest demonstration of a new international structure of inequality in the world trading system. The global underground economy is a necessary by-product of the new restructuring unfolding in the international trading system. The moral consequence of this restructuring is globally tenacious inequalities between the rich and the poor.

Workforce segmentation. The new global economy, as an extension of what Mehmet (2002) identified as Eurocentric capitalism, is restructuring the types of jobs that are available in each country. A global labor market is emerging in which workforce of the world is hierarchically recast into primary, secondary and informal sectors, as an integral part of the web of globalized production. The cornerstone of this globalized production is the new global assembly line, controlled and managed profit-seeking monopolistic multinational corporations. These corporations are able to shift investment, technology, and in the process jobs, across national boundaries, in order to optimize profits and returns to shareholders at the expense of the rights and welfare of workers. The workers of the world are being restructured because jobs are being redefined along the global assembly line. Thus, primary (i.e. highly-skilled, well-paying, knowledge-based) jobs are being concentrated in rich countries, while secondary (i.e. semi-skilled, manual and low-paying jobs, especially suited for women) are relocated to poor countries. While these primary and secondary jobs are in the formal sector of the economy, in the sense that typically an employment contract exists between an employer and an employee, there is now an increasingly trend of job informalisation and marginalisation of work, sometimes based on outsourcing and subcontracting.[xxii] These workers, in other words, are no longer employed by the producer; instead, they might be employed on casual and insecure terms by a labour contractor, or they may be treated as self-employed suppliers of services. In this way, they add to the ranks of the traditional informal sector, engaged in subsistence self-employment (e.g., day labour, hauling and other transportation by the job) or petty street commerce.

This three-way workforce segmentation is clearly a transnational inequality. The cross-border activities and relationships that would impede efforts to resist it are those of globalized trade, production, and investment.[xxiii] For most people, precarious employment is disadvantageous compared to job security, and the growth of informalisation and underground economy is more disadvantageous still. There are prima facie reasons, then, for thinking that domestic justice might require shrinking both the secondary and informal sectors. But the likelihood that, in every country, a sustainable state operating in *this* kind of international environment, without *further* international cooperation, could reverse workforce segmentation, is small. Informalization of the labour process is lucrative in some countries in that it provides a large pool of cheap insecure labour, which can act as a magnet for foreign capital. Worse still is the prospect that, unless checked by concerted international action (e.g. with the introduction of higher labour standards), these trends can be expected to worsen. This follows from "a race to the bottom" whereby investment-seeking countries compete with one another pushing wages and working conditions down.[xxiv] By contrast, any reversal of "a race to the bottom" by policy intervention would require extensive investment for education and empowerment (providing access to business skills, credit, and markets).

The drug trade. The trade in addictive substances creates inequality in various ways. First, and perhaps most importantly, it exposes different sections of the population unequally to being harmed as a result of addiction. Second, it exposes underlings to more of the risks of criminality (i.e., getting caught), and third, for those highest in the hierarchy the wages of crime are highest, while the risks are lowest. These inequalities are *transnational* insofar as cross-border activities and relationships prevent states from reducing, suppressing, avoiding or extinguishing them. Some of the cross-border activities are obvious: smuggling and money-laundering. Drug production is lucrative, adding to underground economies of producing and consuming countries, and it is costly to suppress, especially if the economic dependency of producers on drug crops is factored in. Clearly further international cooperation of some sort is required, if the drug trade and the inequalities it generates are to be reduced.

Healthcare. Differences between health care resources create differences in the practice of medicine in parts in the North and parts of the South, and needless to say, there are concomitant disparities in the health care received. This is a case in which the global inequality is internalized locally, since Southern elites can avail themselves of health care meeting standards that are more typical of the North. Even in the best of circumstances, raising the standards of medical care anywhere takes time, and we should not assume that better care always means more technology. Moreover, we are talking here only about medical treatment; there are other social factors that affect how healthy people are. Nevertheless, we have here a case in which states cannot raise standards of medical treatment within their borders because doing so is costly, and a state that attempted to do so in spite of the cost would be undermined by the effects of international financial markets and institutions.[xxv]

Global Public Reason

Do these inequalities matter? Are they unjust, and would it be wrong to allow them to persist? These, of course, are normative questions, and I will assume, contrary to international-relations realism, that it is not pointless or meaningless to raise them. I will also assume that the best means by which to reach answers to questions like these is global public reason, and, in order to explain and defend this assumption, four things might be said.[xxvi]

First, I should begin with what public reason is and how it can be analyzed. Public reason is ongoing deliberation about questions of practical public importance. Like public opinion, public reason includes what people actually believe at any time about such a question, but it also includes reasons given for those beliefs. Giving an analysis of public reason, on any given topic, starts with observing these actual reasons and conclusions, but it does not stop there. The analysis should also include reasons that are relevant but have not been adduced so far in fact. It should also assess the comparative strength of the various arguments, both by the weight of evidence supporting their premises and by the inference strength connecting these premises with their conclusions. Finally, if possible, such an analysis should determine whether there is any particular answer (or course of action) that, compared with the alternatives, enjoys greater support by the better arguments.

Second, I should say why I think we should look to public reason for answering questions about inequality and justice, rather than some other theory, for instance a social contract theory. The short answer is that these theories are to be considered within public reason, and in that sense we do not have to choose between public reason and any particular theory. On the other hand, what does distinguish public reason is that it cannot be monopolized by any single theory.

Third, this recognition of moral pluralism is necessary in order to preserve the credibility of public reason, especially on the global scale. In modern history – especially colonial history – we find far too many cases in which domination of a people is accompanied by dismissal of their values and moral knowledge, their ways of making sense of common morality and working out differences between right and wrong behaviour. We may acknowledge that such dismissals and exclusion are not permitted in global public reason by adopting a *principle of global inclusivity,* which is that global public reason must give due consideration to everyone's values and moral thinking, insofar as they are relevant to the question at hand. In this way, public reason is impartial towards everyone's values and moral thinking, though giving due consideration will not always result in agreement.

Fourth, if deliberation must be so open to diverse and conflicting moral perspectives, it is reasonable to ask how agreement might ever be reached, even if weaker arguments are discounted. Here, a second principle is required: that the deliberation must show equal concern for everyone's well-being and agency. I call this a *principle of global solidarity*, though more precisely it is a principle of universal impartiality towards persons. It can be implemented in deliberation by what I (2011) have called *responsible pluralism*, which screens out particular applications of a general moral perspective where the consequence would be to inflict unequal and avoidable harm.

Before considering how the transnational labour inequalities are likely to be treated within public reason, within these constraints, it will be useful to consider how the capabilities approach can help to render both public reason itself and the analysis of public reason more resolute and decisive, narrowing the range of disagreement that is allowed by responsible pluralism.

As Sen (1992, 1993, 1999, 2009) has shown, the capabilities approach provides an informational base for assessing inequalities, and this informational base is especially helpful for understanding which inequalities matter most. The capability approach abstracts from the detailed conceptions of what it is to live well, to identify broadly described functionings that people might all value, as elements of a good life, despite differences in taste and preference. For instance, we all value eating well even if you prefer rye bread and I prefer chappatis. We all value learning even if you prefer learning labour economics and I prefer learning philosophy. The important inequalities may not be in the functionings that we achieve: for instance, you may prefer to fast when I prefer to eat. But if you and I are both capable of eating well today, whereas others may have to miss meals, you and I have the greater capability of eating well, and this is the inequality that matters. While Sen has argued that the capabilities that matter most may vary according to context, Nussbaum (2000, 2006) has claimed that there are ten specific capabilities that are central to most political deliberations: life, bodily integrity, health, senses/imagination/thought, practical reason, emotional life, human relationships, play, good relations with the natural environment and other species, and control over the social environment.

Other things being equal, public reason will favour eliminating or at least reducing inequalities of these capabilities. These are, after all, capabilities for living well, so tolerating conditions in which some people are less capable of living well than others would not show equal concern for the good of both groups, violating the principle of global solidarity.

On the other hand, capabilities do not comprise the only evaluative space, according to the capability approach. Agency comprises another such space. As the capability approach has developed, the meaning of 'agency' has evolved considerably within it, and, rather than rehearsing this history, I will focus here on one of the outcomes. From Sen's thinking, Crocker and Robeyns (2009) have reconstructed an 'ideal of agency'. Agency can be exercised to different degrees, and the degree of one's agency depends on the degree to which four conditions are met. Agency requires that (a) a person either performs an activity or plays a role in performing it, (b) this activity has an impact in the world, (c) the activity was chosen by the person, (d) for reasons of their own (in individual or group deliberation). In other words, 'agency' is about the degree and extent to which one's activities are one's own. Insofar as the principle of global solidarity calls upon public reason to show equal concern for everyone's well-being *and agency*, the capability approach once again provides an interpretation that renders the principle able to apply more readily to detailed questions about public problems.

Once public reason avails these evaluative spaces, it becomes clear why forced labour is among the worst kinds of inequality that a human being can endure. While forced labour does involve activities with impacts on the world, the labourers do not choose them for reasons of their own. Suppression of agency could only be worse in cases where all outward activity is blocked, for instance in solitary confinement. Typically, capabilities are also suppressed, since the labourers' goals of living well are subordinated to their owners' goals of extracting labour. Historically, forced labourers have had short lives, no freedom from bodily assault, ill health, only furtive escapes of mental life (such as escape into religion), emotionally damaging disruption of personal relationships, and no control over social environments. In the evaluative space of capabilities as well as agency, any time spent in forced labour is among the worst of the worst. Other things being equal (i.e., in the absence of evidence that these inequalities cannot be reduced, without sacrificing something of comparable importance), if we cannot find rationales, within public reason, for reducing or eliminating forced labour, then clearly we fail to show equal concern for the good and for the agency of the forced labourers.

Now consider the more complex case of global labour market segmentation, with primary sector jobs (i.e. highly-skilled, well-paying, knowledge-based) concentrated in rich countries, while secondary (i.e. semi-skilled, manual and low-paying jobs) are relocated to poor countries, where an underemployed workforce also relies upon earnings from the informal sector, based on cash transactions for services instead of any ongoing labour contract.

The workforce in poor countries faces continued tradeoffs between capability and agency. The informal sector necessarily demands agency: finding buyers for one's services, satisfying them, coping with competing demands when business is good, coping with reduced cash flow when business is bad. In comparison, the apparent security of a labour contract can seem desirable, even at the cost of agency lost through acceptance of an industrial labour regime. And, while secondary sector jobs may raise family capability levels, compared with livelihoods supported by the informal sector, capability levels supported by primary sector jobs are far higher.

Other things being equal, public reason must attend to close the gaps between capability levels afforded by primary, secondary, and informal sector jobs. Otherwise, it would not be showing equal concern for the good of people labouring in the secondary and informal sectors. But how should it attend to their agency? Concern for agency might be reflected in favouring strategies of 'graduating' informal sector enterprises into small businesses with employees under ongoing labour contract – as an alternative to strategies focused exclusively on drawing people into industrial labour. Such transformations also enhance the capability for control over the economic environment, which according to Nussbaum is a central human capability.

Increased freedom for trade-union activity should also enhance both capabilities and agency. Collective bargaining would seem to be indispensable for fully reducing wage gaps between secondary and primary labour markets; at the least, suppression of trade union activity can be expected to retard that reduction. Where a large pool of informal sector labour holds down secondary sector wage levels, a strategy of 'graduating' informal sector enterprises could arguably contribute in its own way to raising secondary sector wages. These living standard considerations all pertain to prospects for reducing capability shortfalls. In addition, trade union freedoms not only expand workers' control over their social environment but also raise workers' prospects for agency. While industrial regimes reduce workers' scope for agency on the job, trade union activity can be empowering, giving workers a greater range of choices to become better able to shape their own lives.

Other things being equal, then, global public reason should be favourable towards shrinking informal sectors and reducing gaps between secondary and primary sectors, by expanding agency through such means as 'graduating' the informal sector and freeing up trade union activity. Both inequalities of capability and inequalities of agency are to be reduced, and both processes of reduction can be thought of as 'upward harmonization' of standards – living standards, business standards, and labour standards.

On the other hand, perhaps everything is not equal. Arguments can be made that inequalities like these are not, properly speaking, unjust, and, so, they do not demand action on the basis of global public reason. In what follows I will consider just one such type of argument, which contends that inequalities between countries do not have the same standing in public reason as inequalities within countries. On this view, inequalities matter only within countries, and a just world is simply a world including and conducive to just countries. What transnational inequalities show, I will argue, is that this view violates the principle of global solidarity by accepting double standards for justice in different parts of the world.

Nationalist Approaches to Inequality and Justice

Nationalist approaches in general

The 'nationalist' approaches that I have in mind make two assumptions, the first of which is that domestic justice is *independent* of international justice, and the second of which limits our conception of justice to what is *feasible* within the capabilities of states. Examples of the independence view would include the following:

1. We can have a coherent view of what justice requires in a self-reliant country without having any particular view of what justice requires in the way of cooperation between countries.

Examples of the feasibility view would include the following:

2. Justice requires nothing in a country which cannot be implemented by a

state that can govern that country.

The feasibility view seems persuasive. Justice-talk, after all, has a place in political agitation and leadership. These are contexts in which it is irresponsible and misleading to advocate ends without strategies that could at least imaginably bring them about. At the present juncture, we cannot imagine a plausible strategy for justice anywhere, locally or globally, in which no role is played by states in some form – with or without the extent of sovereignty they now possess. Moreover, the version of the feasibility view stated above is open to various sorts of international cooperation and support. It does not mean that justice can require nothing in a country which cannot be implemented there by a state governing self-reliantly, without any international institutions, regulation, public sphere, or solidarity. What it means is that, no matter whether international cooperation is nonexistent or highly organized – even dominant – states will in any event have some important and necessary functions to carry out in the removal or mitigation of injustices.

However, when these views are applied jointly to transnational inequalities, they run afoul of the principle of global solidarity. I will demonstrate this both in general terms and with specific reference to workforce segmentation.

First, consider the nature of a transnational inequality. Any state that tries to reduce such an inequality locally will face resistance, in the absence of international cooperation. In addition, as transnational, this is also a global inequality, which implies that some states have been better able to reduce it than others.

Now consider how the independence and feasibility conditions work together. A given inequality that exists within a country cannot be considered unjust unless that country's state can somehow manage to reduce that inequality within its borders. That follows from the feasibility requirement. According to the independence requirement, our belief that this inequality is unjust locally cannot depend on any belief that the same type of inequality is unjust globally. Together, these two requirements entail that an inequality is unjust in a country only insofar as that country's state is independently capable of reducing it. Typically, poorer countries have fewer resources for reducing transnational inequalities. Therefore, inequalities that may be reducible and hence unjust in rich countries may not be unjust (because they are not reducible) in poor countries. So, between rich and poor countries, there is a double standard for social justice. If it involves inequalities of capability and agency, this double standard fails to show equal concern for everyone's well-being and agency, and so it violates the principle of global solidarity.

This can be illustrated with the case of forced labour. Rich and poor countries alike may find it more difficult to protect their citizens against human trafficking without international cooperation. However, poor countries find it far more difficult, and so their citizens are more susceptible to be drawn into cross-border trafficking of forced labour. But the degree of forced labour that is unjust in a country depends, according to the requirements of independence and feasibility, on the degree to which a state can suppress it self-reliantly, without international cooperation. In weaker states, therefore, more forced labour can take place, without being unjust: there is a double standard. But condoning forced labour for some while condemning it for others fails to show equal concern for the well-being and agency of all, in rich and poor countries alike, and so it runs afoul of public reason's principle of global solidarity.

The Nationalism of John Rawls

The Rawlsian approach to international relations is 'nationalist' in the sense I have specified (as I will show), but it is also nationalist in a broader sense. He believed that deliberations about justice are fundamentally the purview of peoples – a people comprising the inhabitants of a nation-state. The nature of justice for the basic structure of each society or nation-state should be a function of a conjectural fair deliberation amongst its people: justice is what a people would agree to through fair deliberation, and hence Rawls (1971) called his theory 'justice as fairness'. Similarly, if there is a just structure internationally, this too should be knowable through some kind of fair deliberation – at least conjecturally. But whose deliberation should this be? Rawls's answer was decisive: it should be conceived as a deliberation among the worlds' several peoples, not among the world's population at large.

The particular difficulty he faced on the international scale is that the world, as he saw it, includes different kinds of states. Some are *outlaw* states that are either expansionist or, in addition, not at all well-ordered internally by any conception of justice.[xxvii] That is to say, in these states, officials and leaders are not answerable for much of what they do; there may be no conception of justice that is shared, known to be shared, and moreover known to be an effective and instititutionalized basis for adjudicating conflicting claims. *Liberal* states, on the other hand, are those which, if they were well-ordered, would be well-ordered by principles that rest in an important way on what Rawls has been calling the 'reasonableness' of citizens. This is, in part, their sense of reciprocity, their sense that what makes a set of arrangements right is simply that each could agree to it, supposing that all others do as well, without intolerably compromising rational pursuit of their own good. But 'reasonableness' in Rawls' usage also means recognizing that reasonable people do not always agree. It is this combination of desire for reciprocity and recognition of difference that is to be modeled by such devices as the original position and the veil of ignorance. It is this combination, fundamentally, that would drive a society to formulate a list of basic liberties, to give high priority to them, and to provide citizens with sufficient resources to make use of them. By adopting these as defining features of liberal societies, then, Rawls broadens his conception of liberal societies beyond those satisfying his own two principles to include any that would be well-ordered by principles that satisfy their citizens' sense of reasonableness – their combined desire for reciprocity and recognition of diversity.

A third category is made up of non-liberal, common-good publics, which Rawls called 'well-ordered hierarchical societies'. Their institutions may not be very liberal, and their principles may rest less on reciprocity than on history, tradition, and perceived common good, but they are nevertheless functional *publics* in which officials and leaders are expected to account for their actions,[xxviii] and there are some inequalities that are considered arbitrary and unjustifiable for *anyone.*[xxix]

The first step, then, for liberals to be reasonable about international relations is to recognize *this* diversity: that there are these non-liberal but still well-ordered common-good publics in the world. The second step is to work out what arrangements might be required if reciprocity among societies of both kinds were the basis.

To capture this complexity, Rawls has proposed that the deliberative metaphor of the original position be split into two sessions. In the first session, representatives of liberal societies meet, not knowing which liberal societies they represent. In the second, they are joined by representatives of hierarchical societies, and in this case the veil of ignorance has the further effects of making liberals unaware of their liberalism and making hierarchicals unaware of their illiberalism.

Thomas Pogge (1994) has argued that, had Rawls understood his own procedures correctly, he would have concluded that international justice requires a far more extensive scheme of international cooperation than the "Law of peoples". Pogge thinks that extensive poverty reduction should be included on Rawls's international agenda, and the only reason that it is not is that Rawls mistakenly set up the original position internationally in such a way that the representatives of countries pursue only one interest: conditions for implementation of their society's conception of justice. Pogge asserted that these representatives should also represent conditions for their peoples' well-being, and if they did that, they would favour a global scheme of poverty alleviation through a mechanism such as a Global Resource Dividend (or Tax). I think Pogge has not quite gotten this right, because I think the problem really does lie quite deeply in the procedures of Rawlsian nationalism, and not in details of Rawls's interpretation of these procedures. To illustrate this, I want to show what happens when these procedures are followed in a context defined by four assumptions.

First, we will assume that deliberations on international justice must arrive at some ruling on what we have called "transnational" inequalities, and, in particular, on the inequalities embedded in the globalised workforce segmentation that I discussed previously, section 1.

My second assumption is that Rawlsian international justice will be largely silent on free trade. There are many other issues of trade policy that might be issues of justice. Trade inequalities, neo-colonialism, and the use of trade sanctions might indeed pose risks that any nation might wish to avoid, no matter what its conception of domestic justice might be. But free trade is a different kettle of fish. Free trade poses some risks to countries both rich and poor, as does protectionism; at some times for some countries, free trade will pose the greatest risk, while at other times the greatest threats will be protectionist. The choice between free trade and protectionism is not one on which justice-seeking countries *could* speak consistently with one voice. So far as international justice is concerned, then, each country may set its own policy on whether to raise or lower its own trade barriers.

The third assumption I will introduce is that there are at least two different conceptions of the common good that non-liberal publics might introduce. Let us say that "aggregators" think of the common good in terms of national wealth or income, while "equalizers" think of the common good in terms of building and equalizing capabilities – for instance, by raising the literacy rate, or lowering the rate of infant mortality, or raising and equalizing participation rates in the workforce or in institutions of higher education.

My fourth assumption is that there are some tenacious transnational inequalities that would be judged unjust by all liberal societies. Inequalities revealed by some major social indicators such as literacy rates, participation rates in education, and life expectancy might be plausible examples; workforce segmentation may not be, although there are certainly some liberal conceptions of justice against which it offends.

Suppose, then, that we know these inequalities are unjust by the standards of all liberal societies, and we want to know whether they are unjust internationally. That is, we know that removing these inequalities is required by fair terms of cooperation in each liberal society, and we want to know whether fair terms of cooperation *among all well-ordered societies* requires mutual aid and international cooperation in this endeavour.

(i) First session: liberal societies. As a preliminary step, Rawls would have us check whether this would be agreed to in fair deliberation among the liberal societies. Clearly the answer is *yes.* The goal of fair deliberation in this context would be to set international terms of cooperation so as to give each society its best chances for realizing the particular conception of justice by which it is well-ordered. If each is committed to removing inequalities of a particular kind, then none would wish to be in the position of lacking resources to do so.

For instance, imagine a poor but well-ordered liberal society that could not on its own resources raise its standards of education or health protection to those enjoyed elsewhere fifty years ago, without taking a beating by world financial markets. I take it that this is an outcome that representatives of all liberal society would want their societies to avoid, an outcome from which they would want their societies to be protected. Fair deliberation among them, then, would conclude that this is an outcome from which they must protect each other, through some scheme of international cooperation.

(ii) Second session: all well-ordered societies. So this is what the liberals would propose at the next state of deliberation, at which they are joined by the well-ordered but non-liberal common-good publics. But here they would meet decisive resistance. Justice, as understood by these non-liberals, requires arrangements that promote the common good, which is understood by some, the "aggregators", as national wealth or income. For some economically weak countries, reversing tenacious transnational inequalities is costly, while preserving them can be lucrative. If they are "aggregators", then from their point of view justice rules in favor of retaining these inequalities rather than reducing them.

This is illustrated well by the case of workforce segmentation. Shrinking the informal sector can be done, but it is costly. Development funds may be required to provide the subsistence self-employed with sufficient literacy, numeracy, and business skills, not to mention credit and business connections to enable some of their micro-enterprises to grow into sustainable enterprises that might ultimately provide formal employment to others. Moreover, keeping the informal sector large can be lucrative, in that it keeps labour competition high and wages low, which can induce capital flows from higher-wage countries. Shrinking the informal sector, then, carries not only direct costs, but possible indirect costs of foregone investment as well. However, aggregators would have nothing to gain by providing such aid to their weaker cousins: there need be nothing about workforce segmentation to offend against their conception of justice, while financing the reduction of workforce segmentation elsewhere would have the effect of reducing their own national income, which, according to their own conception of justice, would bring the legitimacy claims of their leadership into question.

In this deliberation, then, no one should expect agreement among liberals and common-good publics that workforce segmentation is internationally unjust.

We can expect similar conclusions to be drawn about similar inequalities. Because these inequalities are lucrative, low-income aggregators will deny an obligation to reverse them, unless this project is externally funded and leads to rapid growth. Because the reversal project is costly, wealthy aggregators will deny an obligation to support it. This much will be known to the parties in fair deliberation, even if, in order to model fairness, we suppose that they do not know which societies, territories, or conceptions of justice they represent. So, the parties will know that they cannot all be told, "you would not be able to implement your conception of justice, unless we all pitched in against these types of inequality." So what seems to hold for workforce segmentation should also hold for other types of inequality that, like it, are local, global, costly and lucrative. Under Rawlsian procedures, none of them should count as *internationally* unjust.[xxx]

But this has implications for domestic justice as well. Consider a poor society in which everyone wanted to be well-ordered by Rawls' two principles. What should they do about workforce segmentation?

Subsistence self-employment is not an advantageous position, nor is having a large informal sector necessary in order to promote growth and raise living standards for the self-employed. The same argument could be made (though less uncontroversial) concerning insecure labour. Moreover, the larger these sectors are, the more likely it is that people will be unable to escape them. In this way, workforce segmentation undermines equal fair opportunity as well as equality in basic goods, twice violating Rawls's second principle of justice.[xxxi]

Now consider what a poor liberal society might do about this. Attempting to shrink the informal sector with resources that the country does not possess would require either of two things: either international support or indebtedness. If international support is not to be had, then, the weaker that this liberal society is, the more likely the indebtedness is to work to the disadvantage of future generations, and thus to violate the just savings principle. The country could attempt to reduce the extent of insecure labour unilaterally by means of national legislation. Given that international justice would be silent on issues of free trade vs. protectionism, the effect of such unilateral legislation would be capital flight and disinvestment, driving insecure jobs from this poor country to some other poor country. This would deprive unemployed and subsistence self-employed people of what, from their vantage point, is the relatively advantageous opportunity to work insecurely in maquiladoras, export processing zones, and the like. Therefore, in the absence of international support, attempting to remove either of the two inequalities that constitute workforce segmentation would likely work to the further disadvantage of some people who are already among the most disadvantaged. In other words, if they cannot count on international support, the citizens of a liberal society following Rawls's two principles of justice would have to conclude that *allowing* those inequalities to continue *would not be unjust.*

As a result, we face the following anomaly: in a rich Rawlsian country, with sufficient resources of its own to eliminate these inequalities, it would be unjust not to do so, but in a poor Rawlsian country, lacking the resources to eliminate these inequalities, they are not unjust. The kind of inequality we are talking about is part of the basic structure of a society, and yet whether it is just or unjust seems to depend on *which* society it is part of. It is difficult to see fairness in this double standard.

Conclusions

One essential feature of transnational inequalities is, so to speak, that they cling to the boundaries between states and are for that reason especially difficult to eliminate. More precisely, they enter into countries through transnational activities or transactions, and in the absence of international cooperation, states find it difficult to reduce them. I have mentioned only four examples, but there are doubtless many more to be discovered by further research.

Transnational inequalities are important because they are instructive in two ways: both about nationalist approaches to justice and about public reason. Another way to put this is that a nationalist on justice in effect also takes a nationalist approach to public reason. As Rawls saw it, public reason could only deliberate about justice in one country at a time, and only once that was done could just relations between justice-seeking countries be worked out. As I have tried to show, this model is bound to suffer two faults. It will be unable to recognize important inequalities (including transnational inequalities) as unjust *internationally*. In addition, it will generate double standards for domestic justice in poor countries as compared with rich countries: even with the same ideals or principles, a poor country will not be able to afford the same standards of justice that can be realized a rich country.

This is not only an argument against Rawls, it is an argument against 'nationalising' public reason. As I have shown, global public reason seems quite capable of concluding (other things being equal) that change towards greater justice should involve reducing transnational inequalities such as forced labour and global workforce segmentation. Of course, I have not considered the rich panoply of arguments that might be brought to bear on this issue, but what I have shown is that the basic principles of global public reason incline in that direction. The principle of global solidarity, which commits global public reason to showing equal concern for everyone's well-being and agency, promises to screen out ideological arguments that would vindicate or excuse these inequalities. But, however, these further arguments might play out, it is clear that the global model of public reason that I have presented is at least relevant to transnational inequalities, while nationalized models of public reason yield results that are not only silent on these inequalities but incoherent when faced with them, condoning double standards which, by the better lights of global public reason, can be seen as clearly unacceptable.

References

Charney, D. (1991). 'Competition among jurisdictions in formulating corporate law rules: An American perspective on the "race to the bottom" in the European Communities', *Harvard International Law Journal,* 32.

Crocker, D, and Robeyns, I. (2009). "Capability and agency", In: C. Morris, (ed.) *Amartya Sen.* Cambridge University Press, Cambridge, 60-90.

Drydyk, J. (2011). "Responsible pluralism, capabilities, and human rights", In: D. Elson, S. Fukuda-Parr, and P. Vizar (eds.), *Human Rights and the Capabilities Approach: An Interdisciplinary Dialogue.* New York: Routledge.

Koivusalo, M., and Ollila, E. (1997). *Making a Healthy World.* London: Zed.

Mehmet, O. (2002). *Westernizing the Third World: The Eurocentricity of Economic Development Theories,* second edition. London and New York: Routledge.

Mehmet, O., Mendes, E., and Sinding, R. (1999). *Towards a Fair Global Labour Market: Avoiding the New Slave Trade.* New York: Routledge.

Nussbaum, M. (2000). *Women and Human Development: The Capabilities Approach.* Cambridge: Cambridge University Press.

Nussbaum, M. (2006). *Frontiers of Justice: Disability, Nationality, Species Membership.* Cambridge, MA: Harvard University Press.

Paden, R. (1997). "Reconstructing Rawls's law of peoples", *Ethics and International Affairs,* 11, 215-232.

Pogge, T. W. (1994). "An egalitarian law of peoples", *Philosophy & Public Affairs,* 23(3), 195-224.

Rawls, J. (1971). *A Theory of Justice.* Cambridge, MA: Harvard University Press.

Rawls, J. (1999). *The Law of Peoples; With the Idea of Public Reason Revisted.* Cambridge, MA: Harvard University Press.

Sen, A. (1992). *Inequality Reexamined.* Cambridge, MA: Harvard University Press.

Sen, A. (1993). "Capability and well-being", In: M. Nussbaum and A. Sen, (eds.), *The Quality of Life.* New York: Oxford University Press, 30-53.

Sen, A. (1999). *Development as Freedom.* New York: Knopf.

Sen, A. (2009). *The Idea of Justice.* Cambridge, MA: Harvard University Press.

Standing, G. (1999). *Global Labour Flexibility; Seeking Distributive Justice,* London: International Labour Organization and Macmillan.

Thomas, H. (ed.) (1995). *Globalisation and Third World Trade Unions: The Challenge of Rapid Economic Change.* London: Zed.

Chapter Six

Labor-Capital Conflict: From Eurocentric Capitalism Towards A Humanistic World Order[xxxii]

Ozay Mehmet

"In the closing years of the nineteenth century it was assumed...to be a natural and inevitable thing that all the world should fall under European dominion. ... the European mind prepared itself to take up what Rudyard Kipling called 'the White Man's Burden' – that is to say the lordship of the earth." H.G. Wells, The Outline of History, Doubleday & Co, NY, 1971, Vol. II, p. 851.

"Today, market capitalism has no major ideological rival. Its biggest threat is from within itself. If it cannot promote both prosperity and justice, it will have failed." Kofi Annan, former UN Secretary-General, The Gazette (Montreal), Feb. 2, 1997: A7.

"Indian electricity consumption per capita in 2035 will reach the US level that prevailed in 1947." Fatih Birol, Chief Economist and Director, Global Energy Economics, International Energy Agency, in a public lecture at Carleton University, Ottawa, Ont., Canada, 26/11/2012.

Introduction

What Wells summarized in the first quote above was Eurocentric capitalism. It has now become the principal source of instability and inequality in the world. Speculation, not profit, is its driver; profit has taken a back-seat. Capital market, the arena for speculation, is disconnected from the real economy, particularly the labor market which rewards less and less the workers and producers. Rewards[xxxiii], as private wealth are increasingly in speculative capital gains which accrue to the top 1% elite, made up of stock market players and financial institutions, while the rest [workers, middle class and those in lower segments of the socio-economic pyramid] fall behind.

For Marxists and neo-Marxists, the post-2008 financial crisis in the USA and EU may signal the end of capitalism. Here we argue differently: that what we are witnessing is yet another crisis shaking, but not destroying, the Eurocentric foundations of the system, a system moving inherently from crisis to another, but always working to enrich the West and impoverish the Rest. Well's summation, written as WWI was ending, was right on! A century later, greed-driven aggressive capitalism is crushing down in debt and deficits.

Looking ahead, a peaceful and stable world is viewed as the noblest GPG [global public good], and sustainable development (SD) as the policy instrument to lead to a Humanistic World Order built on shared prosperity of the entire global family. This chapter argues that what we are witnessing now is the difficult transition to the next stage of world governance. In such a world, international taxation is seen as essential to make global justice, peace and prosperity as GPG a reality.

The chapter is organized in four Parts. In Part II, we focus on the weakest link of Eurocentric capitalism, i.e. the increasing disconnect between the capital market and the labor market. Capital is now driven by speculation, delinked from the real economy of production, employment and earnings. The labor mobility is blocked and unable to serve as a mechanism of social justice. The systemic failure has assumed global proportions. In Part III a Race-to-the-Bottom global market is formulated to account for systemic failure of capitalism. In the spirit of positivism, Part IV outlines transition to a Humanistic World Order, using the GPG paradigm in the case of international taxation and autonomous SD.

Globalisation of Speculative Capital Mobility

The capitalist system, a Western invention with deep-rooted mercantilist roots, has enriched the West but impoverished the Rest (Mahbubani, 1992). However, the Rest and the West are simply too big, too diverse and too complex to fit or be reduced into a single mould. Ideology, religion and economy subdivide the Rest [i.e., Third World] no less than in the West. Furthermore, where does Japan, with its unique culture, fit in? Or a market-driven People's Republic of China, or such outposts of the West as Australia, New Zealand, or South Africa?

Crises in the Western capitalist system are self-generated from within the dynamics of the system itself. In perfectly competitive market, equilibrium implies zero profit [Mehmet 1999: Fig. 1.1, p. 21]. The system re-generates itself, creating speculation and havoc in markets, re-shuffling wealth anew between losers and gainers. In the end, the capitalist system survives with the Eurocentric interests always winning, while the Rest experience yet another round of impoverishment. After waves of crises, capital, [defined as not just finance, machines and equipment, but increasingly technical knowledge and know-how as well], is systematically concentrated in the West, home of technology and innovation, whereas the Rest is further drained of such resources.

As a rough generalization, the impoverishment of the Rest is the product of approximately two centuries of aggressive imperialism, all driven by aggressive or "pioneering" capitalist/investors, taking risk in new markets through speculative ventures, moving capital from the center to the periphery, but always ending with yet further concentration of surplus, as return on capital, in the center. Certainly classical economics, particularly Adam Smith, Malthus and Ricardo, wrote theories which facilitated colonialism and imperialism; but free trade and market theory alone, without a strong navy and military power, efficiently utilized by colonial administrators, could not subjugate British India, China and Africa. The subjugation had a self-centered commercial interest: It eliminated speculators' risk and safeguarded the extraction of surplus drained from the periphery to the center. The Eurocentric capitalist/investor could count on a guarantee of profitable business venture overseas by the powerful home-government. Military might, as gunboat diplomacy, always came to the rescue in risk-laden environments.

The period of aggressive imperialism, with gunboats and armies, may be dated from the publication of the system's "bible", i.e., Adam's Smith's masterpiece, The Wealth of Nations in 1776 till the mid the 20th century when the final gunboat confrontation over Suez was fought. Egypt's Abdul Nasr, a new anti-imperialist voice from the Third World, won a pyrrhic victory over the combined forces of Britain, France and Israel. Leadership of the West passed to the USA with an expanding influence in the oil-rich Middle East.

In the preceding 200 years, Europe and by extension the USA emerged, thanks first to the Industrial Revolution which brought in the Age of Machine, and then the French Revolution, which promised the Age of Human Rights, as H.G. Wells so aptly, put it, to assume the "lordship of the earth."

In the Age of Eurocentricity, economists, literary figures and missionaries as well as natural scientists like Darwin, globalized whatever comparative advantage the West had, demeaning and devaluing assets in the Rest. Free Trade was aggressively applied in empire-building at the heels of Industrial Revolution. It de-industrialized India and the Ottoman Empire; it subjugated China. Earlier, the Portuguese and Spaniards hard carted back to Europe the gold of the Incas and Aztecs causing a huge inflation in Europe, but also financing the Industrial Revolution, the Triangular Trade and created an unequal world.

Colonial administrators, backed by gunboat diplomacy, constructed a Eurocentric world in order to enrich the West and impoverish the Rest. Ethics and the rights of non-European man were ignored in this construction. For example, the East India Company controlled the Opium Trade, growing the drug under monopoly cultivation in India. The monopoly output was then dumped on an unwilling China, enslaving the Chinese for the exclusive profit of Britain. Similarly, the Dutch exploited ruthlessly Indonesian Archipelago, and the likes of Cecil Rhodes built the South African gold mines, impoverishing the natives and reserving the riches to the privileged Europeans and their descendants in what became the Apartheid system. How was this any different than the earlier Triangular Trade? African slaves had built the Cotton Civilization in the Deep South, so beautifully described in Gone with the Wind that was an integral part of the manufacturing system of Lancashire and Midlands.

Yet, remarkably, this Eurocentric capitalist system was reinforced and justified by evolutionist theories of survival of the fittest. Aggressive capitalism was ennobled as "natural" that evolved from nature-ordered competitiveness; it was natural because it meant survival of the fittest in the marketplace. One step further, in the logical deduction, was the derivation that the White Man was superior; the "Other" [Non-White] was inferior, lazy, as in the Myth of the Lazy Malay [Alatas, 1977]. Accordingly, colonial schemes such as Apartheid, Colonial Cheap Labor Policy, Settlement of the American and Canadian West, genocidal policies to eliminate the native people, were all justified on economic, philosophical and religious grounds as in "Manifest Destiny."

The Age of Imperialism coincided with the scientific age which reinforced a Eurocentric hegemony. From Enlightenment, universities led rationalism. Research and development produced inventions and investment opportunities. Risk-taking speculators and investors were always ready to monetize these new opportunities. The rewards, as huge surplus, would enrich risk-takers. Schumpeter put it in a context when profit was still significant. Pioneer profits worked as incentive for aggressive capitalists like the Vanderbilts and Rothschilds. Steam engine, electricity, automation and mass-production techniques ushered in the Factory System. The West became the Center of industry, capital, management and technology, the Rest its Periphery, source of raw materials. Western knowledge did not aspire to a global solidarity or creation of a sharing global family.

On the contrary, it contributed to the creation of an unequal world driven by aggressive capitalism. The new industrial system, processing and producing ever-expanding products, was hungry for raw materials as inputs and, at the other end of the assembly-line, it needed consuming markets. The Periphery, in the decolonization period after WWI, was redefined as the target of "global reach" [Barnet and Muller, 1973, Barnet, 1993]. Earlier, literary figures, from Rudyard Kipling to Joseph Conrad joined in the Great Game, painting the Rest in "Orientalist" or self-serving images [Edward Said, 1978], Western Arts and Science, soldiers and merchants, missionaries in particular, working as one gigantic team in the service of Imperialism and neo-Imperialism.

Marx had something to say on the subject.

Marx and the Third World

Slowly but surely, industrialization has been globalized, but not the proletariat or socialism. The factory system, the supremacy of machine over working class, alienating workers and pushing them, in Marxian terms, to violently overthrow the capitalist system, failed to occur, first in Germany in the aftermath of the Bolshevik Revolution of 1917 as the leaders of the Communist regime in Russia at the time expected. Instead, and during the course of the next half century, USSR itself collapsed under the weight of its own militarist, super-class aristocracy.

None of this makes Marx the humanist wrong. Nor was his critique of injustice and inequality in 19th century Europe misplaced. The questions put by a recent Marxian analyst are right on: "Why is it that the capitalist West has accumulated more resources than human history has ever witnessed, yet appears powerless to overcome poverty, starvation, exploitation, and inequality? What are the mechanisms by which affluence for a minority seems to breed hardship and indignity for the many? Why does private wealth seem to go hand in hand with public squalor?" [Eagleton, 2011].

Nevertheless, we must ask: how valid is Marxian analysis at the present time? Some, of course, continue seeing much relevance [Eagleton, 2011; Kitchen, 2001]. In an eclectic, non-ideological perspective, in the early decades of the 21st century, in the West, the class system has to be judged in decline. So is socialism: the middle class is shrinking as capital and investment [and with them jobs] are being exported to cheaper labor destinations like China, India, and several other emerging economies are rising into prominence. With declining real income in working households, not only savings, but consumer spending too, the life blood of capitalism, is only being propped up by increasing private debt and public sector deficit. This is unsustainable rendering survival of Western capitalism questionable, but not for Marxian reasons. There is no evidence of an "international working class" [Negri, et. al., op. cit., 1991] or working class consciousness emerging.

What has been globalized is the speculative nature of the capital market, not the labor market. Capital and its biggest owner the West enjoy global freedom of movement. Here 'freedom' implies speculation, the ability of the capitalist to convert risk and uncertainty into surplus extraction. Former colonies, now the Third World, have two special characteristics, high risk and labor surplus. Risk aversion techniques include blocking international migration so that "freedom of mobility" is restricted only to capital. This asymmetry is an essential feature of Western capitalism and constitutes market failure of contemporary capitalism. This as well as other systemic failures are ignored by defenders of the system and triumphalists [Fukuyama, 1989].

Marxist prospects in other parts of the world are no better. Free mobility of capital together with technology along with immobility of labor, have created a Race-to-the-Bottom world [Part III]. Industrialization has turned out to be far more capital-intensive than Marx or anyone ever anticipated. Early leaders in the Third World, such as Nehru, opted for capitalism choosing import-substituting industrialization and welcoming foreign investment while paying lip-service to feeble Third Wordlist movements like the Non-Alignment Movement. As a result, the growth of the proletariat has not occurred, and an indigenous labor union movement even under African Socialism with Nkrumah or Nyerere failed to emerge. In the West 'labor aristocracy' rose with little or no concern for global labor solidarity. Post-Apartheid South Africa has followed capitalist growth. If, the more mature industrial countries have not gone the way Marx predicted what about late-developing countries?

The answer is even more discouraging for Marxism. In developing economies identity emerged more on ethnic, national or religious lines than Marxist notions of material dialectics. Confucian, Hindu, Muslim or born-again Christian values now shape behavior of the masses. Marxist/Communist regimes, outside top-down, single-party systems in Cuba and PRC, generally failed during post-colonial phases of nation-building. In non-Western societies, as we shall argue at a subsequent section of this paper, there are home-grown varieties of cultural traditions, with several different manifestations such as Gandhian [Ghosh 2006], Muslim or Confucian. Marxism is alien, imported ideology that often clash with these traditions.

Not just Marx, but other economists who reasoned in terms of inevitable laws of economic development have gone astray. For example, Walter Rostow, the architect of the Stages-of-Growth Theory [Mehmet, 1999: 70-2] or Colin Clark's Structuralist Theory [Mehmet, 1999: 95-6] failed to help developing countries escape poverty. Neither was Arthur Lewis was any more helpful: Originally from West Indies, Lewis formulated his Dualistic Growth paradigm [Mehmet, 1999: 74-9], as did Rostow and Clark, from empirical evidence of the economic history of Western economies. Their prescriptions for Third World development was based on the assumption that late-developer countries, would inevitably follow the same path as Western advanced countries. Lewis was the more Marxian: his dualistic theory was purely non-empirical and totally abstract. Like Marxian "Asiatic Mode of Production", Lewis' agrarian sector was characterized by negative marginal productivity of labor [i.e. it was a reservoir of surplus labor] and therefore, could be squeezed for transfers of workers to the modern industrial sector for greater value-added. Both Lewis and Marx theorized heuristically, with no empirical evidence; both theorists constructed empty boxes!

Without empirical evidence theories are non-testable and as Karl Popper has argued, the scientific method that advances human knowledge is the method of refutation, not confirmation. For this, empirical evidence is a necessity. Popper's critique of Marxism, and the Communist system it spawned, as a totalitarian system, is well-placed.

In the case of economic and social development, home-made or indigenous development, at once autonomous and anti-imperial, is the norm on which to judge Marxism. Empirically, the world has gone much beyond Marxism [Mills, 1968: 130].

The Mindset of Aggressive Capitalist

To understand aggressive capitalism, we need to explore the motivating force of greed. How does the mind of a capitalist/trader work? What are the motives at play? What ethical values are present in market behavior?

These kinds of questions were uppermost concerns of Adam Smith who, it must be remembered, was a professor of moral philosophy very much occupied with ethical issues. Smith, along with contemporaries like David Hume, argued that self-interest is what drives the economic man. Economic man is a calculating decision-maker, passions determining reason in the articulation of self-interest.

The foundations of capitalism were laid and its institutions created after Smith in conformity with the new doctrines of the Invisible Hand of the market, Division of Labor and Laissez-Faire, all driven by self-interest. Much can be learnt of the creation of the capitalist system by examining the behavior of some leading capitalists of the 19th century at the height of Western imperialism. A few examples from the Opium Wars, The Dutch Monopoly in Indonesia, and the Firestone Plantation in Liberia are instructive. Similar cases from oil, mining or other commodities can just as easily be given.

Opium Wars: Traders like Jardine and Dent were among the most successful in terms of the pursuit of profit. Driven by unbounded greed, they believed in freedom of trade, i.e. buying cheap Indian-grown opium and selling it at high prices to Chinese tycoons, wholesalers and middlemen. These men were, first and foremost, free traders. The law of free trade, to them, trumped ethics. Never mind that they were smugglers, no different than pirates, breaking Chinese laws that prohibited importation of opium into the country. How did they see themselves? As betters, superior, who knew better than the Chinese, even when it came to Chinese welfare. The Chinese were "uncivilized", the Emperor and the Mandarins were all corrupt, no different than children. Accordingly, their desire to control opium addiction in China by supply management could not be regarded as serious. Why should these Traders pay the folly of the Chinese? Chinese demand for opium would somehow be met, so why not them? Besides, Chinese laws did not apply to these Traders who operated under extra-territorial laws, recognizing only their own rules in unbelievable arrogance. Their amazing life in Canton has been beautifully narrated in River of Smoke by Amitav Ghosh, a novel based on extensive archival sources.

The remarkable thing is that the British Traders were so mercantilist, they could not see that they were victims of their own greed. These free traders in China saw nothing wrong with the monopoly cultivation of opium in India: Opium was grown in India under the monopoly of East India Company, the mother of all oriental trade, in effect reserving all the profits from opium to itself. In China, these free traders, who resisted any government interference in their trading, unhesitatingly sought protection under gunboat diplomacy once the Chinese authorities applied legal sanction against opium smuggling.

In the end, the British traders effectively, adopted a position that Might is Right. The dispute over opium was decided, ultimately, by force of arms, the Chinese losing two Wars, and having to accept Unequal Treaties that humiliated the Chinese, and led to the Boxer Revolution and the bloody and long wars finally culminating in Mao's triumph with the establishment of PRC. So much for the triumph of free trade theory.

The Dutch Monopoly in Indonesia: The behavior of the Dutch imperialism in what is now Indonesia was similar, driven by the same mindset of European superiority over the local population. Monopoly created a plantation economy judged ethical by a master convinced to be superior. This superiority justified enslavement of Indonesian people, while enriching Europeans through a brutal system of exploitation.

Attracted by the lure of profit of the spice trade, the Dutch, by force of arms, subdued the Indonesian Archipelago, well before the colonization of South Africa and the creation of the Apartheid system there. In 1511, the Dutch overcame the Malacca Sultanate and in 1602 they established the Dutch East Indies Company as a state monopoly. From the imperial capital Batavia, they established a comprehensive monopoly system for the production and trade of spices, in the process subjugating the native population into slavery and forced labor on plantations, brutally suppressing any resistance. The Dutch colonialists justified their imperialist exploitation even under ethical policy intended to put a human face on forced labor and cultural oppression [Higgins, 1968].

The Dutch economic policy in Indonesia, however, was the most ruthless monopoly system: Production quotas, prices and wages were all determined by the Dutch and the native princes and people had no option but to comply. The Dutch masters, super class made all the decisions, the Indonesians toiled on their own land. Whenever, the native people rioted against injustice, the Dutch countered with brutality such as the 1740 massacre in Batavia or in Moluccas, Java and Aceh. The inequities of the Dutch in Indonesia have been well captured in the movie, Max Haavelar, the story of rebellion against exploitation on Java's coffee plantations in the 19th century. In 1949 the Dutch finally formally apologized to Indonesia. However, the historical fact remains unaltered: Dutch imperialism was mercantilist in the extreme, and it laid the foundations for Holland's prosperity.

Dutch prosperity was not home-made; without imperialism in Indonesia and South Africa, it would have been impossible for Holland to achieve the level of prosperity and high living standards that had enslaved Indonesians and Africans.

Firestone in Liberia: The Firestone Rubber and Tire Company of the USA was launched in 1896 by Harvey Firestone with assets of $20,000. Today it is a multinational corporation with annual sales of over $4 billion. There were two landmark events which shaped the company's growth. Firstly, the arrival of the automobile age and Harvey Firestone's success in becoming the first supplier of rubber tires to Henry Ford. Secondly, in 1926 he was granted a huge tribal land in Liberia to for a rubber plantation believing that "Americans should grow their own rubber" to end dependence on S. Asian sources (www.academyofachievement .org/honorees/ harvey_firestone.htm).

Firestone prospered, but Liberia has remained poor. What is the explanation? Liberian politics and misrule [Mehmet 1978: chap. 6], is a good part of the answer. However, the principal explanation must be sought in the dynamics of aggressive capitalism which drove Harvey Firestone, as a pioneering investor to Liberia in the first place. While Firestone got the land, the indigenous tribes were dispossessed. Rubber was not processed locally, it was shipped raw to the USA to launch a rubber and tire industry. In Liberia, come what may in the course of the next several decades, but always in collusion with the ruling leadership [Americo-Liberian oligarchy till mid-1970s, warlords including the notorious Charles Taylor during the civil war from the 1980s, and since the end of this conflict], Firestone in Liberia has prospered.

In early phases of the plantation at Harbel, Firestone used dubious labor practices, such as forced labor and slavery, to plant, weed and harvest rubber. In the highly corrupt Liberian political environment, it was easy to buy off political leaders who willingly co-opted security forces to raid tribal areas and force peasants to work on Firestone's plantation. As a result, the Company has had poor relations with international labor organizations which found Firestone in violation of basic labor codes and standards.

As the Firestone Company grew and prospered, it engaged in all kinds of noteworthy philanthropic works in the USA, including contributions to such well-known centers of learning as Princeton University. However, beyond paying off political leaders in discretionary ways, the Company contribution to Liberia has been meager; in education for example, Firestone's contribution pales in comparison with the Chinese-built University at Fendall. Needless to say, the Chinese are investing in Liberia, and elsewhere in Africa, for the same motive as Western investors, i.e. to gain access to raw materials for surplus extraction. As a late-comer, Chinese capitalism is yet to prove itself: Whether it will end up any different than the Western pro-type remain to be seen.

In each one of these three cases, a number of key features emerge about the nature of Western imperialism and its mercantilist roots:

1. Homeland of the capitalist is always the Center, and homeland nationalism of the capitalist puts the economic and political interest of the home country first.

2. The host country is Periphery and its resources [whether land, labor, or markets] are readily available for expropriation or exploitation by the capitalist.

3. Therefore, the welfare of the native population in the Periphery does not matter because they are uncivilized or inferior to Europeans or Americans.

4. Hence, as the quotation from HG Wells at the outset puts it, "it is natural" that these Westerners should exercise "lordship over the earth"

and for Eurocentric minds it is not, unethical to drain surpluses and profits for enrichment of the homeland at the Center.

5. In short, in a Eurocentric world, it is natural (i.e. objective) that global riches should be appropriated by at the Center with the Periphery in permanent poverty[xxxiv].

Speculation and Casino-Economics

Financial innovation [i.e. using new information technology to create new financial products and internationalize their ownership in a globalized capital market] is now a key function of the capital market. In mainstream economics, the capital market intermediates between saving and investment to supply the life-blood of the economy. That is no longer the aim of capital market: It is, rather, to seek maximum return in a highly mobile global capital market, moving assets in response to interest rate variations or speculative currency transactions. The aim is short-term gain, typically quarterly capital gain for stake-holders of large pools of assets. These assets are controlled by fund managers, including hedge funds and other assets that, in an unregulated market, may be of dubious quality, sometimes referred to as toxic assets [see moral hazard problem below].

Rational expectations theory, formulated from monetary economics, has been harnessed by speculative financial management as a tool of foot-loose capital, or "hot money" transactions. These are short-term flows moving into this stock market today, another one the next and so on. The gainer is free to take his capital gains to tax havens, thus escaping tax obligations at home.

The trigger behind these speculative flows is monetary policy, specifically the interest rate differential. Involving huge amounts, these hot money transactions leave a country the moment a better interest rate is available some place else. In the process, they destabilize currencies and may undermine economic performance. Some countries have been obliged to impose capital flow restrictions to avoid such negative consequences. Even under normal conditions, hot money flows they are quite removed from the real economy of investment, production and employment. Monetary policy, set by central banks, has effectively been captured by the financial elite dominating the market.

With the advantage of modern financial innovation and high-tech management tools, hot money flows are on the rise. Normally measured in a residual manner as the difference between the total capital account flows less trade balance and change in official reserves, globalisation of capital markets has expanded this type of capital transactions, generating instability and inequality in the world economy. Stock markets channel funds not into investment for growth in the real economy, but into option and future trading promising large capital gains.

The future prospects are particularly worrisome. Inherently, these speculative capital transactions are similar to betting in gambling. One wins similar to a successful bet in a casino. Accurate predictions of expectations bring in huge "wins" as capital gains. Eurocentric capitalism, as Keynes stated, is fast becoming casino-capitalism. If not checked, in future casino economics will create a world with diminishing employment opportunity and rising non-labor income. Consumer spending will be increasingly financed from non-earned income. The latest frontiers of casino-economics are such fields as erotica, TV shows and books on sex as freedom, and luxury services such as golf courses that only the rich can afford. For the dwindling middle-class stake-holders, the best hope is a share in some pension or mutual fund.

Under casino-capitalism stake-holders in pension or mutual funds, receive their yield not from real investment [infrastructural projects or mining or industrial development], but rather from "winnings" as in chance games. So long as quarterly expectations are met, rating agencies and the stock market actors are satisfied, the outcome is rewarding, yielding impressive capital gains. In the real economy ledger, however, jobs may be lost or real earnings hit the bottom. This is the Race-to-the-Bottom world described below.

A Race-to-the-Bottom World

In a closed economy, firms and entrepreneurs produce solely for the domestic market and profit, $\prod$ is the excess of revenue, R, over cost, C:

$$\prod = R - C \qquad (1)$$

In a globalized economy, $\prod$ consists of two parts, $\prod_1$ and $\prod_2$ where subscript 1 and 2 refer to domestic and international sources respectively.

$$\prod = \prod_1 + \prod_2 \qquad (2)$$

Dividing (2) through by $\prod$, we get return ratios

$$1 = r_1 + r_2 \qquad (3)$$

Where r represents return ratio, subscript 1 referring to home and subscript 2 to international ratio. Given that capital and technology are mobile, but labor is not[xxxv] [due to visa and residency requirements], in a global economy, $\prod_2$ will continuously increase as firms go international seeking production platforms in labor-cheap regimes.

In this process, home countries and host countries get locked in a zero-sum game in investment and employment. As one gains investment and employment, the other loses. For example, jobs are exported from North America and Europe to China and other cheap-labor regimes that operate as magnates for multinational firms.

What happens to wages and labor incomes in this zero-sum game? In home countries (of North America and Europe) job exports generate casualisation of employment, as part-time or time-share jobs increasingly replace full-time, secure, pensionable jobs. Workers in primary job markets are obliged to enter casual job markets, sometimes having to accept two or more part-time, temporary jobs to make the same real incomes as before.

In host countries, too, there is a matching race to the bottom in labor markets. This occurs because inflow of investment and technology creates a small primary labor market with high wages attracting the most productive [or skilled] labor and other complementary resources. In fact, these primary labor markets are effectively sub-markets of a globalized High-Level Manpower (HLM) market concentrated in the West. As the literature on brain-drain shows, host countries are net losers of HLM to capital-rich, high-technology abundant home countries. Indeed, it may be more useful to consider HLM as a form of specialized capital, embodying technical knowledge and know-how which, over time, is systematically concentrated in the West.

The residual labor, of declining quality and productivity is forced to flood into the secondary or informal markets of host countries. In these markets, child labor, female exploitation and informalization accelerate [Mehmet, Mendes and Sinding, 1999: 46-54]. Real wages per hour decline. In the terminology of labor market flexibilization [i.e. absence of wage rigidity], real wages fall toward the bottom.

What exactly is the "bottom"? The bottom is where bad jobs exist, dirty, dangerous and poorly paid. It is the zone of mass poverty: long hours and low wages. The worst is that at the bottom, new rounds of poverty are bred in the next generation as poor parents produce poor children. Underfed and uncared poor households live in sickness and disease. Mass poverty not only reproduces itself in the next generation, it also breeds crime, radicalization and terrorism. Alienated youth, with no hope and no future, are easy victims of extremism ready to blow up the unequal system.

Some have argued that bad jobs are better than none. "Better" for whom? Rising social costs of poverty and criminality make the world unsafe and increase the cost of global security. In free market theory, wages decline until some kind of low-wage equilibrium is established in the labor market. Whether this equilibrium wage is below or above minimum subsistence level of wages is uncertain. There is no reason why the "bottom", as discussed above, may not be below minimum subsistence wages with vulnerable groups depending on charity and humanitarian aid.

Overall, as the share of $\prod_2$ increases, globalisation turns into a race to the bottom in the global labor market: Workers must continually lose in order that profits keep rising. But, in the end profits compared with speculative gains decline as well. An unjust, greed-driven capitalism is like cancer inside a body. It ultimately becomes self-destructive, a sober warning voiced by the former UN Secretary General Kofi Annan quoted at the outset.

Debts, Deficits and Moral Hazard

If and when profits fail to increase, or they do not rise in tandem with expectations, then debt, deficits emerge; speculation overtakes profit as the system's driving force. Speculative behavior creates moral hazard problems. In the post-2008 phase of a globalized capitalist system, significant restructuring is producing new winners and losers.

China has emerged as the largest creditor nation in the world while the USA is the biggest debtor in part because the US $ has become international currency. Europe has attempted to gloss over huge structural and institutional rigidities by accumulating unmanageable deficits.

In the meantime, several emerging countries have forged ahead in global economic ranking, BRIC and G20 countries and these trends can only be expected to accelerate in the years ahead. One thing is certain: global economy is rapidly changing and new economic actors will crowd the stage of global trade, investment and capital markets.

Capital-labor conflict and the disconnection between capital and labor markets may keep on worsening. In the next decade, China, if it is able to manage its own internal stability, may overtake the USA as the biggest economy. For a while, the Chinese authorities may devalue the Yuan to boost exports, but in the long-run investment opportunities for Western corporations overseas, including China may decline causing Π_2 to fall short of expectations. In the end, private and sovereign debt would rise.

In Europe and North America the politics of debts and deficits will persist for the foreseeable future. Indeed, it may be fuelled by moral failure on the part of auditors and rating agencies that are professionally responsible for corporate integrity. Moral hazards appear to be systemic in the capital and financial markets, suggesting the system either collapses or undergoes serious structural change. Assuming the second is the more likely scenario, the global economy in the decades ahead will be radically different than at present: linear projections whether of income growth or energy requirements are bound to go wrong. Already there are far-reaching shifts in emerging economies as China, India, Brazil and others. If, in addition Europe remains stuck in recession for the next 5-10 years, or a Green economy is created, the world capitalism will look different in 2025 than in 2015.

One thing is certain: Fossil-fuel intensity of economic growth is rapidly coming to an end. As world oil and gas reserves diminish, energy markets may be expected to experience shocks. While greater energy efficiency may occur, for example in passenger cars, ecological and environmental sustainability will become critical constraints on capitalism in the decades ahead. Heavy energy-consuming countries, principally in rich countries, will be obliged to shift away from coal, oil and gas, toward renewable alternative sources more friendly to the environment. Yet, as the quote at the top of this article suggest, high-energy using capitalist countries like the USA will dominate the energy markets for the next several decades.

The capitalist dominance of global economy may, however, be a source of instability as recently argued by the French economist Thomas Piketty in his comprehensive book, Capital in the 21st Century (2014) due to increased capital flows, especially private and speculative in nature, un-taxed and un-regulated. These capital flows are motivated by private capital gains, resulting in excess of r relative to g, as pointed out above (Piketty, 2014: 353-356). Piketty is concerned that private capital accumulation over time is leading to concentration of private wealth in rich countries, or what he calls "patrimonial capitalism." (Piketty, 2014: 173, 473). His policy recommendation is international taxation, applied regionally as, for example, "a European Wealth Tax" (Piketty, 2014: 527-529). We shall discuss international taxation in detail in a later stage in this paper.

The projections above are based on the continuation of the status quo. However, the status quo capitalism is unsustainable. Can the 1% rich in the West living off speculative trading and capital gains in stock markets matched by mass poverty in the Third World survive in confidence that the pyramid is safe and sound? Greed at the top of the global wealth pyramid, and poverty at the base is unlikely to persist for the next half century on "business as usual."

Rather than a violent revolution and civil wars, including those in volatile regions like the Middle East, better to cooperate together for a rational world order: When all is said and done, capitalism is a creative system and it may yet create a Green economy, less dependent on hydrocarbons and more driven by solar and alternative energy. Most significantly, greed must be replaced by justice. Reason must prevail over Passion. Unrestrained self-interest needs regulation in the wider public interest. That is the way to give the system a human face, to ensure the sustainability of capitalism. That much persons of good will may endorse. For collective good, it is time that aggressive mercantilist mindset is replaced by something ethically sound. The Eurocentric economic system can be reformed for the good of humanity as a global family. The next Part will examine such a transition.

Towards a Humanist World: Global Fiscal Policy and Institutional Reform

Speculation, greed must be checked to save the system and profit, as fair rate of return, must be restored as the driver of capitalism. The question is how to manage surplus value now cornered by speculators at the top? Here we propose channeling it via a global fiscal policy to finance transition towards a humanistic world.

The history of Eurocentric capitalism demonstrates one thing: A humanist world cannot evolve automatically from market forces unaided by human hand. The West certainly has a role and a significant contribution to make in efforts to establish such a world. In particular, western decision-makers can endorse transition to such a world. Left unregulated to operate on a laissez-faire basis, guided by the "invisible hand", the market is inherently unstable, as bears and bulls generate fluctuations for speculative gains. Moreover, such a market process is devoid of ethical standards. The non-Christian world, the Muslim world currently war-torn in particular, is crying for fairness and social justice in global governance. Terrorism is the voice of the dispossessed and the irrational who want to tear down everything in blood because they themselves have nothing left to lose.

A humanist world is one in which every member of the human family contributes to global wellbeing according to one's capability and in return is entitled to basic human needs such as food, shelter, education and freedom. This is Amartya Sen's capability analysis based on viewing development as freedom [Sen, 1999], a blend of welfare economics, ethics from east and west [Sen, 1987], and some updating of Marx, in his most celebrated saying in the Critique of the Gotha Program.

The global family is pluralistic and diverse: many languages, religions, cultures and economic and political systems. The humanist world runs on peaceful co-existence, co-ownership and co-management of world's resources. Capabilities, individual as well as collective, differ. Each can contribute to the maximum of one's capability. All have basic needs and entitlements. Global justice must evolve out of this principle through universalization of Best Practice norms and conventions based on consent. The ultimate aim is world governance with a level playing field. However, no world government is feasible without international taxation. Universalization of Best Practice rules need funding generated from progressive (ability to pay) principles, for resource equalization (transfer) payments in aid of social and economic development from the rich to poorer regions.

The 1998 Nobel Prize winner Amartya Sen has gone furthest in the promotion of a humanist world order. Sen's is unique because, although an economist living in the West, his agenda is truly global, not Eurocentric. This sets him apart from most business school academics, and narrow-range economists or econometricians. He is unafraid to mix ethics, culture and economics in favor of multi-disciplinariaty. For Sen, in keeping with his Indian roots, development is "enlarging people's choices, capabilities and freedoms so that they can live a long and healthy life, a decent standard of living, and participate in the life of their community."

[http://hdr.undp.org/en/media/Capabilities%20and%20Human%20Development,%20 Sabina%20Alkire.ppt].

To give substance to this definition, Sen has played a key role in the construction of the UNDP's Human Development Index (HDI). The Index consists of three components: Income, Education, and Health. UNDP has utilized this Index to classify countries on their performance in terms of Human Development. Moreover, the

UNDP has gone further and designed Millennium Goals (MG) to provide policy guidelines for developing countries. But these countries, especially the poorest, need resources even more.

Without resources, however, HDI, MG or Sen's ideas are bound to stay merely ideas on paper. It is essential to break out of the existing [and insufficient] system, the Eurocentric mindset. The largest resource flow from the rich to the developing world is direct foreign investment (DFI) through multi-national corporations (MNCs). Notwithstanding reforms enacted through the World Trade Organization, the global trade system inherently generates an unequal world because it favors the former colonial powers. Even DFI tend to contribute to a Race-to-the-Bottom world since both DFI flows occur within a monopolistic and unfair system generating monopoly gains for the powerful and rich actors. Foreign aid and charitable donations are also inadequate and, like missionary aid, often pursue ideological or bilateral policy objectives.

In the transition towards a more democratic and humanistic world order, the major question which emerges is a question of finance and resources: How can the monopoly gains of the existing global system be harnessed for a humanistic world order? Such a world would require an agreed system of world governance. It would have to evolve from the existing architecture of the UN and international financial institutions. As with any governance system, taxation must be central. What is required for transition to a more humanistic world is international fiscal authority to raise tax revenue and pay for sustainable international development.

Such taxation should be levied on world trade, both on capital account flows as well as on trade in goods and service. Multinational corporations (MNCs), the key players in international trading system are the logical actors to pay international taxation. After all, MNCs, and the trading system are extensions of the old Colonial System. Global justice would be served if MNCs were to pay their fair share in the promotion of a more peaceful and stable world. Towards this end, MNCs need to be come taxpayers of international governance, for example, through the World Bank and IMF if only the required political will would be forthcoming. Taxing MNCs would be the most practical and efficient method, compared to alternative methods of international taxation mentioned above. It could be implemented via national tax authorities, with the revenues thus generated transferred to an international financial institution on the basis of multilateral agreements as in the case of UN organizations. These agreements could be drawn in such a way as to overcome any concerns against the proposal on grounds of sovereignty.

Upward Harmonization: Creating Global Justice

International sustainable development (SD) must become autonomous, funded independently as proposed above. As with other forms of taxation, international taxes must be progressive, administered efficiently by responsible institutions and create global justice. Global peace, stability and justice are Global Public Goods (GPG), a subject further discussed below. Consistent with GPG is Upward Harmonization in labor markets based on core labor standards, defined by the International Labor Organization (ILO). These standards are examples of Best Practice for application in national labor markets to eliminate slavery, child labor, female exploitation through investment in education and skill training. With higher worker productivity, wages and earnings would rise promoting a more just "level playing field" for all workers producing for world trade.

There is a further, equally fundamental rationale of Upward Harmonization in developing country labor markets: To stop the brain-drain outflow which impoverishes the Rest. Under Upward Harmonization the supply of HLM in developing countries would increase but, thanks to better earnings and working conditions it would not be drained away. Rather HLM would be retained in developing countries themselves creating value-added locally and contributing to social and economic development.

Funding of Upward Harmonization is the key. Who will pay for skill training, monitoring of standards and for enforcement of rules? Our view is that Upward Harmonization is Global Public Good[xxxvi] (http://www.globalpolicy.org/social-and-economic-policy/global-public-goods-1-101.html): Consumers in high-income countries and workers in low-income countries have a common interest in fairly-produced tradable goods and services as opposed to goods produced by workers under exploitation and unfair production conditions. Such exploitation and unfairness production represent market failure generating monopoly profits for MNCs and speculative gains for financial elites. In short, these gains are value expropriated from unjust conditions in global labor markets. Unfairness can be converted into GPG through global fiscal policy: International taxation offers[xxxvii] an equitable method for leveling the field, specifically by resolving the fundamental capitalist problem of labor-capital conflict.

As with progressive taxation, global tax is a justice-creating step toward global governance by putting a "human face" on capitalism. More precisely, taxing capitalists in the unregulated global market, the inherent instability of capitalism is checked and the danger of "patrimonial" wealth accumulation in the hands of the top 1% in rich countries is prevented.

The fundamental premise here is global equity: The desire is to treat labor in the global market fairly by taxing capital. The proposal here for international taxation enables some kind of compensation of the workers whose contributions have generated those monopoly profits of capitalists in the first instance. That is what global justice must mean as argued several years ago (Mehmet in Drydyk and Penz, eds., 1997) before George W Bush invaded Iraq unilaterally.

In a post 9/11 world, the "war on terror" has set back the internationalist agenda decades. In particular, the Bush doctrine has created a new "Crusade" mentality, effectively destabilizing the Islamic world. US-led military interventions in countries like Iraq, Afghanistan, Libya and Syria have bred more, not less, terror and violence. Poverty, marginalization and human displacement have increased creating an unprecedented refugee crisis.

Will the internationalist agenda aimed at creating a humanistic world return to reclaim the unfinished business that led to the UN and the Bretton Woods reforms at the end of WWII? Or is mankind condemned to permanent violence between the haves and the have-nots? Other-directed global ethics has become essential as a first step in global reform to tackle terrorism, injustice, environmental degradation and unequal access to health and other benefits of economic development.

This paper is an argument in favor of renewed internationalism for global justice. For this, institutional reforms in the UN system are essential, in line with the GPG theorem above. These reforms should be the guiding principles for the next phase of global governance, starting at the G8 and G20 meetings. In 1945, a good start was made with the establishment of the UN system of multilateralism. Now, after almost three quarter century later, the system is urgently in need of a democratic and representative transition.

Global Fiscal Policy and Institutional Reform

To promote this transition, in particular the following two urgent reforms are proposed: (1) creating more democratic global governance and (2) global governance must have global fiscal policy, i.e. international taxation.

First, the permanent veto system in the Security Council, a reward system, a legacy of WWII now totally outmoded, needs to be replaced by something more workable, democratic and representative of the global family. Permanent veto creates super powers and is hegemonic; it should be replaced with a rotational system all 15 members enjoying equal status. In the Muslim world there is widespread belief that Muslim problems get no hearing because in the existing global governance Muslim voices are not heard; there are no Muslim voices "at the table." UNSC should have Muslim representation.

Secondly, to give equality real meaning in global governance, there is an urgent need to link finance and global justice. Existing international financial institutions, such as the World Bank and IMF must become fiscally autonomous through international taxation as argued above [similar to what Keynes had originally proposed]. Their articles of incorporation could be updated, by international consent at G8, G20 and at the UN, so that they are authorized to levy and collect tax revenue from MNCs and currency transactions. These renewed WB and IMF would then become accountable to a global parliament, as the UN General Assembly, constituted on a "one-man-one-vote" basis and some suitable acknowledgement of MNCs, maybe in some Council of MNCs, as global corporate citizens. The exact formulae would be determined by international negotiation which, of course, inter alia, would require arrangements to avoid double taxation.

In short, global fiscal policy must go hand in hand with institutional reform for global justice. The logical starting point of such reform would be bodies such as G8 and G20 leading to reforming the existing UN system. Middle-power countries such as Canada and Turkey could perhaps take a lead in such initiatives together with other like-minded actors.

Conclusion

The current global financial crisis which began in 2008 is by no means over. This is a systemic crisis of capitalism with many simultaneous manifestations of instability and conflict: US and EU debt crises, petro-dollar driven Islamic extremism and radicalization of the Middle East, along with the rise of emerging economies. China may overtake the USA as the biggest economy, but equally significantly there is a convergence of Chinese and American interests that may become stronger in future for a peaceful world.

Clearly a new Post-Modern world is unfolding before our eyes. We are at the early stages of a new multilateralism, the 1945 world order having been shuttered by unilateral invasions in Afghanistan, Iraq and elsewhere. But, the world will not achieve stability and sustainability unless and until global equity is achieved, until a new order is attained effectively globalizing the benefits of technology and progress to all members of humanity. Indeed, with the on-going conflict in the Middle East, the refugee crisis may get worse before it is finally resolved.

Moving from the current world of disorder and conflict toward a humanistic world order looks utopian and unrealistic. Some may also argue that reform comes in small steps, not the giant leap premised and grand vision outlined in the article above. This may bring to mind Marxist utopian visions and, for that reason, it might be dismissed for ideological considerations. That would indeed be short-sighted. This paper is neither utopian nor ideological. What we are proposing is an extension of the present market economy with a human face on it. A progressive global fiscal policy is the path to follow in the transition to the next phase of multilateralism.

Rather than the greed-driven, selfish gene-oriented Eurocentric capitalism, we need an Other-directed global ethics in which the wellbeing of others, as members of the global family, is priority action in a post-modern world. Selfishness and greed can only lead to more conflict and instability in a divided world.

Global justice, as entitlement by all members of humanity to basic human needs, is feasible only by collective human action at the highest level of multilateral political will. It must be a free good, independent of ability to pay for it. As such, global justice should be seen as the essential foundation for world peace, the greatest example of GPG. Nothing less than foresight, vision and courage for the collective good can bring it about. Hopefully, the current global chaos and economic instability will lead to a new dawn and push humanity to a grand vision for building a humanistic world.

Furthermore, and in defense of the grand vision, the following may be said in conclusion and in the spirit of neo-institutionalism and multilateralism. The UN system itself, created in the closing days of WWII, was a giant leap for humanity. Nothing less is required now for the next step forward to create a better world. As argued above, the logical step for the reform agenda would be to launch it most appropriately at G20 meetings.

A new humanistic world requires going beyond a Eurocentric construction. It must be built by a true global partnership. Western and non-western voices must be heard and, moreover, all members of humanity should provide meaningful input into a redesign of the UN system, without a permanent veto system, and international taxation for autonomous SD for growth, peace and justice simultaneously.

References

Barnet, R. and R. Muller (1974). *The Global Reach*, New York: Simon & Shuster.

Barrett, S. (2007). *Why Cooperate? The Incentive to Supply Global Public Goods*, New York: Oxford University Press.

Burnet, R. (1993), “The end of jobs”, *Harper's*, September.

Drydyk, J. and P. Penz (1997) (eds.). *Global Justice, Global Democracy, Society for Socialist Studie*s, Winnipeg/Halifax: Fernwood Publishing.

Eagleton, T. (2011). *Why Marx Was Right?* Yale University Press.

Ghosh, B.N. (2006). *Gandhian Political Economy*, London: Ashgate.

Higgins, B. (1968). *Economic Development - Principles, Problems and Policies*, New York: Norton & Co.

Kitchen, G. (2001). *Seeking Justice Through Globalisation: Escaping a Nationalisst Perspective*, Pennsylvania University Press.

Mahbubani, K. (1992). “The West and the Rest” the National Interest, Summer.

Mehmet, O. (1978). *Economic Planning and Social Justice in Developing Countries*, London: Croom Helm.

Mehmet, O. (1995 and 1999). *Westernizing the Third World - The Eurocentricity of Economic Development Theories*, London: Routldege, second (and expanded) edition.

Mehmet, O., E. Mendes and R. Sinding (1999). *Towards a Fair Global Labor Market - Avoiding A New Slave Trade*, London: Routledge.

Riketty, T. (2014). *Capital in the 21st Century*, Harvard.

Wright Mills, C. (1968), *The Marxists*, New York: Dell.

Negri, A. (1991). *Marx Beyond Marx, Lessons on the Grundisse* – translated by Henry Cleaver, Michael Ryan, Mauricio Vianno, edited by Jim Fleming, London: Pluto Press.

Said, E. (1978). *Orientalism*, New York: Random House.

Sen, A. (1987). *On Ethics and Economics*, Oxford: Blackwell.

Sen, A. (1999). *Development as Freedom*, Oxford: Oxford University Press.

Chapter Seven

The Past has No Future: Revisiting Danish Flexicurity[xxxviii]

Johannes Dragsbaek Schmidt and Jacques Hersh

Without wishing to underestimate the role of international finance in the launching of the current "Great Recession" as it has been called, it is the position of this contribution that over-emphasizing such causality contributes to reducing the scope of the phenomenon. From this viewpoint, the understanding of the multi-layered crisis affecting a number of core capitalist countries is constrained by the conceptual frame of reference which in the past decades has achieved predominance in socio-economic theorizing and policy-making as well as socio-political practice.

As a result, the proposed resolutions to the impasse which seems to have impacted most economies of the world depend on this conceptualization. In the dominant mainstream political conversation, the policy choices offered have been either a course of austerity (neo-liberal shock therapy and decrease of living standards) or one of audacity (Keynesian "pump priming" and activating of demand). However, assuming a binary opposition between the two approaches may lead to false expectations as the proposed strategies belong to the same theoretical toolbox of policy-making under modern capitalism. That does not of course mean that the social and political consequences of each strategy are inconsequential. While the austerity discourse is based on the assumption of "no pain, no gain", the audacity approach is based on the supposition of "unlimited prosperity".

It is in this context that the following reflections will attempt to establish a general framework that can be used to analyze the Danish model's response to the turbulent times confronting capitalist societies. According to a number of economists, the scope of the dysfunctioning of the world economy is reminiscent of the Great Depression in the 1930s; others see it as a conjunctural and temporary crisis or simply as "business as usual". In this context, it may be relevant to look at the way a small economy has navigated in coming to terms with the vagaries of late capitalism. In later years, the so-called "Danish Flexicurity Model" has been hailed by the international media as a success-story (Zhou, 2007) becoming almost the exemplar to follow in European labor market reform (Viebrock and Clasen, 2009).

A former Danish social democratic finance minister published a book with the title *The Danish Model: A European Success Story* where he emphasizes the positive turn in employment and socio-economic activity in Denmark in comparison with large countries such as Germany and France on the European continent. "For a long time, Danes have had no ambitions of dominating other large and small countries. But we do believe that we can contribute with good experience and ideas on how social democracy and social relations can enrich a society" (Lykketoft, 2009: 6).

Calling the Danish example of industrial relations and social organization a model implies that it can be generalized and emulated which is a problematic proposition. Furthermore, its viability needs to be tested with the passing of time and the evolution of politics and social conditions in Denmark and changes in the international political economy. In this respect, it is doubtful that multinational corporations would relinquish willingly the so-called "global labor arbitrage" pattern, whereby the differences in wage levels and other production costs between countries are exploited in order to extract surplus profits (Bellamy Foster and McChesney, 2012: 15).

The framework of the Danish flexicurity model — characterized by flexible hiring/firing rules, generous social safety net, and active labor market policies — has been challenged in the past decade by a liberal-conservative government and yellow unions even before the crises hit the economy. Flexicurity as a conflict prevention scheme based on labor market regulations has been further weakened by EU legislation and various governments promoting a strategy of reductions and cuts in social security and unemployment benefits in addition to the marginalization of a growing pool of non-wage earners outside the labor market. Rising unemployment and a drastic reduction in unionization has created a new situation where the sustainability of the model is in question. Already prior to the crisis, the right-wing government of Anders Fogh Rasmussen (who later became General Secretary of NATO) introduced a work first strategy - i.e. a milder version of workfare – changing labor market relations towards a more individualized type of employability where economic incentives and sanctions replaced general upgrading of qualifications and skills (Jørgensen, 2008).

Pressure from the EU and the competitive austerity impact of the crisis also raises the issue and challenges of corporatist democracy as a specific form of capitalist governability. If an EU institutional straightjacket imposes itself on its member countries, this thereby weakens the notion of national sovereignty. Tendencies pointing in this direction seem to be at work. Examples are numerous: The financial treaty which lays a conservative, monetarist and restrictive fiscal policy in essence ties governments' hands in terms of combating unemployment and meeting the immediate social impact of the crisis with national expansive policies; the pegged exchange rate of the Danish currency to the Euro hinders a flexible exchange rate as an alternative macro-economic measure to decrease production costs and enhance the internal and external competitive position of the economy. Such a policy rather than a strategy of "flexicurity" would improve the competitiveness of an economy with balance of trade problems and high production costs. Another contradictory position of the new "Red" government that came to power in 2011 can be grasped when in its capacity of Chairmanship of the European Union, it opposed the so-called Tobin tax ("Robin Hood") on financial transactions favored by the rightwing governments in Germany and France. Furthermore, the reforms of the German labor market under social democratic leadership have led to a negative spiral of wage cuttings putting tremendous pressure on government and trade unions in Denmark in terms of job insecurity, loss of productivity and competitive downsizing.

This chapter explores how the protracted multi-layered crisis has affected the Danish model in the past decades and focuses on the policy options and institutional responses in the attempt of adjusting the economy to the demands of neo-liberalism and globalisation while moderating and/or managing the impact on social and labor market conditions. More specifically, it offers an analysis of the collective agreements, income support, and wage negotiations and specifically on the strength/weaknesses of organized labor as a collective partner in the workings of the corporatist model. The first part questions the mainstream explanations of the crisis and strategies offered as a way out of the crisis. It also introduces the conceptual framework embedded in the "social structure of accumulation" for understanding the essence of the crisis and rather than its symptoms. The second section is devoted to a reconstruction of the historical background behind the shift from the corporatist welfare state (the so-called Danish model) to the corporatist competition state leading up to the crises of the private sector in the United States and Europe. The third part proposes a brief re-reading of the restructuring of the Danish welfare state while the fourth part offers an analysis of the impact of the crises on the labor market regulation model of flexicurity in Denmark. The fifth section discusses the options and limits of the Left under the current crisis while the last part presents some concluding remarks.

The Problem of Conceptualization

An important analytical problem in working with the current contradictions and conflicts of capitalism concerns the ambivalence of the term "crisis" as the *explanatory* paradigm. Mainstream definitions offer various choices. Hence, should it be understood as the expression of acuteness in a disease which will lead either to recovery or death — i.e., as a crucial moment or turning point? Its use in the neo-classical and Schumpeterian vocabulary of "economics in command" is to consider crisis as the culminating point of a business cycle prosperity followed by a period of liquidation. The latter definition is the working hypothesis propagated by the dominating discourse in the world of academia and the mainstream media. Even self-proclaimed opponents of capitalism adhere to this interpretation and their proposed remedies thus remain within the box.

As a consequence, the political essence of the crisis has been assigned secondary importance while the financial aspects are given most attention. Nevertheless, as solutions are sought whereby the debt of financial institutions is nationalized or socialized by making populations assume the burden of repayment through decreasing standards of living and reforms of the labor market, it can be expected that a politicization of the crisis will emerge despite the present low starting point of the process. Far from representing a boon for anti-systemic forces, especially in Europe, the current crisis of capitalism has revealed the limbo in which they find themselves trapped in. This confusion is first related to the Social Democratic tradition's implicit conversion since World War II to the Keynesian macroeconomic model of state interventionism in the national economy during the Golden Age of capitalism and then in the 1980s to its acceptance of economic neo-liberalism with its emphasis on supply economics, liberalization of market forces, lean and new public management leading to what Cerny (1994, 2007) has called "embedded financial orthodoxy".

It has somehow fallen out of the collective memory that, following the Great Depression and the Second World War, the balance of political forces in the core countries was rather unstable with socialist or anti-capitalist forces on the ascendance. It is in this context that the strategy of Keynesian economics should be understood — i.e., putting "politics in command". In the words of John Kenneth Galbraith, capitalism was saved by the social-democratic tradition: "[T]he survival of the modern market system was in large measure, our accomplishment. It would not have survived had it not been for the successful efforts of the social left ... Let us not be so reticent: we are the custodian of a political tradition that saved classical capitalism from itself" (Galbraith, 1997: 5). This is very much akin to Keynes' own view that capitalism is an imperfect machine that needs to be maintained and updated if it is to function and work to meet peoples' needs (Backhouse and Bateman, 2011: 56). Not to be ignored, however, is the high degree of political mobilization that existed in capitalist societies at the time. It has to be recognized that social and political pressures — and not pure Keynesian economic intervention and policies — paved the way for a so-called social compact, albeit without challenging the dominant position of capital, whether in the short run or the long run, neither internally nor externally (Schmidt and Hersh, 2006: 77).

Furthermore, while the social democratic Left assumed credit for the implementation of a counter-program to liberalism it did not have a monopoly on the strategy. It is interesting to note that prior to the 1970s all political forces aspiring to government responsibilities adhered to state interventionism which was understood as a necessary tool in order to avoid a rupture within the system. As written in a Washington Post essay: "Keynes was a lifelong member of Britain's centrist Liberal Party. He wanted to save capitalism, not replace it. It is a mark of his ingenuity that his policies were adopted not only by those on the left but also by conservatives from Winston Churchill and Harold Macmillan to Dwight D. Eisenhower and Richard Nixon" (Wapshott 2011). Although the limits to Keynesian inspired deficit spending have been reached in both Europe and the United States, it is not an exaggeration to say that Barack Obama's rescue of banks and the automobile industry turned to Keynes for inspiration in order to temporarily save capitalism from its worst excesses in more than 50 years. The same applies to European crisis management where in effect the current sovereign debt crisis has been nationalized creating a double burden for taxpayers. This was both self-inflicted and predictable from the very beginning.

The backdrop to the resurgence of the free market orthodoxy, which the Great Depression had discredited, was, on the one hand, related to the difficulties encountered by the statist regime of macroeconomic management on the domestic and international levels in the core countries and on the other hand, the over-accumulation of capital as a consequence of overproduction leading to a return of the secular stagnation tendency. Equally important, however, was the ideological and political neutralization of the working classes whose conditions had been improved through the establishment of the "Welfare State".

The social contract that was established during the hegemonic period of Social Democratism had been under attack by conservative rightwing forces even before the Keynesian model began to show its relative weaknesses. However, in the 1970s, the problems of Keynesian economics/Welfare State became apparent as a result of the rising unemployment and increasing public expenditures, stagflation, limitations of interventionism, fiscal deficit, and inflationary tendencies caused by the dollar export by the United States and the loss of that currency's value. The so-called "Nixon Shock" of 1971 whereby the convertibility of the dollar into gold was unilaterally rescinded by the American government was followed by a decade of one of the worst inflations in American history and the most stagnant economy since the Great Depression. In addition, the *de facto* devaluation of the US dollar caused havoc in the international economy, opened for foreign exchange speculation on a grand scale and prepared the ground for the financialization of the global economy.

Although the model of "dirigisme" implied in Keynesian economics faced difficulties, there was no natural law dictating a reversion to (neo)liberalism as the solution. The return of the "second movement" (Polanyi, 1957), this time with capital recouping on the years of state interventionism in favor of a relatively more equal distribution of the socially created wealth, was the result of political decisions promoting the interests of capitalist forces. Ideologically and academically, the transition from "interventionist state" economics to "turbo" market capitalism was given legitimacy in 1974, when both the Swedish Keynesian economist, Gunnar Myrdal, and the leading figure of classical economic liberalism, Friedrich Hayek, shared the Nobel Prize in economics that year.

While the "rolling back" of the social compact of the Welfare State had been on the ideological agenda of the hardcore rightwing capitalist class since its inception, the debacle of the Keynesian model was accentuated at a time when the strengthened financial sector was liberating itself from the constraint of capital control and the technological revolution had made means of communication instant and reduced transportation costs. The growth and internationalization of the financial sector as well as the export of capital and outsourcing of production to low cost areas in the world economy (first and foremost China) played havoc with the sovereignty of the national state giving international organizations and volatile capital a large say in the economic policies of individual countries.

In its essence, the liberalization of the financial sector worldwide contributed to laxity in the regulation of speculative activities. While the much heralded current financial crisis can be seen as a self-inflicted wound by speculative capital, the solution proposed by the financial sector and the international organizations (i.e., the International Monetary Fund, the European Central Bank, and the European Commission), has been the nationalization of the debts incurred by the private financial institutions. The bottom line is to make the nation-state assume responsibility for the servicing and repayment of the debts by socializing them. As a consequence, acceptance of rescue packages for bailing out the banks and the servicing of the sovereign debt by governments with taxpayers' money dictates a course of state spending cuts and radical austerity. What first appeared as a financial crisis quickly morphed into a sovereign debt crisis of the state leading to an economic and social crisis with severe consequences for the increasing informalization of labor markets (Schmidt, 2006; 2008) and the creation of a precariat (Standing, 2011). The fact is that most of the debt of vulnerable countries increased — not because of excessive consumption or generous welfare benefits — but rather as a result of the nationalization of the losses of banks and other credit institutions. The problem arose in the private sector but the bill was passed on to the public sector.

In the last instance, the implication of such a blatant transfer of socially produced wealth to the financial sector demands a high degree of statecraft on the part of the authorities. The democratic challenge facing governing political parties is to have the social consequences of cutbacks in wages and pensions and public welfare internalized in the ideological superstructure of what can be called "a kind of collective Calvinism" (Petras, 2012). Depending on one's view of the longevity of the crisis, what is politically taking place is a repudiation of the social contract as epitomized by the welfare state and Keynesian macro-economic management.

In the historical context of capitalism, it would be an error to juxtapose state and market as antagonistic institutions. While the state was a precondition for Keynesianism, the financialization and liberalization of the economy likewise depended on the state. This was recognized by Thomas Friedman during the "High Noon" of globalisation and financialization of the world economy in the 1990s: "The hidden hand of the market will never work without a hidden fist" (Friedman, 1999). The direct state help given banks during the ongoing crisis makes a mockery of the "Minimal State" vs. Maximal State dichotomy. The more essential question concerns the role of the state in the redistribution of wealth from the real economy to the private "fictive" economy.

In order to comprehend the tools at hand for the implementation of the adjustment program of austerity, it is useful to grasp, as the "Social Structure of Accumulation" approach proposes, the political and cultural as well as economic institutions and arrangements which have been institutionalized in highly developed countries. Awareness of the complexity of supportive institutions allows for a holistic approach to the *modus operandi* of modern capitalism. The *domestic institutions*, according to this school of political economy, can include the arrangement overseeing labor-management relations; the organization of the work process; the character of industrial organization; the role of money and banking in relation to industry; the role of the state in the economy; the project and discourse of political parties; the race and gender relations; and the character of the dominant culture and ideology. The *international institutions* behind the accumulation process influence trade, investment climate, monetary-financial arrangements as well as the domestic political environments (Kotz et al., 1994: 1). Under this framework the relative bargaining power of labor and capital is always the main determinant of changes in wages and working conditions although there are other factors as well to be taken into consideration.

Just as important, or even more significant, as these institutions are, it is of primordial importance — as the current crisis reveals — to realize that the socio-economic system of capitalism is not only defended and promoted through the material resources of the state apparatus and the existing productive, financial and commercial enterprises. As Antonio Gramsci has shown, it is necessary to take into account the question of ideological hegemony and manipulation of popular opinion by the "chiens de garde" of the system, i.e. the army of ideologues, journalists, academics and publicists. As a consequence, the deconstruction of the definitional and ideational power of the ruling elite is a task which alternative political forces, sooner or later, will need to come to grasp with.

In the present circumstances, however, the established political forces claiming to represent the interests of the working population have themselves been infected by the virus of neo-liberalism or remain at a reformist level. Essentially, they belong to the same historical bloc. The dilemma is that, while self-declared progressive political forces show themselves to be at the service of financial capital in the implementation of austerity measures, others perhaps yearning for a return to a glorious era of Social Democratism still remain in the context of the two orthodoxies of modern capitalism.

In this relation, what we see is the degradation of advanced capitalist societies through social turmoil as well as erosion of living standards and working conditions at the same time as trade unions and political opposition cling to a reformist dominant ideology. The politics of this "resistance" movement proposes to defend the structure of social benefits, public spending and investment by expanding the role of the state in the areas of the economy where the private sector is failing to create employment. In other words: "[T]he left proposes to conserve a past when capitalism was harnessed to the welfare state" (Petras, 2012). Contrary to this opinion, we may wonder whether the reality was not the other way around, i.e., the welfare state being (temporarily) harnessed to capitalism.

Whatever the case, the call for a "capitalism of the past" is a non-starter as that socio-economic construction is gone, giving way to the reemergence of a more naked capitalism which is more virulent and intransigent. Seen in this light, the "crisis" which core capitalist societies are going through is less of a tipping point than the beginning of a transition process towards a more unadulterated "lean and mean" capitalism.

The Historical Dimension of the "Danish Model"

The attempt to square the circle created by a strategy of catering to the economic interests of a minority ruling elite while wanting to promote and preserve the social gains of the majority is a political exercise that finds expression in institution-building. A case in point is the societal innovations which have taken place in a nation like Denmark during the last decades. In this relation, it ought to be pointed out that Danish political culture and society have been adaptive to the demands required of a developed industrial state. The country's relative socio-political harmony is often ascribed to that society's traditions of corporatist bargaining involving the labor market's partners, the Danish Confederation of Trade Unions (LO) and the Danish Employers' Confederation (DA) with the government as overseer. It is needless to say that consensus is easier to be reached in periods of high economic growth than during recessions or structural crisis. At the same time, while this tripartite arrangement can work as a shock absorber to the fluctuations of the international as well as the national economy, it should not be considered to be a game-changing institution.

The mode of functioning of this system of industrial relations is based on the regulation of the conflicting interests between wage earners and employers in the context of a capitalist labor market. In praxis, this means that agreements on a basic framework for wages and working conditions are reached between the different organizations for a period of two years at a time. Thereafter, all major groups of employees are expected to accept and conform to the results of these negotiations. These institutionalized labor market relations form the dominant aspect of the so-called Danish Model which has played a determining role in shaping the social and political evolution of Danish society for the past century.

The foundation of the Welfare State has been based on the workings of this collective bargaining system as an arena of consensus-making whereby conflicts of interest between the different actors of the labor market could be resolved or reduced. The mode of operation of this consensus-seeking institution contributed to a high degree of stability, consensus and trust by creating economic growth, social well-being and reducing political contradictions. Nevertheless, it would be inaccurate to portray Danish society as inherently more harmonious than other capitalist formations. At the same time though, the institutional innovation of collective bargaining did contribute to reducing potential conflicts and disharmony. A student of the Danish labor market put it in the following way: "This constant capacity for releasing tensions, defusing threatening situations and breaking crippling deadlocks has made the relationships between the social partners the main pillar of the Danish model" (Petersen, 1997).

There is a tendency among political scientists and economists belonging to the social democratic tradition to ascribe societal innovations encompassing the "Danish Model" to the intrinsic ingenuity and political culture of the Danes. Although this aspect ought not to be disregarded it should be put in the proper perspective. As an export-oriented economy (agriculture, shipbuilding, shipping, industrial products, high-tech, pharmaceutical production, oil, etc.), there is a built-in Danish dependency on the fluctuations and transformations that take place in the world market and especially the nearby main export markets of Germany and Sweden. The implication of this state of affairs is that the domestic political conversation and policy-making is highly reactive to the external influence and the need to adjust to those demands.

The Mother (Muster kind) of All Welfare States

The relationship of the Danish political class to the construction of the welfare state, from its inception in the 1930s to the recent process of adjustment to the demands of the world market and the ideological gains of neo-liberalism, reveal a somewhat bipartisan approach. When the country's voters returned the Social Democratic party to power in January 1993, the new government implemented a continuation of some of the measures that had been proposed by the conservative coalition but unable to put through. The sale by the Social Democratic government of the state-owned telephone company which, relatively speaking, represented one of the largest examples of privatization in Europe for the entire decade is a case in point. The new government also remained committed to balanced budgets leading to more low-level spending cuts, de-regulation of the financial sector, and introduction of new public management in the public sector. Important reforms of the unemployment system were introduced impinging on the living standard of the unemployed. Previously, unemployment benefits had been both generous — 90 % of lost wages — and unlimited in time. With the new scheme unemployment assistance was limited to four years and under the condition that the recipients worked or enrolled in job training.

In order to make this policy effective, large government funds were invested in worker-counseling and job training with the intention of up-grading the qualifications of the working force in order to make the economy competitive for attracting foreign investments and accessing export markets. In those years, Denmark spent approximately 4 percent of its GDP on its labor market program. The explanation was of course that Denmark had a tax level to match these expenditures. As a commentator in the American magazine *The New Republic* put it: "Half of the country's annual output goes through government in the form of taxes — again, among the highest in the developed world and well above the U.S. rate of just under 30 percent" (Cohn, 2007). However, tax on work is comparatively speaking very low in Denmark almost half of that in Belgium and much lower than Germany and France. It is the high value added tax (VAT) on goods and services that makes Denmark a high tax country (Goul Andersen, 2011).

In fact, various studies have shown that a majority of Danes are willing to pay taxes although the complaint is that multinational corporations pay no or little taxes for their activities in Denmark. Dissatisfaction also comes to the fore when the conversation revolves around immigrants and refugees who are accused of coming to Denmark in order to “sponge” on the country’s welfare state. Although the established center-right parties were reluctant to tie the question of taxation to xenophobism, the populist Progress Party’s success built precisely on this connect which resonated in the ranks of the working class and petite bourgeoisie.

The Social Democratic-led government which had come to power in 1993, until its demise in 2001, did relatively well in reducing the level of unemployment in the country. By the time the government was defeated, the rate of unemployment had been reduced from a peak of 9.6 percent in 1994 to 4.3 percent on 2001. The problem for the Social Democratic-led government was, however, that during the 1998 electoral campaign, the party leader and Prime Minister, Poul Nyrup Rasmussen, had made the promise that the early retirement arrangement, that had had its roots in the Social Democratic-Liberal government in the closing years of the 1970s, would not be tempered with. Originally, the early pension scheme had intended to relieve unemployment pressures on the economy by making room for younger people to enter the labor market as well as giving elderly workers a better old age. But a few months after the 1998 electoral victory, the Social Democratic party reached an agreement with the same Liberal party reducing the early pension benefits which had been a key issue for the party’s working class constituency. Squeezed by its own voters because of this broken promise and the inroad of the populist anti-foreigner Progress Party in the ranks of the working class, the Social Democratic party was soundly defeated. The incoming liberal-conservative government in the 2001 election continued along the same lines with a gradual reduction of social welfare benefits and introduced “employment policy” to de-activate the corporatist compromise between labor and capital. This marked a significant shift from labor market regulation to employability and not less significant gradual exclusion of organized labor’s influence on the evolution of the flexicurity model. Competences and decision-making power have been altered: labor unions’ institutional power has weakened, “opportunity structures have been recalibrated, and the legitimacy of collective action have been openly questioned. Now social dialogue and partnership function mostly as a kind of ‘damage control’ mechanism.” It is indeed a double-farewell to unions and activation policy (Jørgensen and Schulze, 2012: 642).

This evolution partly explains the gradual transformation of the Danish welfare state into a work first state and may end in a workfare state or what some commentators have termed a “competition state” which somehow is a paradox in itself by its peculiarity which demands more regulation and intervention “in the name of competitiveness and marketization” (Cerny, 2007: 251).

The Big Trade-Off: Social Security-Flexibility-Competitiveness

The point to emphasize when discussing the politics of the welfare state and labor market relations is that the measures and schemes adopted are problem-solving initiatives which balance between catering to different social and economic interests while at the same time promoting the competitiveness of the country's economy. This is especially the case for export-oriented economies. In this light, it is important to realize that while measures affecting industrial relations and the organization of the society find their origin in the domestic socio-economic and political conditions their viability will be reflected by the degree they promote the interests of the export oriented sector. This aspect is often not given the attention it deserves.

Consequently, innovations in the sphere of labor market relations should not only be evaluated for their capacity to initiate and carry out policies conducive to internal social harmony between the different social groups around the inherently conflictual process of creation and division of the economic surplus.

In the last two decades, Denmark has had remarkable success in carrying out a relatively harmonious transition from Keynesianism and adapting the economy to the agenda of neoliberalism. Under the slogan of reforms, attempts were made to gradually reform the public and social sectors with the privatization of many service functions, often with the active help of the state. There have been systematic downsizing of unemployment benefits, reduction of the entitlement period from four to two years and further tightening of social welfare benefits for those falling outside the labor market. With regard to labor market strategy, while Keynesian macroeconomics puts emphasis on aggregate demand-creation by the state, the neoliberal mantra, which gained predominance in the political sphere and academia, has put emphasis on supply-side economics in order to satisfy the demands of the market. That is not only creating an ideal investment climate for domestic and foreign investors in the private sector of the economy but concurrently devising the specific type of labor market flexibility known as flexicurity.

Seen from the point of view of employers, the scheme offers a comparative advantage in the form of having access to a qualified and flexible workforce without the burden of paying for the upgrading of qualifications nor for paying laying-off compensation to the dismissed employees. For organized labor, it secures an autonomous collective bargaining position of unions in the protection of the interests of wage earners as well as other groups. It ought to be noted that although this model of industrial relations is corporatist, the structure of the private economy is dominated by small and medium-sized enterprises.

The essence of labor market regulation and flexicurity is "a policy strategy to enhance, at the same time and in a deliberate way, the flexibility of labor markets, the work organization and employment relations on the one hand, and security —

employment security and social security — notably for weaker groups in and outside the labor market, on the other hand" (Wilthagen and Tros, 2004; Tros, 2012). In the Danish context, it can be understood as a post-deregulation strategy as well as a historical compromise between labor, employers and the state. It may consequently not only be characterized as a form of integration and synchronization of economic and social policy but also as an instrument for conflict preemption and resolution (Crumlin and Schmidt, 2009; Tros, 2012). The fundamental aim of the strategy is to increase mobility in the labor market simultaneously with income and employment security. In other words, it signifies the continuation of industrial relations by other means. In this line of thought, the opinion has been voiced that, in fact, governments and social partners had practiced flexicurity "without knowing it" long before the concept made its way into the vocabulary of industrial relations and welfare state. It was after policy-makers began to use the term to describe employment policies in a more coherent and deliberate way that the notion gained traction in labor market discussions (Clement and Goul Andersen, 2006).

The favorable reputation of the Danish flexicurity model is principally due to the "activation" policies of the Social Democrat-led government of Poul Nyrup Rasmussen which introduced an active labor market policy (ALMP) in the 1990s that simultaneously denoted a significant kudos to neoliberalism. As a result, a transition from distribution of welfare entitlements to labor market upgrading of qualifications was introduced by the back-door. The centerpiece of these policies is that they offered "people further job training, education, and other measures that improve their skills and abilities to help them re-enter the labour market. Macro-economic initiatives supported the goal of full employment. Because of the economic progress and improved employment, the length of the unemployment benefit period could be shorted from seven to four years" (Jørgensen, 2011: 3). Danes change jobs more frequently than elsewhere in Europe and they have the shortest tenures (Bredgaard, 2012: 184). In such a volatile job market it might be expected that there would be demands for protection as is common in the rest of Europe. But most people seem to agree that the combination of welfare programs and job-training means that the newly unemployed do not fear becoming destitute. Polls show that, despite the high rates of job turnover, Danes are seemingly among the most optimistic working populations about prospects of finding work again once laid-off. One may say that in principle the Danish system promotes employment security rather than job security.

A precondition for a well functioning labor market is of course growth of the economy. As we know, the capitalist world economy has since the post-World War II reconstruction shown stagnation tendencies. In fact, the real growth rate of the Triad (North America, Europe, and Japan) has been in decline since the 1960s (Bellamy Foster and McChesney, 2012: 3). As a matter of fact, during the past decade or so, only the BRICS countries have shown some semblance of vigorous economic growth which is mostly accountable to China's emergence.

As in other core capitalist countries, the impact of the current economic downturn has been serious in Denmark thus putting flexicurity to the test. Compared to other economies (Holland and Germany) there has been a sharper decline in the growth of the Gross National Product which went down from +3.4 % in 2006 to -5.2 % in 2009 — the sharpest decline since WWII (Madsen 2011: 7; Andersen et al. 2011: 118). This downturn has taken place in spite of the fact that the country spent much on activating the workforce. Compared to other OECD countries, Denmark has one of the highest total expenditures on labor market policies (2.56 percent of GDP in 2008) as well as the highest expenditure on active labor market policies (1.35 percent of GDP in 2008) (cf. Bredgaard, 2012: 185). The explanation is perhaps to be found in the fact that as a consequence of its flexible labor market with low severance costs for employers, the immediate reaction to the crisis was a fast increasing level of unemployment. The results were that the Danish unemployment rate is well above EU average and some reduction in income security for the jobless workers.

Besides seeing the loss of workplaces as an inevitable effect of the model of low job protection it can also be seen as a result of the policies of the former liberal government (2001-2011). During those ten years, the privatization of job centers and the reduction of skill-upgrading took place as drastic savings on adult and vocational education expenditure were implemented. As noted by a researcher, the new stress on obligation departed from the original model: "More 'work first' elements were introduced in the system, giving social discipline a prominent position. Sanctions were introduced. Integration policy was also used as a lever to obtain more general changes in the activation and security system" (Jørgensen, 2011: 4).

Another accompanying issue affecting the Danish labor market is related to the relative loss of trade union bargaining strength which has been revealed by the crisis. One of the three pillars of the flexicurity regime is a relatively strong central organization representing a high percentage of the organized wage earners. However, the monopoly position of the social democratic unions has in later years been challenged. Although the European Union has approvingly included the concept and political strategies encompassed in flexicurity (Jørgensen, 2011: 3), several European High Court decisions against so-called exclusive rights in the labor market have moved in an opposite direction. Together with a substantial increase in yellow union membership and influence (more than 100,000 in a decade), the strength of the traditional trade unions has declined (a loss of more than 250,000 in a decade) (see Andersen and Redder, 2011), thus weakening the bargaining power of the third component of the corporatist flexicurity structure. A 2006 ruling by the International Court of Human Rights in Strasbourg went against the Danish practice of exclusive (i.e., closed shop) agreements in a limited part of the labor market (Due and Madsen, 2008: 526). Furthermore, the European High Court rulings in the Laval, Viking, Luxemburg and Rüffert cases have had grave repercussions on industrial relations generally and more specifically on the tripartite flexicurity institutional model itself.

Before these rulings, the labor unions had the exclusive responsibility to safeguard wages and employment conditions. The power of the unions was implicitly strengthened by their threats of using industrial action against employees who did not belong to any labor organization and thus not bound, as union members were, to conclude "accessory agreements", i.e., collective contracts in which the employer undertakes to apply the contents covering the branch of activity in question. Although there was stiff opposition to the rulings among trade unionists and no real change in Danish legislation was made, the decisions of the International Court of Human Rights and the rulings of the European High Court have nevertheless strengthened the encroachment of yellow unions. If implemented these rulings would result in increased social dumping and threaten the distributive justice system in Denmark and would represent a further step in the direction of the neoliberal project of dismantling the welfare state.

The unfolding difficulties affecting the Danish labor market are thus influenced by the country's membership in the European Union and the inclusion of the former socialist countries in it. The freedom of movement for labor, capital and enterprises within Europe has brought to the fore a whole new set of problems with regard to the application and implementation of Danish labor laws regarding migrant labor. As a direct outcome of EU legislation, the problem becomes acute when foreign companies operate in Denmark outside the flexicurity frame of industrial arrangements between employers' organization and labor's organization. A number of cases have exposed that foreign workers have been subjected to intensive exploitation by being paid low wages, long working hours and bad working and living conditions.

Social dumping is probably one of the most severe potential problems for organized labor leading to a race-to-the-bottom as wages are squeezed and trade unions are pressurized by membership flight and the lowering organizational rate of employees. In the last instance, this represents a threat to the flexicurity model itself. It ought to be mentioned that the decreasing interest for the traditional labor organizations on the part of wage earners is also related to the bureaucratization of unions and their willingness to compromise with the employers' organization. As in other countries, the increases of labor productivity in the past decades have not been accompanied by corresponding wage increases in Denmark. Incomes for large sections of the population have depended on the rise of stock market shares as well as the housing bubble which permitted people to borrow on their properties in the expectation of a permanent rise of housing prices. As a consequence, the Danish people are the most indebted populations in Europe. Of course as part of the financial crisis, the housing bubble has also busted in Denmark (Bergmann Moll, 2011).

It is clear that the present version of the flexicurity model of industrial relations promotes a variant of supply-side economics. In essence, this means the creation of an investment climate capable of attracting capital, i.e., low taxation and other favorable conditions. With regard to the labor market it implies the availability of a qualified work force assuring a high level of productivity and relative competitive wage level. In the past ten to fifteen years, a discourse concerning a potential labor shortage bomb threatening Danish society has been put on the political agenda of all political parties.

This has given rise to various proposals for increasing the working time of the employed and raising the retirement age in order to avoid bottlenecks. Such a position, however, overlooks the fact that modern means of production are based on labor saving technologies and the fact that also Danish labor intensive enterprises are outsourcing their activities to low production costs areas in the world. As Robert Boyer and Daniel Drache (1996: 18) point out the dichotomy between the need for less labor input and living wage is yet to be put on the agenda: "The deeper question is: can a wage-based system of capitalism overcome the disorientation of its labor-saving efficient technologies creating more wealth with less and less labor?"

The immediate Danish response to the crisis has been a number of state rescue packages for the banking sector and of growth packages attempting to kick-start the economy and create jobs. However, this was soon replaced with a far more restrictive praxis which among other issues saw a maximum of tax deduction for union membership and increasing fees charged for labor market training (Madsen, 2011: 12). Oblivious to the new trends of modern production and globalisation, the present Social Democratic-led government (which includes the Socialist Peoples' Party) has been at the forefront of the general offensive for increasing the working hours of employed labor. In the spring of 2012, this government made several suggestions for immediately reducing the number of religious free days and decrease the rate of taxation for employed people. This caused havoc in the labor movement putting added pressure on the unions as the reduction of work time is an essential demand of the working population. Consequently, union leaders rebelled and the popularity of the "red" coalition hit the doldrums and in fact may not survive four years.

In addition to the malaise of the labor market, the socio-economic conditions of present Danish society leave much to be desired. In this relation, it should not be forgotten that in the past few years Denmark has experienced a drastic increase in official unemployment to approximately 160,000 persons. These figures, however, hide the fact that more than 850,000 individuals form a precariat outside the labor market and are thus not covered by these statistics. (The number of persons receiving public benefits has increased from 769,600 full-time participants in 2008 to 857,200 in 2010 — an increase of 11 percent. The 857,200 full-time participants correspond to 24 percent of all inhabitants in Denmark between 16 and 64 years) (Danmarks Statistik, 2011: 85). Related to this state of affairs, the key questions to ask are whether the social safety net is capable of absorbing such an increase of joblessness and whether the relatively high level of job creation and turnover characterizing the labor market can be sustained. The latter is important in order to avoid a more persistent increase in unemployment (long-term unemployment) or a reduction of labor force participation in the productive activities of society (Andersen, 2012: 118). It is interesting to note that as the workfare structure of Danish labor market policy was gradually strengthened, the accompanying legislation has also become a potential source for the creation of a divide between insured insiders and uninsured outsiders. In the early 1990s, Danish law contributed to counteracting such divisions by seeking to combine the needs of job seekers with the needs of local communities and municipalities. The risk of an insider/outsider divide has, however, increased since these original aims lost priority with the strengthening of workfare (Kananen, 2012: 8). This problem is evident in the way "tripartism" has been challenged by the crisis — the work-sharing schemes previously widely used have been cancelled as the rightwing government in the 2,000s was not willing to extend their continuation to combine them with further educational measures (Jochem, 2011: 137).

The Re-Commodification of Labor and the Competition State

The on-march of neo-liberalism which ideologically and politically framed the offensive against the social compact of the welfare state was accompanied by the so-called imperative of adjusting national economies to the requirements of globalisation. This frame of reference legitimized the movement away from welfare as countries had to face new constraints in balancing concerns for the maintenance of the social contract while adjusting to the demands of competitiveness in the international division of labor. The conundrum affecting all the advanced economies including Denmark is thus related to the transformation of the previous "social structure of accumulation" — with its welfare dimension — into a new pattern of accumulation prioritizing workfare at the expense of social considerations. While the welfare system to a certain degree liberated wage earners and other social elements of the population from complete dependency on the market through a partial de-commodification of labor (Esping-Andeersen, 1990), what is happening with the weakening of welfarism is a re-commodification of wage labor and society.

The Danish transition to the competition state was the Social Democratic attempt to achieve a "soft landing", i.e., to combine retaining some features of the former arrangement while introducing measures to satisfy market demands by raising the productivity of its labor force without increasing production costs. The latter aim was general for all core countries with a welfare system, but the policy approaches did differ. Thus, as a commentator writing in the *New York Times* put it, Europe was more sociably minded than the strategy pursued in the United States: "...[J]ust as the U.S. was dismantling much of its welfare system — replacing it with the welfare-to-work reforms of the mid-1990s — Europe was (somewhat nobly) trying to show that an economy can be humane and competitive. In 1994, Denmark modernized a system, which came to be known as 'flexicurity', that offered American-style flexibility (layoffs, transitions into new lines of business) coupled with traditional European security. Laid-off workers were offered generous benefits, like 90 percent of their last salary for two years and opportunities to be retrained" (Davidson, 2012).

The parameter for measuring competitiveness in the international division of labor is not the degree of welfare or social satisfaction but the availability of a qualified and disciplined workforce as well as a relatively competitive wage level, i.e. in comparison with other economies. Besides the constraints on the state to adjust to the new economic orthodoxy of neo-liberalism and the demands of globalisation, European countries have additional burdens to cope with. These are related to the policy-making straightjacket which membership of the European Union imposes. In the case of Denmark, although the population declined — by voting down a referendum — to be included in the European Monetary Union thereby retaining its own currency, the political class pegged the Danish Crown to the Euro. Adherence to the exchange rate of the Euro prevents countries from increasing their competitiveness through devaluation measures. Although conditions have not demanded such a course to improve Denmark's foreign trade, having pegged the Crown to the European currency removes one of the tools available for autonomous nation-states to manage their macro-economy. Another measure, which is being pushed by the current Danish social democratic government, is the EU finance treaty aiming at imposing budget discipline on the member states in order to prevent "countries from living above their means" by having their deficits not exceed 3% of their gross domestic product. With very few exceptions, the treaty has been adopted by 17 member states without a popular referendum, raising the legitimacy question of the decision-making process in the EU.

The point is that these institutional measures imposed in a non-democratic manner remove macro-economic instruments from the toolbox of sovereign states. Not having access to other means of economic management, sitting governments have only the possibility of applying some variant of austerity measures on the labor force and societies in order to participate in the race to achieve competitiveness. This moves the goal post of established politics in a non-democratic direction and reduces statecraft to following the dictate of external power centers. As Amartya Sen (2012) sees it the democracy edifice is at risk: "Perhaps the most troubling aspect of Europe's current malaise is the replacement of democratic commitments by financial dictates — from leaders of the European Union and the European Central Bank and indirectly from credit-rating agencies, whose judgments have been notoriously unsound."

Consequently, while the ideological discourse promoting increased national competitiveness resembles that of economic nationalism, the implemented policies of neo-liberalism tend to go in the direction of deconstructing the national economy and in the case of the EU reducing the nation-state construct.

The Crisis of the Left

Far from offering a vision of an alternative socio-economic model, the social democratic forces in the European context do their utmost to balance their acceptance of the demands of the market with efforts to preserve their image as defenders of the working populations and the underprivileged. Thus, during the Danish electoral campaign of November 2011, the Danish Social Democratic Party and the Socialist Peoples' Party criticized the sitting liberal government both for its lack of audacity in the use of macro-economic instruments in order to put the economy on right track and for streamlining the welfare sector.

But upon assuming power in 2011, the new government (in conjunction with the

Finance Ministry) issued a 2020-plan for the Danish economy which bases itself on the assumptions of supply-side economics. In other words, it is assumed that an increase in the qualified labor reserve army and a lowering of taxes for high income wage earners together with a reduction of capital gain taxes will incentivize the creation of jobs and intensify the activities in the private labor market. The plan furthermore foresees low growth of the public sector which has in the past decades been a main source of employment for a large segment of the population. Tellingly, the employers' organization together with the liberal opposition have voiced approval of the plan while the government's supporting party, the Left Green Alliance has criticized it and refused its support.

The political context for decision-making is similar in most core countries. The multi-faceted crisis which has hit the capitalist system has opened a path for the deconstruction of the various welfare state models that originated following the Great Depression of the 1930s and the Second World War. As President Obama's former White House Chief-of-Staff Rahm Emanuel said: "You never want a serious crisis to go to waste. And what I mean by that is an opportunity to do things you think you could not do before" (WSJ 21 November, 2008). What the world has seen since the financial sector busted has not only been the socialization of the losses incurred by banks and other financial institutions, but the strategic offensive on remaining state welfare structures.

The response of the "Left" to the crisis engendered by the shortcomings of neoliberal economics has nevertheless been to accept the premises laid-down by the protagonists of neo-liberalism. Ever since, the problem of the financial crisis of the state was put on the political agenda of countries with generous welfare states, this has resulted in the de-politization of the welfare question. A Swedish commentator on the left puts it in the following manner: "The cuts in public expenditures during the past 20 years are no longer considered as neoliberal politics, but as 'necessary' adjustment to an 'inescapable' reality" (Ankarloo, 2012). Without breaking out of the bind of this discourse which ties the financial problem to the question of welfare, no vision of the future can emerge and the political initiative grasped (Ankarloo, 2012).

Another misconception of the liberal left is related to the belief that the crisis of their society can be resolved by raising the competitiveness of the domestic economy and establishing a semblance of full employment of labor and production capacity at a time when globalisation has transformed the structure of production. On the one hand, the structural problem is connected to the existence of productive over-capacity and on the other, the fact that the capital-intensive means of production reduces the relative need for labor input. Secondly, the fact that globalisation has generalized industrial capitalism to the rest of the world and introduced large numbers of producers and consumers in the world economy is a factor which Left forces in the old core countries still have not taken into their strategic considerations.

Historically, the rise of colonialism and imperialism was primordial to the emergence of industrial capitalism. Besides fulfilling the role of markets for European production and source of raw material for industrial production, the gains of this relationship could be used to neutralize the societal contradictions of emerging capitalism. Imperialism, as Cecil Rhodes said, was the alternative to revolution. The colonial tribute could be used to alleviate the conditions of the proletariat and other social classes.

The mutation in the making which the international division of labor is experiencing is the result of the internationalization of production with the inclusion of the so-called emerging economies on the scene. According the International Labor Organization (ILO), the global workforce between 1980 and 2007 grew 63 percent from 1.9 billion to 3.1 billion, 73 percent of the labor force located in the developing world, and 40 percent in China and India alone (Bellamy Foster et al., 2011). This is accompanied by the emergence of an Asian working and middle class in populous countries whose political system's legitimacy is based on continuous economic growth revolving around competitive low labor costs. This inclusion of billions of producers and consumers in the modus operandi of global capitalism will, of course, also put an additional burden on the carrying capacity of the planet earth.

It is in the context of global over-capacity and huge reserve labor army that the gradual transition to the "competition state" ought to be understood. The relationship between wage labor and competitiveness will impose itself on all economies in the system in what some have called a "race to the bottom". The societies, who resolve this problematique best, will be those with a pliant labor force willing to accept less than a fair wage for a fair day's work — i.e., less than their increase in productiveness. In the current European crisis, Germany has proven itself to be the strongest economic power on the continent. In this connection, it has to be taken into account that "in no other EU country have unit labor costs increased as little as in the past ten years as in Germany. German companies have procured competitive advantages for themselves through wage restraint" (Sablowski, 2012). Consequently, the key to the success of Germany is determined to a great extent by the austerity that it practices at home and is pushing for in the rest of Europe while previously having lend money to Southern European economies to import German made goods.

Without resistance based on audacity, such a pattern will be the benchmark for the success of the competition state in future years. The lesson of what has taken place since the Great Recession of 2008-2009 has yet to be entirely absorbed. The recession was not only a short-lived downturn of a business cycle but it revealed a systemic crisis whose resolution is not yet in sight. Under the banner of economic necessity and increasing competitiveness, many components of welfare capitalism is either being rolled back or dismantled. This is not only done as a temporary measure to resolve the short-term difficulties facing many countries, but as a general political offensive against welfarism. As the editors of the *Socialist Register* put it in the 2012 volume: "We are witnessing the onset of permanent austerity in the advanced capitalist world" (Panitch, Albo, and Chibber, 2011).

Concluding Remarks

It is evident that contemporary capitalism is reaching a qualitatively new stage where the relative socio-political harmony based on dynamic economic growth is in the process of being replaced by a leaner and meaner "social structure of accumulation" on a world scale.

While the welfare state was a political construction aiming at the management of production and distribution of the economic surplus, the workfare state of 21st century capitalism is not only the result of neoliberal economics but a political project of re-distribution of wealth — both at the national as well as at the global levels — at a time when the stagnation tendency has again become the major characteristic of capitalism. This has resulted in a marked decline of the world GDP growth rates since the "Golden Age" of capitalism to the present. This is an evolution that is not in accordance with neo-liberalism which is theoretically unable to foresee the possibility of long-run excess capacity because according to standard neoclassical micro theory such a possibility is not supposed to take place (Crotty, 2002).

Governance of modern industrial capitalism has fluctuated between two orthodoxies: expansive Keynesian economics (demand creation by the state) and (neo) classical economics which celebrates the market as a self-regulatory institution without government intervention. The financial crisis under the reign of neo-liberalism has, however, seen states and other international institutions coming to the assistance of banks and finance capital after the bubble bust. Departing from the original doctrine, government bailouts of banks and other institutions has raised the specter of shifting the costs of this strategy on the shoulders of the working populations through so-called austerity measures — i.e., the audacity of socializing financial capital's losses.

It is in the context of over-production and under-utilization of productive capacity in the world economy that the evolution from welfare state to flexicurity to the competition state — that has taken place in Denmark — should be understood. The Danish model of flexicurity was a political and institutional model of labor market relations which attempted to effectuate a smooth transition to the competition state by straddling the market demands of flexibility with that of security for wage earners while retaining a residual social dimension in the process. The explicit objective of this hybrid was to reduce indirect costs to enterprises or those involving the decrease of social benefits provided by the state through "flexibilizing" laws protecting labor employment.

The analysis has critically evaluated the internal strength and weaknesses of this corporatist structural pattern of labor market management while at the same time responding to the challenges of the world economy and the institutional demands of the European Union on its member states. Whether the Danish model can prove to be the proto-type exception to the transformation of advanced capitalism while managing employment levels and working conditions in the national economy is questionable. The flexicurity model belongs to the toolbox of supply-side economics which besides taking responsibility for the continuous up-grading of a qualified workforce is an indirect subsidy to employers. As a follow-up to this strategy, the recent agreement between the Social Democratic-led government and the bourgeois parties to reduce taxes on high incomes to a certain degree reduces pressures on wage bargaining. At the same time, reducing public expenditures for people outside the labor market divides the working population between a well paid qualified workforce ("labor aristocracy") and a low qualified and low paid "lumpen proletariat" and unemployed people on the dole or physically or mentally unable to work.

We have shown that the Danish political class has in later years promoted the competition state structure while retaining the claim that such an adjustment was a precondition for the retention of residual welfarism. One ideological reason for this approach is that the welfare state construction has until recently been embedded in the political culture of the Danish population making a complete rupture politically difficult. The consensus-seeking institutional framework of labor market bargaining has thus attempted to protect employment while not drastically (as has been the case in other countries) cut welfare benefits. The offensive against deficit spending puts this strategy in question, however.

The structural crisis of the system which the financial crisis revealed has affected most core capitalist nations. Under such conditions, the promotion of the competitive state only accentuates the dilemma. The generalization of the competitive state will bring about cuts in social programs and impoverishment as part of the "Age of Austerity" in all major countries (McNally, 2012: 36). The proposed solutions and strategies have reduced the sovereignty of nations with an ensuing encroachment on democracy. It is in this context that the "Left" alternative has accepted the rule of neo-liberalism and globalisation and is unable to protect the interests of its constituency. The victory of a Social Democratic-led government in Denmark in the 2011 election is a case in point.

References

Andersen, Torben M. (2012). "A flexicurity labour market in the Great Recession: The case of Denmark," *De Economist*, 160 (2), 117–140.

Andersen, Iver Houmark and Gitte Redder (2011). "Unge Strømmer til Gule Fagforeninger", in *Ugebrevet A4*, Copenhagen, 16 November, at http://www.ugebreveta4.dk/2011/201146/Onsdag/unge_bliver_gule.aspx.

Ankarloo, Daniel (2012). "Myten om finansieringsproblemet", in *Modkraft*, at http://www.modkraft.dk/artikel/myten-om-finansieringsproblemet.

Backhouse and Bradley Bateman (2011). *Capitalist Revolutionary: John Maynard Keynes*, Cambridge: Harvard University Press.

Bellamy Foster, John, Robert W. McChesney, and R. Jamil Jonna (2011). "The global reserve army of labor and the new imperialism," *Monthly Review*, 63(6), November.

Bellamy Foster, John and Robert W. McChesney (2012). "The endless crisis", *Monthly Review*, 64(1), May.

Bergmann Moll, Jytte (2011). "Danmark har rekord i private klatgæld", in *DR*, at http://www.dr.dk/DR1/penge/2011/02/23145411.htm.

Boyer, Robert and Daniel Drache (1996). "Introduction", In: Robert Boyer and Daniel Drache (eds), *States Against Markets: The Limits of Globalisation*, London: Routledge, 1-30.

Bredgaard, Thomas (2012). "Flexibility and security in employment regulation: What can be learned from the Danish case?", In: Katherine V.W. Stone and Harry Arthurs (eds.), *After the Standard Contract of Employment: Innovations in Regulatory Design*, New York: Russell Sage.

Cerny, Philip (1994). "The infrastructure of the infrastructure? Toward 'Embedded Financial Orthodoxy' in the international political economy", In: Ronen P. Palan and Barry Gills (eds), *Transcending the State-Global Divide: A Neostructuralist Agenda in International Relations*, Boulder, Co.: Lynne Reinner, 223-275.

Cerny, Philip (2007). "Paradoxes of the competition state: The dynamics of political globalisation", *Government and Opposition*, 32(2), 251-274.

Clement, S.L. and Goul Andersen J. (2006). "Ledighed og incitamentseffekter: Hvad ved vi? En forskningsoversigt", *Delrapport 5 til Kulegraving af Kontanthjælpsområdet.* Aalborg: CCWS.

Cohn, Jonathan (2007). "Great Danes", *The New Republic*, at http://www.tnr.com/article/politics/great-danes.

Crumlin, Jens Voldby and Johannes Dragsbæk Schmidt (2009). "Er Flexicurity ved vejs Ende?" (Has Flexicurity reached its dead-end?, in *Nordjyske*, 16 February.

Danmarks Statistik (2011). "Offentligt Forsørgede 16-64 årige", Copenhagen, November.

Davidson, Adam (2012). "The other reason Europe is going broke", *The New York Times*, at http://www.nytimes.com/2012/01/08/magazine/the-other-reeason-europe-is-going-broke.html?pagewanted=all.

Due, Jesper and Jørgen Steen Madsen (2008). "The Danish model of industrial relations: Erosion or renewal?", *The Journal of Industrial Relations*, 50(3), 513-529.

Esping-Andersen, Gøsta (1990). *The Three Worlds of Welfare Capitalism*, Princeton, New Jersey: Princeton University Press.

Friedman, Thomas (1999). *The Lexus and the Olive Tree*, New York: Farrar, Straus and Giroux, Inc.

Galbraith, John Kenneth (1997). "Preface," *New Political* Economy, 2(1), 5-9.

Goul Andersen, Jørgen (2011). "Danmark som lavskatteland?", *Information*, 25 October.

Jochem, Sven (2011). "Nordic employment policies: Change and continuity before and during the financial crisis", *Social Policy & Administration*, 45(2), 131-145.

Jørgensen, H., and Schulze, M. (2012). "A double farewell to a former model? Danish unions and activation policy". *Local Economy*, 27(5/6), 637-644.

Jørgensen, Henning (2011). "Danish flexicurity in crisis – Or just stress-tested by the crisis?", *International Policy Analysis*, Berlin: Friedrich-Ebert-Stiftung.

Jørgensen, Henning (2008). Fra arbejdsmarkedspolitik til beskæftigelsespolitik - kosmetisk eller indholdsmæssige forskelle? *Tidsskrift for Arbejdsliv*, 10 (3).

Kananen, Johannes (2012). "Nordic paths from welfare to workfare: Danish, Swedish and Finnish labour market reforms in comparison", *Local Economy*, 2 (5–6), 1-19.

Kotz, David M., Terrence McDonough, and Michael Reich (eds.) (1994). *Social Structures of Accumulation: The Political Economy of Growth and Crisis*, New York: Cambridge University Press.

Lykketoft, Mogens (2009). *The Danish Model: A European Success Story*, Copenhagen: Arbejderbevaegelsens Erhversråd.

Madsen, Per Kongshøj (2011). "Flexicurity i Modvind – en analyse af den danske flexicurity-model under den økonomiske krise", in *Tidsskrift for Arbejdsliv*, 13 (4), 7-20.

Panitch, Leo, Greg Albo, and Vivek Chibber (2011). "Preface", In: *Socialist Register 2012: The Crisis and the Left*, London: Merlin Press.

Petersen, Kåre F.V. (1997). “The Danish Model under threat?”, In: *EIROnline: European Industrial Relations Observatory On-line*, at http://www.eurofound.europa.eu/eiro/1997/08/feature/dk9708122f.htm.

Petras, James (2012). “The politics of language and the language of political regression”, In: *Global Research.ca: Centre for Research on Globalisation*, at http://www.globalresearch.ca/index.php?context=va&aid=31018.

Polanyi, Karl (1957). *The Great Transformation.* Boston, MA: Beacon Press.

Sablowski, Thomas (2012). “Impoverishing Europe”, in *MRzine: A Project of the Monthly Review Foundation*, at http://mrzine.monthlyreview.org/2012/sablowski160512.html.

Schmidt, Johannes Dragsbaek and Jacques Hersh (2006). “Neoliberal globalisation: Workfare without welfare”, *Globalisations*, 3(1), 69-89.

Schmidt, Johannes Dragsbaek (2010). “A cacophony of crises: Systemic failure and reasserting people's rights“, *Human Geography*, 18-33.

Schmidt, Johannes Dragsbaek (2006). “Flexicurity, casualization and informalization of global labor markets”, In: B. N. Ghosh and Halil M. Guven (eds.), *Globalisation and the Third World: A Study of the Negative Consequences*, Palgrave, Macmillan, Houndsmills, Basingstoke, Hampshire and New York.

Sen, Amartya (2012). “The crisis of European democracy”, *The New York Times*, 22 May, at http://www.nytimes.com/2012/05/23/opinion/the-crisis-of-european-democracy.html.

Standing, Guy (2011). *The Precariat: The New Dangerous Class*, Bloomsbury Academic, London and New York.

Tros, Frank (2012) “Flexicurity in Europe: Can it survive a double crisis?”, Working Paper for the ILERA World Congress 2012, at http://ilera2012.wharton.upenn.edu/RefereedPapers/TrosFrankUPDATED.pdf.

Viebrock, Elke and Jochen Clasen (2009). “Flexicurity and welfare reform: A review”, *Socio-Economic Review*, 7(2), 305–331.

Wapshott, Nicholas (2011). “Was Keynes a Keynesian?” in Theory.”, in *The Washington Post*, 4 September, at http://www.washingtonpost.com/wp-srv/special/opinions/outlook/whats-in-a-name/keynes.html.

Wilthagen, Ton and F.H. Tros (2004). "The concept of 'flexicurity': A new approach to regulating employment and labour markets", *Transfer: European Review of Labour and Research*, 10 (2), 166-186.

WSJ (2008). In Crisis, Opportunity for Obama, Wall Street Journal 21 November, http://online.wsj.com/article/SB122721278056345271.html?mod=googlenews_wsj#articleTabs%3Darticle

Zhou, Jianping (2007). "Danish for all? Balancing flexibility with security: The flexicurity model", *IMF Working Paper*, European Department, WP/07/36, Washington DC.c

Chapter Eight

The Dynamics of Labour Market in a Global Economy: A Multivariate Causal Pathways Model

Parvesh K. Chopra

Introduction

The dynamics of labour market in an economy have been a focus of meticulous theoretical and empirical research over the past few decades. As the world is becoming increasingly integrated and interconnected in terms of economic, political, social and cultural life, the outcomes of labour markets across the globe are also changing rapidly. Since the phenomenon of globalisation affects us all in different ways, it somehow has been influencing directly or indirectly the labour markets dynamics in both developed and developing economies. More precisely, the process of globalisation and its forces such as trade liberalisation, capital mobility, global migration, foreign direct investment, offshoring, skill-based technical change, and so on, have been deteriorating labour market performances. As a result, communities, individuals and social groups have been experiencing diverse labour market experiences. Some people in an area have been immensely benefited from globalisation while others have been marginalised or excluded. Therefore, globalisation has been witnessed as an uneven world market development. It has been negatively contributing to the drop in mobility of low quality manpower, rise in unemployment rates, fall in real wages, social exclusion, wage inequalities, discursive localisation of poverty in low-income as well as high-income economies, and the like (Stiglitz, 2002 and 2006). What is, nevertheless, controversial is the *nature and degree of relationship* between different elements comprising globalisation and labour market outcomes. Considering the widely divergent claims made in the literature on globalisation and labour market dynamics, there is a call for apposite theoretical framework that enables a systematic and scientific evaluation of empirical work on the problem in hand.

Rationale

This chapter focuses on the interplay between the pathways of globalisation and labour market dynamics. It is a theoretical study of *causality* and *mechanisms* among the elements of globalisation and labour market outcomes. It is comprehensible that labour market performances are heterogeneous among different countries. Then, what are the actual dynamics behind labour market outcomes that might help in explaining these differences? To this aim, it is understood that the functioning of labour market in an economy is determined within the prevailing global economic system that fabricates various channels through which the outcomes of labour market are influenced. The fundamental aim of this chapter is to propose a *new* theoretical structure to examine the relationship between globalisation in its current form and its effects on labour markets. It, for the first time, introduces and constructs a robust, structural and multivariate causal pathways model to understand and analyse the dynamics behind labour market outcomes in a global economy. It contributes to this domain of research by building and proposing a multivariate framework that reveals how the key labour market aggregates/outcomes are statistically related to various internal and external shocks, failures and interventions in a global economy.

The distinct processes of globalisation are essentially producing increasing international socio-economic, cultural and environmental integration, mobility of resources, and growing interdependency among national economies. Considering this, the present chapter delineates diverse channels of globalisation associated with various activities in a country that may inauspiciously affect the dynamics of labour market in a global economy. It investigates theoretical linkages between globalisation channels and labour market movements and flows. Based on systems thinking, structural equations modelling, and multivariate data analysis, this chapter succinctly illustrates the theoretical scaffolding of multivariate structural model of labour market effects of globalisation in an economy with special reference to the causal pathways that involve distinct dimensions of globalisation, different movements and flows of labour market and environment of an economy. It outlines a chain of models that are both generic as well as specific in nature.

The conceptual notion of the phenomenon of globalisation is holistic, multidimensional and multidisciplinary. The chapter further divulges how *critical globalisation forces* simultaneously intensify labour market outcomes in a multiplicative way or may interact producing reciprocal compensatory and attenuating effects. The constructs and relationships of the proposed structure can be rigorously tested by means of data derived from various sources for an empirical analysis. A *labour market dynamics matrix* may be constructed to illustrate the effects of economic liberalization, human mobility, technology and innovations and shocks, failures and interventions. This theoretical framework that contains a conceptual model, operational model, latent variable structural model, measurement model and multivariate causal pathways model in order to drive the dynamics of labour market pertaining to a country within certain boundaries of the overall global economic system. For the purpose of the practical use of the model, the measurement software based on Partial Least Squares method can be used to calculate and analyse the causal pathways, and to construction of overall labour market dynamics matrix from the collected information. Results from empirical analysis may be used to pinpoint the practical policy options to regulate and manage the outcomes of labour market in any economy.

Globalisation and Labour Market Dynamics: The Background

Globalisation has been defined as a set of processes that increase integration and interdependencies between national economies by reducing barriers to flows of trade, migration, capital, ideas, technology and other aspects. It enhances international mobility of national resources and increases inter-reliance of national economies (Chandra, 2007; Das, 2004). Thus, three main characteristics of globalisation are: increasing international economic integration, mobility of resources and growing interdependency. Globalisation is understood here as a process of increasing interconnectedness fostered by accelerating communications and the emergence of global systems of banking, trade, legal arrangements and diverse forms of cooperation amongst areas of the world previously separated to varying degrees by geography, culture, language, religion, politics and numerous other distinctions.

The labour market is a key part of the economy and long-term trends have major implications not only for the economy but also for society more generally. Since the beginning of the 1980s, the labour markets in many economies have witnessed many drastic changes in terms of rise in unemployment, increase in self-employed, proletarisation of labour, feminization of labour market, widening wage gap between skilled and unskilled workers, and so on (Goos and Manning, 2003). These changes have coincided with the processes and outcomes of the third and current wave of rapid globalisation[xxxix] with falling barriers of international economic transactions between developed and developing countries, integrating economic ideas and many other fast changes in the emerging markets. All of this may be both a consequence and cause of globalisation.

There has been a debate regarding the flexibility and polarisation of labour market. Some authors have used vigorous polemic to examine and analyse the social goals based on values. McLaughlin (1994) confronts the notion that unemployment represents a lack of flexibility in the labour market, and that successful policies against unemployment have been those which engender a higher degree of flexibility. Macnicol (1987) critically examines the view that the core of unemployment is an 'underclass' based on anti-social, anti-work values and welfare dependence. McLaughlin particularly focused upon the evidence that non-employment *is* becoming a problem on a par with unemployment, and argues that when this is taken into account, the apparent successes of flexible labour market policies tend to evaporate. Similarly, Macnicol points to the complex and large-scale changes in fertility, family formation and lone-parenting which are taking place, changes which transcend simplistic notions of an 'underclass' or of welfare dependence.

The basic question is: what drives the changes in the outcomes of labour markets across the world. However, there is no straight and clear-cut universally applicable answer to the question. Building on David Ricardo's theory of comparative advantage in international trade, Heckscher–Ohlin model has been used to analyse the effects of international trade on labour market in terms of real wages in a two factors, two products and two countries framework (Ohlin, 1933; Leamer, 1995)[xl]. Trade with the South causes the North to specialize in the production of skill-intensive manufacturers, in which it has a comparative advantage because of its relatively large supply of skilled labour, and to reduce production of labour-intensive manufacturers. In the North, there is a rise in the relative price of skill-intensive goods and the relative demand for skilled labour, and a widening of the wage gap between skilled and unskilled workers and vice-versa in the South (Wood, 1998). Although Heckscher–Ohlin model is still a useful framework to understand international trade, but it is not a suitable model with regards to the recent changes in labour markets due to globalisation process as it ignores unemployment and has little predictive power (Bernstein and Weinstein, 2002).

It will be worthwhile to review the relevance of the theories of international trade developed since Heckscher-Ohlin model in context with the changes in labour markets in the North (Greenaway and Nelson, 2000). Stopler-Samuelson model (1941) of international trade and lower wages questions: what is the effect of changes in the prices of goods caused, for example by changes in tariffs, on the prices of factors of production? The model concluded that if the world price of capital-intensive goods increases, it will increase the relative rental rate as well as decrease the relative wage rate (the return on capital as against the return to labour). Also if the price of labour intensive goods increases, it will increase the relative wage rate as well as decrease the relative rental rate (Deardorff and Stern, 1994). Thus, when import-competing goods are relatively labor-intensive, wage-earners gain and capital-owners lose, irrespective of which bundle of goods they consume. Put simply, protection unambiguously raises real wages (Neary, 2004). The model has also been applied to a range of empirical issues, including to address the "trade and wages" debate, Leamer (1998) and Feenstra (1998), the effects of increased globalisation on income distribution in developed countries (Jones, 2000), and the long run political allegiances of classes and interest groups (Rogowski, 1989). However, Stopler-Samuelson model is not relevant in fully capturing the totality of the labour market changes both in Western and developing worlds.

The Rybczynski theorem (1955) states that at constant relative goods prices, a rise in the endowment of one factor will lead to a more than proportional expansion of the output in the sector which uses that factor intensively, and an absolute decline of the output of the other good. The theorem is useful in analyzing the effects of capital investment, immigration and emigration within the context of a Heckscher-Ohlin model. Paul Samuelson (1948) and Abba Lerner (1952) independently developed factor price equalization theorem which states that the prices of identical factors of production, such as the wage rate, or the return to capital, will be equalized across countries as a result of international trade in commodities. When two countries enter a free trade agreement, wages for identical jobs in both countries tend to approach each other and this is what is happening recently in various countries of the European

Union. However, further contribution to the debate of international trade and wages were made by Leontief paradox (Leamer, *1980).* [xli] in 1954 and Linder hypothesis[xlii] in 1961.

More recently, two main factors that have contributed significantly in widening the wage gap between the skilled and unskilled workers in the Western world and increase in unemployment of unskilled workers are: the defensive innovation along with reducing costs in transport and communication and large immigration of unskilled workers into the West. Technology changes the skill structure in the economy and hence adversely affects the real wages and employment levels. It is well documented that the unskilled workers in most of the European countries are affected to a much greater extent than in the USA by low employment rather than low wages due to the introduction of minimum wage level (Blau and Kahn, 1996 and Nickell, 1997). Computer use has changed the wage structure (DiNardo and Pishke, 1997; Haskel and Slaughter, 1998). Recently, there has been a debate between 'trade' (reduction in barriers in trade) and 'technology' (skill-biased technical change) as the driving forces (alternative and non-overlapping forces) of the recent changes in the labour markets in the Western world. Another debate being developed in this context is the technology hypothesis vis-à-vis globalisation hypothesis. In fact, trade, technology and globalisation are closely interlinked with one another. Therefore, it will be a very narrow approach just to rely on either 'trade hypothesis', 'technology hypothesis' or 'globalisation hypothesis' alone, rather they should be studied together under one analytic umbrella.

Assar Lindbeck and Dennis Snower (1984, 1986) propounded the insider-outsider theory of employment that examines the behaviour of insiders as more privileged than outsider workers of the firms. This behaviour results in two situations. First is the absence of wage underbidding even when many unemployed outsider workers are willing to work at lower wage rate as the firms do not want to replace the insiders with outsiders due to high replace costs or insiders do not co-operate with outsiders. Second is existence of permanent higher unemployment after negative shocks and hence causing hysteresis (Blanchard and Summers, 1987). The issues of globalisation and labour market are also analysed from another point of view, taking into consideration expected migration flows from developing countries to developed countries. Another perspective from which the links between globalisation and labour market are analysed gives importance to the interaction between unfavourable macroeconomic policies and real labour market rigidities. Effects of globalisation on labour market dynamics are seen through labour mobility and the integration of the product market (Ederveen, Nahuis and Parikh, 2007). There have been various recent attempts in literature evaluating different aspects of the link between globalisation, economic integration and labour market (Fertig, 2003). These theories, however, are very narrow in their approach in addressing labour market changes in the presence of constant changes in global economic system, economic liberation, international migration, science and technological inventions and shocks, failures and interventions in an economy. Therefore, there is a need to take all driving forces into account simultaneously in explaining the labour market changes.

The Theoretical Framework

The critical driving forces inherent in the process of the proliferation of globalisation are diverse and complex. They are intertwined and interconnected. Therefore, a study of these forces helps us to understand the global economy better and also the effects of globalisation on labour market outcomes. To the extent such forces of globalisation persist in an economy and the magnitude of their multivariate casual connections may cause negative or positive consequences for labour market dynamics. These critical forces hover around economic, financial, political, operational, socio-cultural, legal, religious, technological, linguistic and other factors of our global economy. The liberalisation, migration, financial and technological forces are by far the most important, even though the political and socio-cultural milieu cannot at all be neglected. The following are the critical forces of globalisation that influence labour markets:

(a) Global Economic system

The key driving forces of globalisation that bring changes in labour markets lie within the prevailing global economic system that subsumes the networks, subsystems and arrangements that unite the economies of the world into one global marketplace. It is concerned with international economic relationships that exist among different countries of the world. Ever since the Industrial Revolution era, between 1820 and 1890, the global economic system has undergone various changes and transformations introduced by factors such as systematic application of science and technology; overseas trade; capital and population movements; creation of global financial system, emergence of international patterns of specialization in production and trade; and so on. However, a meeting of delegates from 44 nations in 1944 in Bretton Woods, New Hampshire, United States, laid the foundation for the modern global economic system. International organizations such as the International Monetary Fund (IMF) and the World Trade Organization (WTO) are important institutions in the global economic system. Global trade agreements such as the North American Free Trade Agreement (NAFTA) and the General Agreement on Tariffs and Trade (GATT) helped accelerate globalisation, opening markets around world to an expanding range of goods and services. Thus, the domestic and global economy, society and institutions have witnessed great renovation over the last many decades.

However, the main features of the prevailing global economic system include liberal global trading order, international migration, capital movements into overseas territories, fluctuating exchange rate system, elastic payment systems in globalised financial and capital markets, capital-embedded technology and energy intensive growth, high productivity specialized agriculture, global political and market institutional framework building, faceless communication system, globalisation of production and consumption, rapidly rising economic and social inequalities both within and across nations, and so on. Ever since Industrial Revolution, the information and communication revolution is in the process of altering all aspects of the national and global economy, society and polity. It is transforming the industrial structure, industrial organisation, workplace, destroying old and creating new jobs, altering working patterns, permitting a new level of decentralization of productive employment, changing the international patterns of division of labour, new kinds of international firms in different fields have emerged. A liberal economic trading order is in process of being forged (Adelman, 1995).

Institutions are systems of established and prevalent social rules that structure social interactions (Hodgson, 2006). Economic institutions or organisations are those institutions that perform economic functions, regulated by formal regulating agencies, of establishing and protecting property rights; facilitating transactions; and permitting economic co-operation and organisation (Wiggins and Davis, 2006). The functioning of institutions depends upon many other factors such as administrative requirements, efficacy of legal systems, underlying norms of society, and individual freedom versus obligations to wider collectives, and so on. Institutions are often embedded in social and cultural characteristics of the particular context. Institutions affect economic growth, investment, human capital formation and technological innovations through secure intellectual property rights (Nabli and Nugent, 1989).

There are mainly four pathways through which global economic system affects labour market outcomes such as economic liberalisation, international mobility of resources including human, information technology and communication innovations and shocks, failures and interventions. The extent to which the growth in an economy depends upon its political structure and the nature of economy also influences its labour market dynamics and pattern of employment. Thus, global economic system allows economies to engage in international trade of goods and services and permitting entrepreneurs, labour, capital, technology, and ideas to move freely around the world.

(b) Economic Liberalisation

Strong wave of liberation induced by the World Trade Organisation (WTO) as well as unilateral negotiations and decisions undertaken by the countries world-over introduced the process of economic liberation in many countries. Economic liberalisation includes internal (domestic) and external (international) as well as stabilisation and structural adjustment. It refers to the process of the opening up of a country to the rest of the world with regards to international trade, international investment, regulations, taxation, capital mobility, legal issues, labour market flexibility, open market in terms of interbank trade in securities and other areas by reducing protectionist policies, relaxing barriers and relinquishing some control over the direction of the economy to the private sector (Kotz, 2002). This often involves deregulation and privatization of state owned companies.

The economic liberalisation dimension mainly includes real, monetary and financial liberalisation such as freedom in interregional and international trade, capital mobility, financial remittances, foreign direct investment (inward and outward FDI flows), and multinational corporations. When FDI increases, unemployment increases or decreased depends in which sector the investment is being made. One possibility is that if FDI is made in state enterprises, the labour force in these enterprises might be laid off. Unemployment decreases as exports grow when exporting goods that are produced with labor intensive techniques. However, the main indicators for economic liberation have been used in this study are intra-regional trade index ratio between the intra trade (internal trade of the region in which the country falls) and total trade; global trade index (ratio between total trade and the GDP, it measures the degree of participation of a country); financial market integration index; reforms in exchange rates, fiscal, monetary and labour market policies, opening up the economy to competition from abroad (global competitive index) or country contestability; lower taxes on the rich and foreign investors; trade deficit as a percentage of GDP; extent to which the economy is import-dependent for its production inputs and consumption activities; extent to which the economy is export-dependent for its earnings; extent of capital flows in terms of foreign aid, foreign direct investment, and foreign loans

(c) International Migration

Migration is a complex phenomenon and research on this subject mainly brings out three aspects. First, migration flows are spatial enabling us to distinguish between international and international migration. The second facet distinguishes between microeconomic (individual decisions to migrate) and macroeconomic approach (role played by macroeconomic variables). The third aspect is concerned with the determinants of migration or to explore the consequences of migration. This paper focuses on consequences of international migration flows, following a macroeconomic approach, on the labour market dynamics.

The globalisation of the market economy is the prime reason for migration that includes both spatial and occupational mobility of productive resources. Increasing globalisation has escalated the migratory flow of workers across the world. Human mobility include international networks of migrants (immigration and emigration) and diasporas (which facilitate trade and investment), circular migration, labour mobility, skill selectivity, productivity-wage mismatch, overseas educational opportunities, female migration, quest for better quality of life, better remuneration abroad, concerns about livability, political stability, human rights and media freedom, and remittances from expatriates living abroad constitute a significant proportion of foreign revenue for many developing countries. International migration affects both supply of labour and demand for labour. It is also useful to distinguish among mobility of individuals, knowledge workers mobility, ambitious entrepreneurs, and managerial power.

(d) Science and Technology Inventions

With modern technology, the connections between economics, politics and the environment are growing stronger every day and are frequently described within the framework of globalisation. Geographers' abilities to examine issues such as trade between nations, regional economic policies, global political networks, and environmental issues provide geographers an excellent understanding of global issues.

The endogenous relationships between labour market dynamics and skills, training and innovations are highly controversial with varying results and impacts (Pieroni and Pompei, 2008). It is controversial as to if innovation crate many jobs or lead to productivity crisis. Technology is labour replacing so a positive technology shock leads to a decline in labour inputs (Mandelman and Zanetti, 2008). Mortensen and Pissarides (1999) model of equilibrium unemployment asserts that 'skill-biased' technology shocks that increase the spread of labour productivities, interacting with different policy regimes, explain the rise in unemployment in Europe relative to the United States in the 1980s and 1990s. Moreover, labour market rigidities in terms of technological rigidity affect the age structure of a firm's work force in equilibrium. Firms using relatively flexible technology care only about total hours of labor input, but not hours of work per worker. Older workers with a desire for short or flexible hours of work are attracted to such firms. Firms using a more rigid technology involving team production impose a minimum hours constraint, and as a result tend to have a younger age structure (Blau and Shvydko, 2007). Thus, unemployment structure is also changing and unemployment is rising in the UK and other advanced countries due to labour market rigidities.

Over the last three decades, the gap between wages and unemployment rates of skilled and unskilled workers has widened in the UK (Wood, 1998). The demand for skilled relative to unskilled has increased, relative to its supply. Due to the introduction of skill-using technological progress such as computers, internet, new products, new forms of business organisations, new processes and so on, both the relative demand for skilled workers and its relative supply have risen sharply more or less in similar magnitudes. This has resulted in the rise in income generated by the employment of highly skilled labour and through externalities even generating more needs and opportunities to hire even more skilled workers. Capital is replacing labor in the production process as technology advances. The growth in fixed capital investments was found to be positively correlating with unemployment. So producers are replacing machines for workers. For example, new technology platforms are replacing traditional high street banking branches and thus replacing labour, e.g., smart phone based current accounts. Most of the super markets have now introduced self-checking tills in their stores. This has further reduced the number of jobs available in the market.

In the digital global economy of the internet era, the faster and cheaper technology has broken the national barrier of time and space. Hence, technology and innovations have easily brought the national markets together. The main technological factors affecting labour market in an economy are the extent of technology transfer, investment in R&D, number of researchers per million population in R&D, publication in scientific and technical journals can be taken as summary indicator that captures output in science and technology knowledge-creation, extent to which the country has the research expertise, trademark applications that offer the possibility of research that has commercial value, extent of technology transformation, and intellectual property rights.

(e) Shocks, Failures and Interventions

The role of the forces of shocks, failures and interventions in an economy can hardly be exaggerated. These are also likely to have profound influence on the patterns of employment and unemployment within and between economies (Nunziata, 2002). Shocks are the large unexpected and unpredictable external events that bring out changes in real economic growth, employment and inflation, as a result, produce significant negative welfare effects. For example, a shock in supply of staple commodities, such as oil, can cause prices to skyrocket, making expensive to use for business purposes. Similarly, a rapid devaluation of a currency would produce a shock for the import/export industry leading to job losses and business closures. Broadly, there are *aggregate demand side shocks* taking place due to economic downturn in a major trading partner, unexpected tax rises, financial crisis, etc, and aggregate supply-side shocks because of steep rise in commodity prices, political turmoil, natural disaster, unexpected breakthroughs in production technology, and so on.

A failure is a condition wherein desired objectives are not met. It represents imperfections and structural rigidities in a system. With a globalisation of markets comes a globalisation of failures. A labour market failure is a situation in which a market fails to allocate resources efficiently, to provide a free movement of labour, to provide perfect information among buyers and sellers, monopsony power of employers leading to discrimination on the basis of race, gender, age, ethnicity, sexual preference, etc., and disincentive to find and take paid work due to income tax system, cost of travelling to work, cost of childcare, low wages, lack of qualifications and skills, and so on. Government interventions to resolve labour market failures can also fail to achieve the desired goals due to information failure, excessive bureaucracy, incentives, welfare benefits, and subsidies payments. Government price fixation creates distortions which may lead to shortages or surpluses, for example, setting a minimum wage is likely to create an excess of supply of labour in markets where the 'market cleaning equilibrium' is less than the minimum. Welfare benefits such as unemployment benefits lead to the problem of *moral hazard* as the unemployed individuals are less likely to improve their employability.

Even if there is no shock in an economy, labour market performance may be adversely affected by *coordination failure* as the real market conditions might prevent individuals and firms from coordinating their decisions properly due to lack of complete knowledge (Mankiw and Romer, 1997). Therefore, two economies with same technologies, policies, labour forces and other conditions, could achieve different activity rates, unemployment rates and labour market performances (Cooper and John, 1988). The main sources of labour market coordination failures are mismatch between hiring decisions of firms and the job search efforts of workers, existence of multiple equilibria because of labour market policies, lack of human capital accumulation due to loss of skills when unemployed, and existence of various frictions in labour markets (Manning, 1992).

Besides coordination failure, labour markets suffer from collective action problem. Collective action occurs when a number of people work together to achieve some common objective. However, it was recognized as early as in 1740 by David Hume in his *A Treatise of Human Nature,* that individuals often fail to work together, e.g., two neighbours may agree to drain a common meadow, to have a thousand neighbours agree on such a project becomes too complex a matter to execute. Mancur Olson (1965) popularized the problems of collective action. A collective good, economically infeasible to exclude people from using it, such as collective wage bargain for an industry by trade union, also poses *a problem of free ride* as the fruits of bargaining (wage increase, better working conditions, less working hours, etc.) are also enjoyed by the workers who do not contribute anything to union dues and are not part of union. In game theory, one shot 'prisoner's dilemma' game represents a series of more complex situations, where individual rational action leads to a suboptimal outcome. Thus, if the network effects are allowed in a game played by more than two parties, the possible outcome includes both cooperation and free riding.

The labour market deficiencies such as costly information, adverse selection, and coordination and collective action failures call for job-searching and job-matching intermediaries or institutions like the 'medical match' that allocates young doctors completing medical schools to medical jobs/residencies (Autor, 2009). With a sharp fall in information costs, labour market intermediaries such as on-line job boards (information only intermediaries), job-search engines, newspaper advertisements, job banks, job centres, private agencies supplying workers to firms, temporary help agencies, and so on, step-in to co-ordinate between job vacancies and job seekers. However, labour market intermediation also suffers from many failures such as market congestion, expensive job co-ordination commission charged by private agencies both to workers and firms, cheap information not sufficient to solve labour market failures, pitfalls in the technology of job-matching, and so on.

(f) Labour Market Dynamics

Labour market dynamics simply means movements in labour markets. It may be defined as the outcomes of labour market in terms of the changes in jobs (number of jobs), changes in jobs of employed persons (flows within employment, i.e., between full-time and part-time employment; industries, occupations, between employee status) and self-employment and economic activity status of individuals (employed, unemployed and inactive) in an economy. A system labour accounting provides a comprehensive framework for the description and analysis of the state and dynamics of labour market and its interaction with the rest of the economy. Labour market dynamics is a measure of gross changes, movements and flows in the number of jobs and persons and their activities[xliii].

Figure 8.1 Labour Market Dynamics among Labour Market States

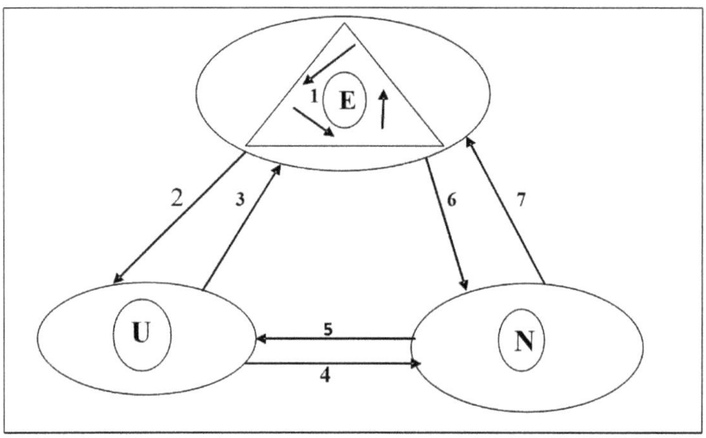

Source: Stibbard, P. (1999). "Labour market dynamics: A global survey of statistical activity", International Labour Office, Employment and Training Papers, No. 38, p. 5

Figure 8.1 shows the gross flows between labour market states of employment (E), unemployment (U) and not in the labour force (N). The first set of dynamics, shown by 1 in the Figure 8.1, is within employment (E), such as between jobs; full-time and part-time employment; industries; occupations; or between employee status and self-employment. The second set of dynamics is unemployment turnover, i.e., inflows and outflows of unemployment, represented by arrows 2, 3, 4 and 5 in Figure 8.1. The third set of dynamics is the labour and job turnover rates represented by herrings represented by arrows 1, 3, and 7 and separations (layoffs and quits) represented by arrows 1, 2, and 6. The aspects of labour market flexibility and mobility are represented by arrows 1, 2, 3, 4, 5, 6, and 7. The transition from full-time education into the labour force is represented by arrows 5 and 7. Similarly, the move from work into retirement is shown by 2, 4 and 6 arrows. Depending upon the work history records, the profile of individuals' earnings over time are represented by arrows 1, 2, 3, 4, 5, 6, and 7. Thus, the dynamics of labour market includes the magnitude of labour force in an economy, unemployment turnover, full-time employment, extent of part-time unemployment, magnitude of self-employed individuals, job turnover rates, labour turnover rates, and the earnings profile of workers.

Research Methodology

In this model the global economic system provides the foundation for economic liberalisation, international migration, science and technological inventions and shocks, failures and interventions. The way these are developed and supported will determine the degree of labour market dynamics; thus a major challenge for the policy makers to effectively manage the relationship among the globalisation components. In this case, the latent variable structural model is used to represent the causal relationships among latent variables (global economic system, economic liberalisation, international migration, science and technological inventions and shocks, failures and interventions). The purpose of the approach is to estimate the strength of the causal connections among the latent variables and to test the goodness of fit of the structural model. For the requirements of labour market evaluation, it is necessary for the system to delivery meaningful results in terms of causal (cause-effect) relationship and a structural approach; that is to say that the analysis shall be model-based. Structural equation modeling[xliv] (SEM) provides a means by which relationships can be tested. To estimate the strength of these causal connections, it is necessary for each of the latent variables to be operational in terms of manifest variables (measurement items). In reality, the manifest variables are measured by using measurement items, also, they serve as indicators of the latent variable.

A measurement instrument is then developed and used to obtain scores from respondents on a variety of attributes that provide an empirical content to the model's constructs. The labour market matrix is obtained using structural equation models that simultaneously measure the impact of all the dimensions of globalisation. SEM traditionally has some assumptions, namely: independence of variables, random sampling of respondents, linearity of all relationships, multivariate normality of distribution, no kurtosis and no skewness, appropriate data measurement on interval or ratio scale, and sample size between 100 and 400. The other postulate of our model is that labour markets are characterized by the presence of a monopolistic structure and mechanisms.

The Theoretical Model

(a) The Conceptual Model

The conceptual foundation of this model links the components of globalisation with labour market dynamics under one umbrella. However, globalisation is a complex multidimensional phenomenon. It can be conceptualised as the combination of various interconnected and interwoven critical driving forces such as global economic system, economic liberalisation, international mobility of resources, science and technology inventions, shocks, failures and interventions that separately or jointly influence the labour market outcomes in a region, country or global economy. In turn, each critical dimension of globalisation is comprised of multiple sub-factors that are often a combination of subjective evaluations and more objective macroeconomic statistics. The extent to which the labour market of a country exhibits a risk to globalisation forces depends upon the system of positive and negative linkages.

Figure 8.2 The Conceptual Model of Globalisation and Labour Market Dynamics

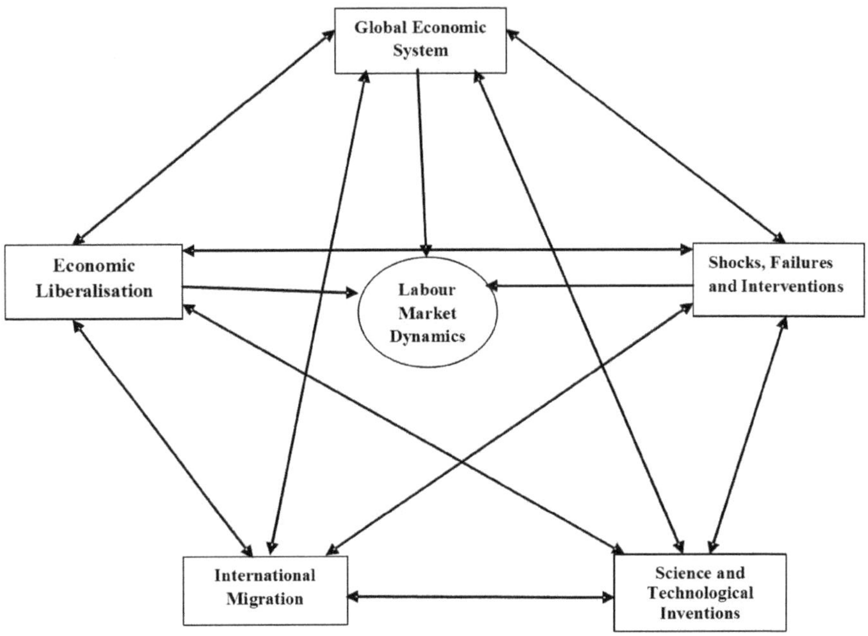

Source: Own construction

Figure 8.2 illustrates a complete conceptual model demonstrating the multivariate causal pathways (indicated by the arrows) interlinking the critical forces of globalisation with labour market dynamics. All these are interwoven with each other (as shown by double ←→ pathway arrow) and they all are jointly leading to and contribute to labour market dynamics (as shown by the single pathway arrow ⟶). All these factors have multiple causal relationships with each other. Global economic system interacts with economic liberalisation, international migration, science and technological inventions, and shocks, failures and interventions and in turn, impacts the labour market dynamics. Similarly, international migration is also interwoven with other four constructs and contributes to labour market dynamics. It can be concluded that all these constructs are significantly interdependent and interwoven with each other and singly and/or jointly contribute to overall labour market dynamics.

(b) The Operational Model

The second stage transforms the conceptual model into operational model by unfolding the complexity via looking deeper into all forces of globalisation causing labour market dynamics. It is at this stage that one needs to identify various critical factors generating labour market outcomes in a region, country or global economy. As adumbrated earlier, there is a whole range of critical factors contributing to labour market dynamics. The model identifies and takes into consideration 48 such factors that are key areas that may be managed which improve the overall conditions and performance of labour markets if managed properly. The choice and selection of such factors will depend upon the researcher's judgment, justifications, extensive literature review, emerging empirical evidences and so on. However, these factors can be arranged on the basis of their degree of importance. There may be different ways of assigning weights or importance to these factors. However, in the case of this model, the measurement of labour market dynamics will involve determining weights of these factors automatically by the measurement software. Depending upon the nature and type of the factors, they are grouped into the following six latent variables, namely, global economic system, economic liberalisation, international migration, science and technology inventions, shocks and institutions and labour market dynamics (See Chopra, 2011).

(c) The Latent Variable Structural Model

Figure 8.3 A Latent Variable Structural Model of Labour Market Dynamics

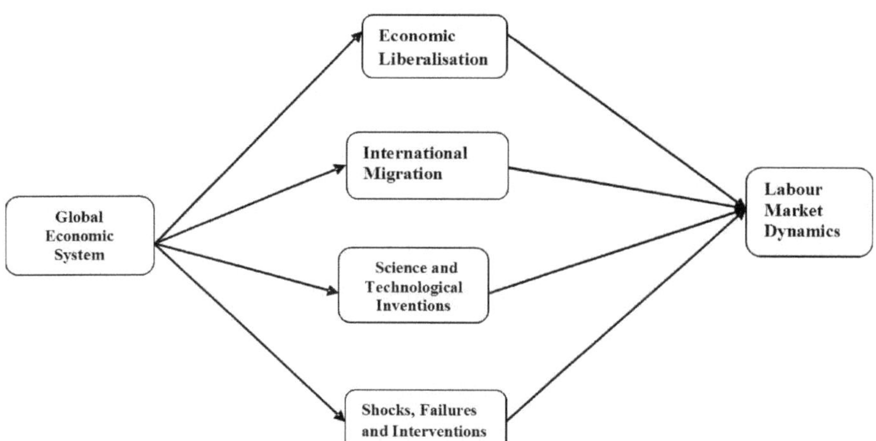

The third stage transforms the operational model into latent variable structural model that unfolds the complexity in each dimension of globalisation by looking deeper into different factors causing labour market dynamics. A latent variable structural model is a theoretical construct, that is an unobserved variable presumed to exist within a structural model but for which direct measurements are not available. A latent variable structural model is a graphical model that specifies the presumed structure of causal connections among latent and manifest variables (Chopra and Kanji, 2010 and 2011; Chopra, 2011, 2012 and 2015). The latent variable structural model is used to represent the casual relationships among latent variables (Figure 8.3). The present study identifies and takes into consideration six dimensions and 48 critical factors.

The mathematical equations that express the relationships among latent variables are referred to as the *structural model*. In a latent variable structural model, the *inner model* is the part of the model that describes the relationships between the latent variables that make up the model. In this sense, the *path coefficients* are inner model parameter estimates (inner coefficients)[xlv]. The inner models are also frequently referred to as the structural models. Latent variables as opposed to observed variables are variables that are not directly observed but are rather inferred (through a mathematical model) from other variables that are observed (directly measured). A latent variable structural model is expressed in a system of simultaneous equations known as structural equations for the original model. The structural equations generate hypothetical variance/covariance matrix of manifest variables. The degree to which a structural equation model reflects reality is given by the degree to which the hypothetical variance/covariance matrix is similar to, or has a good fit with, the empirical variance/covariance matrix for the same manifest variables. The chi-square for goodness-of-fit statistic is used to evaluate whether manifest variables are related to their respective latent variables. It is also used to test whether the structure among the latent variables is consistent with the data. This new model will provide a deeper understanding and greater theoretical knowledge about the management and the measurement of labour market dynamics.

The model contains one latent exogenous[xlvi] variable (ξ_1), five latent endogenous[xlvii] variables (η_1 to η_5), eight observed (manifest) exogenous variables (x_1 to x_8) which feed the exogenous latent variables, and forty observed (manifest) endogenous variables (y_1 to y_{40}) which feed the endogenous latent variables resulting in total forty-eight manifest variables. Thus, ξ_1 is operationalised by eight indicator variables (x_1 to x_8) and is a cause of latent endogenous variables η_1, η_2, η_3, η_4, and η_5 as indicated by arrows from ξ_1 to η_1, η_2, η_3, η_4, and η_5. Eight manifest endogenous variables (y_1 to y_8) serve as indicators of η_1 as indicated by the arrows from η_1 to these variables in squares in Figure 8.4. The subscript numbers indicate a particular variable's location within the matrices, which are used for calculation purposes. Each operationalisation of the model's latent variables is made in a similar way. The model recognises that the measures are imperfect, and we make an attempt to model this imperfection. Thus, the model includes terms representing measurement errors or structural disturbances or errors in equations. The measurement error terms associated with 'x' measures are labeled with the eight Greek character 'delta' (δ_1 to δ_8) and each 'x' is also associated with structural parameter[xlviii] (regression coefficient) relating measurement error to manifest exogenous variable (e_{11} to e_{88}, i.e., these are used to indicate the effect of a disturbance variable on an exogenous manifest variable. The measurement errors associated with 'y' (y_1 to y_{40}) are labeled with Greek letter 'epsilon' (ε_1 to ε_{40}) and each 'y' is also associated with structural parameter (weight or coefficient) relating measurement error to manifest endogenous variable (α_{11} to α_{4040}, inner coefficients, i.e., these are used to indicate the effect of a disturbance variable on an endogenous manifest variable). The measurement errors associated with endogenous variables are labeled as ζ_1 to ζ_5 and the structural parameters relating these disturbance variables to latent endogenous variables are labeled as $\alpha_{\zeta 11}$, $\alpha_{\zeta 22}$, $\alpha_{\zeta 33}$, and $\alpha_{\zeta 44}$ (inner coefficients). The characters γ_{11}, γ_{21}, γ_{31}, and γ_{41} are the structural parameters relating exogenous variable to endogenous variables (inner coefficients). The Greek characters β_{51}, β_{52}, β_{53}, and β_{54} are structural parameters relating the endogenous variables to another endogenous construct.

Figure 8.4 A Latent Variable Structural Model of Globalisation and Labour Market Dynamics

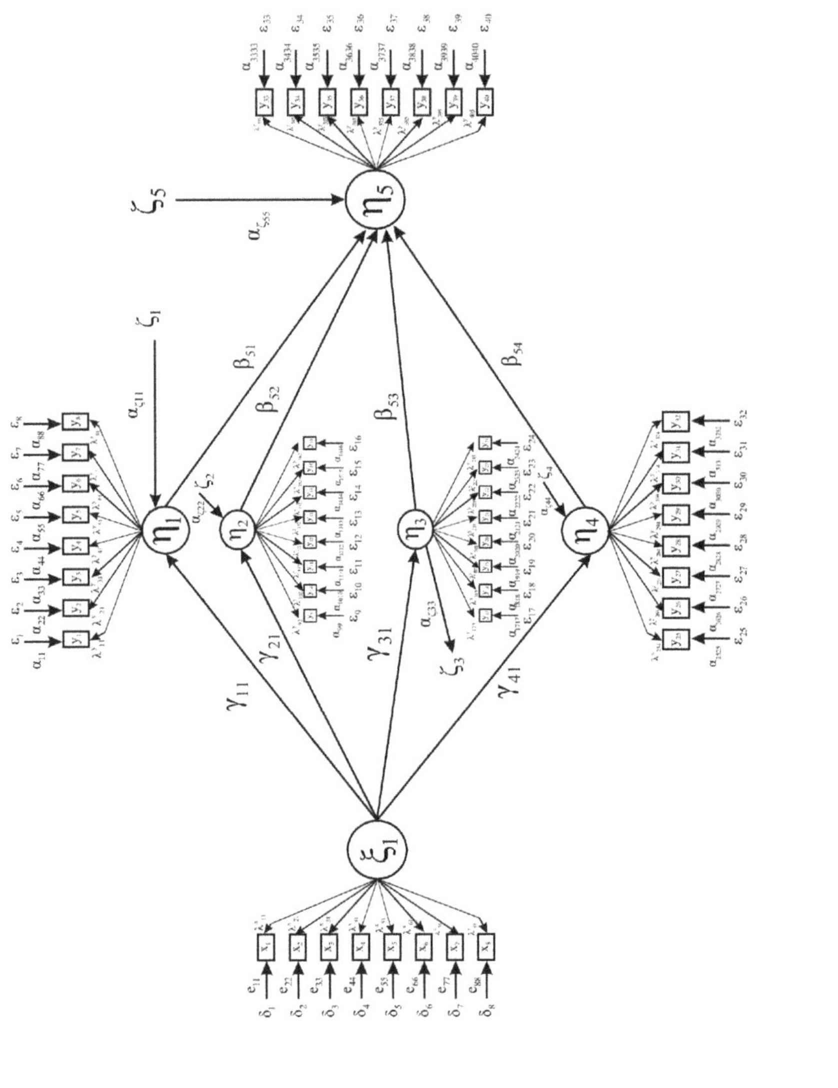

Source: Own construction

The model in Figure 8.4 can be expressed by a system of simultaneous equations. One variable is developed for each latent or manifest variable, which means that there are although fifty three equations. Each equation includes the latent and/or manifest variables that have a direct effect on the endogenous variable, including disturbance variables. Thus, the components of a structural equation are the latent variables, structural parameters and a disturbance term. Other endogenous variable will have similar equations. Latent variables structural model is expressed by a system of simultaneous equations. This system of equations is as follows:

$\eta_1 = \gamma_{11}\ \xi_1 + \zeta_1\alpha_{\zeta 11}$
$\eta_2 = \gamma_{21}\ \xi_1 + \zeta_1\alpha_{\zeta 22}$
$\eta_3 = \gamma_{31}\ \xi_1 + \zeta_1\alpha_{\zeta 33}$
$\eta_4 = \gamma_{41}\ \xi_1 + \zeta_1\alpha_{\zeta 44}$
$\eta_5 = \beta_{51}\eta_1 + \beta_{52}\eta_2 + \beta_{53}\eta_3 + \beta_{54}\eta_4 + \zeta_5\alpha_{\zeta 55}$
$x_1 = \lambda^x_{11}\xi_1 + e_{11}\ \delta_1$
$x_2 = \lambda^x_{21}\xi_1 + e_{22}\ \delta_2$
$x_3 = \lambda^x_{31}\xi_1 + e_{33}\delta_3$
$x_4 = \lambda^x_{41}\xi_1 + e_{44}\delta_4$
$x_5 = \lambda^x_{51}\xi_1 + e_{55}\delta_{58}$
$x_6 = \lambda^x_{61}\xi_1 + e_{66}\delta_6$
$x_7 = \lambda^x_{71}\xi_1 + e_{77}\delta_7$
$x_8 = \lambda^x_{81}\xi_1 + e_{88}\delta_8$
$y_1 = \lambda^y_{11}\eta_1 + \alpha_{11}\varepsilon_1$
$y_2 = \lambda^y_{21}\eta_1 + \alpha_{22}\varepsilon_2$
. . . .
. . . .
. . . .
$y_{37} = \lambda^y_{375}\eta_5 + \alpha_{3737}\varepsilon_{37}$
$y_{38} = \lambda^y_{385}\eta_5 + \alpha_{3838}\varepsilon_{38}$
$y_{39} = \lambda^y_{395}\eta_5 + \alpha_{3939}\varepsilon_{39}$
$y_{40} = \lambda^y_{405}\eta_5 + \alpha_{4040}\varepsilon_{40}$

In the above equations, we have the following definitions:
ξ_1 = global economic system (latent exogenous variable)
η_1 = economic liberalisation (latent endogenous variable)
η_2 = international migration (latent endogenous variable)
η_3 = science and technological inventions (latent endogenous variable)
η_4 = shocks, failures and interventions (latent endogenous variable)
η_5 = labour market dynamics (latent endogenous variable)
λ^x_{11} = structural parameter or regression coefficient linking exogenous construct to its measures (exogenous manifest variables)
λ^y_{11} = structural parameter (regression coefficient) linking endogenous construct to its measures (endogenous manifest variables)
γ_{11} = structural parameters (regression coefficients) relating exogenous variables to endogenous (inner coefficients)

e_{11} to e_{88} = measurement errors associated with manifest exogenous variables
ζ_1 to ζ_5 = measurement errors associated with endogenous variables
ε_1 to ε_{40} = measurement errors associated with manifest endogenous variables

Structural Errors

As it is very rare to expect to perfectly predict the dependent constructs, so it is important to include error term in the latent variable structural model, labeled as the Greek character 'zeta' (ζ). In order to achieve consistent parameter estimation, these error terms are assumed to be uncorrelated with the model's exogenous constructs. The violation of this assumption comes about as a result of the excluded predictor problem. However, the structural error terms have been modeled as being correlated with other structural error terms. This specification indicates that the endogenous constructs associated with those error terms share common variation that is not explained by predictor relations in the model.

Matrix Equations

A matrix of equations representing the fifty-three-variable-model is created. *Dependent variables* are represented in a random vector η^* that may be portioned as $\eta^{*\prime} = [\eta', x', y']$, where η' is a (transposed) random sub-vector of latent endogenous variables, x' is a (transported) random sub-vector of manifest exogenous (independent) variables and y' is a (transposed) random sub-vector of manifest endogenous (dependent) variables. The number of latent dependent variables in η' is indicated by m_1, the number of manifest exogenous variables is indicated by m_2, and the number of manifest dependent variables in y' is indicated by m_3. The total number of dependent variables is indicated by m, where $m = m_1 + m_2 + m_3$. The order of η' is thus m x 1.

Independent variables are included in a single random column vector ξ^*. Thus, we may write $\xi^* = [\xi', \eta_1']$ where ξ' stands for a (transposed) sub-vector of latent exogenous variables, and η_y' stands for a (transposed) random sub-vector of manifest endogenous variables. The number of latent exogenous variables included in ξ' is n_1: the number of manifest endogenous variables in η_y' is equal to m (the number of dependent variables). The number of independent variables in ξ^* is thus $n_1 + m = n$, and so the order of ξ^* is n x 1.

The *path coefficients* (inner) γ_{ij} that relate independent to dependent latent variables, path coefficients (inner) β_{ij} that relate pairs of dependent variables and path coefficients (outer) λ^x_{ij} and λ^y_{ij} that relate latent variables with their manifest variables are included in matrix A. Each row of A corresponds to one of the dependent variables and contains structural parameters corresponding to the variable's connections with independent variables that cause it. The *path coefficients* (outer path coefficient or structural parameter) λ^x_{ij} relate latent exogenous variable to its manifest variables and the path coefficients (outer) λ^y_{ij} relate latent endogenous variables to their manifest variables. The elements of diagonal of A are thus ordinarily zero, meaning that a dependent variable does not cause itself, i.e., A zero element of ith row and k^{th} column of means that the kth exogenous variable is not the cause of the variable.

The *structural errors* (ζ_{ij}) associated with latent endogenous variables, structural errors (e_{ij}) linking measurement errors to manifest exogenous variables and structural errors (α_{ij}) linking measurement errors with manifest endogenous variables are contained in the matrix Γ^*. The matrix $\Gamma^* = [\Gamma: e: \Delta]$ is partitioned into 'm x 1' matrix; Γ into 'm x n' and 'm x m' for matrix Δ. The rows of Γ correspond to the different dependent variables. The column of Γ corresponds to only one exogenous variable. In the present example, Γ is a 5 x 1 sub-matrix. The sub-matrix 'e' contains measurement errors relating to manifest exogenous variables, and 'e' is a 8 x 8 sub-matrix. The sub-matrix Δ contains structural errors linking measurement errors to manifest endogenous variables. The rows of Δ, thus, also correspond to the different manifest variables, which the columns of correspond to different disturbance variables.

The *disturbance variables* are included in a single random column vector ε^*. This vector may be partitioned to distinguish between manifest and latent exogenous disturbance variables. Thus, we may write $\varepsilon^* = [\alpha_\zeta', \delta', \varepsilon']$ where α_ζ' stands for a (transported) sub vector of latent disturbance variables, δ' stands for a (transported) sub-vector of manifest exogenous disturbance variables, and ε' stands for manifest endogenous disturbance variables. The number of latent disturbance variables in α_ζ' is n_1, the number of manifest exogenous disturbance variables in δ' is m_1, and the number of manifest endogenous disturbance variables in ε' is equal to m_2. The number of disturbance variables in ε^* is thus $n_1+m_1+m_2$.

A more compact for the general matrix formulation of the linear structural equation model with latent manifest variables is given by

$$\begin{bmatrix} \eta \\ x \\ y \end{bmatrix} = A \begin{bmatrix} \xi \\ \\ \eta \end{bmatrix} + [\boldsymbol{\Gamma} : \mathbf{e} : \boldsymbol{\Delta}] \begin{bmatrix} \alpha_\zeta \\ \delta \\ \varepsilon \end{bmatrix}$$

or simply

$$\eta^* = A\xi^* + \boldsymbol{\Gamma}^*\varepsilon^*$$

The goal of structural equation model is to show how relationships among manifest variables (given by either correlation or covariance) can be explained in terms of structural equations relating manifest variables to other (possibly latent) variables of the model. To reach this goal it is required that a certain ‘selection’ equation draws out manifest variables in the sub-vectors x and y, from the larger vectors η* and , of variables. The selection equation is

$$\mathbf{y=[0:I]} \begin{bmatrix} \eta \\ \quad x \\ y \end{bmatrix}$$

or

$$y = G_y \eta_1{}^*$$

G_y = **[0:I]** is a partitioned (m_2 x m) ‘selection’ matrix with **0,** an m_2 x m_1 null matrix and **I**, an m_2 x m_2 identity matrix. In other words, G_y contains zero elements everywhere except for a single element of unity in each row placed in the appropriate column of G_y to ‘select’ a corresponding manifest dependent variable for η*.

The matrix reflecting the variances and covariance among independent variables of the model is

$$\boldsymbol{\Phi} = E(\xi^* \, \xi^{*\prime})$$

The model requires that exogenous variables are independent of disturbance variables. This requirement is expressed mathematically by the requirement

$$E\,\varepsilon[\xi']$$

Where, E is the expectation operator

The effect of this requirement appears in the matrix and may be seen in a partitioning of this matrix as

$$\Phi = \begin{bmatrix} \eta & 0_{\varepsilon\varepsilon} \\ y & \Phi_{\varepsilon\varepsilon} \end{bmatrix}$$

Where $\Phi_{\varepsilon\varepsilon} = E(\xi\xi')$ and $0_{\varepsilon\varepsilon} = E(\varepsilon\varepsilon')$

$$
\begin{pmatrix} \eta_1 \\ \eta_2 \\ \eta_3 \\ \eta_4 \\ \eta_5 \\ x_1 \\ x_2 \\ x_3 \\ x_4 \\ x_5 \\ x_6 \\ x_7 \\ x_8 \\ y_1 \\ y_2 \\ \vdots \\ y_{37} \\ y_{38} \\ y_{39} \\ y_{40} \end{pmatrix}_{\eta^*}
=
\begin{pmatrix}
\gamma_{11} & 0 & 0 & 0 & 0 \\
\gamma_{21} & 0 & 0 & 0 & 0 \\
\gamma_{31} & 0 & 0 & 0 & 0 \\
\gamma_{41} & 0 & 0 & 0 & 0 \\
\beta_{51} & \beta_{52} & \beta_{53} & \beta_{54} & \beta_{55} \\
\lambda^x_{11} & 0 & 0 & 0 & 0 \\
\lambda^x_{21} & 0 & 0 & 0 & 0 \\
\lambda^x_{31} & 0 & 0 & 0 & 0 \\
\lambda^x_{41} & 0 & 0 & 0 & 0 \\
\lambda^x_{51} & 0 & 0 & 0 & 0 \\
\lambda^x_{61} & 0 & 0 & 0 & 0 \\
\lambda^x_{71} & 0 & 0 & 0 & 0 \\
\lambda^x_{81} & 0 & 0 & 0 & 0 \\
\lambda^Y_{11} & 0 & 0 & 0 & 0 \\
\lambda^Y_{21} & 0 & 0 & 0 & 0 \\
\vdots & \vdots & \vdots & \vdots & \vdots \\
0 & 0 & 0 & 0 & \lambda^Y_{375} \\
0 & 0 & 0 & 0 & \lambda^Y_{385} \\
0 & 0 & 0 & 0 & \lambda^Y_{395} \\
0 & 0 & 0 & 0 & \lambda^Y_{405}
\end{pmatrix}_{\Lambda}
\begin{pmatrix} \zeta_1 \\ \zeta_1 \\ \zeta_1 \\ \zeta_1 \\ \eta_1 \\ \zeta_1 \\ \zeta_1 \\ \zeta_1 \\ \zeta_1 \\ \zeta_1 \\ \zeta_1 \\ \zeta_1 \\ \zeta_1 \\ \eta_1 \\ \eta_1 \\ \vdots \\ \eta_5 \\ \eta_5 \\ \eta_5 \\ \eta_5 \end{pmatrix}_{\zeta^*}
+
\begin{pmatrix}
\zeta_1 \cdots 0\,0\,0\,0\,0\,0\,0\,0\,0 \cdots 0\,0 \cdots 0 & 0 & 0 & 0 \\
\zeta_2 \cdots 0\,0\,0\,0\,0\,0\,0\,0\,0 \cdots 0\,0 \cdots 0 & 0 & 0 & 0 \\
\zeta_3 \cdots 0\,0\,0\,0\,0\,0\,0\,0\,0 \cdots 0\,0 \cdots 0 & 0 & 0 & 0 \\
\zeta_4 \cdots 0\,0\,0\,0\,0\,0\,0\,0\,0 \cdots 0\,0 \cdots 0 & 0 & 0 & 0 \\
0 \cdots 0\,0\,0\,0\,0\,0\,0\,0\,0 \cdots 0\,0 \cdots 0 & 0 & 0 & 0 \\
0 \cdots e_{11}\,0\,0\,0\,0\,0\,0\,0\,0 \cdots 0\,0 \cdots 0 & 0 & 0 & 0 \\
0 \cdots 0\,e_{22}\,0\,0\,0\,0\,0\,0\,0 \cdots 0\,0 \cdots 0 & 0 & 0 & 0 \\
0 \cdots 0\,0\,e_{33}\,0\,0\,0\,0\,0\,0 \cdots 0\,0 \cdots 0 & 0 & 0 & 0 \\
0 \cdots 0\,0\,0\,e_{44}\,0\,0\,0\,0\,0 \cdots 0\,0 \cdots 0 & 0 & 0 & 0 \\
0 \cdots 0\,0\,0\,0\,e_{55}\,0\,0\,0\,0 \cdots 0\,0 \cdots 0 & 0 & 0 & 0 \\
0 \cdots 0\,0\,0\,0\,0\,e_{66}\,0\,0\,0 \cdots 0\,0 \cdots 0 & 0 & 0 & 0 \\
0 \cdots 0\,0\,0\,0\,0\,0\,e_{77}\,0\,0 \cdots 0\,0 \cdots 0 & 0 & 0 & 0 \\
0 \cdots 0\,0\,0\,0\,0\,0\,0\,e_{88}\,0 \cdots 0\,0 \cdots 0 & 0 & 0 & 0 \\
0 \cdots 0\,0\,0\,0\,0\,0\,0\,0\,0 \cdots \alpha_{11}\,0 \cdots 0 & 0 & 0 & 0 \\
0 \cdots 0\,0\,0\,0\,0\,0\,0\,0\,0 \cdots 0\,\alpha_{11} \cdots 0 & 0 & 0 & 0 \\
\vdots & \vdots & \vdots & \vdots \\
0 \cdots 0\,0\,0\,0\,0\,0\,0\,0\,0 \cdots 0\,0 \cdots \alpha_{3737} & 0 & 0 & 0 \\
0 \cdots 0\,0\,0\,0\,0\,0\,0\,0\,0 \cdots 0\,0 \cdots 0 & \alpha_{3838} & 0 & 0 \\
0 \cdots 0\,0\,0\,0\,0\,0\,0\,0\,0 \cdots 0\,0 \cdots 0 & 0 & \alpha_{3939} & 0 \\
0 \cdots 0\,0\,0\,0\,0\,0\,0\,0\,0 \cdots 0\,0 \cdots 0 & 0 & 0 & \alpha_{4040}
\end{pmatrix}_{\Gamma^*}
\begin{pmatrix} \alpha_{\zeta 11} \\ \alpha_{\zeta 22} \\ \alpha_{\zeta 33} \\ \alpha_{\zeta 44} \\ \alpha_{\zeta 55} \\ \delta_1 \\ \delta_2 \\ \delta_3 \\ \delta_4 \\ \delta_5 \\ \delta_6 \\ \delta_7 \\ \delta_8 \\ \varepsilon_1 \\ \varepsilon_2 \\ \vdots \\ \varepsilon_{37} \\ \varepsilon_{38} \\ \varepsilon_{39} \\ \varepsilon_{40} \end{pmatrix}_{\varepsilon^*}
$$

The terms $E(\varepsilon\xi')$ and $E(\xi\varepsilon') = 0$ in above equation.

The variance/covariance matrix among manifest variables is given by

$$\Sigma_0 = \Sigma_{yy}$$

Where according to the model,

$$\Sigma_{yy} = \Sigma(yy') = G_y B^{-1} \mathbf{\Gamma^*} \Phi\Lambda^{*\prime} B^{-1\prime} G_y'$$

The above equation implies that a predicted or hypothetical variance/covariance matrix Σ_0 for the set of observed variables in random vector $\mathbf{y}$ may be derived from the parameter values of a hypothetical structural equation model. Therefore, the degree to which the hypothetical structural equation model reflects reality is given by the degree to which the hypothetical matrix Σ_0 is the same as the empirical variance/covariance matrix Σ for the same variables (in $\mathbf{y}$) obtained from measurements of these variables in the world. To make the comparison between the hypothetical matrix Σ_0 and the empirical matrix Σ is the goal of a confirmatory analysis using structural equation models with latent and manifest variables. In practice, Σ_0 and Σ are replaced with sample estimates namely, Σ_0' and $\mathbf{S}$ respectively.

Model Identification and Path Coefficients

Before the values of path coefficients can be obtained, the structural equation model must be specified in such a way that the 'model' is 'identified'. Identifying a model involves fixing the values of some coefficients (fixed parameters) and using data to estimate values of other coefficients (free parameters) that would result in a unique hypothetical population covariance matrix of manifest variables (James, Mulaik and Brett, 1982). The least squares estimation method is used to minimise the sum of squared differences between the elements of sample covariance matrix (S) and the hypothetical population covariance (Σ_0') matrix for manifest variables.

Analysis of path coefficients begins with the outer path coefficients. For every relationship, all measurement items with values of path coefficients that are less than 0.1 is removed from the model. This is to ensure that only manifest variables that adequately reflect the empirical content of latent variables are retained for further analysis. Usually PLS has to be run several times to remove all manifest variables that are poorly linked to latent variables. The outer coefficients of remaining manifest variables are then used to compute critical food crisis factor and global food crisis indices for the study samples by using a mathematical expression that takes into account item mean scores and number of points in the scales. Following the analysis of outer coefficients, the research is then concerned with inner coefficients, which represents the amount of change in a dependent variable, expressed as multiples of standard deviation, when the value of its independent variable is changed by one unit.

Standardised inner coefficients cannot be compared across groups of sample nor can those that are produced by the same population over time. However, standardisation of data simplifies the computation of path coefficients because correlation matrix of manifest variables is used instead of the covariance matrix. In the PLS method, the values of inner coefficients for causal connections that do not involve a single dependent variable can be easily determined by reading their values directly from the correlation matrix. The values of inner coefficients for causal connections that involve a single dependent variable, however, have to be solved from the following equation (Namboodiri et al., 1975):

$$r_{ij} = \sum_{k} p_{ik} r_{kj}$$

where i = endogenous variable (I >k,j); j = causal variable; and k begins with I-1 and ranges down to 1 (i.e. η_1).

The Measurement Model

The fourth step in this model is to convert the structural model into a measurement model. The equations that express the relationships between latent variables and indicators are referred to as the *measurement model.* The *outer model* is the part of the model that describes the relationships between the latent variables and their indicators. The outer models are also frequently referred to as the measurement models. Thus, the outer models containing weights and loadings are also referred to as measurement models. At this stage, the latent constructs, which, though not directly measurable, are translated into a set of indicators (manifest variables). Each latent variable is usually associated with multiple measures. The measurement model is the mapping of measures onto theoretical constructs.

Figure 8.5 The Measurement Model

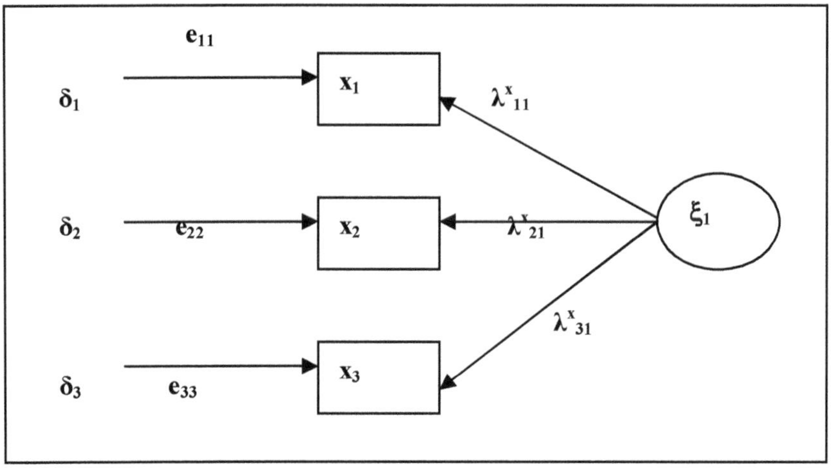

The latent constructs are most commonly linked to their measures (manifest variables) through a factor analytic measurement model, i.e., each latent variable construct is modelled as a common factor underlying the associated measures. These 'loadings' linking latent constructs to measures are labeled with the Greek character 'lambda' (λ) and there are two separate 'lambda matrices', one on the X side (λ^{x}_{11})and one on the Y side (λ^{y}_{11}) as shown in Figure 8.5. The labour market dynamics measurement model is the congeneric measurement model, where each measure is associated with only one latent construct, and all covariation between measures is a consequence of the relations between measures and constructs. Most of the models in use are indicative or non-prescriptive models, whereas measurement model is an improvement or prescriptive model. For the measurement of the phenomenon, the main objective is to develop a suitable latent variable structural model that shows relationship between latent variables, other intervening variables and ultimately labour market dynamics.Measurement Error

Almost every measure is acknowledged to include some error since the measures are imperfect and this imperfection is modelled by including terms representing measurement error in the equation. These measurement error terms are uniquenesses or unique factors associated with each measure. Measurement error terms associated with X measures are labeled as the Greek character 'delta' (δ) while terms associated with Y measures are labeled with 'epsilon' (ε).

To estimate the strengths of causal relations, it is necessary to operationalise each of the latent variables in terms of manifest variables that are believed to be caused by a latent variable. In this sense, each latent variable has the role of a common factor, and the manifest variables serve as manifest indicators of the common factor. The empirical content of each manifest variable is reflected directly by assigning observable events to values on the measurement scale of the variables. The measurement model contains the following:

Multivariate Casual Pathways Model

Figure 8.6, a graphical representation of the model, matches the paths and interrelationships to the variables. In this step, a model is used to establish the set of structural and measurement elements that link the diagram to the constructs of the theory. Structural equations can be used to link the constructs. Variables were assigned to the specific constructs showing which variables measure which constructs. A set of matrices is used to indicate the hypothesized constructs from the critical globalisation factors to the constructs or variables. The model has been designed to identify the manifest variables to the latent variable constructs.

Figure 8.6 Multivariate Casual Pathways Model

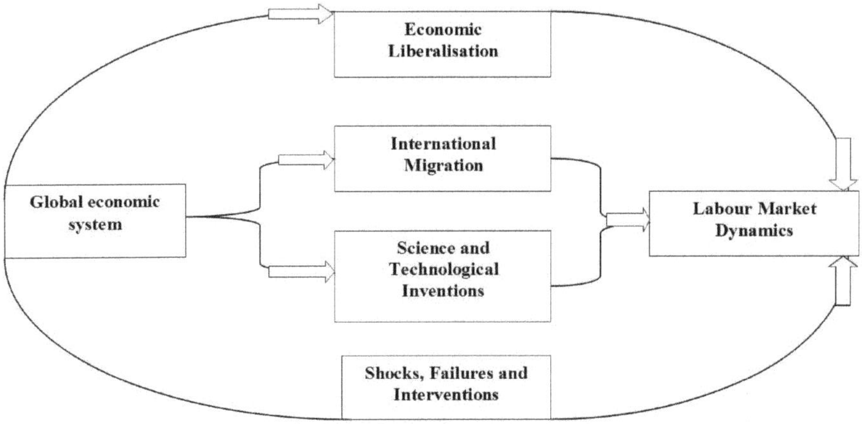

All the variables in the model are dependent variables except global economic system, which is independent variable. All dependent variables are directly connected with independent variable except labour market dynamics. Therefore, dependent variable labour market dynamics is indirectly linked with independent variable global economic system through four causal pathways. In PLS, functional equations are formatted for every causal connection. These equations take into account path coefficients and variable mean scores. It is possible to calculate the contribution of each variable toward labour market dynamics from the value of path coefficients. The model has four pathways going through it each starting from global economic system and ending with labour market dynamics, as shown in Figure 8.7.

The arrow ←→ shows that the pathways is on both sides, it means that a unit change in global economic system produces change in international migration and subsequently in labour market dynamics and vice versa.

Figure 8.7 The Four Pathways through the Causal Pathways Model

Path 1	Global Economic system	←→	EL	←→	Labour Market Dynamics
Path 2	Global Economic system	←→	IM	←→	Labour Market Dynamics
Path 3	Global Economic system	←→	STI	←→	Labour Market Dynamics
Path 4	Global Economic system	←→	SFI	←→	Labour Market Dynamics

Measurement of the Elements

The measurement of the elements is based on the Analysis of Covariance Structures. The model used matrix notation in a statistical package to set up the simultaneous equations. All structural parameters assume values that reflect the strengths of causal relationships. Specially, each structural parameter reflects the amount of change in an effect (endogenous variable) that results from a unit of change in a cause (exogenous variable or preceding endogenous variable) with all other causes of that effect held constant. A key objective of representing the model as a latent variable structural model is to do a confirmatory analysis to estimate the values of the structural parameters. The ε_i's associated with each endogenous variable are the 'disturbance terms'. Disturbance terms involve variation in an endogenous variable that is not to be attributed to the causes of that variable included explicitly, in a structural model. In the structural model, the sources of variation include (a) random shocks and/or unmeasured or omitted causes, (b) random measurement errors in the effect and the causes, where the primary concern is error in one or more of the causes, and (c) non-random measurement, such as bias in scales of measurement and method variance. The inclusion of the disturbance variation in the model makes it a probabilistic model.

Functional Relations

The causal relations in the model can be expressed as functional relations, that is, a function of an effect on one or more causes. The functional relations are asymmetric because their causal directions are unidirectional. It can be observed from the structural model that there are four types of functional relations: (a) relation between an exothermic latent variable and endothermic latent variable; (b) relation between an exothermic latent variable and manifest indicator variables; (c) relation between an endothermic latent variable to one or more endothermic variable(s); (d) relation between a latent endothermic variable with manifest indicator variables. In structural models, functional relations are analysed by using structural equations.

Structural Equations

The above four types of functional relations can be expressed as a system of equations known as functional equations. For the model, there is one endogenous variable and forty eight manifest variables, which mean that altogether there would be forty eight equations in the system of functional equations.

Empirical Support for Functional Equation

The confirmatory analysis using manifest variables may proceed only if the manifest variables are reasonably accurate representations of the constructs. The objective of such an analysis is to check whether a structural model can be confirmed. Confirmation implies that a structural model and functional equations representing the model are useful for making causal inferences to explain how variables occur (excluding purely exogenous variables). Non-confirmation implies that the structural model (functional relations and equations) are not useful in this respect. The functional relations and equations in a linear structural model may be used to drive a set of predictions regarding the observed correlations (or variance/covariance) among the manifest variables. A structural model is confirmed if the predictions regarding correlations (variance/covariance) among manifest variables are consistent with the observed (i.e. empirically derived) correlations (variance/covariance) among manifest variables. Non-confirmation is implied if predictions and observed correlations (variances/covariances) are inconsistent.

Confirmation of predictions implies support for the structural model represented by the functional relations as equations. Non-confirmation of predictions implies that one or more components of structural model (functional relations and equations) is (are) false, in which case it is concluded that the structural model proposed originally is invalid. Predictions regarding correlations (variances/covariances) among manifest variables and confirmation/non-confirmation of these predictions can be addressed empirically by testing predictions regarding the magnitudes of estimates of structural parameters.

Solutions and Estimates of Structural Parameters

Structural equation modeling (SEM) provides a means by which relationships can be tested. The purpose of the approach is to estimate the strength of the causal connections among the latent variables and to test the goodness of fit of the structural model. To estimate the strength of these causal connections, it is necessary for each of the latent variables to be operational in terms of manifest variables (measurement items). In reality, the manifest variables are measured by using measurement items, such as questionnaires; also, they serve as indicators of the latent variable. A measurement instrument is then developed and used to obtain scores from respondents on a variety of attributes that provide an empirical content to the model's constructs.

The importance of meeting these conditions depends on the estimation methods used. Some estimation methods can adjust for the violation of some of these assumptions. In structural models with latent variables, we make the assumptions that the distribution of the manifest variables is a function of their variance/covariance matrix. By making this assumption, it is possible to determine the non-fixed parameters of the model. The estimated and fixed structural parameters of a structural equation model determine a hypothetical variance/covariance (correlation) matrix for the manifest variables (Y_o) under the assumption that the model is valid. The structural parameters y and α computed are actually unstandardarised regression coefficients of the structural equations. In the PLS method, the structural parameters of structural equation linking latent variables and manifest variables are called structural weights.

Measurement Software

The statistical reasoning behind model is relatively complex, but the user will not need to have any particular mathematical expertise, although some basic skills and statistical knowledge will help. To support the implementation of model, there are many user-friendly statistical software products such as SPSS/AMOS, LISREL, EQS, SEPATH, and so on, that calculate the estimates of the parameters of structural equation models, all the associated indices and produces some standard graphics. It is based on a structural equation modelling technique which combines aspects of multiple regression and factor analysis to estimate simultaneously a series of interrelated dependence relationships. The software essentially uses the Partial Least Squares (PLS) method in the simultaneous estimation of the weights of the constructs of the model, calculates these weights in a way that maximises the goodness of fit of the model and thus has the ability to explain labour market dynamics as the ultimate endogenous variable. It is not necessary to have any particular expertise to work with the software package. Anyone who feels comfortable working with Windows usual software programs will soon become familiar with this package. The software generates several types of outputs: outer coefficients (γ, a); inner coefficients (γ, a); Pearson correlation coefficient square (inner r^2); Pearson correlation coefficient (inner r) and Cronbach coefficient (α).

Outer Coefficients (Structural Weights)

The outer coefficients are the unstandardized structural weights of manifest indicator variables. Structural weights must have values significantly different from zero for a confirmation or non-confirmation of a model. Specially, each structural weight reflects the amount of change in an effect (endogenous variable) the results from a unit of change in a cause (exogenous variable or endogenous variable), with all other causes of that effect held constant.

Inner Coefficient (Structural Parameter of latent variables)

Structural parameters are the coefficients of functional equations linking latent variables. Structural parameters must have values significantly different from zero for confirmation or non-confirmation of the model. These values reflect the strengths of causal relationships. Specifically, each structural parameter reflects the amount of change in an effect (endogenous variable) that results from a unit of change in a cause (exogenous variable or preceding endogenous variable), with all other causes of that effect held constant.

Variability Analysis

The variability analysis has been undertaken by taking into using: (a) Standard Deviation: The standard deviation is the standard error of sample estimate of a structural parameter associated with a causal connection. It provides information on the spread of the parameter estimate from the mean.

Coefficients

The t-coefficient of a structural parameter is the confidence interval around the estimate of the structural parameter. By using the standard error of the parameter, if the confidence intervals constructed around the structural parameter differ significantly from zero, then it can be concluded that there exists a causal connection between the variables in question.

Causality Analysis

The causality analysis is done with the help of: *(a) Correlation Matrix (γij):* This is the Pearson correlation, r, matrix among all the exogenous and endogenous variables in the model. Values in the matrix corresponding to latent variables that have cause and effect relationship provide additional indication of strength of their relationship. (b) *Coefficient of Determination (r2):* The coefficient of determination (r2) represents the proportion of regression sum of squares corresponding to latent variables. The regression model explains the proportion of the total variation due to the cause-variable and the proportion due to randomness and other variables. (c) *Pearson Correlation Coefficient (r):* Pearson correlation coefficient r is the correlation of latent variables that have causal connections. The closer this value is to ±1, the stronger is the relationship between the variables in both directions.

Cronbach Alpha (Coefficient α)

Coefficient α value provides an indicator of internal consistency of latent variables that are being empirically reflected by manifest variables. It is calculated using variance of individual questions and covariance between items. The formula is:

$$\alpha = \frac{k}{k-1}\left\{1 - \frac{\Sigma\sigma_i^2}{\Sigma\sigma_i^2 + 2\Sigma\,\Sigma\sigma_{ij}^2}\right\}$$

Where, k = the number of items in the scale, σ_i^2 = the variance of item i, and σ_{ij} = the covariance of the items i and j. Computing alpha divides total variance into signal and noise components. In other words, the total variance that is equal to the signal is equal to alpha. The second term in brackets represents the noise in the model. A coefficient α value of more than 0.7 indicated the consistency of the questions as appropriate to the reliability of the measurement scale.

The Labour Market Dynamics Derived

The model uses a ten-step scale in order to provide reliable data. All these variables are scored based on the average score on their respective data. This average is useful when analysing how well labour market is performing in a country. Labour market dynamics are not the total average of all the variables, the dynamics are based on how well or badly all other dimensions of globalisation are performing. The labour market dynamics are dependent on how the variables correlate and thereby produce certain outcomes.

Knowing the relationship between critical globalisation forces and labour market dynamics is useful in examining the strength of these forces to determine which one needs to be controlled by policy options and by how much, and in what ways in order to improve labour market dynamics. The labour market matrix is also influenced by the structural weights and the scores of manifest variables that are linked to it as specified by the mathematical formula as follows:

$$\text{LMD} = \left[\frac{\sum_{i=1}^{n} w_i x_i - \sum_{i=1}^{n} w_i}{(N-1)\sum_{i=1}^{n} w_i} \right] \times 100$$

Where N = number of points on the scale; x_i = manifest variables for each latent variable; and w_i = outer coefficients. A step-by-step procedure for analyzing the dynamics of labour market is discussed in Chopra and Kanji (2011).

Concluding Remarks

The labour markets suffer from a number of frictions and problems such as mismatch between the worker and employer, imperfect and asymmetric information, market imperfections, global and local shocks, coordination, collective action, intermediation and other failures, labour replacing technological inventions, wage disparities, outsourcing or offshoring, negative consequences of free trade, challenges and effects of immigration on wages, and so on. Considering this, this present chapter takes into consideration a whole range of factors and variables, both latent and manifest, and develops a theoretical framework to analyse their simultaneous effects on outcomes of labour market in a global economy. In order to achieve this aim, it uses PLS path modelling as a way to build casual pathways for globalisation forces and to estimate the relationships between them. The procedure is free from the danger of tendency to overestimate or underestimate outer or inner relationships. Many studies have concluded that the estimates so obtained are robust since when the number of observed variables and sample size increase, the quality of the PLS path modelling estimates increases. The present chapter develops a model encompassing four interlinked multivariate models of labour market dynamics. After specifying the model, it needs to be identified, estimated, tested and manipulated. The relationships among the variables (both measured and latent) are shown in the measurement model.

Only the relationships between the latent variables are shown in the structural model. One important benefit of using latent variables is that they are free of random error. The error associated with the latent variables is statistically estimated and removed in the structural equation modelling analysis. Only a common variance remains. Each construct of globalisation is operational using collected data and the entire system is estimated using PLS method. This modelling methodology offers a number of advantages over other measures. First, the use of collected data for each construct increases the provision of the estimate of labour market dynamics. Second, the collected qualitative and quantitative data are converted and measured on a ten-point scale in order to enhance reliability. Third, the labour market dynamics are constructed by weighting the individual items such that the resulting matrix has a maximum correlation with critical globalisation forces. Last but not the least, the identification and assessment of various critical forces provide a feasible means for strategically integrating various concepts and captures, validates and distributes new knowledge fast enough to change strategic direction of labour market policy makers and resource allocation to manage labour market dynamics in a global turbulent environment.

References

Adelman, Irma (1995). "The long term impact of economic development in developed countries on developing countries since 1820", *Evolutionary Economics*, 5, 189-208.

Acemoglu, Daron (2002). "Technical change, inequality and the labour market", *Journal of Economic Literature,* (XL), 7-72.

Allen, Jim and Rolf van der Velden (2001). "Educational mismatches versus skill mismatches: Effects on wages, job satisfaction, and on-the-job search", *Oxford Economic Papers,* 53 (3), 434-452.

Autor, David H. (2009). *Studies in Labour Market Intermediation*, Chicago: The University of Chicago Press.

Autor, David H., Frank Levy and Richard J. Murnane (2003). "The skill content of recent technological change: An empirical exploration", *The Quarterly Journal of Economics* 4, 1280 – 1333.

Bauer, Thomas K. (2000). "Educational mismatch and wages: A panel analysis", *Economics of Education Review,* 21, 221–229.

Bernhardt, Annette, Martina Morris, and Mark S. Handcock (1995). "Women's gains or men's losses? A closer look at the shrinking gender gap in earnings", *American Journal of Sociology* 101, 302–28.

Bernstein, J. R. and Weinstein, D. E. (2002). "Do endowments predict the location of production?: Evidence from national and international data", *Journal of International Economics*, 56 (1), 55–76.

Blanchard, O.J. and Summers, L.H. (1987). *Hysteresis and the European Unemployment Problem*. NBER Working Paper No. 1950.

Blau, D.M. and Shvydko, T. (2007). "Labor market rigidities and the employment behavior of older workers", IZA DP No. 2996, http://ftp.iza.org/dp2996.pdf.

Cahuc, Pierre and André Zylberberg (2004). *Labor Economics*, Cambridge Massachusetts: The MIT Press.

Card, David and John E. DiNardo (2002). "Skill-biased technological change and rising wage inequality: Some problems and puzzles", *Journal of Labor Economics,* 20 (4), 733-783.

Chandra, N. (2007). *Bound Together*: *How Traders, Preachers, Adventurers, and Warriors Shaped Globalisation*, Yale University Press.

Chopra, Parvesh K. (2011). "A Kanji-Chopra Model of Global Food Crisis", *Journal of Human Development*, 3 (2), 197-230.

Chopra, Parvesh K. (2012). *On Measuring Global Food Crisis: A Multivariate Approach,* Leeds: Wisdom House Publications.

Chopra, Parvesh K. (2015). "Country risk: A theoretical and empirical analysis with special reference to Northern African economies", *Economia Internazionale*, 68(1), 81-137.

Chopra, Parvesh K. and Kanji, Gopal K. (2010). "On measuring country risk: A new system modeling approach", *Economia Internazionale*, 63(4), 479-515.

Chopra, Parvesh K. and Kanji, Gopal K. (2011). "On the science of management with measurement", *Total Quality Management & Business Excellence*, 22(1), 63-81.

Cooper, R. and John, A. (1988). "Coordinating coordination failures in Keynesian models", *Quarterly Journal of Economics*, 103, 441-63.

Das, Dilip K. (2004), *The Economic Dimensions of Globalisation*, New York: Palgrave Macmillan.

Deardorff, Alan and Robert M. Stern, eds. (1994). *The Stolper-Samuelson Theorem: A Golden Jubillee*. Ann Arbor: University of Michigan Press.

DiNardo, John E. and Rischke, J. (1997). "The returns to computer use revisited: Have pencils changed the wage structure too?", *The Quarterly Journal of Economics*, 112 (1), 291-303.

Ederveen, S., Nahuis, R. and Parikh, A. (2007). "Labour mobility and regional disparities: The role of female labour market participation", Utrecht School of Economics, Tjalling C. Koopmans Research Institute, *Discussion Paper Series*, 05-31.

Feenstra, R. (ed.) (1988). *Empirical Methods for International Trade*, Cambridge, MA: MIT Press.

Fertig, M. (2003). "The impact of economic integration on employment – AN assessment in the context of EU Enlargement", *IZA Discussion Paper Series*, 919.

Goos, M. and Manning, A. (2003). *Lousy and Lovely Jobs: the Rising Polarization of Work in Britain*, Centre for Economic Performance, London School of Economics and Political Science.
http://eprints.lse.ac.uk/20002/1/Lousy_and_Lovely_Jobs_the_Rising_Polarization_of_Work_in_Britain.pdf.

Greenaway, D. and Nelson, D. (2000). "The assessment: Globalisation and labour-market adjustment", *Oxford Review of Economic Policy*, 16 (3), 1-11.

Haskel, J.E. and Slaughter, M.J. (1998). "Does the sector bias of skill-based technical change explain changing wage inequality?", NBER Working Paper 6565, National Bureau of Economic Research.

Hodgson, Geoffrey M. (2006). "What are institutions", *Journal of Economic Issues*, XL (1), 1-25.

James, I.R., Mulaik, S.A. and Brett, J.M. (1982). *Causal Analysis: Assumptions, Models and Data*, Beverly Hills, CA: Sage Publications.

Jones, Ronald W. (2000). *Globalisation and the Theory of Input Trade*. Cambridge: MIT Press.

Jubilee. Ann Arbor: University of Michigan Press.

Kanji, Gopal K. and Chopra, Parvesh K. (2007), "Poverty as a system: Human contestability approach to poverty measurement", *Journal of Applied Statistics*, 54 (9), 1135-1158.

Kotz, D. M. (2002). "Globalisation and neo-liberalism", *Rethinking Marxism*, 12(2), 64-79.

Layard, R., Nickell, S.J. and Jackman, R. (1991). *Unemployment: Macroeconomic Performance and the Labour Market*, Oxford University Press.

Leamer, Edward E. (1980). "The Leontief Paradox, Reconsidered". *Journal of Political Economy*, 88 (3), 332–349

Leamer, Edward E. (1995). The Heckscher-Ohlin *Model in Theory and Practice. Princeton Studies in International Finance* 77. Princeton, NJ: Princeton University Press.

Lerner, Abba (1952). "Factor Prices and International Trade", *Economica*, N.S., 19 (73), 1–15.

Lindbeck, A. and Snower, D.J. (1984). "Involuntary Unemployment as an Insider-Outsider Dilemma,Seminar Paper No. 39, Institute for International Economic Studies, University of Stockholm, Sweden.

Lindbeck, A. and Snower, D.J. (1988). *The Insider-Outsider Theory of Employment and Unemployment*, MIT Press, Cambridge, Massachusetts.

Machin, S. (2004). "Skill-biased technical change and educational outcomes", In: Johnes, Geraint and Jill Johnes (eds.), *International Handbook on the Economics of Education*, Cheltenham: Edward Elgar.

Macnicol, J. (1987). "In pursuit of the underclass", *Journal of Social Policy*, 16(3), 293-318.

Mandelman, F.S. and Zanetti, F.(2008). "Technology shocks, employment and labour market frictions", No 390, *Bank of England working papers* from Bank of England. http://www.bankofengland.co.uk/publications/workingpapers/wp390.pdf.

Mankiw, N.G. and Romer, D. (1997). New *Keynesian Economics: Coordination Failures and Real Rigidities*, Cambridge, Massachusetts: MIT Press.

Manning, A. (1992). "Multiple equilibria in the British labour market", *European Economic Review*, 36, 1333-65.

Mclaughlin, E. (1994). "Flexibility or polarisation?", In: M.WHITE (ed.) *Unemployment and Public Policy in a Changing Labour Market,* London: Policy Studies Institute.

Mortensen, D.T. and Pissarides, C.A. (1999). "Unemployment responses to 'Skill-biased' technology shocks: The role of labour market policy", *The Economic Journal*, 109(455), 242-265.

Nabli, M.K. and Nugent, J.B. (1989). "The new institutional economics and its applicability to development", *World Development*, 17(9), 1333-1347.

Namboodiri, N.K., Carter, I.F., and Blalock, H.M. (1975). *Applied Multivariate Analysis and experimental Designs*, New York: McGrow-Hill.

Neary, J. Peter (2004). "The Stolper-Samuelson theorem", In: J.J. McCusker et al. (eds.), *Encyclopedia of World Trade Since 1450,* New York: Macmillan Reference.

Nickell, S. (1997). "Unemployment and labour market rigidities: Europe versus North America", *Journal of Economic Perspectives*, 11 (3), 55-74.

Nunziata, L. (2002). "Unemployment, labour market institutions and shocks", Nuffield College Working Papers in Economics,

Ohlin, B. (1933). *Interregional and International Trade*, Cambridge, MA: Harvard University Press.

Olson, M. (1965). *The Logic of Collective Action: Public Goods and the Theory of Groups*, Harvard University Press.

Pieroni, L. and Pompei, F. (2008). "Evaluating innovation and labour market relationships: the case of Italy", *Cambridge Journal of Economics*, 32 (2), 325.

Rybczynski, T. M. (1955). "Factor endowment and relative commodity prices", *Economica*, 22 (88), 336–341.

Samuelson, P. A. (1948). "International trade and the equalisation of factor prices", *Economic Journal*, June, 163-184.

Stiglitz, J. (2002). *Globalisation and its Discontents*, New York: W. W. Norton.

Stiglitz, J. (2006). *Making Globalisation Work*, New York: W. W. Norton.

Stolper, W. F.; Samuelson, Paul A. (1941). "Protection and real wages", *The Review of Economic Studies. Oxford Journals*. 9 (1), 58–73.

Wiggins, S. and Davis, J. (2006). "Economic institutions", IPPG Briefing Paper No. Three, July, www.assets.publishing.services.gov.uk

Wood, A. (1998). "Globalisation and the rise of labour market inequalities", *The Economic Journal*, 108(450), 1463-1482.

White, M. R. M. (ed.) (1994). *Unemployment, Public Policy and the Changing Labour Market*. London: Policy Studies Institute.

Chapter Nine

Malaysia's Labour Market: Globalisation and Its Challenges

Shankaran Nambiar

Introduction

Malaysia's labour market faces new challenges following the economy's transformation from one that is agricultural to an export-oriented manufacturing economy. Indeed, now the Malaysian economy aspires to be services-driven. The demand for labour in Malaysia at a time when the agriculture sector was predominant is different from the nature of labour that is demanded now (Inagami, 1998 and Kuruvilla, 1998). The challenges that the labour market faces has changed with a change in the structure of the economy. There is a shift in production methods with the transformation of the economy. Labour-intensive production methods are no longer desirable or optimal. Besides, as a matter of policy the government seeks to make Malaysia a knowledge-economy. These changes have had repercussions on the labour market.

On the external front, globalisation has exerted its pressures. The changing nature of the economies in the region adds a further source of pressure on the supply of labour. Malaysia used to be a favoured destination for foreign direct investment (FDI) because of its labour endowments: labour was cheap, abundant and pliant. These characteristics encouraged foreign investors to base their factories in Malaysia. In present times, labour of this nature is more cheaply available in Vietnam, China and Indonesia. Malaysia cannot count on cheap labour costs as a source of its comparative advantage.

Globalisation means that multinational corporations (MNCs) seek economies with the attributes that are most favourable to their investments. At one end of the favoured spectrum are those countries that offer low-cost labour; at the other end of the spectrum, MNCs prefer economies where there is an abundant supply of skilled labour that can produce technologically intensive, high value-added goods. Malaysia's labour force does not quite fit the bill, since its labour force is neither cheap, nor does it have an abundant supply of highly skilled labour. Malaysia has to change the character of its labour force to fit the demands of the changing global landscape. The labour force that can drive Malaysia to a higher level of development will have to be knowledge-based, creative and skilled. It is these features that the workforce has to develop, and thus reach developed country status. However, the labour force has certain constraints. Most importantly, it does not have an adequate supply of skilled labour.

Macroeconomic Background

As Malaysia integrates itself more firmly in the global economic structure, two features emerge in regard to the Malaysian economy. First, although Malaysia's economy is closely linked to the global economy, it has developed a measure of economic resilience that enables it to withstand global fluctuations. Second, because of its integration with the global economy, the Malaysian economy has been able to mature and transform itself accordingly, moving from an agricultural economy to one that is services-driven.

Malaysia has managed to maintain high growth rates over the last two decades. In the decade after 1990, Malaysia's annual growth rate was close to ten per cent; and it is only in 1998, following the Asian financial and economic crisis, that growth rates dropped. In fact, Malaysia recovered rapidly from the effects of the crisis, and the economy rebounded. In 1999, the growth rate was six per cent, and it rose to 8.9 per cent the following year. It was in the years stretching 2002 to 2008, the Malaysian growth rate was more sedate, averaging about six per cent.

The Malaysian has been resilient to global economic disruptions. The economic fluctuations in Malaysia mirror fluctuations in the global economy. There has been a good understanding of global requirements and the economic transformation in Malaysia has been well poised to take advantage of these changes. Although Malaysia was a predominantly agricultural economy soon after its independence in 1957, and remained so for the next 20 years, this changed with Malaysia's judicious use of industrial policy. From the late 1970s, and particularly from the 1980s, there was a shift to the industrial sector.

Presently, the services sector contributes most to gross domestic product (GDP). The services sector contributes close to 57 per cent of GDP. This is followed in importance by the manufacturing sector, which accounts for about 30 per cent of GDP. The agriculture sector, which used to drive the growth of the economy, now accounts for about eight per cent of GDP. Agriculture is followed in importance by mining and quarrying (six per cent). The construction sector is largely domestically driven, in terms of the demand for its output, and has a sectoral share of about three per cent.

The effect of globalisation has much relevance to the Malaysian economy in several ways. First, being an open, export-oriented economy, Malaysia is affected by global fluctuations. This is immediately clear in the case of exports from the electrical and electronics sector, which is largely an export-oriented sector. Fluctuations of demand in this sector have a direct effect on retrenchments in this sector of the economy in Malaysia. At a broader level, the economic crises that affect the global economy are relatively well-contained by Malaysian authorities.

The relative importance of the different sectors in contributing to the total GDP has implications on the characteristics of the labour market, as we shall see later. But the relative importance of the economic sectors has some relationship with the export structure of the economy. The manufacturing sector contributed as much as 82 per cent to total exports in the period spanning 2000 to 2003. However, since 2004, the manufacturing sector dropped in its contribution to exports from Malaysia. In 2009, this sector contributed 70 per cent of total exports. Exports from the agriculture sector have remained at about nine per cent in recent years. These exports are mostly due to palm oil. In relative terms, from about 2004, the exports from the manufacturing sector have been declining.

As the evidence indicates, the services sector is an important component of GDP, but it is not a substantial contributor to exports from Malaysia. Clearly, services are largely meant for domestic consumption rather than for exports. While the manufacturing sector has been declining in its performance, it still remains a significant contributor to GDP and also to the export structure of the economy. But there is evidence that the services sector is increasingly becoming a component that enters into exports as a source of growth. As for agriculture, it has been declining over the long term, in terms of its contribution to GDP, but its share as a component of total exports is not negligible since it amounts to about nine per cent of exports.

The contribution of the various sectors to GDP has some impact on the employment structure of the economy. This will throw clearer light on the structure of employment and it will also help evaluate the incidence of employment patterns on the different sectors. By examining the pattern of employment in the different sectors, the issue that we turn to in the next section, it will be possible to discuss the relationship between employment and its contribution to the economy.

Employment Trends

Through the years, as the Malaysian economy has increasingly integrated itself with the global economy, the structure of the economy has changed and with it the patterns of employment. As noted in the previous section, agriculture has ceased to be an important contributor to the economy's GDP. With increasing globalisation, agriculture which used to be the mainstay of the economy has ceased to be so. The manufacturing and services sectors are now more important as contributors to the economic growth and sources of employment.

In 1995, the services sector accounted for about 47.7 per cent of total employment and the manufacturing sector contributed to 23.3 per cent. In the same year, employment in agriculture contributed to 20 per cent of employment. As these figures indicate, the services sector was the most important source of employment in the economy, followed by the manufacturing and agriculture sectors. In 1995, although agriculture was not the main source of employment, it was a significant source of employment.

However, the profile of employment has been changing over time. The sectoral demand for labour has been shifting, with the agriculture sector witnessing a sharp decline in being a source of employment. The shift in the employment pattern has been strongly in favour of the services sector, and this is particularly pronounced in more recent years. Agriculture as a source of demand for labour has decreased to 13.5 per cent. The services sector, however, has recorded an increase in employment in 2009 that is 11.8 per cent higher than it was in 1995. The construction sector accounts for a slightly higher percentage of employment for the same reference years, increasing marginally by about one per cent since 1995. Thus, while the services sector has assumed more importance, this has been at the cost of employment in agriculture and manufacturing. Employment in mining has remained fairly constant over the years.

It is not surprising that employment in agriculture has been declining, since government policy has not been targeted to the agriculture sector. In fact, it is only palm oil that has been a major export commodity. And palm oil plantations have faced severe labour shortages. The fact that manufacturing is not as attractive a source of employment as it used to be is cause for concern for several reasons. First, Malaysia is an export-oriented economy, and this sector may, reasonably, be expected to be a labour absorbing sector. Second, the manufacturing sector as a driver of GDP is shrinking. This by itself is not a cause for concern because as countries develop there is a tendency for their services' sectors to grow. But in the case of Malaysia, which depends on export-led growth, rather than domestically driven growth, it is a phenomenon that has special importance. Nevertheless, the reduction in employment that originates from the manufacturing sector is an indication that the sector is becoming less labour intensive.

The pattern of employment within the manufacturing sector does not show any major shifts in recent years. The non-resource based component continues to dominate over resource-based activities in generating employment. But the composition of employment due to the earlier has declined, albeit slightly. The electronics and electrical (E&E) sector is significant for the employment it creates, in that it accounted for 55 per cent of employment in manufacturing in 1996, declining somewhat to 52 per cent in 2005. Nevertheless, even in recent years the manufacturing sector constitutes an important source of demand for labour. There has been an increase in employment within the chemicals sub-sector. Within the resourced-based component, wood products and furniture are most important, and they have employed 11.9 per cent of labour, moving up from 10.7 per cent in 1996. Employment in textiles, which used to be important activity in the resource-based manufacturing component of manufacturing, has declined, and that is line with the nature of the industry which is labour-intensive. Malaysia does not have the comparative advantage that Bangladesh or China have since Malaysia no longer possesses the characteristic of a low-wage economy, and so it is not a thriving industry.

Globalisation has clearly altered the patterns of employment in Malaysia. Agriculture was the dominant economic activity in Malaysia at the time of its independence in 1957. However, with the increasing interest to take advantage of global markets using what was then Malaysia's comparative advantage in cheap labour, there was a shift in importance to the manufacturing sector. Demand for labour was largely generated by the export-oriented manufacturing sector in the 1970s to 1980s. To be more specific, the electrical and electronics sub-sector contributed significantly to employment generation, then, and, indeed, does so even now. Given the fact that Malaysia is a small, open, trade-oriented economy, it is only natural that there was a winding-down of the agriculture sector, resulting in changes in employment patterns within this sector. An over-riding phenomenon in this sector has been the employment of migrant labour since local labour has tended to shun employment in agriculture.

Malaysia has taken advantage of trade to drive its growth. Accordingly a labour shortage situation has emerged, giving rise to various strategies that have been employed to cope with the excess demand for labour (Ducanes and Abella, 2008). As Malaysia has become more industrialised, the use of capital has increased. This has taken place at a rapid pace. The investment in capital can be decomposed into the capital formation by the public and private sectors. In the early 1990s, the contribution to gross fixed capital formation (GFCF) by the private sector far outstripped that of the public sector. This trend continued till the mid-1990s, after which the private sector's investment in gross fixed capital formation declined. It was not till 2002 that the private sector played a more active role in increasing GFCF. In more recent times the private sector's participation in GFCF has, once again, declined. However, the public sector's participation has consistently been on the uptrend.

Another response to the excess demand for labour has been the increasing labour force participation among almost all age groups. The only exception to this is with those in the 15-19 age group, where the decline in participation is noticeable. With those in the 20-24 year age group, the rate of increase in participation is not encouraging either. Otherwise, there is an uptrend among all other age groups, and this applies for those from 20 to 59. Even the 60-64 age group demonstrates a mild increase in participation.

However, the gender details regarding participation in the workforce are interesting. Quite unexpectedly, male participation in the labour force has been steadily declining since the early 1990s. In 1996, almost 85 per cent of the labour force was made up of males, but in 2010 it came down to 79 per cent. This is not the case with female participation, which has been above male participation since 1999. It is certainly encouraging to note that there is more female participation in the labour force. It is indicative of the changing social norms in Malaysia; but from an economic point of view, it indicates how the level of employment has been extended by including women into the workforce.

Considering Malaysia's dependence on FDI to drive growth, it is certainly necessary to examine trends relating to FDI flows. Inward FDI flows declined considerably after the 1997 financial and economic crisis, and it was not until 2002 that the figures improved. FDI is important to the economy because it contributes to the growth of capital in the economy. It is also crucial because of the demand for labour that it generates. In this regard, it is a matter of concern that outward FDI flows exceed that of inward flows, and this pattern is on the increase. With increasing outward investment flows, not only will the economy be deprived of opportunities that give rise to labour creation, but capital formation will also be stifled.

There are two serious issues that confront the Malaysian labour market as it continues to participate in the global economy. First, the labour intensive economic activities in Malaysia do not pay sufficient wages to attract domestic workers. This has led to a continued and increasing inflow of migrant workers. Second, although Malaysia wishes to move up the value chain it is not able to supply the market with sufficient numbers of highly skilled workers. These are the two central issues that constrain the labour market in Malaysia, and the gains of globalisation can be enjoyed only if these restrictions are relaxed.

Globalisation and Labour Market Constraints

A serious constraint to the development of skilled labour in Malaysia arises from the lack of an adequate allocation of resources for research and development (R&D) (see Fleming and Soborg, 2010). Malaysia's investment in R&D is not encouraging when compared with other countries in the region. Malaysia's GERD is a mere 0.6 per cent, and it has remained stagnant in the last few years. By comparison, Singapore has a GERD that exceeds two per cent. India, which has a lower per capita GDP, has a higher GERD. If Malaysia seeks to reach the ranks of the developed economies, it must be more willing to invest in R&D. The progression to a knowledge-based economy will be restricted until Malaysia is able to engage in R&D.

The number of researchers in R&D is very low in Malaysia as compared to Singapore. Singapore has a pool of researchers that out-stretches its population. In fact, Singapore's number of researchers as a proportion of its population is greater than Japan's, Korea's, and definitely that of the United States. While the US had about 4,663 researchers per million people, Japan had 5,568 researchers and Korea had 4,186 researchers per million people.

The low number of researchers in Malaysia is aggravated by the low number of technicians in R&D. Technicians in R&D are required to possess sound technical knowledge and experience in engineering, physical and life sciences (technicians). It is expected that R&D technicians will participated in R&D, but under the supervision of researchers. This class of knowledge workers are expected to support the researchers, and a low figure points to the fact that the researchers will not be sufficiently assisted by the requisite technicians.

Publication in scientific and technical journals can be taken as summary indicator that captures output in science and technology knowledge-creation. The US has the highest achievement for the publication of scientific and technical journal articles. Of the countries that have been selected for comparison, in recent years China has performed creditably. China has improved tremendously well on its achievement in this indicator, as compared with its performance in the early 1990s. Japan's publication record is currently not as high as China's, and, indeed, it has not increased as substantially as China has. Malaysia's achievement is low, and it is poor in comparison to that shown by Singapore and Thailand.

Malaysia's low record of publications in scientific and technology journals is consistent with its performance in other related indicators. Since expenditure in R&D is low, and combined with the lack of research expertise as well as poor support from research technicians, outcomes such as publication in scientific and technological journals will necessarily be poor. Another concomitant outcome of research expertise and R&D capacity and expenditure is the number of trademark applications. Although, Malaysia performance on journal publication is no impressive, it has achieved satisfactory outcomes on trademark applications. Malaysia has done well as compared to Singapore and Korea on this criterion. Trademark applications offer the possibility of research that has commercial value. In that respect, the level of trademark applications is an indication of the preparedness of residents to produce research that has commercial value in the market. While journal publications do not necessarily have value in the market, trademark applications are specifically meant to be commercially viable. There is a positive aspect to this because Malaysia's poor performance in journal publication is somewhat mitigated by its encouraging record in trademark applications. However, although Malaysia has shown good progress in trademark applications, China's is simply astounding.

There is undoubtedly a shortage of skilled labour. This places Malaysia at a disadvantage since Malaysia cannot take advantage of global industrial developments and be a hub for value-added production. The bulk of the migrant labour inflow into the country is prompted by unskilled labour. The sustained rates of growth in the mid-1970s necessitated the inflow of migrant labour, which was drawn to support the agricultural sector. Malaysia, in this phase, was undergoing rapid industrialisation, as a consequence of which there was a net inflow of labour into the industrial areas of the country. The movement of domestic labour to urban areas created a situation of excess demand for labour in the agriculture sector. This was met with the supply of migrant labour, with the majority of workers who came into the country during this period being from Indonesia. They were brought into the country on an informal basis and employed in the agricultural sector to fill the gap that arose due to the domestic movement of labour.

Indonesia was a logical choice for foreign labour at that time because of geographical proximity, besides sharing a similar religious and cultural background. These factors have, perhaps, laid the setting for continued authorised and unauthorised labour inflows. The bulk of foreign workers may have been Indonesian, but there were also workers from Thailand and the Philippines. The influx, and accommodation, of illegal migrant workers has its origins during this period. It was estimated that there were almost one million foreign workers in the country during this period, most of whom were in the plantation and construction sectors. Official sources, on the other hand, note that a small proportion of these workers held valid documents. For instance, in 1985 only about 3,500 foreigners were registered as workers in the country.

There was a decline in commodity prices (principally palm oil and rubber) in 1985, leading to a recession. The recovery was swift, and in 1988 growth rates were high, reaching almost 8 per cent. By the early 1990s there was, again, a situation of labour shortage. This led to an excess demand for skilled and unskilled labour, pushing wages of local labour up. In 1994, there were about 640,000 registered migrant workers; this number rose to about 745,000 in 1996. The number of legal migrant workers sky-rocketed to about 1.5 million in 1997, only to drop to 1.2 million the following year. Once the full impact of the East Asian financial and economic crisis was felt, the need for migrant workers declined, sliding to about 900,000 workers in 1999, and settling at about 630,000 migrant workers by the year 2000. The number of illegal migrant workers in 1997 was put at one million by the Ministry of Home Affairs implying that the economy was home to as many as 2.5 million workers in that year alone, constituting close to one-third of the total labour force requirements of the country. Once again, the bulk of the foreign workers were employed in the plantation and construction sectors.

Following the 1997 crisis, the economy faced a slowdown and that helped to moderate the demand for unskilled migrant workers. The GDP sank to -6.7 per cent as a result of the recession and the unemployment rose to 3.9 per cent. While an economy that has unemployment rate that is within the boundary of four per cent is often considered to be in full employment, in the Malaysian context, given the previously high levels of growth that had been achieved and the excess demand for labour that had come to be expected, an unemployment rate of 3.9 per cent was perceived as being high. The total number of retrenchments that workers had to face because of the crisis was unprecedented. A total of 83,865 workers were retrenched in 1998, most of whom (88 per cent) were local workers. This led to adjustments in government policies on migrant labour and a stricter enforcement of laws to curb the illegal entry of migrant workers, particularly from Indonesia. There was a turn-around in policies and efforts to restrict the inflow of foreign workers were instituted.

The number of foreign workers has been increasing tremendously over the years, and in spite of the bans on them the number has been steadily rising. In the early 1980s, there were about 136,000 foreign workers, but this number swung up to almost 1 million in 2000. The proportion of foreign labour was estimated to be about 10 per cent of the total labour force in 2004. As at July 2004, it was reported that there were about 1.5 million migrant workers. In the following year (at the end of May, 2005) official sources report an increase to 1.6 million that, again, rose in 2006 (1.8 million) and inched up yet again by the end of May, 2007 to 1.9 million. Presently, there are about four million migrant workers in Malaysia. This is a huge figure, considering that the labour force in Malaysia is about 12.5 million. It is estimated that there are presently around two million illegal workers in Malaysia, close to 70 per cent of whom are of Indonesian origin.

Most of the migrant workers are employed in the agriculture sector, specifically in the plantations. By July 2004, there were 335,200 foreign workers in agriculture as compared to 115,800 in 1990. These figures tend to be deceptive in the sense that although the absolute numbers have more than number, the share of foreign workers in the total employment in the sector has been declining. In 1990, foreign workers constituted almost 48 per cent of the total labour in this sector, but dwindled down to roughly 17 per cent in 2003, and accounted for 24.7 per cent in July 2004.

The sector that now employs most of migrant labour is the manufacturing sector, where 30.5 per cent of the workers are foreigners. The share of foreign workers was about 10 per cent in 1990 and more than doubled in 1995 (24.1 per cent), moving up to its present value by 2001 (31.5 per cent). The construction sector, too, has come to employ a higher percentage of foreign workers, shifting from about 10.4 per cent in 1990 to 23.6 per cent in 2003. The mining and services sector show are different trend in the composition of migrant workers. The share of migrant workers is declining in the services sector, slipping from 31.3 per cent in 1990 to 25.0 per cent in 2004. On the other hand, mining has little need to foreign workers who account for less than one per cent of the labour force. This is hardly surprising since mining, with the closure of tin mining, is not a substantial economic activity in the country.

The profile of foreign workers corresponds to the changing pattern of Malaysia's economic development. In the early 1970s, the booming agriculture sector necessitated the inflow of migrant labour, and came to take up almost half the labour force employed in that sector. With the winding down of agriculture and the rising importance of manufacturing, the phenomenon of domestic rural-urban migration took place and the sum total of these factors pressed for more foreign workers in the unskilled sections of the sector, that, anyway, was labour-intensive. Indonesian workers with no formal education quite easily filled this gap since domestic labour was more attracted to working in the urban-based manufacturing sector. These factors triggered the inflow of foreign labour from Indonesia. Generally, there has been a situation of policy neglect over the presence of illegal migrant workers and, aside from occasional official outbursts, the inflow of migrant labour has not been effectively stemmed, something that encourages the continued presence of undocumented labour in this sector.

Nonetheless, the number of documented foreign workers has increased considerably since the 1970s. A structurally similar set of circumstances explains the inflow of foreign labour into the manufacturing sector. The excess demand for low-cost, unskilled and labour-intensive operations in manufacturing acts as a pull factor for foreign labour as it does for the construction sector. The construction sector requires labour that can undertake considerable risk, particularly in the construction of high-rise buildings. Construction activities can be carried out beyond regular working hours and at times round-the-clock and domestic labour is noted to be reluctant to participate in such work at the prevailing wage rates.

The services sector is growing rapidly and is set to be the engine for economic growth as Malaysia moves towards developed country status. Accordingly, the demand for labour in this sector will increase. Nevertheless, the increasing participation of migrant workers in the services sector stems from the low-cost, unskilled segment of the labour demanded. Typically, the migrant workers in this sector are employed in restaurants, hotels and as domestic maids. Domestic maids account for slightly more than 50 per cent of the total foreign labour employed in the services sector. The foreign workers employed in restaurants and as domestic maids work very long hours (18 hours is not unusual in many restaurants), without medical benefits and with no leave. Under these terms of employment and at the wage rate that is offered to migrant workers it is impossible to find locals who are willing to supply their labour. This explains why the number of domestic maids has increased sharply from 75,300 persons in 1997 to 261,006 persons as at July 2004.

There is a slight change in the landscape of migrant workers with the excess demand for highly skilled and knowledge-intensive workers. This is a fairly recent category that has come up with Malaysia's own development towards being a knowledge economy. However, this is a small segment of the migrant labour supply, and at present accounts for about three per cent of the migrant workers in the country. These workers, or expatriates, are professionals and highly skilled workers who are typically employed in the technical aspects of manufacturing, the oil and gas (O&G) industry, construction and services. A significant number of expatriates supply the labour needs of the more knowledge-intensive sections of the services sector, particularly in health, education and the ICT related industries. For instance, there are 700 expatriates employed in the Multimedia Super Corridor (MSC), 70 per cent of whom are software developers, systems analysts, web designers and systems engineers. Similarly, there are expatriates employed in Malaysia's public hospitals most of whom are medical officers and medical specialists.

Globalisation, Labour and Economic Transformation

The Malaysian government recently launched the New Economic Model (NEM). The goals of the NEM are ambitious; it includes a target of creating 1.4 million jobs mostly in the services sector and achieving full employment by 2015. The unemployment rate that is implied by this target is set at 3.1 per cent. Noting that the present rate of unemployment is low, it is expected that a more severe shortage of labour will result if this goal is achieved. Fundamental to the NEM is the transformation of the economy through the creation of a labour force that is skilled and knowledge-based. Although not quite measurable, the anticipated workforce is expected to be creative and innovative, empowered with greater job mobility and more highly skilled. It is expected that these goals will have a positive impact particularly on those from the bottom 40 per cent of households.

Aside from the NEM, the government, through the Tenth Malaysia Plan (10MP) has announced that it expects a transformation of the Malaysian economy that cannot be undertaken without a higher level of human capital. The 10MP has been specific about the labour market reforms that it wishes to accomplish. There are three key areas that the 10MP seeks to improve: (a) to make the labour market more flexible, (b) upgrade the skills and capabilities of Malaysia's workforce, and (c) enhance the country's ability to attract and retain top talents. Within this scheme of things, unskilled migrant labour has little role to play. And the 10MP wants Malaysia's dependence on foreign unskilled labour to be reduced. However, it is accepted that for the sectors where labour shortages persist, such as the construction and plantation industries, foreign labour will be permitted, based on needs. In an effort to encourage the move towards a highly-skilled workforce or for employers to hire skilled foreign labour, a new multi-tiered levy system will be implemented for employers of unskilled workers. The new levy system is aimed at controlling the entry of unskilled foreign labour as the levies will be borne by the employers and not the employees.

The 10MP directs its attention on labour market reform in two ways. First, it attempts to reduce the issue of the overall labour shortage that the economy faces. Second, the plan document recognises the importance of addressing the specific question of labour shortages that are associated with developing a skilled workforce. An allocation of RM80 million (about US$26 million) has been made for a Relief Fund for Loss of Employment. This allocation is spread over the years spanning 2010 to 2012, and it is meant to provide assistance to workers retrenched without compensation. On one hand, this fund functions as a social safety net, but beyond that it also ensures that workers do not get demotivated and fall out of the active search for employment, as can happen when workers have difficulty getting employed within a short period of time. Another measure that is directly targeted at relieving labour shortages is through Part-Time Work Regulations under the Employment Act 1955. This amendment is to be introduced so as to introduce housewives, retirees and disabled persons into the workforce. Further, the government wants to increase female participation in the labour force, increasing it from 46% in 2010 to 55% in 2015.

The government realizes that only 28 per cent of the workforce in Malaysia is highly-skilled, and a large segment of the workforce has low levels of educational attainment. Consequently, the 10MP has put forth various instruments to upgrade the skill levels of the existing labour force. The 10MP has indicated that it will offer incentives in the form of loans to workers and school leavers for training and skills upgrading, also matching grants will be offered for the training and skills upgrading of small and medium enterprise employees. Further, a fund will be provided to assist employees obtain industrial PhDs. In addition, partial financial assistance will be offered for PhDs in local universities.

There are three components to the labour market strategies suggested by the 10MP. They include: (a) increasing the participation of individuals in the labour force, (b) improving the skills of the existing workforce, and (c) increasing the talent pool of the labour force. The last mentioned of these strategies involves the following measures:

- Setting up the Talent Corporation to source global talent, not excluding Malaysians currently living overseas,
- Simplify the hiring of foreign talent,
- Permitting spouses of individuals hired as foreign talent to engage in employment,
- Open visas for highly skilled foreign professionals.

It is definitely useful to bring in foreign talent into the local labour market to ease the labour constraints on skilled labour. However, this policy measure faces certain limitations. First, this is a short-term measure because it does little to address the need for policies to develop endogenous sources of labour. Second, it is doubtful if Malaysia can offer incentives and opportunities that are comparable to countries such as Singapore to attract skilled foreign labour. Third, this proposal assumes that ventures requiring skilled foreign talent abound. Also, this proposal assumes that Malaysians will establish concerns on the assumption that they will be able to attract the skilled foreign talent they need. This requirement is better suited to those firms that are already in operation and require special expertise to advance their transformation or growth. Finally, it is interesting to note that the government has approved this policy ahead of any definite picture on the skills needs of the various sectors. The National Talent Blueprint 2011 is expected to identify the talent needs of priority economic sectors, but has yet to be published.

The more recent plan documents, viz. NEM, 10MP and the National Talent Blueprint 2011, indicate the government's clear intention to place Malaysia in a position whereby it is able to keep abreast with the opportunities that arise in the global economy. The heightened competition in the region implies that Malaysia has to improve its competitive edge, and this can only be accomplished by improving the quality of its human capital. It is in this context that the plan documents have outlined ways in which the supply of skilled labour can be upgraded so as to make Malaysia a regional production hub and a key player in the value chain hierarchy. There is the danger of not being able to attract FDI if these structural changes are not made.

Conclusions

The structure of the Malaysian economy has changed since its independence in 1957. At that time Malaysia was a predominantly agricultural economy. With its increasing integration into the global economy, first heralded by the inflow of FDI into Malaysia during the 1970s, it has turned to a more highly developed manufacturing sector. The services sector, as with all mature economies, is also gains more ground in this country. There have been corresponding changes in the pattern of employment in Malaysia. Employment in agriculture has been diminishing and the main sources of employment are in the manufacturing and services sectors.

Two issues constraint the supply of labour in Malaysia, and these have to be addressed if Malaysia is to benefit from the challenges of globalisation. First, there has been an increasing presence of unskilled migrant workers in the country, mostly employed in agriculture and in the more labour-intensive aspects of the manufacturing, services and construction industries. Although, the inflow of labour is very much a part of globalisation, it does not fulfill Malaysia's long-term economic goals. Second, the development of skilled, knowledge-intensive labour has not been progressing as well as needed. This is a constraining factor if Malaysia wishes to maintain its attractiveness via the high quality supply of skilled labour that it possesses, a matter that is of importance if it wishes to move up the value chain.

Recent policy announcements indicate that Malaysia wishes to produce high quality, skilled workers. Various incentive schemes have been developed to attract the growth of such a workforce. However, present achievements do not match announced intentions. Nevertheless, the goals and plans of the government are correct in so far as they have rightly identified the niche areas for human capital development and growth. Unless these goals are achieved, Malaysia will have difficulty in moving up the value chain and maintaining its lead in the region. Clearly, these are the demands that are placed on the Malaysian economy in the context of current global developments. It is imperative that Malaysia as an economy that is outward-looking and heavily dependent for its growth on FDI and trade meet these challenges.

References

Ducanes, G. and M. Abella (2008). "Labour shortage responses in Japan, Korea, Singapore, Hong Kong and Malaysia: A review and evaluation," Working Paper No.2, Bangkok: ILO.

Fleming, D. and H. Soborg (2010). "Malaysia's human resource strategies for a knowledge-based economy - Comparing the influence of different labour market relations," *European Journal of Social Sciences,* 16(2).

Inagami, T. (1998). "Labour market policies in Asian countries: Diversity and similarity among Singapore, Malaysia, the Republic of Korea and Japan," *Employment and Training Papers* No. 34, ILO, Geneva.

Kuruvilla, S. (1998). "Linkages between industrialization strategies and industrial relations/human resource policies: Singapore, Malaysia, the Philippines, and India," *Industrial and Labour Relations Review*, 49, 635-657.

Malaysia (2010). *Tenth Malaysia Plan: 2011-2015*, Kuala Lumpur: Government Printers.

National Economic Advisory Council (2009). *New Economic Model for Malaysia*, Kuala Lumpur: Government Printers.

Thangavelu, S.M. and H. Guangzhou (2005). "Structural change, labor market dynamics and economic growth: Comparative study of Ireland, Korea and Malaysia," National University of Singapore, mimeo.

Vandernberg, P. (2008). "Is Asia adopting flexicurity? A survey of employment policies in six countries," *Economic and Labor Market Papers* 2008-4, ILO, Geneva.

Wad, P. (2001). "Transforming industrial relations: The case of the Malaysian automotive industry," CLARA Working Paper No.12.

Chapter Ten

Globalisation, Inequality and Unemployment: A Case Study of Two Giant Asian Countries: India and China

Raj Kumar Sen and Somnath Hazra

Introduction

There are different origins of globalisation such as social, political, cultural etc, but our concerned parameters are related to economic globalisation and its consequences in the society of two giant economies of Asia. Jagdish Bhagwati made a distinction of economic globalisation as, " integration of national economies into the international economy through trade, direct foreign investment (by corporations and multinationals), short-term capital flows, international flows of workers and humanity generally, and flows of technology" (Bhagwati, 2004, p. 3). He also argued that the integration into the global economy promotes economic growth, as a consequence which helps to solve inequality in the society, problems of poverty, lack of democracy and pollution, and empirics suggest a considerable reduction in poverty amid globalisation, especially in the case of India and China (Bhagwati, 2004; Zhou et al., 2011).

Globalisation is not a new phenomenon. The process in recent times has started in eighteenth century. According to O'Rourke (2001), O'Rourke and Williamson (2000) and Maddison (2001) and Williamson (2002) the period of 1870-2000 is classified into different stages, these are: (1870-1913) the first wave of globalisation, (1913-1950) the de-globalisation period, (1950-1973) the golden age, and from 1973 onwards the second wave of globalisation has started.

India is the second most populous country in the world, and has started officially the globalisation process in 1991 as one the three components of the strategy of economic reforms, the other two being liberalization and privatization although since the mid1980s she actually started the globalisation process in the form of liberalization of international trade. India adopted the policy of economic reforms in the face of a serious balance of payment crisis and as dictated by the IMF and World Bank. This process of globalisation got accelerated since 1995 when India became one of the founding members of the WTO.

Globalisation is not a new concept and that cannot be easily defined. A number of definitions of it can be found, depending on the source. In general it may be said that, it is interdependent close relationship between the countries and people from around the world. In globalisation, technology plays an important role. As per the different definition around the world, the globalisation has been accepted by the different countries to promote global economic growth and social progress, but it is also seen that the globalisation has generated growing income inequality and environmental degradation, social degeneration and lack of competition. Since the last two decades the causal effect of globalisation on income inequality is a significant issue. As per OECD, 'Globalisation refers to a comprehensive process of economic integration which enhances international mobility of national resources and increases interdependency of national economies' (OECD 2005, p. 11).

The positive views are not accepted globally; some of the economists are opposed and they believed that the globalisation is the root of economic uncertainty and contributes to the increasing inequality in both the developed and developing countries (Stiglitz, 2002; Borjas & Ramey, 1994; Cornia, 2004; Bergh & Nilsson, 2011). As per Stiglitz (Stiglitz, 2006, p. 8), 95 per cent of the world's populations are living in countries with growing inequality, with only 5 per cent in countries with declining inequality. Even in most of the developed countries, the rich are getting richer while the poor are often not even holding their own".

As per ILO about globalisation, "our primary concerns are that globalisation should benefit all countries and should raise the welfare of all people throughout the world. This implies that it should raise the rate of economic growth in poor countries and reduce world poverty, and that it should not increase inequalities or undermines socio-economic security within countries" (ILO, 2004). In fact, globalisation is considered to be an integration process of national economies into the international economy and also as the engine of growth, technical advancement, raising productivity, enlarging employment and bringing about poverty reduction along with modernization. But unfortunately, today unemployment is not only a theoretical possibility, but also it is in fact a grim reality of increasing concern in the world of work in the last two decades since when globalisation has become a buzzword and the whole world has willingly or otherwise has accepted it as an established fact. The ILO report has also examined the global trends of employment in this period and analyzed unemployment as one of the areas of increasing global concern to prove that this trend is resulting in most cases, in increased insecurity for workers. It has shown further that 'in the current phase of globalisation, labour markets have generated greater economic insecurity and greater levels of most acute forms of inequality, adversely affecting decent work and employment opportunities'. Hence, it concludes that productive employment for all is not a policy option, but it is an imperative for the twenty-first century.

In our paper an attempt has been made to analyze the incidence of income inequality and unemployment as a consequence of the current phase of globalisation especially in the two giant Asian countries, viz., India and China. Of course, it does not mean that the process of the ongoing globalisation process has only negative impacts; but it is more or less clear that it does not affect all regions or all sections of the people throughout the world uniformly. Further, in many countries the globalisation has been adopted as a package along with other requisites like privatization and/or liberalization (e.g., economic reforms programme of 1991 in India). Again, globalisation has been understood and interpreted differently by many and also implemented in different ways in different countries.

In this paper, apart for the introduction we will also discuss the gains from trade through increase in trade and employment, theory of convergence and inequality in the world economy. In the second section, we will discuss why this globalisation is a truncated globalisation, and in the third section we will analyze the link of globalisation- income inequality- unemployment for the two Asian giant countries. The final section is devoted to conclusions and policy requirements.

Globalisation and Income Inequality

In the recent decades the researchers have been concentrated on the theoretical research of relation between globalisation and income inequality, but the empirical analysis is very limited. The fundamental relation between globalisation and inequality in the developing countries are well accepted in different schools. In the empirical research, it is seen that there is no such structural relationship between the growth and inequality but side by side it is also argued that the income inequality in the pre-globalisation era is motionless and in India including the South Asian countries there is a long period (1951-52 to 1993-94) near constancy in income distribution (Hashim, 1997-98) before the reform period measured in terms of Gini index (for rural India it varied between 0.329 and 0.367). But it was not so for China.

If we go through the comprehensive literature survey on historical perspective of globalisation and its impact on income inequality, we can have the process of globalisation and the sources with the relationship of inequality and number of channels of globalisation. The channels are commodity price equalization, factor price convergence due to international migration and capital mobility and disparity in marginal products and rate of returns of capital among countries, and dynamic convergence in growth of per capita income.

In our case, if we see the situation of India and China it is seen that both the countries have a positive trend in income inequality with the globalisation. During 1990 and 2010 it is seen that in China the globalisation has been increased by 74% side by side the income inequality has also been increased by 31%. In case of India globalisation has been increased by 66% where as income inequality was increased by only 5%.

Table 10.1 KOF, HDI and Gini for India and China

Country	Year	KOF	Change (%)	Gini	Change (%)	HDI	Change (%)
China	1990	34.09		32.43		0.49	
			74%		31%		39%
	2010	59.36		42.48		0.682	
India	1990	31.26		31.88		0.41	
			66%		5%		32%
	2010	51.88		33.38		0.542	

Sources: KOF: Dreher, 2006; updated in Dreher et al 2008; Gini: World Development Indicators; HDI: Human Development Report, UNDP 2011.

Table 10.2 Rankings (R) are based on the raw data for the year 2010

Country	R	Globalization Index	R	Economic Globalization	R	Social Globalization	R	Political Globalization
India	107	51.57	128	42.71	144	31.63	18	92.21
China	73	59.43	109	51.12	90	48.94	44	85.85

Source: 2013 KOF Index of Globalisation

The KOF index is used as a measure of globalisation. KOF globalisation index depends on three globalisation index these are economic globalisation, social globalisation and political globalisation. If we look into these three parts of globalisation it is seen that in India and China only political globalisation has been done and ranked in top 20 and top 50 respectively, where as social globalisation is very poor but economic globalisation has taken place.

The increased overall inequality has been seen mostly to growing differences between rural and urban household incomes and irregular growth in incomes among urban households. Focusing on inequality between 1988 and 1995, Wei and Wu (2007) have examined the effect of trade globalisation on Chinese income inequality using two unique data sets on urban and rural Chinese regions. Through the first data set, they have examined the urban rural inequality and through the second data set, they have examined within-urban and within-rural inequality.

In this context, we may refer to the analysis by Bardhan (2007), where he has analysed the impact of globalisation on poverty and inequality in China and India. He has defined globalisation in the limited sense of openness to foreign trade and long term investment where both China and India have made major strides over the last two decades. Going by the World Bank poverty line of $1 a day per capita at 1993

PPP, the proportion of people below poverty in China fell from 63.8% in 1981 to 9.9% in 2004. If one takes a national poverty line of 850 yuan per year for rural China and 1200 yuan for urban at 2002 prices than the poverty proportion declined from 53% to 8% during 1981 to 2001. However, there is no convincing statistical analysis of this as no one has tested a causal model for this result. Similarly, the link between globalisation and inequality is also not very clear. As many changes have taken place in the last quarter century in China and also in India, it is difficult to identify the effect of globalisation from that of other ongoing changes. Secondly, in both the countries there are reasons to suspect that economic inequality or its rise is underestimated because of a fact facing household surveys of large non- response by rich households. It is also difficult to compare China and India as most of the inequality data usually are for income inequality for China and consumption expenditure inequality for India. Further, while the Gini coefficient of income in coastal China went up from 0.35 in 1991 to 0.39 in 2000, the corresponding rise was as much as 0.48 in the interior provinces.

So, we have seen a positive relationship between inequality and globalisation. From the literature, it is also seen that only the explanatory variable follows a considerable long term trend to income inequality is the durable goods trade deficit as a percentage of GDP (Borjas and Ramey, 1994). But, it is not always true for all the countries. There is no proper evidence to suggest that trade liberalization, or increased globalisation has any significant impact on income inequality worldwide (Edwards, 1997). Sometimes economic reforms seem to increase inequality mainly in the North, whereas social globalisation is more important in the South. It is also seen that monetary, legal and political globalisation may not be liable to increase inequality (Bergh and Nilsson, 2011).

But World Development Report (WDR) for the years 1990 on 'Poverty', WDR 2000/01 on 'Attacking Poverty' and WDR 2010 indirectly show that there has been an increase in countrywise range of per capita GDP in each decile. In 1988, it was $100 (Mozambique) –27500 (Switzerland), increased in 1998 to $100 (Ethiopia) – 44640 (Luxemburg) and further increased in 2008 to $140 (Burundi) – 87070 (Norway). This means that in 20 years roughly coinciding with the present era of globalisation, the ratios between countries with lowest and highest per capita GDP moved from 1:275 to 1: 446 and ultimately to 1: 622. And so far as India is concerned, she is still the habitat of largest number of poor in the world with increasing malnutrition though she experienced a slow decrease in poverty over time.

According to a WIDER study by Cornia (1999), it is observed that while income inequality declined in several nations between the 1950s and 1970s, this trend has been reversed during the last 20 years in two-thirds of countries based on an econometric analysis of inequality trends for 77 countries accounting for 82 percent of world population and 95 percent of world GDP-PPP. Also in China, inequality rose quickly between 1985 and1990 and rapidly after 1990.

Globalisation and Unemployment

1995 is the year of acceleration of the on-going globalisation process with the formation of the World Trade Organization (WTO) which hoped for global prosperity through global expansion of trade in goods and services. It is really a coincidence that in the same year, the World Summit for Social Development at Copenhagen declared as its Commitment (No.3) 'to promote the goal of full employment as a basic priority…' Following this, the UN also has emphasized the role of productive employment in reducing poverty and promoting social development. After a decade in 2005, in the World Summit, the world leaders again reiterated this as a central objective of their national and international policies. In 2006, the UN has included it as a target (goal 1) under Millennium Development Goals (MDGs). However, this has its origin in the 1948 Universal Declaration of Human Rights, where it is stated (Art.23 (1)) that 'everyone has the right to work, to free choice of employment, to just and favourable conditions of work and to protection against unemployment.' But in reality we find that throughout the world, many people face sufferings 'in the form of unemployment and underemployment, poor quality and unproductive jobs, unsafe work and insecure income, loss of hard-earned rights, gender inequality, exploitation of migrant workers, lack of representation and voice, and inadequate protection and solidarity in the face of disease, disability and old age' (UN, 2007). In 2006, 1.4 bn. workers were earning below $2 per day and as many as 507 mn workers (including over 200 mn youth) lived below the $1 per day poverty line. 130 mn young people are illiterate. Out of 650 mn people with disabilities, about 470 mn are of working age, and they are most likely to be unemployed or underemployed. It is estimated, as relevant statistics are often missing, that the indigenous people constitute 15% of the world's poorest though they constitute only 5% of the total population. And all these statistics after two decades of ongoing globalisation are not at all encouraging to say the least.

As noted earlier, the current globalisation process has affected the labour market with different sets of challenges for different categories of labour. This is, however, in built in the nature of the process itself as it affects different groups differently. It should also be mentioned that this globalisation is primarily meant for free movement of finance and capital and much less or nil for labour and in particular for unskilled labour. Branco Milanovic, economist at the Carnegie Endowment for International Peace, has mentioned that 'globalisation means free movement of capital, goods, technology, ideas and people. Any globalisation that omits the last one is partial and not sustainable'. (Datt and Sundharam, 2007). This has prompted many to call this as a truncated globalisation (Sen, 2004) compared with the process observed in the ancient period with completely free movement of capital and labour. As currently it is agreed that knowledge is power, the globalisation process is almost sure to favour the skilled, employed, educated, rich, strong, organized, urban, sophisticated and the capitalist at the cost of the unskilled, unemployed, uneducated, poor, weak, unorganized and marginalized, rural, tribal and the labourer. Consequently, we note that under the present scenario, while the former groups dominate and gain, the others lose. Some of the social groups are more vocal and thus more visible, while others are voiceless and invisible. Thus, the figures in Tables 10.1 and 10.2 show that the joblessness could not be cured under globalisation; it has accentuated the inequalities among various groups. This pattern of jobless growth, therefore, has also led to voiceless growth for the vulnerable groups of the society including workers and unemployed, women, migrants and other marginalized categories of people and it is urgently required that their views on matters affecting their lives are properly heard.

There has been also a decline in formal employment in many parts of the world as there has been external labour market flexibility for the sake of competitiveness and this flexible system has been also unstable leading to contractual and unprotected employment for a majority of workers. In contrast with the conventional economic theory, economic growth is found to be no longer associated with the growth of formal employment and informal activities are growing both in absolute and relative terms. This feature results in casualization of labour associated with insecurity of labour both in job and in social life. The constant insecurity makes the worker further voiceless as he/she does not want to object changes in job conditions including loss of existing rights and/or benefits, out of fear of losing their jobs. The long tradition of social security slowly built up over the years with the development of the concept of welfare state is now getting fast eroded with the present policy of marketization, privatization and deregulation of social services. Short term contracts, outsourcing and subcontracting are fast replacing the permanent nature of employment with right to form trade unions. While all these policies are reducing labour costs, it is really doubtful if these are increasing labour productivity especially in the long run. The associated social costs also need not be overlooked as they can accumulate and lead to grave social tensions and disruption.

A few other factors are relevant in this context to show the tilt in the balance of power against the labourers: (i) The new emergence of agency labour for short term work assignments where the worker has no attachment to a particular company. Such moving workers do not develop any sense of collective bonding and hence do not possess any bargaining power. (ii) So far as the level of open unemployment is concerned, it is estimated (ILO, 2004) that 'for the world as a whole, ...(it) has increased over the last decade to about 188 million in 2003.' Of course, the results are varied over regions. In Latin America between 1990 and 2002, these rates were 6.9% and 9.9% respectively while they were 3.6% and 6.5% for South East Asia while Japan experienced a rise from 2.1% to 5.8%. The rates are highest for Sub-Saharan Africa (increased from 13.7% in 2000 to 14.4% in 2002) and Middle East and North Africa (the corresponding figures being 17.9% and 18%). Between 1995 and 2002, these rates went up also for East Asia (3.1% and 4.0%) and South Asia (2.9% and 3.4%), but declined for EU (10.5% and 7.6%) and remained unchanged for USA at 5.6%. This also amply proves that globalisation has not only been a case of jobless growth for most of the developing countries including the developed country like Japan, but also it has been beneficial for the EU and did not hurt USA. (iii) Another controversial aspect of globalisation is transferring jobs by the MNCs of high income countries to low income labour surplus economies which engender fear and insecurity among workers of the rich countries altering fundamentally the balance of bargaining power between the workers and employers. Perhaps without this feature, USA would have experienced a decline in her unemployment rate. (iv) The question of rising working hours for the workers is also no less important in this context. An ILO study by Lee and Messenger (2007) estimated that only 614.2 mn workers, i.e., 22% of the global workforce, are working within the legal limit of 48 hours per week. Such labour exploiting situation is putting pressure on other sectors and other countries too to follow these practices violating the law in the name of industrialization and growth. (v) The creation of SEZ (Special Economic Zone) in different countries following the Chinese model is another area where the rights of a labourer are drastically curtailed. This policy goes against the competitive policies followed by the globalisation itself. Gradually other industries also are demanding the facilities of SEZ for investment to earn supernormal profit in poor economies. (vi) Under globalisation employment of women labour has increased no doubt but that took place mainly in the unorganized, casual, informal, unskilled and part-time sectors and in many cases they are subjected to inhuman working conditions and sexual harassment.

In case of India, we note that the merchandise exports during the period 1990-2003 increased at an annual rate of 9.1% compared to the world average rate of 6.1% in this period. Thus, so far as the exports growth rate is concerned, India performed better than the world average. But India's share in world merchandise exports improved only marginally from 0.51% in 1990 to 0.73% in 2003. However, if we combine India's exports in the merchandise and the services sectors, this share improved from 0.53% in 1990 to 1.0% in 2003 as India's performance in services sector exports was relatively much better. Even here considering the size of India's economy, her gain is much smaller than that of South Korea, Mexico and China.

In the background of this increase in exports from India, the increase in imports from abroad has been far greater. Throughout the period 1990-1 to 2005-6, trade balances were always negative with an increasing trend with a net positive balance in invisibles coming to rescue in this situation. This clearly shows that the foreigners have been able to penetrate the Indian market more effectively than Indians have been able to access the foreign markets. The present increasing negative trade balance (-4.9 in 2004-5 and -6.4 in 2005-6 as percentage of GDP at market prices observed from Economic Survey, Government of India 2006-7) is also of much concern which led to the reappearance of a negative balance in the current account.

Another important aspect of globalisation is to achieve a greater flow of foreign investment in the form of foreign direct investment (FDI) and foreign portfolio investment (FPI). During 2000-01 and 2005-6 the share of FDI was 46.1% and that of FPI was 53.9% showing that less than half of the amount of total foreign investment was available for increasing productive capacity which can enhance the level of employment and more than half of it are of highly volatile and undependable nature.

So far as the FDI inflows are concerned, it is noted that during January 1991-March 2004 nearly 69% accrued to five high priority sectors namely Energy, Telecommunications, Electrical Equipments (including computer software and electronics), Transportation and Metallurgical industries, most of which are not employment intensive and with falling employment elasticity. In other words, the impact of FDI inflows in India on employment generation in this period has been also not appreciable (Economic Survey, 2003-4). Further actual FDI inflows reveal a wide gap between FDI approvals and actual inflows. In fact, it has been 26.8% in the ten listed sectors attracting highest FDI approvals. This huge gap only highlights the slow progress in the actual help rendered by the FDI to promote development and hence employment in India. If globalisation has to make an impact and prove its effectiveness, the gap between approved FDI and actual inflows must be reduced. The situation has been complicated since 2000 when there have been FDI outflows as some Indian firms have been establishing investment projects in other countries. Hence, there has been a sizeable reduction in the net FDI inflows, which is the real factor to increase the rate of investment, productivity and employment of the Indian economy from this source. An overview of the world situation in FDI inflows shows that nearly two third of it has gone to benefit the developed countries, while the share of India has been, as per the World Investment Report 2004, a minuscule amount of 0.8% in 2003. It has been further demonstrated by ILO (2004) in its report titled ‘A Fair Globalisation: Creating Opportunities for All’, shows that in the decade of nineties, the distribution of FDI inflows to developing countries has been highly unequal as only 12 countries could corner 74.7% of the FDI inflows leaving the remaining 25.3% only for the whole set of 176 countries and territories. This distribution of FDI has been utterly unfair for India as she does not find a place within this group of twelve countries even though she accounts for 16% of the world population. The role of MNCs for using FDI to enhance their economic power has been mentioned in the ILO Report 2004 where it has been observed that by transferring production processes to the developing countries, the FDI investment is used to nullify the comparative cost advantage of such countries in cheap labour and raw materials in most cases. The Report says “Communication technology revolution, coupled with declining transport cost made the growth of far flung multi-country based production of goods and services both technically and economically feasible” (WCSDG, 2004). It is therefore not also true that FDI inflows are all growth-oriented and employment generating as preached by the pro- globalisation lobby. In fact the MNCs and their affiliates actually strengthen their stranglehold over the global production system.

In India, the period under economic reforms is usually identified as one of jobless growth as the employment situation in India like many other developing countries has worsened in the era of globalisation. If we compare the pre-reform period of 1983-94 with the post- reform period of 1994-2000, then it is clearly observed that the growth of employment has come down from 2.04% per year to only 0.98% annually in the latter period. Sector wise, agriculture, mining & quarrying, electricity, gas & water supply have accounted for negative rate of growth of employment and the community, social and personal services sector registered a sharp decline from 2.90 % to 0.55% only. This was the consequence largely of a negative growth rate of employment in agriculture which was neglected during the reform period and which absorbed about 65% of total employed workers. Further, by imposing a continuous ban on recruitment in the public sector units and also not filling up even the positions vacated by retirement of public sector employees, the level of employment growth was drastically curtailed in the public sector enterprises. This has been revealed in the Report (2001) of the Task Force on Employment Opportunities appointed by the Planning Commission, Government of India.

Conclusions and Recommendations

In this context, the ILO has suggested that the current globalisation process should possess a more human face. For this purpose there should be an agenda for a fair and inclusive growth. What we need a proper macro-economic and employment and income generation policy, improving the productivity of employment specially in the informal sector through promotion of skill development with the help of organizations of the working poor, with an emphasis on the development of the social sector and promotion of a balanced regional development. About India, the WBCSDG has mentioned that the lives of the educated and the rich had been enriched by globalisation but the benefits had not yet reached the majority and new risks have cropped up for the losers - the socially deprived and rural poor. Such a situation needs remedial action to achieve the target of a fair globalisation. Under the current macro-economic policy in India, the employment generation has not been a concomitant of accelerating growth rates. While there has been a growth in the employment of urban and educated section of the people, the major source of employment became dry. It is necessary to improve the productivity of employment also as the main problem in India is underemployment and not open employment. As regional disparities have widened in India under globalisation, it is necessary to put more emphasis on the development of backward states to achieve the goal of a more balanced regional development. To save the poor from exclusion from the benefits of globalisation which has increased the need for acquiring skills, it is necessary for the state to increase public investment in social sector. As human development is conducive to economic growth, it is vital to adopt a policy framework to promote employment growth, social security, education, health care and effective poverty reduction program through employment generation and asset creation.

References

Bardhan,P. (2007). "Poverty and inequality in China and India: Elusive link with Globalisation", *Economic and Political Weekly*, September 27.

Bergh, A. and Nilsson, T. (2011). "Do liberalisation and globalisation increase income inequality?" *European Journal of Political Economy,* 26, 488-505.

Bhagwati, J. (2004). *In Defense of Globalisation*, New York: Oxford University Press.

Borjas, G.J. and Ramey, V.A. (1994). "Time-Series evidence on the sources of trends in wage inequality", *The American Economic Review*, 84, 10-16.

Cornia, G.A. (1999). "Liberalisation, globalisation, and income distribution', Working Paper No.157. UNU/WIDER, Helsinki.

Cornia, G.A. (2004). *Inequality, Growth, and Poverty in an Era of Liberalization and Globalisation*, New York: Oxford University Press.

Datt, R. and K.P.M.Sundharam (2007). *Indian Economy* (56th ed). New Delhi: S. Chand.

Dreher, A. (2006). "Does globalisation affect growth? Evidence from a new index of globalisation", *Applied Economics*, 38(10), 1091-1110.

Dreher, A., Gaston, N. and Martens, P. (2008). *Measuring Globalisation – Gauging Its Consequence,* New York: Springer.

Deshpande, L.K. et.al (2004). *Liberalisation and Labour: Labour Flexibility in Indian Manufacturing*. Institute for Human Development, New Delhi.

Edwards, S. (1997). "Trade policy, growth, and income distribution", *The American Economic Review,* 87 (2), 205-10.

Hashim.S.R.(1997-98)."Economic growth and stability of income distribution in the Indian development scenario". *Indian Economic Journal*, 45(4), Apr-Jun.

ILO (2004). *A Fair Globalisation: Creating Opportunities for All*. Report of the World Commission of Social Dimension of Globalisation. Geneva.

KOF Globalisation Index (2013). http://globalisation.kof.ethz.ch/ accesses on 24th March 2013.

Maddison A. (2001). *The World Economy: A Millennial Perspective*, Development Centre Studies, OECD.

OECD (2005). 'OECD Handbook on Economic Globalisation Indicators', pp. 11, viewed 3rd October 2012, http://www.realinstitutoelcano.org/materiales/docs/OCDE_handbook.pdf

O'Rourke K.H. (2001). *Globalisation and Inequality: Historical Trends*, NBER 2001:8339.

O'Rourke K.H. and J.G. Williamson (2000). *Globalisation and History: The Evolution of a Nineteenth-century Atlantic Economy*. The MIT Press.

Pan, S and R.K.Sen (2007). *Foreign Direct Investment and Trade in India*. Deep & Deep Publications, New Delhi.

Pavcnik, N. (2011). "Globalisation and within-country income Inequality", In: Marc Bacchetta and Marion Jansen (eds.), *Making Globalisation Socially Sustainable,* International Labour Office – Geneva.

Reddy, N. (2004). "Challenges of decent work in the globalizing world". Presidential Address, 46th Conference of the Indian Society of Labour Economics.

Sen, R.K. (2004). "An overview of economic globalisation: Its momentum and its consequences examined", In: Clem Tisdell and Raj Kumar Sen (eds.), *Economic Globaization, Social Conflicts, Labour and Environmental Issues.* Edward Elgar Publishing. UK and USA.

Sen, R.K. (2004). "Globalisation and Indian economic thinking in the past and their relevance in the present and future", *Indian Economic Journal*, 51(2), Kolkata, India.

Sen, R.K. (2005). "Indian economy and current globalisation", In: Clem Tisdell (ed.), *Globalisation and World Economic Policies. Vol.2.*, Serials Publications, New Delhi.

Sen, R.K. (2006). "WTO and the south: Past, present and future", In: B. N. Ghosh and H.M. Guven (eds), *Globalisation and the Third World.: A Study of Negative Consequences,* Palgrave Macmillan, UK and USA.

Sen, R.K. (2011). "Globalisation and jobless growth", *Bhutan Journal of Economics and Management*, 1(1) October.

Stiglitz, J. (2002). *Globalisation and Its Discontents*, New York: W. W. Norton.

Stiglitz, J. (2006). *Making Globalisation Work*, New York: W. W. Norton.

UNDP 2012, *Human Development Report 2011*, Data and Indices, viewed 04 October 2012, http://hdr.undp.org/en/statistics

UN Department of Economic & Social Affairs (2007). *The Employment Imperative.* Report on the World Social Situation. New York.

Williamson J.G. (2002). *Winners and Losers Over Two Centuries of Globalisation,* WIDER Annual Lecture 6.

Williamson J.G. (1996). "*Globalisation and inequality then and now: The late 19th and 20th centuries",* NBER Working Paper 1996:5491.

World Bank (2012). 'World Development Indicators', viewed 24 September 2012, http://databank.worldbank.org/ddp/home.do

World Bank (1990,200/2001,2010). *World Development Reports*. Washington DC.

Zhou, L, Biswas, B, Bowles, T, and Saunders, P.J. (2011). "Impact of globalisation on income distribution inequality in 60 countries", *Global Economy Journal*, 11 (1), 1-18.

Chapter Eleven

Sectoral Growth, Unemployment and Globalisation in Turkey

Sule L. Aker and Ahmet H. Aker

Introduction

Unemployment is one of the greatest ills of the Western economic system today. Masses of people are economically and socially in dire straits because they can not find jobs. The classical formulas relating economic growth and employment are not functioning anymore; in many countries unemployment is growing regardless of the economic growth figures of these countries. Nor the Phillips Curve relation presents a remedy to unemployment. The relation claims that unemployment and inflation are inversely proportional. That is, policy makers can reduce unemployment if they increase inflation. Yet, since the beginning of the latest economic crisis that started in 2008, the central banks are increasing money supply vigorously, but the Western world had not witnessed a substantial improvement on employment figures. So in a way, we are out of sound policies at the moment to reduce unemployment in the capitalist economies.

The policy makers are worried about unemployment, because it has economic and social costs to the societies. Economically, unemployment means idle resources, a factor of production, labor is not fully utilized. Socially, the devil tempts the idle, so these unemployed people are open to all sorts of evil suggestions. In many countries, the youth unemployment is much higher than unemployment in middle and older generations. The youth unemployment in the 27 European Union countries is "twice as high as the rate for the total population throughout the last decade", for example. (Unemployment Statistics) This poses an extra threat, because younger people are more impatient and they can take more risks without carefully calculating the consequences of their actions. So they may be involved in illegal activities. Moreover, because of the erosion in moral and ethical values, "proper" behaviour has become a joke for the young people in today's Western capitalist system. There is also not too many values except owning money whatever the means to achieve it. Doing unconventional things are considered even "cool", and violence, killings, toughness, irrespect for the others are encouraged by the media. Of course, that type of culture has been deliberately inserted by global companies producing arms and weapons. If people become violent and full of hate, the agressor will be buying arms and the others, also will be buying arms to protect themselves. That will increase the customer base. A flourishing business. If they want to sell more arms, they can intoduce intercommunal violence in different countries, or animosity between different countries. Unemployment helps these companies, because they recruit unemployed youth as soldiers.

Or unemployed habitually become idle and free-riders, for which they use the term Y-generation. This is given to the generation born after 1980. A typical Y-generation individual spends long hours on the internet. They like material thing and they like money, but they do not want to work for it. They prefer short-cuts for achieving money or wealth; the short-cuts may be ethical or unethical. They are born to very productive and creative parents who are called the X-generation. Most of the parents provide for their children for many years, sometimes until they become middle aged people. Unemployment contributes to this Y-generation culture. The unemployed young demand everything from the parents and/or from the government (like unemployed benefits) because they can not find jobs. Most of the time they don't work, even when they find a job. Their excuse could be "the job is not for them", "the boss is terrible" or "they are waiting for the other opportunity". So, unemployment becomes a habit for them which is difficult to change. For the economy, the youth would be wasted resources, and the system would be missing the energy and creativity of the young people in the production process.

Is globalisation responsible for the increasing unemployment in the capitalist economies? One is tempted to answer this question as "yes" since as economies globalize, the unemployment problem becomes more acute. Additionally, the more the economies of the countries are integrated economically, the more unemployment problems they have. For example, the unemployment figures are worst in the euro area in the European Union (EU) then in 10 EU members outside the eurozone. In January 2013, EU27 unemployment rate was 10.8% while the unemployment rate for the eurozone (17) was 11.9%. (Unemployment statistics).

Of course, countries globalize in many different ways: politically, economically, socially and culturally. In this chapter, the effects of Turkey's economic globalisation on Turkey's employment are analyzed. Turkey liberalized her trade and capital accounts towards the end of 1980's. Turgut Özal was elected as the Prime Minister of Turkey at 1983 and he started the economic liberalization attempts immediately. Towards the beginning of 1990's, Turkish economy had become part of the global economic system to a great extent with all the pros and cons.

Unemployment in Turkey

Table 11.1 illustrtaes employment (to population ratio; individuals employed over the age of 15 as the percentage of the total population) and unemployment (is the total unemployment as percentage of the total labor force) in Turkey over the years.

Table 11.1 Employment in Turkey

Years	Employment, 15+, total (%)	Unemployment
1992	55	8.5
1993	52	9.0
1994	54	8.6
1995	53	7.6
1996	53	6.6
1997	52	6.8
1998	52	6.9
1999	52	7.7
2000	49	6.5
2001	49	8.4
2002	48	10.4
2003	47	10.5
2004	46	10.8
2005	46	10.6
2006	46	10.2
2007	46	10.3
2008	47	11.0
2009	48	14.0
2010	49	11.9
2011	50	9.8
2012	49	9.2

Source:World Development Indicators

As observed in Table 11.1, after the liberalization, in other terms after Turkey became more globalized, unemployment in Turkey has increased, both measured as the percentage of people employed out of total population (above the age of 15) has gone down and as percentage of the unemployed out of the total labor force has gone up.

Several studies on Turkish labor market and unemployment in Turkey show that the unemployment pattern in the country resembles that of other developed countries, especially EU countries. The characteristics of Turkish unemployment are the following in very general terms:

- Unemployment is high among the young in Turkey. 40% of the young, between the ages 15-24 are not working and they are not going to school either (İkinci, 2008). So, 5 million young people in Turkey appeared as unemployed, however, that figure includes unregistered labor.

- Women labor market participation rate is decreasing in years, which means that as percentage of the labor force, women participation is falling. Moreover, duration of unemployment, leaving unemployment and finding a job is lower for women in Turkey than it is for men. (Tansel and Tasci, 2010).

- Unemployed in Turkey find jobs in a shorter period of time than in other developed countries. (Tansel and Tasci, 2010).

One important common characteristic of Turkey's and developed countries' employment figures is increasing unemployment in the last two decades and the measures designed and implemented to change this trend have not been successful. Of course, to cure a problem, the problem must be correctly identified. In this research we try to understand whether the roots of the problem lies in globalisation or not.

To understand up to what extent this increasing unemployment is related to Turkey's globalisation, we analyzed the correlation between unemployment and yearly growth rates of different sectors in Turkey, firstly. The results of this analysis show that unemployment decreases as exports grow in Turkey. Similarly, employment increase as exports increase. So, we can conclude that the export sector contributes to employment in Turkey. One of the explanation for this finding can be found in Heckscher-Ohlin Theory which says that countries export those goods produced with the abundant factor of production in that country. The findings show that Turkey is exporting goods that are produced with labor intensive techniques. Thus, unemployment goes down as exports increase. On this account, globalisation has positively effected Turkey's employment. As Aker (2004) points out the changes in BOP will have an effect on domestic macroeconomic variables sooner or later, this outcome suits the expectations.

Then we also checked how FDI is relating to unemployment, because FDIs are the other change brought by globalisation. As Turkey liberalized capital movements in and out of the country, the FDI in Turkey increased. The results of the analysis show that FDI and unemployment are positively correlating in Turkey which means that as FDI increased unemployment increased, too. One explanation for this finding is that FDI in Turkey was mainly directed towards state enterprises during privatization periods. After privatization of state enterprises, many employees were laid off. This is why the labor unions in Turkey are strongly against privatization of state enterprises. So in this respect, globalisation increased unemployment in Turkey.

The last point analyzed is to see whether the general argument claiming that capital is replacing labor in the production process as technology advances is true or not. This argument was true in the case of Turkey, because the growth in fixed capital investments was found to be positively correlating with unemployment. So, producers are replacing machines for workers in Turkey. This point may be related to FDIs, too. The foreign firms instead of employing local labor, they may be using more imported capital goods then local producers do. The firms underaking FDI in Turkey are generally big global companies, and they use more advanced technology then local small and medium enterprises (SMEs) in Turkey. The reason for this is because big global firms financially more opt to buy latest advanced technology to be used in their production process. Hence, globalisation adversely effected employment in Turkey in this respect, too. Overall, since unemployment is increasing in the last two decades, we can say that negative effects of globalisation are larger than its positive effects on employment in Turkey.

Sectoral Analysis

Multiple regression analysis is used to find the correlations between the variables. In the first part, unemployment (U) is the dependent variable and agriculture (AGR), industry (IND), services (SER), government expenditures (GOV), exports (EXP) and imports (IMP) are the independent variables. The hypothesis tested is that unemployment is a factor of following sectors; agriculture, industry, services, government expenditures, exports and imports. The assumption is that as these sectors grow, unemployment is expected to go down. Observations cover the period between 1988-2010, so there are 23 observations.

$$U = f(AGR, IND, SER, GOV, EXP, IMP) \quad (1)$$

The multiple regression equation is as follows:

$$U = a + \beta_1 AGR + \beta_2 IND + \beta_3 SER + \beta_4 GOV + \beta_5 EXP + \beta_6 IMP + e \quad (2)$$

Where:

U is the total unemployment as percentage of the total labor force (unemployment refers to the share of the labor force that is without work but available for and seeking employment), (World Development Indicators)
a is the constant term of the equation (2),
β_1 is the standardized coefficient of agriculture,
AGR is the yearly value added by the agricultural sector as percentage of GDP of Turkey,
β_2 is the standardized coefficient of industry,
IND is the yearly value added by the industrial sector as percentage of GDP of Turkey,
β_3 is the standardized coefficient for services,
SER is the yearly value added by the services sector as the percentage of GDP of Turkey,
β_4 is the standardized coefficient of the government expenditures,
GOV is the yearly percentage growth of the general government final consumption expenditure in Turkey,
β_5 is the standardized coefficient of exports,

EXP is exports of goods and services as percentage of GDP in Turkey,
β_6 is the standardized coefficient of imports,
IMP is the yearly percentage growth of imports in Turkey,
e is the error term.

The result of the regression analysis:

$$U = 10.101 + 0.268\ AGR + 0.083\ IND + 0.893\ SER - 0.275\ GOV - 0.768\ EXP - 0.741\ IMP + 0.688 \quad (3)$$

R square of equation (3) is 0.428, which shows that equation (3) gives a satisfactory representation for the correlation. The data for unemployment is obtained from world development indicators, 2012. Data for AGR, IND, SER, GOV, EXP and IMP are obtained from World data Bank, 2013.

Table 11.2 The results of the regression analysis when unemployment is the dependent variable and AGR, IND, SER, GOV, EXP and IMP are the independent variables

Sectors	Standardized coefficients	t-value	Significance
AGR	0.268	1.207	0.245
IND	0.083	0.180	0.860
SER	0.893	1.541	0.143
GOV	-0.275	-1.218	0.241
EXP	-0.766	-3.308	0.004
IMP	-0.741	-1.565	0.137

Out of the six sectors analyzed, only exports is correlating with unemployment at a significant level. The t-value is -3.308 which shows a strong negative correlation between the two variables. The significance level is at 99% which means that the two variables are correlating 99% of the time during the observed period (years 1988-2010, including both ends). The sign is negative, therefore, we conclude that as exports are increasing, unemployment is going down.

To check the findings, we did the regression analysis with Turkish employment, too. The equation (4) shows the analysis when employment is the dependent variable and AGR; IND; SER; GOV; EXP and IMP are the independent variables.

$$EMP = c + \delta_1\ AGR + \delta_2\ IND + \delta_3\ SER + \delta_4\ GOV + \delta_5\ EXP + \delta_6\ IMP + \epsilon \quad (4)$$

Where:

EMP is the percentage of the people (above 15 years of age) employed to

total population, yearly (labor force participation rate is the proportion of the population ages 15 and older that is economically active: All people who supply labor for the production of goods and services during a specified period) (World Development Indicators)
c is the constant term of the equation (4),
δ_1 is the standardized coefficient of AGR,
δ_2 is the standardized coefficient of IND,
δ_3 is the standardized coefficient of SER,
δ_4 is the standardized coefficient of GOV,
δ_5 is the standardized coefficient of EXP,
δ_6 is the standardized coefficient of IMP,
ϵ is the error term of equation (4).

The same data is used for AGR, IND, SER, GOV, EXP and IMP as in equation (2).

The results of the regression analysis for equation (4) is as follows:

$$EMP = 46.584 - 0.084\ AGR + 0.367\ IND - 1.619\ SER + 0.173\ GOV + 0.668\ EXP + 0.820\ IMP + 1.652 \quad (5)$$

Table 11.3 The results of the regrssion analysis when employment is the dependent variable and AGR, IND, SER, GOV, EXP and IMP are the independent variables

Sectors	Standardized coefficients	t-value	Significance
AGR	-0.084	-0.353	0.730
IND	0.367	0.689	0.503
SER	-1.619	-2.484	0.027
GOV	0.173	0.739	0.473
EXP	0.668	2.643	0.020
IMP	0.820	1.627	0.128

As equation (5) and Table 11.3 shows, similar results are obtained if employment figures are taken as the dependent variable and sectoral value added rates as percentage of GDP of Turkey are taken as the independent variables. Again, the export sector is positively correlating with the employment figures significantly. This time at 5% level, and correlation is observed at 98% of the time between employment and exports. The R square of equation (5) is 0.442 which shows it is explaining the correlation satisfactorily.

However, in equation (5) there is a significant negative correlation between employment and services sector. It shows that as the value added by the services sector increases, employment falls. In equation (4), there are weak hints about this correlation, too. In equation (4) unemployment increases as the percentage value added of services to GDP grows. This observation is not surprising, because many scholors have pointed out that the employment creating sector is mainly manufacturing and as the prcentage of service production in GDP increase, this trend effects employment adversely. Maybe this is the reason for increasing and sticky unemployment in Western capitalist economies. The percentage of service sector in many European economies and in the USA has been increasing steadily and it is well above 50% of their GDP's lately.

Unemployment and FDI

The other change induced to Turkish economy with globalisation was the liberalization of the capital movements in and out of the country. After the liberalization of the capital account of the balance of payments (BOP) in Turkey in 1989, inward FDI to Turkey increased. In this second part of the chapter we want to see how this change effected the unemployment in Turkey. In this analysis, unemployment is the dependent variable and GDP growth, FDI and growth in fixed capital investments are the independent variables. So the hypothesis is that unemployment is a factor of GDP growth (negatively), FDI (negatively) and fixed capital investments (positively).

$$U = d \quad + \gamma_1 \, GDP + \gamma_2 \, FDI + \gamma_3 \, CAP + \varepsilon \qquad (6)$$

Where:

U is the total unemployment as percentage of the total labor force,
d is the constant term for equation (6),
γ_1 is the standardized coefficient of GDP,
GDP is the yearly percentage GDP growth,
γ_2 is the standardizedcoefficient of FDI,
FDI is net FDI inflows as appears in the BOP in US dollars,
γ_3 is the standardized coefficient of CAP,
CAP is the gross capital formation as percentage of the GDP,
ε is the error term for equation (6).

The results of the regression analysis is as follows:

$$U = 9.759 - 1.697 \, GDP + 0.625 \, FDI + 1.683 \, CAP + 0.509 \qquad (7)$$

Table 11.4 The results of the regression analysis when unemployment is the dependent variable and GDP, FDI and CAP are the independent variables

Independent variables	Standardized coefficients	t-value	Significance
GDP	-1.697	-3.263	0.004
FDI	0.625	3.810	0.001
CAP	1.683	3.243	0.004

As equation (7) and Table 11.4 shows, all the three independent variables are correlating with unemployment at 1% level, which means those three variables explain the unemployment in Turkey at high significant levels. t-values are very high supporting the findings. The R square is 0.519, showing a high explanatory power of the equation. According to findings, GDP growth and unemployment are inversely proportional and as GDP grows by one percent, unemplyment falls by 1.697%. FDI and unemployment are positively correlating showing that as FDI increases by one percent, unemployment rises by 0.625% in Turkey. Thus, globalisation and FDI inflows has increased Turkish unemployment. It can be argued that, FDI inflows directed to privatized public enterprises resulted in reduction in employment in these workplaces. Also fixed capital investments and unemployment are correlating positively at high significance levels. It shows that the classical explanation argueing that "capital is replacing workers" seems to be the case in Turkey. As fixed capital investments increase, unemployment is increasing in Turkey. Of course one of the explanations can be that as the global firms invest in Turkey, they bring in their capital, too. This point needs to be explored further.

Main Findings and Policy Implications

Globalisation is a complicated and tricky phenomenon. Certain aspects of globalisation would look very attractive at the beginning but can cause totally unwanted outcomes after a period of time. For example, FDI may be improving the host country's balance of payments (BOP) when the capital is transferred from the home country to the host country at the beginning, but it can worsen the BOP when profits are expatriated from the host country for many years afterwards. Similarly, when foreign firms are buying country's state enterprises in the process of priviatization, the capital may be flowing in, but when the privatized firm start laying out workers, unemployment increases. Or, foreign firm becomes a monopoly in time pushing the local businesses to bankruptcy, and increases prices and cause inflation in the host country. Additionally, as pointed out in the chapter, probably the foreign investor replaces imported capital with local labor, increasing unemployment as observed in the Turkish example. The major concern of the foreign firms investing in Turkey is increasing its profits. Increasing employment, improving the living standards of the workers, contributing to the local technology and know-how are not foreign firms' primary objectives. So, FDI is negatively effecting Turkish employment, because probably using more fixed capital and minimizing labor input maximize profits.

International trade generally is viewed as a more manageable international economic activity, because it is assumed that a country may stop it if it starts harming the country's economy. However, it is not the case. If a country decides to restrict some imports, the exporting country may retaliate and stop its imports from that country. Hence, once the country is globalized and the rules of globalisation are in action, the domestic control over the economy weakens. The country's economy becomes subject to influences from other major, larger players. The country may become import-dependent, in other words, some productive sectors may be dependent on some raw materials or intermediary goods to continue production. In Turkey, around 60% of inputs in automobile production are imported, for example. Before globalisation, most of these imported car parts had been produced in Turkey. However, as cheaper imports of these products have entered the Turkish market, most of the local producers stopped production and they become importers. The opposite is also true; the country may become export-dependent. Because the exports are creating employment and the economy depends on export-earnings, some countries overemphasize export sector at the expense of local needs. The economies of some oil producing countries, for example, depend on the export earnings extensively. When the international price of oil changes or fluctuates, the economies of these countries become unstable and unpredictable. Turkish economy is far from being export-dependent, so there is room to expand the export sector for the time being. Also the export sector contributes to employment creation in Turkey as found out in this Chapter.

Conclusion and Suggestions

Unemployment is a major problem in Turkey like in many Western capitalist economies. The regression analysis in this research show that the export sector increases employment in Turkey. So, supporting export industries and exporting firms looks like a good policy choice. If the export industry is surviving during the recent global crisis and increasing employment in Turkey, the exporting firms deserve special attention. In this respect, we can say that trade liberalization can help Turkey's employment and benefit Turkish economy if imports can be restrained.

The other factor that effected Turkish economy as a result of globalisation is the increased FDI inflows after the liberalization of capital movements in 1989. The research shows that FDI inflows adversely effected the employment in Turkey. FDI inflows and unemployment are correlating highly significantly in Turkey. It means that FDIs in Turkey is increasing unemployment. So one suggestion on this aspect could be that Turkish policy makers can be more selective in allowing FDI into Turkey. They can require certain number of employees should continue working in privatized state enterprises, for example. They can also ask the firms to reinvest a certain amount of profits in Turkey rather than transferring all of it abroad. It has become a common knowledge that the global companies are not paying too much taxes to the host governments. Through different accounting procedures, the global firms pay very little taxes everywhere, anyway. Thus, Turkish policy makers should find ways to assure that the global firms undertaking FDI in Turkey should contribute to economy and employment in Turkey at least as much as they are expatriating.

After 20 years in the system of globalisation, Turkey's experience as its effects on unemployment has been dissappointing, probably because Turkey's policy makers could not manage the FDI inflows into Turkey in a way that the country benefits from it. If the past mistakes are realized and examined objectively, the tide can be changed. Otherwise, Turkish employment will continue to be harmed and country's resources will be expartiated by some of the foreign firms irresponsibly.

References

Aker, Sule L. (2004). "Domestic stability and balance of payments", In: B. N. Ghosh (ed.), *Contemporary Issues in Macroeconomic Management*, Leeds (UK): Wisdom House Publications.

Ikinci, Sinan (2008). "Turkish youth hit hardest by unemployment", *World Socialist Web* Site, http://www.wsws.org/en/articles/2008/05/turkm16.html

Tansel, Aysit, Mehmet Taşçı (2004). "Determinants of unemployment: Duration for men and women in Turkey", *Turkish Economic Association*, Discussion Paper 2004/6, http://www.tek.org.tr

Unemployment statistics,
http://epp.eurostat.ec.europa.eu/statistics_explained/index.php?title=File:Unemployment_rates,_seasonally_adjusted,_January_2013.png&filetimestamp=20130301091843

World Development Indicators, http://data.worldbank.org/news/world-development-indicators-2012-now-available

World Data Bank, http://data.worldbank.org/indicator/SL.UEM.TOTL.ZS
http://data.worldbank.org/indicator/SL.TLF.CACT.ZS?page=4
http://data.worldbank.org/indicator/NV.AGR.TOTL.ZS,
http://data.worldbank.org/indicator/NV.IND.TOTL.ZS,
http://data.worldbank.org/indicator/NV.SRV.TETC.ZS,
http://data.worldbank.org/indicator/GC.XPN.TOTL.GD.ZS,
http://data.worldbank.org/indicator/NE.EXP.GNFS.ZS,
http://data.worldbank.org/indicator/NE.IMP.GNFS.ZS

Chapter Twelve

Globalisation and Migration of High Quality Manpower from Malaysia

Jacqueline Liza Fernandez and Parthiban Gopal

Introduction

The surge in globalisation after the end of World War II was fuelled chiefly by an international exchange of goods and capital rather than people (Rekharamjeet, 2008; Kotz, 2002). There are signs, however, that international migration is playing an increasingly important role in globalisation in the twenty-first century, given that the global migrant stock increased from 175 million migrants in the world in 2000 to approximately 215 million in 2010 (Foo, 2011).

One of the main issues of this new wave of globalisation is brain drain. What is brain drain? The definition given by Grubel and Scott (1976) states that brain drain constitutes people who have the intention of holding permanent employment in a country other than the one in which they were educated up to a specified, high level. According to Carrington and Detragiache (1998) and Docquier and Rapoport (2004, 2011), brain drain is more specially defined as the emigration of high-skilled individuals, where a high-skilled emigrant is a foreign-born individual, aged 25 or more, with an academic or professional degree beyond high school (i.e., 'post-secondary' or 'tertiary educated') at the census or the survey date. In this chapter, we deploy the latter definition as it is the most commonly used in the literature as well as in the data presented in Section 1.2 which is taken from the Malaysian Economic Monitor report (World Bank, 2011).

Developing countries are the main source of migration to developed countries. The migration of intellectuals, professionals and skilled labour out of their domain, implies an irreplaceable loss to the stock of highly skilled population in developing countries. While it may be advantageous for the individuals involved, brain-drain represents a considerable loss to countries that have invested in workers' training and upgrading of skills. However, countries experiencing brain drain could gain from this phenomenon. Ratha (2003) noted that remittances from expatriates living abroad constitute a significant proportion of foreign revenue for many developing countries. For example, in Bangladesh US$ 2 billion is received from citizens who have migrated overseas, and these remittances are the second largest source of foreign revenue (Sengupta, 2002). Formalising the transfer of remittances might permit the generation of revenue that could be invested nationally in the social and economic development of the developing home country. Dodani and E LaPorte (2005) suggest that the magnitude and economic importance of remittances, economic development and growth, and ultimately social equity, depend on the endogenous capacity of each nation's human resources. If only a small percentage of the multimillion dollar sum sent home by emigrants could be invested in research and development, might create opportunities for highly skilled and educated nationals improve at home? And would this not in turn spur economic development? In addition, developing countries could also benefit from high-skill migration if it can find ways to foster partnerships between sending and receiving countries that result in the repatriation of skills and knowledge (brain circulation).

Theoretical Perspective of Brain Drain

There are various theories on brain drain and each theory focuses on a specific dimension of the issue. Therefore, a single theory is insufficient to explain brain drain. Roghayeh (2012) asserts that the following are salient theories of brain-drain.

World System Theory

In this model, "historical capitalism" is regarded as a system that defines "unlimited capital accumulation" that leads to cultural exchange between countries and centres. Yet this transaction is not equal and it is characterised by net capital flows from many countries (periphery) to the centre. In fact, the process of brain drain is considered as part of the overall process of capital accumulation. In the world system theory, the difference in economic development of the surrounding (periphery) countries and the centre leads to international migration.

Gidden's Structuration Theory

This migration model is considered the result of people interacting with social structures that are in place. The social structures help them to act and the individuals who are motivated also enjoy simulative interaction. Professionals create a society capable of change. If their world is not capable of change, they believe they must leave the country if their society does not accommodate this need for change. Once they are motivated to achieve progress and find better opportunities, people will emigrate. Migration is influenced by social structure, which also forms the structure of society (or causes a change), i.e., cause and effect are intertwined but it cannot be said which one has a stronger effect.

Rational Choice Theory or Game Theory

This model believes that people are looking for maximum benefit. They are influenced by structural requirements because they make reasonable choices based on their actions. In this model, there is a correlation between decisions and actions. People have goals, beliefs, and emotions that lead them to act the way they do. Professionals emigrate to gain benefits and achieve goals such as high levels of knowledge and freedom to pursue these goals, because when professionals have decided to progress, naturally, they migrate to where that progress can be achieved.

Parsons' Theory of Structural Functionalism

This theory puts forth the idea that migration results from a community's lack of adaptability. When behaviour cannot adapt to global change, professionals (due to their need to adjust, something at odds with the system) are compelled to emigrate.

Marxism Theory

In Marxism theory, through activists' awareness in their social status, changes can be produced. Professionals within a society are more aware of its social, political, and economic situation as well as its status in society. This population transforms and requires a change of location. Migration is one of these transformations to achieve true original position (including improved academic achievement situations). With the migration of the elite from their country of origin, this causes increased retardation in scientific development and lack of economic development. In contrast, the destination country makes progressive growth of production. There is advanced capitalist economic growth in the destination country.

To conclude, this study uses a holistic approach through the amalgamation of various theories (expounded above) to address the underpinning factors that determine brain drain. The holistic approach is deemed appropriate as all these theories shed light on the issue of brain drain. Figure 12.1 below shows the flow of discussion in this chapter which begins with the theories of brain drain, followed by a discussion of the determinants of brain drain and finally the strategies to mitigate the outflow of talent.

Figure 12.1 Brain Drain Theories, Determinants and Strategies

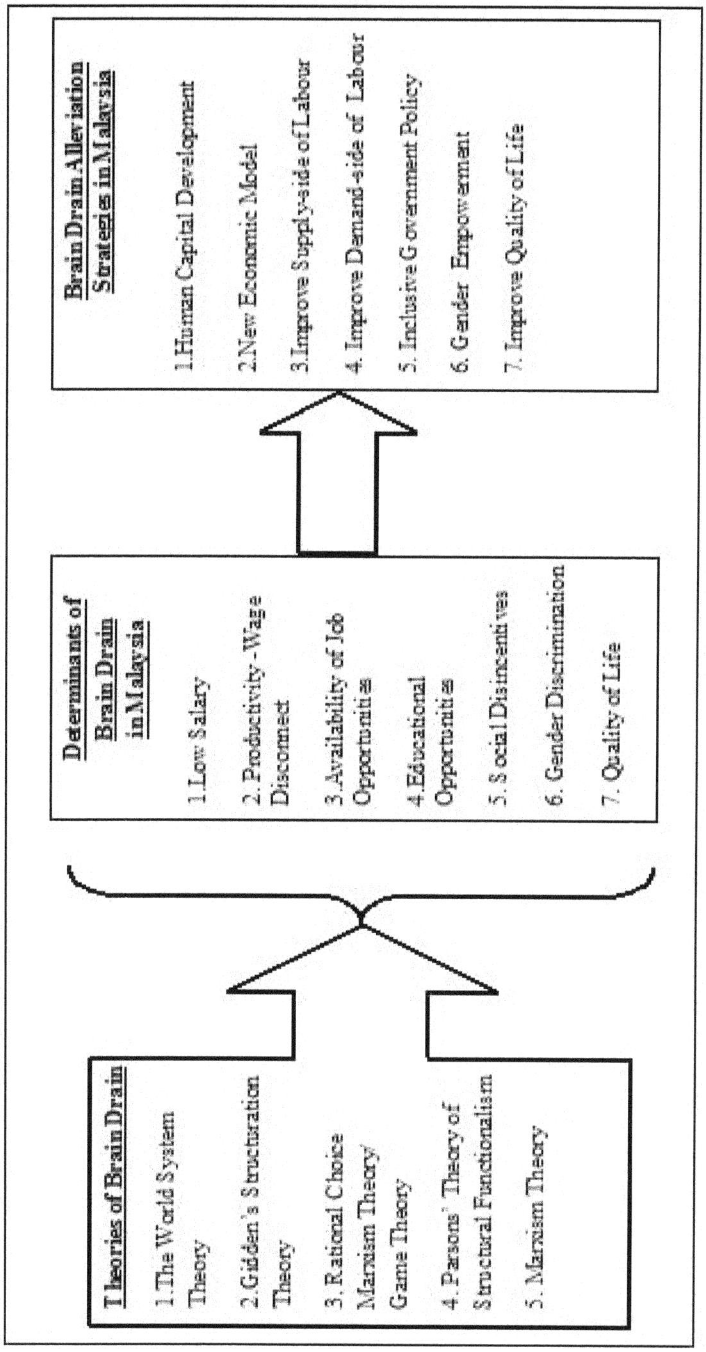

Magnitude and Trends of Malaysia's Brain Drain

In this section, we focus on brain drain in one particular developing country, namely Malaysia. The migration of talent across borders touches the core of Malaysia's aspiration to become a high-income nation by 2020 (Malaysia, 2009). Since human capital is the bedrock of a high-income economy, sustained and skill-intensive growth is requisite for Malaysia's economic transformation. In other words, for Malaysia to succeed in its journey to transforming into a high income nation, it will need to develop, attract and retain talent. The brain drain scenario is not in line with this objective: Malaysia needs talent, but talent seems to be leaving. In fact, Malaysia's brain drain appears to be picking up speed. According to a recent parliamentary report, 140,000 left the country, probably for good, in 2007 (Mariam, 2010). Between March 2008 and August 2009, that figure more than doubled to 305,000 as talented people pulled up stakes, apparently disillusioned by rising crime, a tainted judiciary, human rights abuses, an outmoded education system and other concerns. Wong (2010a) noted that out of a population of 27 million, there are an estimated 1.5 million Malaysians living abroad. Many of these Malaysians are skilled workers who migrated to Singapore and OECD countries like Australia, UK and US.

In what follows, we present the World Bank (2011) data regarding Malaysia's brain drain. We first discuss the overall diaspora, disregarding the skill composition of migrants. Following this, we present the results on brain drain which focuses on the subset of skilled migrants.

Table 12.1 provides an overview of the Malaysian diaspora. This Table shows nine destination countries and lumps the other countries into a residual category. The information is presented at decade intervals, starting from 1980. Most countries have information available up to 2000. There is incomplete diaspora data of most host countries (except Singapore) for 2010 and so intermediate data from by-censuses or other surveys is presented in the table. The aggregate numbers are analysed according to two types of country samples: the balanced sample is for comparisons over time (including only countries that have data for the full 1980-2000 period) and the unbalanced sample is for analysis within a year (including all countries reporting data for that year). The (unbalanced) sample total for 2000 — which is the most recent year where information is consistently available across countries — indicates a diaspora of over 657 thousand people.The data also shows that Malaysia's diaspora has increased significantly over the 20-year period in the last century and this increasing trend continues to manifest itself in the new millennium.

With reference to the above table as well as the data presented in Figure 12.2, the Malaysian diaspora is not only significant but also highly concentrated. In the year 2000, Singapore alone represented 46 percent of the worldwide diaspora — and this accounts for just the Malaysian-born migrants that are registered as Singapore residents. The distant second is Australia, accounting for 12 percent, and the next three preferred destinations are Brunei, United Kingdom and the United States, each with a share of about 8 percent. The five top destinations alone account for 83 percent of the entire diaspora.

Table 12.1 Malaysian Diaspora by Host Country and Over Time

	Historical series			Most recent	
	1980	1990	2000	Value	Year
Balanced sample total	285,623	431,292	611,809	..	..
Unbalanced sample total	286,102	452,109	657,574	..	..
Singapore (residents only)	120,104	194,929	303,828	385,979	2010
Australia	31,598	72,628	78,858	92,334	2006
Brunei	37,544	41,900	60,401	60,401	2000
United States	11,001	32,931	51,510	54,321	2005
United Kingdom	45,430	43,511	49,886	61,000	2007
Canada	5,707	16,100	20,420	21,885	2006
Hong Kong	..	12,754	15,579	14,664	2006
India	23,563	11,357	14,685	14,685	2001
New Zealand	3,300	8,820	11,460	14,547	2006
Other countries	7,855	17,179	50,947	..	..

Source: World Bank (2011)

Figure 12.2 Distribution of Malaysia's Diaspora across Host Countries

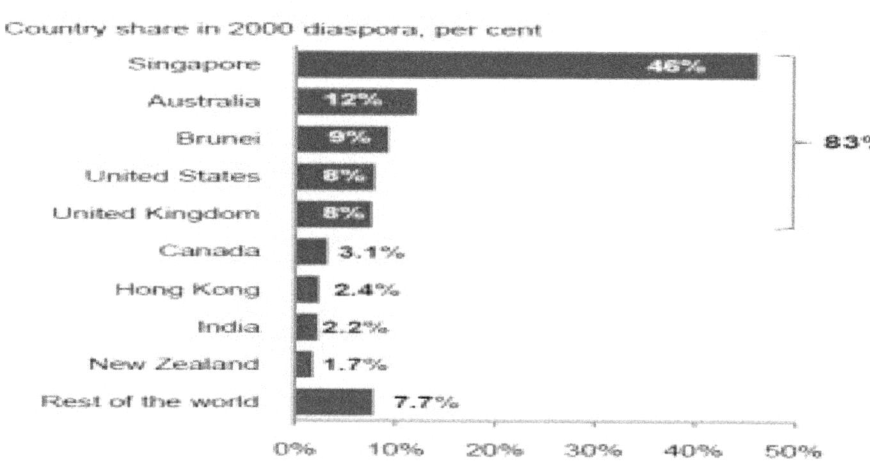

Source: World Bank (2011)

Note: The percentage for Singapore includes resident population only

It is interesting to note that not only is Malaysia's diaspora large and concentrated, but that it has also expanded rapidly over time, even though the momentum has decelerated somewhat. According to the World Bank (2011), the decade-on-decade growth numbers suggest the diaspora expanded rapidly in the 1980s and the 1990s at annualised rates of 4.2 and 3.6 percent, respectively. This growth continued, although at a slightly slower pace, and in 2000 the diaspora was some 40 percent larger than it was in 1990. Although the momentum of migration decelerated, this did not occur across the board. Table 12.2 shows that after the year 2000, migration to Singapore, Canada and United States slowed down but on the other hand, it accelerated for other destination countries like New Zealand, UK and Australia.

Hitherto, the discussion focused on Malaysia's diaspora as a whole, i.e. emigration regardless of age or skill level. But what is the size of Malaysia's brain drain or specifically the migration of skilled workers? Referring to Table 12.3, a few observations stand out when examining the aggregate numbers. It appears that the brain drain is somewhat large, when compared to the overall size of the diaspora. In the year 2000, a total of 524,613 Malaysians above the age of 25 migrated, and of these approximately 184,000 were tertiary-educated individuals. Thus, about a third of the diaspora above the age of 25 in the said year can be considered as brain drain. Migration has also become more skill-intensive over time: the share of skilled migrants rose from 28.6 percent in 1990 to 34.4 percent in 2000 (using the balanced sample numbers).

Table 12.2 Annualised Growth (Percent) in Migrant Stock by Destination

	1980-1990	**1990-2000**	**2000-latest**
New Zealand	10.3	2.7	4.9
United Kingdom	-0.4	1.4	3.4
Australia	8.7	0.8	3.2
Singapore	5.0	4.5	2.4
Canada	10.9	2.4	1.2
United States	11.6	4.6	1.1
Hong Kong	..	2.0	-1.2

Source: World Bank (2011)

Note: Periods for recent growth rates are: 2000-05 for the United States, 2000-06 for Canada, 2001-06 for Australia, Hong Kong and New Zealand, 2001-07 for the United Kingdom and 2000-2010 for Singapore.

Next, we turn to the issue of intensity of the brain drain. Unlike the size of brain drain which is measured in terms of absolute numbers, the intensity of brain drain is measured by the emigration rate of skilled workers. The skilled emigration rate relates how many skilled migrants are leaving to the initial skills base of the sending country — that is the stock of skilled people, which includes both the skilled resident population and the skilled migrants before migration. When the ratio is high, brain drain represents a more significant loss of a nation's human capital than when it is low.

Table 12.3 Size of Malaysia's Diaspora and Brain drain (Both Age 25+), by Country of Destination

	1990		2000		2010	
	Diaspora	Brain drain	Diaspora	Brain drain	Diaspora	Brain drain
Balanced sample total	347,403	99,306	479,064	164,884	..	..
Unbalanced sample total	347,403	99,306	524,613	184,121	..	..
Singapore (resident only)	185,906	19,005	286,048	66,452	350,672	121,662
Australia	44,984	35,366	56,961	38,620	..	..
United States	17,725	13,745	36,994	24,085	..	..
United Kingdom	31,130	15,328	38,147	12,898	..	..
Canada	12,150	8,480	17,150	12,170	..	..
Brunei	49,439	3,142	36,216	6,438	..	..
New Zealand	6,069	4,239	7,548	4,221	..	..
Other countries	..	..	45,549	19,130	..	..

Source: World Bank (2011)

Table 12.4 shows that Malaysia's brain drain intensity is higher than that of Japan, China and Korea; but it is noted that Singapore and Hong Kong have even higher levels of brain drain intensity, which is a characteristic of small, open economies. At the surface it seems as if Malaysia's brain drain is not an issue. After all, as Figure 12.3 shows, other Asian countries (i.e., China, Korea, Singapore and Hong Kong) have experienced more rapid growth in skilled migration over the period 1990-2000. Yet, Figure 12.4, which depicts the emigration rates from Asian countries to OECD countries, gives another perspective. Here it is noted that Singapore — the premier migration destination of Malaysian migrants — is not part of the OECD. But including Singapore as a destination country doubles the estimates of Malaysia's brain drain intensity. Including the Malaysian-born resident migrants in Singapore raises the high-skill emigration rate from 11 percent to 20 percent in 2000 and from 26 percent to 34 percent in 1990. Relative to the domestic skills base, Malaysia climbs up the rankings in the chart on brain drain intensity. This implies that despite the slower emigration growth rate than in other countries, Malaysia's stock of human capital domestically has not grown as fast as elsewhere. In short, the level of brain drain intensity has fallen in Malaysia, as it has elsewhere in the world, but brain drain intensity remains high.

Table 12.4 Comparison of Magnitude and Intensity of Brain Drain by Country

	1990		2000		1990	2000
	High-Skill at Home	High-Skill Overseas	High-Skill at Home	High-Skill Overseas	Brain Drain Intensity	
China	11,593	359	19,893	783	3.0%	3.7%
Hong Kong	379	182	696	292	32.5%	29.5%
Japan	17,399	233	22,128	278	1.3%	1.2%
Korea	3,083	335	7,565	613	9.8%	7.5%
Malaysia	222	79	818	96	26.2%	10.5%
Singapore	84	28	279	47	25.3%	14.4%

Source: World Bank (2011)

Note: Numbers for brain drain to OECD countries only, thousands

Figure 12.3 Growth of High-Skill Migrants to OECD Countries, 1990-2000

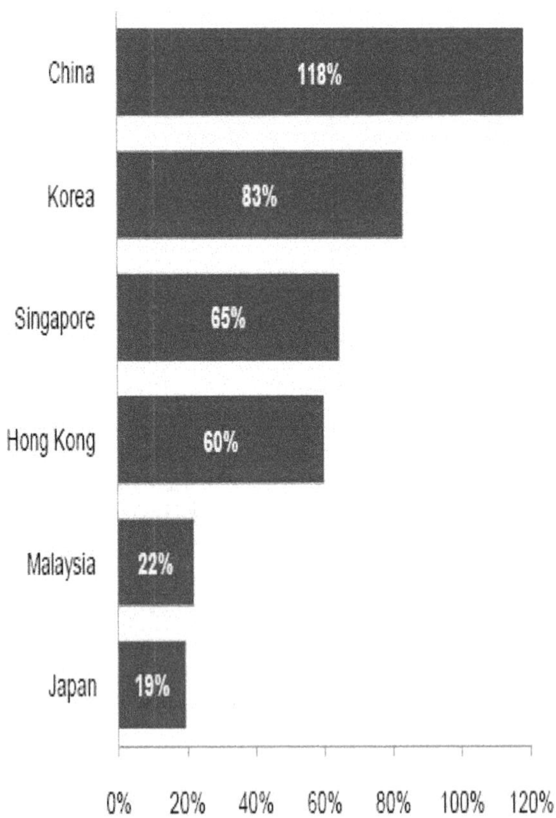

Figure 12.4 Gross Emigration Rates to OECD Destinations

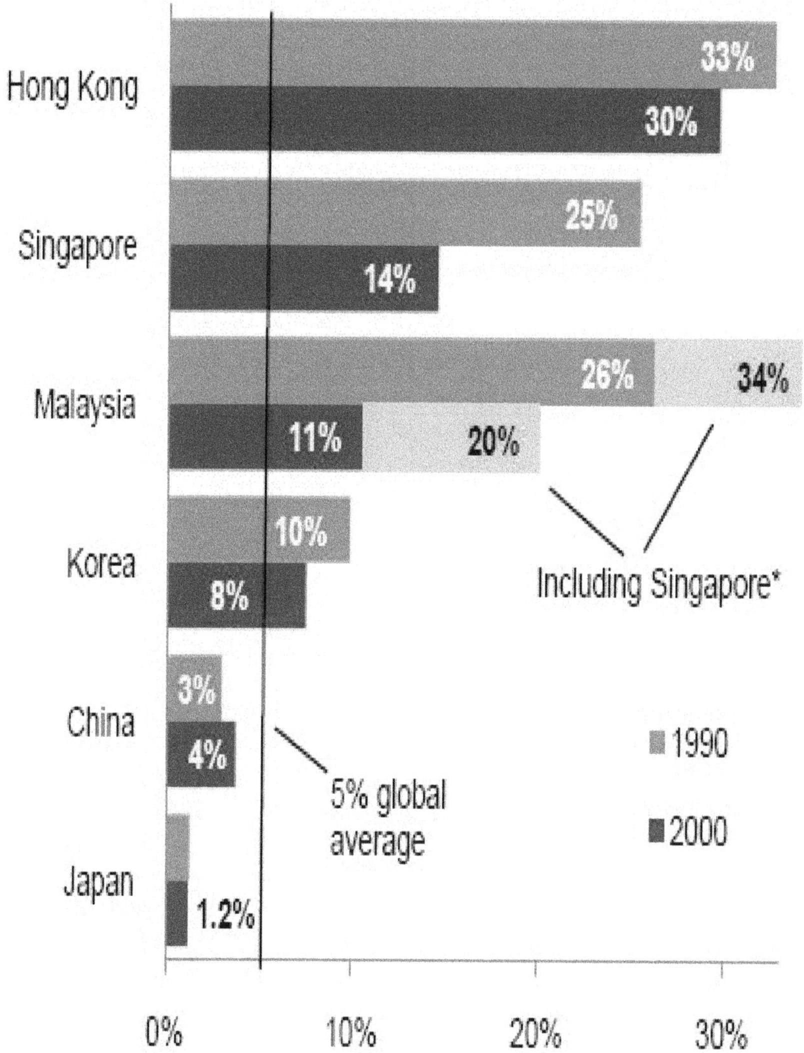

Source: World Bank (2011)

Why is Malaysia's brain drain intensity so high? Returning to OECD countries only, this appears to be related to 'skill selectivity'. The skilled emigration rate can be decomposed into two components, i.e. 'openness' and 'skill selectivity'. Openness captures the overall rate of emigration for all migrants — skilled and unskilled. *Skill selectivity is the ratio of the skill share for migrants to the skill share of the population.* In Malaysia, skill selectivity is the main driver of the emigration rate unlike the case of some other countries like South Korea and Philippines. Examining the sample of emigrants to OECD countries in 2000, the skilled are much more than proportionally represented in the migrant population (56 percent) as opposed to the overall population (8 percent) (Table 12.5).

Table 12.5 Decomposition of Skilled Emigration Rates, 2000

	Emigration rate	Openness	Skill selectivity	
	Share skilled emigrants in total skilled workers	= share migrants in x total workers	(share skilled in / total migrants	share skilled in) total workers
Indonesia	2.0	0.4	34.6	5.2
China	3.8	0.2	46.7	2.7
Global average	6.5	1.7	47.1	12.2
South Korea	7.5	3.9	50.9	26.7
Malaysia	10.5	1.5	56.2	8.3
Taiwan	12.8	3.4	79.2	21.0
Philippines	13.6	5.0	66.2	24.4
Singapore	14.5	3.2	53.7	12.0

Source: World Bank (2011)

International comparisons as shown in Table 12.5 suggest that Malaysia's skill base is narrow, i.e. only 8 percent of Malaysia's workforce is classified as skilled workers. Given the lower skill base, the impact of a person leaving should also be higher in Malaysia than elsewhere, keeping all else constant. The low skill base is inherently related to the challenges Malaysia faces in its education and training sector. Therefore, the brain drain is also closely connected to Malaysia's domestic human capital development agenda. This is an important point when considering policy options to address the brain drain (World Bank, 2011).

Malaysia's Brain Drain: The Underlying Issues

In this section, we focus on the factors that contribute to Malaysia's brain drain. Brain drain is a symptom of underlying issues. The international migration of skilled human capital results from the complex interplay of economic and non-economic factors which can be divided into factors that "push" people out of their home countries and factors which "pull" them to a new or receiving country. The discussion that follows looks at the push and the pull factors which are driving the flight of skilled human capital in the Malaysian context.

Low salary levels and benefits provide a powerful incentive for migration, particularly in the case of highly-skilled workers. The prospect of earning higher wages abroad may serve as a motivation for skilled workers to emigrate. Malaysia is caught in the middle-income trap and workers with higher education have a lower starting salary than individuals with similar qualifications and occupations in other countries. Table 12.6 compares the starting salaries for some occupations across four countries, including Malaysia. A graduate teacher's starting pay is RM 2,500 per month in Malaysia, as compared to RM 6,196 in neighbouring Singapore and RM 15,661 in Hong Kong. An accountant's pay starts at RM 2310 per month whilst the corresponding figure is about three times higher in Singapore (i.e. RM 6,561) and nearly ten times higher in UK (i.e. RM 22,813). The work of clerks and policemen that require a lower qualification (i.e. a high school diploma) also pay significantly less in Malaysia compared to UK, Hong Kong and Singapore.

Table 12.6 Salary Comparisons of Selected Occupations across Four Countries

Occupation/Nation		UK	Hong Kong	Singapore	Malaysia
Policeman (high school diploma)	RM	10,615	9,509	3,788	1,481
		£1,939	HK$21,645	S$1,559	
Teacher (graduate)	RM	11,864	15,681	6,196	2,500
		£2,167	HK$35,693	S$2,550	
Accountant	RM	22,813	12,814	6,561	2,310
		£4,167	HK$29,167	S$2,700	
Clerk (high school diploma)	RM	7,757	3,954	2,916	1,000
		£1,417	HK$9,000	S$1,200	

Source: Fong (2010)

Note: The conversion from Ringgit Malaysia (RM) to UK, Hong Kong and Singapore currency is based on 29/1/2010 exchange rate

In addition to the relatively low starting salaries in Malaysia, the other problem is the productivity-wage disconnect. Wage growth has been slow and lagging behind productivity growth. For instance, labour productivity in manufacturing (i.e. real value-added per worker) grew at an average of 5 percent per annum in the last decade while real manufacturing wages expanded by only 2.4 percent per annum during the same period (World Bank, 2012). The slow wage growth also has an impact on the standard of living given that salaries have not grown in tandem with the increase in cost of living. The data in Table 12.7 indicates that Malaysia's growth in real salary and wages in the various industries dropped after the Asian Financial Crisis and has not returned to the pre-crisis levels. The low starting salary and the lagging wage growth with respect to productivity growth and inflation rates contribute to the migration of skilled workers.

Table 12.7 Growth in Real Wages Pre- and Post-Asian Financial Crisis

Industry		Increase in Real Wages (% p.a.)	
		Pre-Crisis Period (1994-1997)	**Post-Crisis Period (1987-2007)**
Export-Oriented Industries (EOI)	Average Increase for EOI	5.6	1.9
	Electrical & Electronics	6.2	2.5
	Petroleum, Chemical, Rubber, Plastic Products, Real Estate	6.0	1.5
	Textiles & Apparel, Leather Products	5.8	-1.3
	Wood Products, Furniture, Paper Products, Printing, Publishing	2.8	1.4
Domestic-Oriented Industries (DOI)	Average Increase for DOI	6.8	1.4
	Transport Equipment, Other Manufactures	7.9	2.5
	Food, Beverages, Tobacco	6.8	1.2
	Non-Metallic Mineral Products, Basic Metal, Fabricated Metal	5.9	0.6
	Total Manufacturing	5.9	1.8

Source: World Bank (2012)

Another factor that drives brain drain is the availability of the job opportunities in the labour market. As a result of structural changes in the economy that is characterised by the growth in the service sector and decline in the manufacturing sector between 2000 and 2010, most jobs created in the past decade have been at the middle or high-skill levels. On average, professional occupations grew at 5 percent while technical and associate professional jobs expanded at 4.3 percent in the last decade; on the other hand, plant and machine operator positions declined at an average rate of 1.3 percent during this period (World Bank, 2012). The flow of new jobs towards skilled jobs points towards changing trends in the labour market as Malaysia undergoes structural changes in the economy. Yet, the largest percentage (44 percent) of jobs is still relatively low-skilled (Figure 12.5). In Malaysia, not enough high-skilled jobs have been created. According to the New Economic Model report (Malaysia, 2009), the share of skilled labour has declined across industries as a result of the dominance of the production of low-value added goods in Malaysia which use low-skilled labour. This is because in many cases, employers are not willing to pay for skills; instead, they choose to rely on the large pool of unskilled foreign workers to generate profits. Employers' preference for low-skilled labour has led high-skilled workers to seek job opportunities in more advanced job markets.

Figure 12.5 Distribution of Workers in Malaysia by Skill Level, 2010

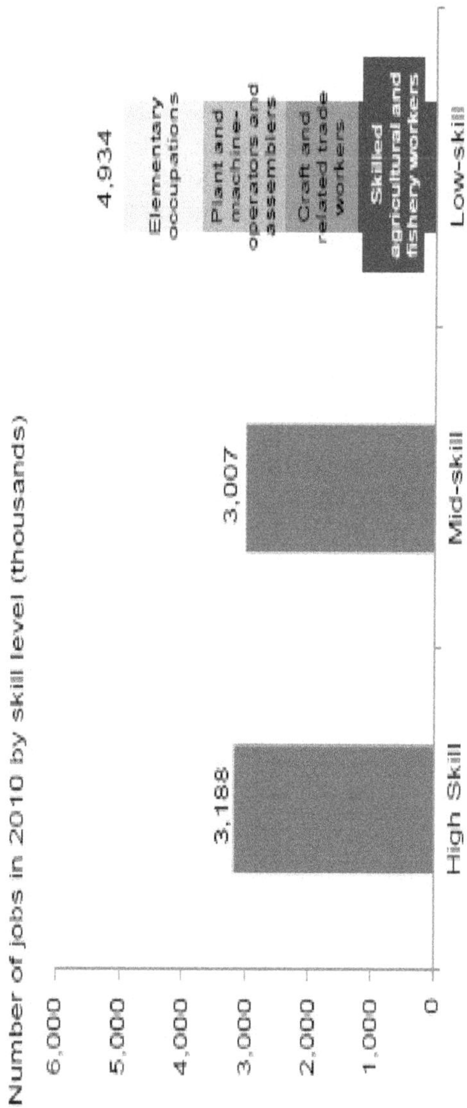

Source: World Bank (2012)

Note: 'High Skill' includes legislators, senior officials, managers, professionals, technicians and associate professionals; 'mid-skill' includes clerical workers, service workers and shop/market sales workers; 'low-skill' includes agricultural and fishery workers, craft and related trade workers, plant and machine operators and assemblers, and elementary occupations.

Another motivation for migration is educational opportunities. Up to the late 1990s, many Malaysians migrated so that their children would have access to higher education since the opportunities to pursue tertiary education (particularly for minority groups, i.e., the non-Malays) were limited by the ethnic-based quota system and financial aid. However, the prospects to pursue tertiary education have increased with the implementation of the 1996 Private University Act and the establishment of the Government University Loan Scheme as well as the availability of government scholarships to excellent students. Nevertheless, Malaysians continue to go abroad for studies given the quality gap between domestic and foreign institutions. The quality of education in Malaysia is found wanting, notwithstanding the heavy public investment in this sector. For example, the data of the Trends in Mathematics and Sciences Study (TIMSS) in Table 12.8 show that eighth-grade students' Science and Mathematics scores in Malaysia have gone down between 1999 and 2007 and rank below the international average level. The quality of higher education in Malaysia is also not up to the mark. This is evident from the high unemployment rates among graduates with a bachelor's degree (i.e. 17% for public universities and 19% for private universities). In a recent survey, nearly half of the Malaysian firms cited the lack of Information Technology skills and lack of English proficiency as key restraints to hiring (Malaysia, 2012a).

Table 12.8 Students Science and Mathematics Scores in Selected Countries

Eighth-Grade TIMSS Scores for Science in Selected Countries					**Eighth-Grade TIMSS Scores for Maths in Selected Countries**			
Economy	**1999**	**2003**	**2007**		**Economy**	**1999**	**2003**	**2007**
Singapore	568	578	567		Taiwan	585	585	598
Taiwan	569	571	561		Korea	587	589	597
Japan	550	552	554		Singapore	604	605	593
Korea	549	558	553		Hong Kong	582	586	572
Hong Kong	530	556	530		Japan	579	570	570
United States	515	527	520		United States	502	504	508
International Average	488	473	500		International Average	487	466	500
Malaysia	492	510	471		Malaysia	519	508	474
Thailand	482	-	471		Thailand	467	-	441
Indonesia	435	420	427		Indonesia	403	411	397
Philippines	345	377	-		Philippines	345	378	-

Source: Malaysia (2012a)

Social disincentives also play an important role in the migration decision. In Malaysia, the perception of social injustice is a long standing problem. In 1970, the government unfolded the New Economic Policy to eradicate poverty and restructure society to eliminate the identification of race with economic function. In order to restructure society and reduce the inter-ethnic disparities between the *Bumiputera* (indigenous groups) and the non-*Bumiputera*, particularly between ethnic Malays and Chinese, the government adopted 'affirmative action' measures on behalf of the mainly Malay *Bumiputera*. The growing dissatisfaction of those deprived of the special privileges accorded to the *Bumiputera* has driven many non-*Bumiputera* to look for greener pastures in other countries. The sense of social injustice is perceived even by young non-Malays as a result of unequal access to scholarships and higher education in specialised fields in spite of the government's efforts to reduce the reliance on racial quotas and lean more towards meritocracy. Discontent with government's inclusiveness policies may be regarded as a critical factor of brain drain given that Malaysia's diaspora has a marked ethnic dimension, i.e., the majority of the diaspora are Chinese descent. Figure 12.6 shows the ethnic profile of Malaysia's diaspora in Singapore, which is favourite destination for Malaysian migrants due to its proximity with Malaysia. In 2010, the share of ethnic Chinese in the diaspora residing in Singapore had risen to almost 90 percent while the share of Indians remained at 5 percent during the last decade.

Figure 12.6 Share of Malaysians of Various Ethnicities Residing in Singapore

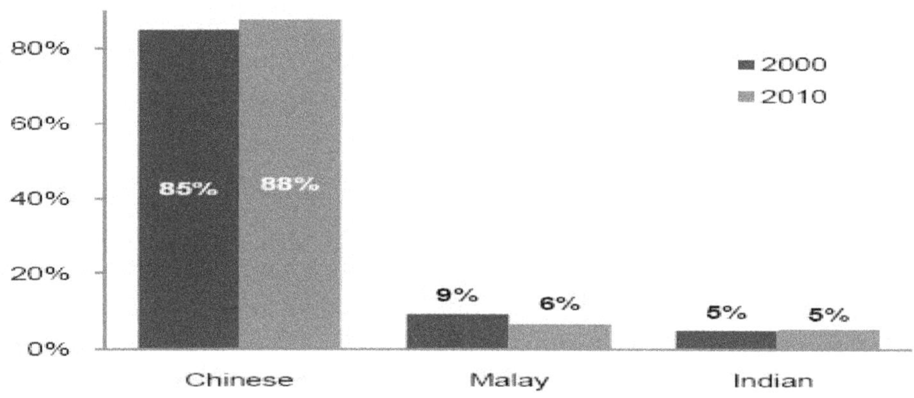

Source: World Bank (2011)

The issue of social disincentive can also be seen from a gender perspective. Although the male-female gap in education has been closed since the 1990s, women's labour force participation rate has still not exceeded 50 percent (Malaysia, 2003; Malaysia, 2012a). There are barriers that make our labour market unattractive for women. Among the main reasons for low female participation rates are inflexible working arrangements and the lack of gender-friendly policies. Efforts undertaken to tackle brain drain should promote inclusiveness along ethnic as well as gender lines in Malaysia.

Finally, another consideration that influences the decision of Malaysians to emigrate is the search for a better quality of life. One measure of quality of life is the Human Development Index which is a composite measure of three basic dimensions of human development, i.e. health, education and income. In the 2012, Global Liveability Survey, Kuala Lumpur which is the capital city of Malaysia was ranked the 77th most liveable city in a list of 140 cities (Malaysia, 2012b). The ranking was based on a set of criteria that included variables such as stability, healthcare, culture and environment, education and infrastructure conditions. Cities with higher ranking were mostly located in developed countries as well as some Asian global cities such as Singapore (52nd position) and Seoul (58th position).

Figure 12.7 Percentage of Malaysian Emigrants Who View Each Factoras One of the Top Three Drivers of Brain Drain

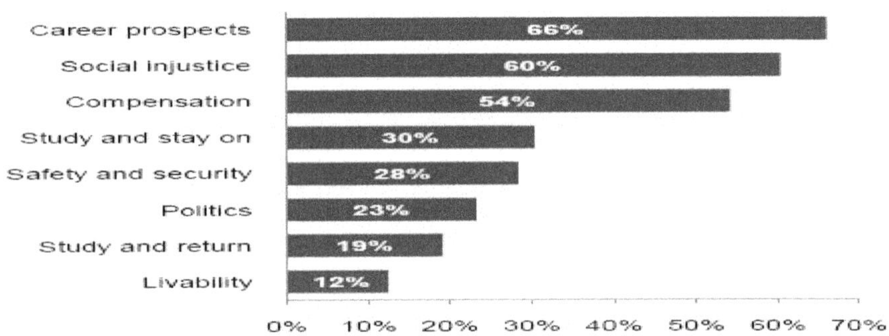

Source: World Bank (2011)

To get an idea of the views of Malaysia's diaspora regarding the reasons for migration, we present the World Bank (2011) findings of an online survey that was carried out in February 2011 that received responses from 194 respondents. Figure 12.7 below shows the share of respondents listing each item as one of the top three reasons for brain drain in Malaysia. The results of the survey suggest that both economic and social factors are the main drivers of brain drain. 'Better career prospects abroad' is at the top of the list, with 66 percent of the respondents listing this factor as one of their top three considerations. Slightly more than half the number of respondents regarded 'better remuneration' as one of the main factors that result in brain drain. In addition to these economic factors, brain drain is also largely attributed to social factors i.e., 60 percent of the respondents' state that brain drain is related to 'a sense of social injustice'. Other factors that influence brain drain include safety and security issues, political factors and concerns about liveability, however, less than a third of the respondents rank these factors as one of their top three considerations that influence the migration decision.

In another study, Wong (2010b) obtained similar results based on an online survey involving of a larger sample of 854 respondents. The survey used a Likert-scale to rank the determinants of migration on a scale of 0 (no effect) to 5 (greatly affected). The share of respondents that give a 4 or 5 rating for factors that influence migration are as follows: Malaysia's economic situation (56 percent), Malaysia's political situation (69 percent), human rights and media freedom (55 percent), inter-racial harmony (58 percent), quality of education (63 percent) and crime rate (63 percent). The results indicate that the majority of respondents regard economic, social as well as political factors as having an important influence on migration.

Policy Approaches to Brain Drain

As discussed earlier, among the reasons for brain drain are the quest for higher salaries and better education. Alienation in the Malaysian labour market along ethnic and gender lines is also a driving force in the brain drain issue, i.e., the pro-*Bumiputera* government policies tend to create a sense of alienation among the non-*Bumiputera* population while the lack of gender-friendly working conditions tends to alienate women from the workforce. Finally, brain drain also arises from the desire for a better quality of life that is offered abroad. Malaysia recognises the need to adopt a holistic approach to tackle the underlying determinants of brain drain. The policies to address the brain drain problem should encompass measures to boost up human capital development as well as provide better job opportunities in order to raise salaries, promote inclusiveness and raise the quality of life (World Bank, 2011).

At the turn of this decade, the government unveiled the New Economic Model (Malaysia, 2009) which outlines Malaysia's goal of becoming a high-income nation and raise the living standard of Malaysians, which is envisaged to reduce brain drain. This goal can be attained by focusing on productivity which involves human capital development issues (affecting the supply of skill) and broader investment climate issues (affecting firms' productivity and the demand for skill) so that productivity and wage levels can rise in tandem.

On the supply-side, the current human capital base in Malaysia is too narrow and insufficiently high quality to support the needs of the high-growth model. The key concerns of firms pertaining to skill deficiencies of local professional workers are in the area of creativity/innovation and IT skills in the manufacturing sector and creativity/innovation, leadership, problem-solving and communication skills in the services sector. To ensure the demand for skill can be satisfied as Malaysia transforms into a high-income nation, measures must be undertaken to improve the quantity and quality of skilled labour. We need to begin by improving the quality of basic education in schools by shifting from the traditional rote learning approach to new ways of teaching and learning that hone students' creativity as well as critical and analytical thinking. Measures must also be taken to nurture talent at the tertiary level and this includes the following: improve university curricula so that graduates are more industry-ready (i.e. the skills of graduates match the needs of employers) and networking opportunities for top talents to link up with critical industries. Developing an employer-led skills development system is also a crucial step in the human capital development agenda. The government should consider implementing measures to encourage employers to play a more active role in skills standard and certification process, designing the curriculum of training programs, providing apprenticeships, and offering internship and scholarship programs to workers to improve their skills. It is only when industries and employers are closely involved in training decisions that the training programs can respond to the changing needs of firms (World Bank, 2011; Malaysia, 2012a).

The other side of the coin regarding the issue of making salaries more attractive is the demand aspect. Firms are concerned about the quality of education and skill deficiencies, but an alternative explanation for low salaries may lie in the unwillingness of firms to offer higher wages to attract the best talents. Given the presence of a large pool of migrant workers, Malaysia's economy has been largely based on production modes that employ low- and semi-skilled workers and this has dampened the demand for skilled workers. In addition, the services sector in Malaysia is highly protected, which does not motivate firms to innovate and move up the value chain, thus further reducing the demand for skills (Malaysia, 2009; World Bank, 2011).

This raises the question of how to raise the demand for skills. The answer lies in the nation's economic transformation. Malaysia's old growth models were based on capital accumulation whereby growth was prompted by large-scale physical capital investment, the export of manufactured goods, natural resource-based goods and petroleum products. Merely increasing investment levels and quantities of low-skilled labour will no longer be sufficient to drive growth to a higher level. The focus for the government at present should be on developing a supporting environment for innovation and providing firms the opportunities to develop higher value-added products. Innovation and the creation of new technology can nurture niches of growth and assist in accelerating growth; these will create demand for skilled labour and increase returns to education and skills upgrading. The factors that would support a more innovative environment include attracting global entrepreneurs, providing government support and infrastructure to build a knowledge-based economy and ensuring the adequate provision of bank finance and venture capital for innovation. To activate innovation, Malaysia will also need to foster competitiveness among firms and industries, which is the driving force of private sector-led innovation. Many services sub-sectors lack both international and domestic competition given the existing restrictions on equity holdings as well as slow liberalisation and deregulation policies. Accordingly, the government should develop a liberalisation policy framework and reform its outdated regulatory framework that deters competition and innovation (World Bank, 2012).

In addition to providing better economic incentives as discussed above, there is also a need to focus on measures that address the issue of social disincentives due to Malaysia's affirmative action policy. Unlike the common practise of bestowing preferential treatment on groups which are economically and socially disadvantaged and politically subordinate, Malaysia's affirmative action policy is unique given that it is the politically dominant majority group (i.e. the Malay *Bumiputera*) which introduces preferential policies to raise its economic status. Although the affirmative action policy has been able to narrow inter-ethnic economic disparities, its prolonged use has created dissatisfaction among the minority Chinese and Indian ethnic groups who feel discriminated. As the government strives to transform the economy into a knowledge-based economy that requires skilled manpower, it must be mindful that the ethnic-based preferential policy continues to be a push factor in the brain drain problem (Lee, 2005). There is a need to shift from ethnic-based affirmative action to a system based on meritocracy to remove negative perceptions and sentiments of the non-*Bumiputera* in order to curb the outflow of talent. In line with its attempt to strengthen inclusiveness as outlined in the New Economic Model (Malaysia, 2009), the government has introduced the concept of *1Malaysia* to foster ethnic harmony. However, it is left to be seen whether the *1Malaysia* concept is merely political rhetoric. It is argued that the concept of *1Malaysia* will only become a reality if there is a lack of political will to introduce substantive changes in socio-economic policies that can create a sense of unity among all Malaysians.

Malaysia's brain drain policy also focuses on strengthening inclusiveness in terms of gender. There are barriers that make our labour market unattractive for women. Malaysia is the only Southeast Asian country with a "single-peaked" profile of labour force participation for women, indicating that many Malaysian women tend not to return to the labour force after marriage and child birth. To optimise the use of our female talent pool in the face of skills shortage, progressive companies and relevant ministries are now implementing initiatives and programmes that will facilitate women to re-enter the workforce, while retaining those already in the workforce. Talent Corp (Malaysia, 2012a) reports that companies such as Agilent, GE, IBM, Intel, MIMOS and SCB have established women councils and cross-border networks. These councils have designed several initiatives dealing with women-centric issues and are making efforts to cater for the well-being of women in the respective organisations. Other than having supportive human resource practices, companies also organise programmes to nurture, attract and retain women. For example, the advocacy and publishing works done by companies like Agilent, IBM and Intel and forums led by in-house Women Councils like the GE Women Network, leverage on its international women network and relationships to share best practices, to retain current women workforce population, and to assist women to return to work. Gender-friendly best practices include setting realistic workloads, creche facilities, flexible work arrangements, and other supportive practices. The benefits of these policies include increased productivity, lower job turnover rates, job satisfaction and women empowerment which can mitigate the brain drain of women to countries that offer better working conditions for the fairer sex.

Finally, we turn to the issue of improving the quality of life in Malaysia as a step towards addressing the brain drain problem. Some of the factors that impinge on the quality of life are safety and security issues, inadequate affordable housing and the lack of an efficient transport system. In addition, there is a need to improve natural resources management and preserve nature. The government is currently taking measures to address these problems but the growing population in Malaysia, which is compounded by the rising number of migrant workers, makes it difficult for the government to provide effective solutions to these problems. Nevertheless Malaysia seeks to achieve sustainable growth that meets the ongoing needs of the population without compromising the needs of future generations as spelled out in the New Economic Model.

Conclusions

Increasing globalisation has escalated the migratory flow of workers across the world. Many countries are competing to attract and retain the global talent pool. No efforts must be spared to increase Malaysia's attractiveness as a destination for top talents, both Malaysian and foreign, as well as to actively source for talent that is critically needed by the nation. To address the problem of skills shortage, Malaysia needs to tackle the underlying causes of the problem.

A holistic approach to this issue is needed rather than the implementation of ad-hoc measures. Only in this way will Malaysia be able to acquire the requisite pool of talent to drive its economic growth till it achieves the status of a high-income nation. Malaysia has embarked on the journey to close the skills gap but it is necessary for the nation to evaluate the strengths and weakness of its existing programmes and policies from time to time with the intent of discarding programmes that are ineffective and introducing new programmes that are able to address present and emerging challenges with regard to attracting, sourcing and retaining talent.

To conclude, for the balance of power and for the staggered development of the world, it is very important for developing nations like Malaysia to regulate the phenomenon of brain-drain. This will help the country to use all local skilled citizens for development and proliferation. But to hold these skilled workers at their native places, it is also important to provide them enough work opportunities and living facilities. For this purpose, developed nations should help developing countries with necessary fund and resources so that each and every nation can transform itself as a developed nation and people everywhere in the world can enjoy a good standard of living.

References

Carrington, W. J. and Detragiache, E. (1998). "How big is the brain drain?" IMF Working Paper WP/98/102. Washington D.C.: International Monetary Fund.

Docquier, F. and Rapoport (2004). "Skilled migration: The perspective of developing countries", World Bank Policy Research Working Paper 3382.

Docquier, F. and Rapoport (2011). "Globalisation, brain drain and development", Discussion Paper 5590. Retrieved from <http://ftp.iza.org/dp5590.pdf> on 25th February 2013.

Dodani, S. and E LaPorte, R. (2005). "Brain drain from developing countries: How can brain drain be converted into wisdom gain?", *Journal of the Royal Society of Medicine*, 98, 487-491.

Fong, C.O. (2010). "Caught in middle-income trap". Retrieved from <http://thestar.com.my> on 12nd February 2013.

Foo, G. (2011). "Quantifying the Malaysian brain drain and an investigation of its key determinants", *Malaysian Journal of Economic Studies*, 48(2), 93-116.

Grubel, H. G. and Scott, A. (1976). "The immigration of scientists and engineers to the United States 1949-61", *The Journal of Political Economy*, 74, 368-378.

Kotz, D. M. (2002). "Globalisation and neo-liberalism", *Rethinking Marxism*, 12(2), 64-79.

Lee, H.G. (2005). "Affirmative action in Malaysia". Singapore, Institute of South East Asian Studies. Retrieved from <http://english.cpiasia.net> on 20th February 2013.

Malaysia. (2012a). "Talent roadmap 2020". Petaling Jaya: Talent Corp Malaysia. Retrieved from <www.talentcorp.com.my> on 20th February 2013.

Malaysia. (2012b). "Kuala Lumpur in global liveability survey 2012". Retrieved from <http://ilmuonline.mpc.gov.my> on 12th February 2013.

Malaysia. (2009). "New economic model for Malaysia". Putrajaya: National Economic Advisory Council. Retrieved from <www.pmo.gov.my> on 23rd February 2013.

Malaysia (2003). *The Progress of Malaysian Women Since Independence 1957-2000.* Kuala Lumpur: Ministry of Women and Family Development.

Mariam, M. (2010). "Malaysia's brain drain. Asia Sentinel". Retrieved from <http://www.asiasentinel.com> on 27 February 2013.

Ratha, D. (2003). "Workers remittances: An important and stable source of external development. In striving for stability in development finance". Washington, D.C.: World Bank, 157–75.

Rekharamjeet. (2008). "Brain drain". Retrieved from <http://www.studymode.com/essays/Brain-Drain-164883.html> on 27th February 2013.

Roghayeh, P. (2012). "Factors affecting the brain drain from Iran", *Journal of Basic and Applied Scientific Research*, 2(3), 3003-3015.

Sengupta, S. (2002). "Money from kin abroad helps Bengalis get by". New York Times World. Retrieved from <http://query.nytimes.com/gst/abstract.html> on 2nd March 2012.

Wong, E. (2010a), "Is Malaysia experiencing a brain drain?" Retrieved from <http://asiapacific.anu.edu.au> on 11th February 2013.

Wong, E. (2010b). "Will you come back to Malaysia? Results of an online survey." Retrieved from <http://pluggingthebraindrain.wordpress.com> on 20th February 2013.

World Bank. (2012). 'Malaysia economic monitor - modern jobs.' Washington, D.C.: World Bank. Retrieved from <http://www.worldbank.org/my> on 22nd February 2013.

World Bank. (2011). 'Malaysia economic monitor-brain drain'. Washington, D.C.: World Bank. Retrieved from <http://www.worldbank.org/my> on 20th February 2013.

Chapter Thirteen

Silence of the Lambs – Dynamics of Female Migration and State Policies

Padmaja D Namboodiri

Introduction

International labour migration is defined as the movement of people from one country to another for the purpose of employment. As per United Nations data, in 2010, 213.9 million persons are working in a country other than their country of birth. International migration in the development context relates both to people who have chosen to move of their own accord, and forced migrants. Labour mobility has become a key feature of globalisation and the global economy with migrant workers earning US$ 440 billion in 2011, and the World Bank estimating that more than $350 billion of that total was transferred to developing countries in the form of remittances. About 70 per cent of total international migrants are born in the South. International migration is not restricted to people from low-income countries moving to high-income ones seeking work. South–South migration has been increasing and is believed to be as significant as South–North movements (UNDESA, 2012). International labour law provides for equality of opportunity and non-discrimination at work for all workers, including migrant workers. However, in the international state system, citizenship confers exclusive rights to nationals of each State. Deprived of these rights and alien to different extents to societies and cultures in their countries of employment, migrant workers are at a disadvantage.

At the same time, there are a number of concrete and potential enabling effects of migration on development. Migration has important effects on fundamental economic conditions related to labour markets, income levels, income distribution, financial markets, trade and investments. The primary means through which migration has an impact on such conditions include financial remittances, labour mobility and circular migration, transfer of skills and knowledge, and the international networks of migrants and diasporas, which facilitate trade and investment. Migration, which is a concrete expression of globalisation, is identified as one of the enablers of development. This enabler has huge development potential, for individual migrants and their families, for their country of origin and for the country of destination.

Historically migration had been the domain of men, but in 2005, for the first time, the number of female migrants equaled that of men. U.N. data on migrant stock indicates that the percentage of female migrants has increased since 1990. Table 13.1 reveals the changing nature of world female migration.

Table 13.1 Female Migrants as Percentage of International Migrants

Year	World	Africa	Asia	Europe	Latin America	North America	Oceania
1985	47.2	44.4	43.8	48.9	48.9	51.9	48.4
1990	49.0	46.2	45.4	52.7	49.7	51.1	49.1
1995	49.3	47.1	45.3	52.4	50.0	50.8	49.7
2000	49.7	46.7	45.7	52.8	50.0	50.5	50.2
2005	49.6	46.7	45.0	52.5	50.1	50.1	50.7
2010	49.0	46.8	44.6	52.3	50.1	50.1	51.2

Source: Trends in Migrant stock, 2008 Revision, Population division of the Department of Economic and Social Affairs (DESA), U.N., (UN data base, pop/DB/MIG/STOCK/2008).

The U.N. data on migrant stock indicates that the percentage of female migrants has increased since 1990, from 47.2% in 1985 to 49% in 2010. The most significant increase took place in Europe, where the percentage of female migrants rose from 48.9% in 1985 to 50.1% in 2010. This data also indicates that the percentage of female migrants has increased since 1985 in all but two regions of the world: Asia and North America (Table 13.1). Africa and Oceania, which includes Australia and New Zealand, also saw increases of about 4% over the same time period.

The United Nations subdivides Asia into four regions: Eastern, South-central, South-eastern and Western. The percentage of female migrants increased in all but Western Asia, which includes most of the countries in the Middle East as well as Turkey. In all the other sub-divisions, the share of female migrants increased.

In Northern America, as the UN classifies the continent, the most significant changes occurred in the two largest countries: the United States and Canada (classified as North America). In the region, meanwhile, the percentage of female migrants decreased from 51.9% to 50.1%. The following figure makes a comparison of the female migration between the more developed and the less developed countries along with the world data.

As the Figure 13.1 reveals, female migration is 49.1% in 1990, 49.4 in 2000 and 49 % in 2010 for the world as a whole. In the more developed regions of the world, there has been a tremendous inflow of female migrants ranging around 52% from 1990 to 2010 (52% in 1990, 51.8 in 2000 and 51.5 in 2010). In the less developed regions, the female migrants were about 45% in the same period (45.9% in 1990, 46.1 in 2000 and 45.3 in 2010). All these data show that women account for approximately half of all global migrants.

Figure 13.1 Percentage of Female Migrants in Developed and Less Developed Regions

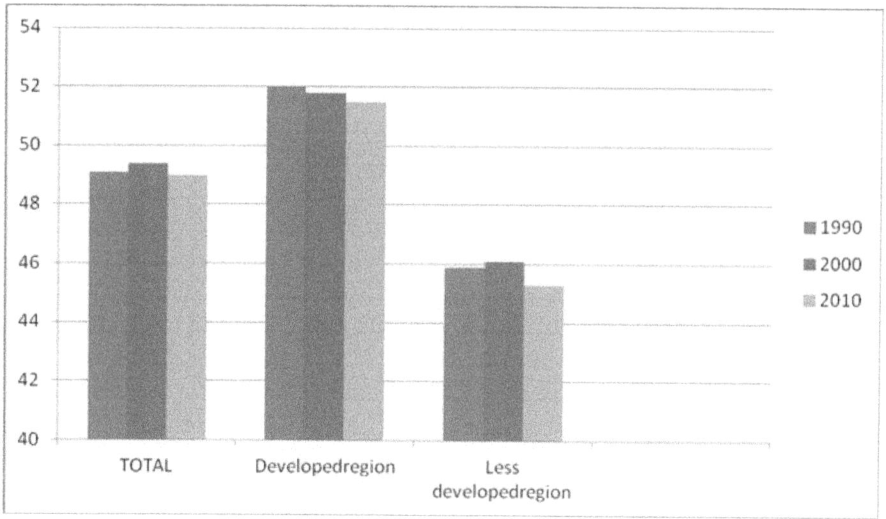

The UN data also reveals some interesting facts about the age distribution of female migrants. Male migrants outnumber their female counterparts until the age group of 50-54. Starting with the age group of 55-59, female migrants are more than males. Women migrants in the age above 65 are more due to their higher life expectancy.

In the developed countries, the number of female and male migrants is same in the age groups from 0-4 to 45-49 showing family migration. In the developing countries, male–female migration is similar as in developed countries in the young age group. But from the age group 20-24 the percentage of females drops rapidly in these economies. However, the percentage of female migrants increases rapidly in the older age groups in the less developed countries. The Table 13.2 gives the sectoral distribution of women migrants employed in OECD countries.

Table 13.2 reveals that female migrant workers dominate the major sectors like health and social work, wholesale and retail, manufacturing, social and personal service activities, hotel and restaurants, education, real estate and business activities. Along with South and Central America and Caribbean countries females from Africa and Asia have a strong presence in OECD countries.

Table 13.2 Percentage of Women Migrant Workers in OECD Countries by Sector and Region of Birth

Sector	Africa	Asia	S & N America	Others	All countries
Health & social work 20	17	18	9	17	
Whole sale & retail	13	15	13	14	14
Manufacturing	9	15	14	14	13
Social & per; services	7	10	15	7	11
Real estate	11	9	6	11	9
Hotel	7	9	11	6	9
Education	10	7	7	5	8
Financial Institn.	5	6	4	5	5
Public Admn.	5	3	3	5	3
Transport	3	3	2	5	3
Agriculture	1	1	2	2	2
Private Households	3	1	2	1	2
Construction	1	1	1	1	1
Others	6	2	2	13	3

Source: http://stats.oecd.org/index.aspx

Legal vs. Illegal Migration

Studies (IOM 2005) that have examined the gender composition of legal immigrant inflows, a population that includes legal permanent residents, refugees and those seeking asylum, show that females very often comprise a majority of arrivals. Of the established 25 million persons displaced by conflicts, more than 70% are women and children. Out of general migration 49% of refugees are female (UNGA, 2004). Another alarming aspect of labour migration from and within South Asia is trafficking of women and children across borders, often for commercial sex work, labour exploitation and other purposes. The working conditions of trafficked persons often amount to slavery, forced labour or debt bondage reflecting serious abuse of their basic human rights. While no firm data exist, an Asian Development Bank study (ADB 2003) noted that Bangladesh and Nepal were the main countries of origin for trafficking, while India and Pakistan were considered countries of destination or transit to other regions, commonly the Gulf States or Southeast Asia. "There are figures quoted and cross-quoted in the literature and reports, but the most cited are: 300,000 Bangladeshi women trafficked to India over an unspecified period and 200,000 to Pakistan. Over 200,000 Nepal sex workers are reported to work in Indian cities, fully one fifth of who are supposedly under the age of 16 years." (ADB 2003: 20)

Factors Affecting International Migration

The Theoretical Scaffoldings

Traditional neo-classical macro theories on international migration as developed by Lewis (1954), Ranis and Fei (1961), Todaro (1976) explain that labour movements across countries are due to geographic differences in the supply and demand for labour and resulting wage differentials. Neo-classical micro economic theory propounded by Sjaastad (1962), Todaro (1969, 1970, 1989) etc., made migration an individual choice. This school conceptualized international migrants as rational economic agents who are focused in maximizing their labour productivity, that is, they except high monetary return from migration. Borjas (1990) also developed an econometric model where potential migrants are conceived as empowered individuals who make migration decisions after estimating the costs and benefits from different international labour markets.

But the ‘new economics of migration school’ put forward by Stark and Bloom (1985), Levhari (1982), Taylor (1986), and Stark (1991) rejects the microeconomic theory of international migration. They say labour movements are collective decisions taken by the members of the households to diversify the risks to household income.

In the 1980s, some sociological theoreticians like Portes and Walton (1981), Petras (1981), Sassen (1988, 1991), and Morawska (1990) developed the theory that international migration is the result of the expansion of world market due to political and economic structural reorganization. World systems theory as it was known considered globalisation of the market economy as the prime reason for migration. Thus, foreign direct investment in developing countries accentuates the inflow of migrants.

Dual market theories consider formal recruitment agencies as the reason for international movements of people. Piore (1979) argues that it is the pull factors in the receiving countries that accentuate the demand for foreign workers. The network theory believes that connections and interpersonal relations that occur within migrant workers community in origin and receiving countries bring forth more migration. They think network between migrants, former migrant and non migrants will speed up population movements. Institutional theory considers the establishment of institutions dedicated to facilitating immigration increases the volume of migration. The theory of cumulative causation states that migration tends to create more migration almost in the similar lines as network theories.

Feminisation of Migration

Feminisation of migration is seen differently by sociologists and economists. They consider female migration to be a highly stratified by different forces of ethnicity, legal status, skill level and mode of entry and exit which affects the rights and entitlements of females in the labour market.

The growth of the migration flows are influenced by supply or push factors which affect the decision of emigrants to leave and demand or pull factors which influence the entry of immigrants. These factors are affected by the immigration controls in the destination economies. The tightening or relaxation of quotas and controls, naturalization policies, evasion in the form of illegal immigration and filing of false asylum claims all affect the flow of migration.

UNINSTRAW ascribes the increasing migration of women to the structural adjustment policies imposed on the developing countries in the last decades of the 20th century by IMF and World Bank. Imposed as a pre condition for loans, these have caused the failure of small and medium term industries, increased unemployment and cuts in social services in developing economies have compelled males and females to seek survival opportunities through migration.

Another explanation for increased female migration is the trans-globalisation of economies which have opened up jobs in service sectors. In many developed countries, the combination of demographic change, increased women participation in work force, and reduced social services for child and aged care has led to a dependency of rich countries on the female workers from poor countries. There is, at present, a great variety of care regimes across industrial countries where elderly care has recently attracted large flows of care migrants, ushering in a new division of labour among family careers (mainly women), female immigrants, and skilled native workers. Thus there is an inflow of skilled and unskilled female migrants from India, Latin America, South East Asia, and Eastern Europe to Europe, America and Gulf countries as teachers, nurses, domestic servants, assistants in hospitality sector, and so on.

Trade liberalization and market orientation through structural adjustment and implementation of General Agreement on Trade in Services (GATS) also brought a change in the demand for labour. There are two modes of service delivery, Mode 1 and Mode -4 which have become the main reasons for increased participation in migration by women in developing countries. Mode -1includes electronics and ITC. Mode -4 involves temporary movement of service suppliers from one country to another. Mode -4 include labour intensive sectors that require proximity between providers and consumers like health, education and social services which employ a large number of females. Since women are ready to work for any wage and perceived as passive and docile, they are in great demand, leading to feminization of labour and feminization of labour migration.

In the advanced economies, the demand for female immigrants increased due to many reasons. The socio-demographic conditions like aging population, increases in longevity plus drastic declines in birthrates as well as rise in divorce rates and extension of formal education have spurred the inflow of female immigrants.

Impact of Migration on Female Labour Market

Migration can contribute to poverty reduction and better access to education and health services. Migration can diversify household risks, can contribute to job creation and steady incomes for more people and can increase gender equality by enabling women to enter the labour market and become more self-reliant. The potential to attain a higher income through migration is also of great importance for social development.

Remittances sent to family back home usually help to cover the daily consumption needs, which can in it contribute to the United Nation's MDG (Millennium Development Goals) to eradicate poverty and hunger. Remittances are, in addition, often invested in health, education and accommodation. Such investments often come with important impacts on the MDGs linked to education and health. This has particularly been found to be the case in situations where women decide on the use of remittances. Sectors with critical skills shortages can benefit from the transfer of skills through circular migration and return (so-called 'brain gain' and 'brain circulation'). The migration experience can empower women, both as individuals and as a group, by helping them to enter the labour market and earn higher incomes. The transfer of values and ideas brought about by migration (so-called 'social remittances') also means that migration can facilitate achieving the gender equality in the MDGs. It can indirectly alleviate poverty by raising the productivity, education and health of the females and their families (World Bank, 2005).

Migration can raise women and men from lower to lower middle class socio–economic ranks (ILO, 2004). Many migrant women tend to remit more of their earnings than men and to exercise control of their households income by ensuring that the remittances are spent on food and clothes for the family back home (IOM, 2005). Increased education seems to encourage more migration of women and in turn foster greater education of females (UNESCAP, 2003).

For many poor women, migration has strengthened their position within structures that normally offer few opportunities. In Kerala, India, in the 1990s, the so-called 'gulf wives' left behind by male emigrants were found to experience loneliness and too high a work burden at home. But today, they and their daughters form a new generation of self–confident, independent female managers in Kerala (UNESCAP, 2003).

Migration increasingly offer women education and carrier opportunities, that may not be available or denied them at home as well as, alternatives to marriage and the traditional role of home maker.

There remain many downsides to migration, including social tensions within families and within societies. Female migrants can be denied their rights. They can be abused and exploited by migrant smugglers, traffickers and unscrupulous employers, and exorbitant fees can reduce their potential savings and investments. Households can become dependent on foreign sources of income and less motivated to seek or prepare domestic opportunities.

In countries of destination, labour migrants often perform important functions, fill skill gaps or labour shortages and thus contribute significantly to the economy. In Thailand, for example, the immigration of lower-skilled labour has contributed to GDP growth and Thai nationals were able to find better employment opportunities as immigrants have taken up the so called 'dirty, difficult and dangerous' jobs (Martin, 2007). In most Organisation for Economic Co-operation and Development (OECD) countries "immigrants have made an important contribution to employment growth during the past decade" (OECD, 2009:12).

Beyond the possible negative effects of brain drain and lost labour, recent research has looked at the complex social and psychological implications and effects on well-being. In Nepal, for example, the predominance of male labour emigration has been affiliated with increasing divorce and elopement. Other studies observe some negative effects on the psychological well-being of children because of the outward migration of their parents (Graham and Jordan, 2011).

Detailed studies in a number of OECD countries have found that female migrant's initial health advantage tends to dissipate over time. Separation from family and social networks and uncertainty regarding job security and living conditions can affect health. In several studies female migrants have reported higher incidence of stress, anxiety and depression than residents; outcomes that were correlated with worse economic conditions, language barriers, irregular status and recent arrival (HDR, 2009).

The impacts of climate change on livelihoods have significant implications for forced migration; simultaneously, migration can be a way for the most vulnerable populations to adapt to negative environmental changes. In this circumstance it is recognized by social scientists that women and children will be the most affected group. Migration was formally introduced to the Climate Change negotiation text in 2010 in the agreements reached at the sixteenth session of the Conference of Parties (COP 16), held in Cancun, Mexico. Paragraph 14(f) of the Cancun Agreements calls for Parties to take "measures to enhance understanding, coordination and cooperation with regard to climate change induced displacement, migration and planned relocation, where appropriate, at the national, regional and international levels" to enhance action on adaptation.

A relatively recent topic on the climate change agenda, loss and damage was formally mentioned for the first time within the UNFCCC framework at the thirteenth session of the Conference of the Parties (COP 13), held in Bali in 2007.The interpretation of the link between migration and loss and damage is manifold. Perhaps the most evident aspect of this nexus is the impact of loss and damage on human mobility. On the one hand, loss and damage can cause migration: loss of arable land caused by desertification or soil degradation – or long-term damage to the agricultural potential caused by floods or droughts – can, for example, force farmers to migrate to cities in search of alternative sources of income. On the other hand, loss and damage may have the opposite effect on mobility, leaving people without the means to adopt migration as an adaptation or even survival strategy, or to move to less vulnerable areas.

Status of Female Migrants

Most migrant workers from South Asia to Middle East and other Asian destinations are low-skilled or semi-skilled such as construction workers and female domestic workers. These workers face numerous problems in protection in both origin and destination countries compared to skilled workers and professionals. Most important trend in total migration from the viewpoint of protection of migrant rights in Asia is the high incidence of 'irregular migration' – commonly referred to as 'illegal', 'undocumented' or 'clandestine' migration. There are no proper estimates of incidence which can range from simple border crossings to organised trafficking and smuggling. The incidence of irregular migration is believed to be high in India and Pakistan, largely due to cross border movements from Bangladesh into India and from Afghanistan into Pakistan. In addition, there is continuing trafficking of women and children across the border from Bangladesh and Nepal into India.

There is also high incidence of South Asian workers in irregular status in the Gulf and Malaysia as shown by numbers availing of amnesties and those deported. The visa trading system in the Gulf States results in making migrants irregular when sponsors bring in more workers than needed. It is estimated that nearly 100,000 undocumented migrants left the UAE for their homelands during a 2003 amnesty and about another 150,000 in 1996 (workpermit.com 2007b). Studies by the Centre for Development Studies in Trivandrum show that many Indians working in the Gulf have reached there on other than regular work visas, suggesting widespread collusion and abuse of the system (Kumar, 2010).

Another observed tendency has been the increasing share of female workers migrating on their own for overseas employment. The bulk of them migrate for low wage occupations such as domestic work. In South Asia, the share of female migration is high only in Sri Lanka where currently about 50 per cent of migrants are female. Since women migrants are one of the most vulnerable groups, policy ambiguities concerning their migration have limited such movements from Bangladesh, India, Nepal and Pakistan.

Bangladesh had banned the migration of women as domestic workers at certain times while India now permits women only of 30 years and more to migrate for low skilled occupations. Hong Kong (China), Malaysia and Singapore represent the major destinations for domestic workers in Asia. A sizeable number migrate to the Middle East, especially Lebanon, Kuwait, Jordan, Saudi Arabia and UAE. This is also reflected in Pakistan's new emigration policy which has assigned female migration as priority area no. 11 for the policy. It states: "This is the era of "Feminization" of migration. Currently, the share of Pakistani female workers is very low in the overall migration; it has to be substantially increased especially in occupations considered safe. A task force will be appointed to look into the problems and prospects of emigration of women workforce as well as mechanism needed to mainstream them in the overall emigration process" (Government of Pakistan, 2009: XIII). One objective of the Nepal foreign Employment Act of 2007 is also promoting safe migration for women.

Abuse and exploitation of South Asian migrant workers occur in both in countries of origin and destination. Misleading information on jobs and destinations, exorbitant fees and high migration costs have already been mentioned. Retention of identity documents by employers is a common practice in many destination countries which severely restricts mobility of workers. For instance, the UAE law makes it illegal for employers to withhold their employees' passports. Yet Human Rights Watch found that employers routinely ignore this law and confiscate employee passports (Human Rights Watch, 2006). A migrant survey in Kerala has cited the following problems faced by migrant workers in the Gulf (Irudaya Rajan et al., 2008): taking away passport, signing of new contract with low wages, modified work and living conditions and reducing other employment benefits such as overtime and leave salaries and return airfare payment. It found that returns migration in one in three cases was due to low remuneration and poor working conditions

Labour Migration Policies – Are They Gender Sensitive?

Labour migration policies consist of two components: a) emigration policy relating to national workers migrating for employment; and b) immigration policy relating to foreign workers who come into the country for employment. Most developing countries give priority to foreign or overseas employment policies, related institutions, and remittances, and are hardly concerned about immigration policy.

There is also lack of coordination and coherence between development, trade, labour and finance and migration policies, which is common to many developing countries. The background report to the UN High Level Dialogue on Migration and Development noted that countries would benefit from "better coordination and coherence between migration and development policies," which would require "closer cooperation among the authorities in charge of migration and those working on development strategies and development cooperation (United Nations, 2006:16).

Female migration policies must address the plight of unskilled female workers working as domestic workers as skilled women workers are protected under the general emigration policy. Therefore, in this section an overview of migration policy of developing countries concerning unskilled workers, are taken as these workers are the major suppliers of this group of migrants.

The ILO has highlighted specific vulnerabilities and abuse of migrant domestic workers (ILO, 2009): inequality of treatment between migrant domestic workers (MDW) and nationals (e.g. especially regarding social protection); vulnerability to abuse: tying of workers to specific employers named on the work permit; requirement for MDW to live in their employer's house; withholding of passport by the employer used as a form of control; risk of potential abuse by unaccredited employment agencies; restrictions of personal freedoms, including forced labour; lack of coverage under generalized national healthcare schemes; and, pregnancy or HIV status often resulting in the worker's dismissal. The following table shows the plight of female domestic migrants in South Asian countries.

Table 13.3 ILO's Women Migrant Domestic Workers' Surveys (2009)

	Baharin	**Lebanon**	**Costa Rica**	**Kuwait**
Average working hours per week	102	72	97.5	108
No overtime paid (%)	100	n.a.	98	100
Number of days off per month	n.a.	4	1.5	n.a.
No resting days per month at all (%)	88	0	n.a.	90
Health fees or social security coverage (%)	n.a.	29.5	57	n.a.
More than five household residents per domestic worker (%)	n.a.	50	41	n.a.
Physical, verbal or sexual abuse cases (%)	37	14	51	47
Non-payment of wages or wages withheld (%)	19	0	n.a.	20.5
Number of domestic workers interviewed	70	54	301	34
Percentage of female domestic workers interviewed	100	100	69	100
Freedom of movement	controlled	not controlled	controlled	controlled
Withholding of passport by sponsor or employer	common	inexistent	common	common

Several reports by Human Rights Watch have documented the poor conditions of work and exploitation of migrant female workers in Gulf countries (Human Rights Watch 2004; Human Rights Watch 2006; Human Rights Watch 2008). In the case of domestic workers in Saudi Arabia, the HRW study found: "While many domestic workers enjoy decent work conditions, others endure a range of abuses including non-payment of salaries, forced confinement, food deprivation, excessive workload, and instances of severe psychological, physical, and sexual abuse. Human Rights Watch documented dozens of cases where the combination of these conditions amounted to forced labor, trafficking, or slavery-like conditions."

There are three major international legal instruments on migrant workers – two ILO Conventions and the International Convention on the Protection of the Rights of All Migrant Workers and Members of Their Families (ICMW), 1990. It is only Sri Lanka which has ratified at least one international instrument concerning migrant workers – the ICMW – in 1996. Bangladesh signed the ICMW in October 1998 – normally an indication of eventual ratification – but has not ratified it up to now. No country in the Asian region has ratified the two ILO Conventions on migrant workers. They are the following:

- ILO Conventions

1. The Migration of Employment Convention (Revised), 1949 (No. 97) – 49 ratifications;
2. The Migrant Workers (Supplementary Provisions) Convention, 1975 (No. 143) – 23 ratifications

- United Nations

International Convention on the Protection of the Rights of All Migrant Workers and Members of Their Families (ICMW), 1990 – 42 ratifications. (In force since mid-2003). Ratification of ILO Convention No 97 and 143 and the International Convention on the Protection of All Migrant workers and members of their Families (1990) (ILO, 2008b) was considered particularly important for the promotion of fair recruitment practices, promotion of safe migration of women, development of a supportive migration infrastructure, and effective services to migrants, skills development of migrant workers, and ensuring that migration promotes development (ILO, 2008b).

The summary of conclusions of the ILO Regional Tripartite Meeting on Challenges to Labour Migration Policy and Management in Asia summed up the Asian situation well (ILO, 2003). "While market forces are driving labour migration, there are several signs of market failures associated with its related processes. A number of risks have been associated with migration including racism and xenophobia, trafficking and forced labour, recruitment malpractices such as fraudulent job offers and exorbitant placement fees, debt bondage, sexual and physical harassment, employment in hazardous jobs, and under or non-payment of wages. Experience suggests that state intervention by sending and receiving countries through transparent, efficient, and appropriate regulatory institutions and measures are essential to the efficient and equitable working of the labour market."

Only a few countries have spelled out clear migration policies. Sri Lanka has a well defined National Labour Migration Policy. Pakistan also elaborated a National Emigration Policy in 2008 and adopted it at a national consultation in December 2008. (Government of Pakistan, 2009). Bangladesh had issued an *'Overseas Employment Policy'* in 2006 since "manpower is a major export sector for Bangladesh economy and since the government has taken decision to undertake long term program for ensuring the welfare of the Bangladeshi expatriates and to enhance and streamline employment opportunities for Bangladeshis in abroad". But other countries in South Asia do not have spelled out a clear or transparent policy statement on migration. For instance, India which is the largest source and destination country lacks a consistent policy which addresses both emigration and immigration.

For a number of countries, a major protection issue has been the protection of female domestic workers whose conditions are similar to slavery confined to households. The 2008 ILO Regional Symposium in Dhaka highlighted the problem experienced by women migrant workers in general and argued for a gender sensitive migration management policy (ILO, 2008). It recommended a package of measures: protection and fair treatment of women migrants; lifting the restriction for women migrants; recognition of their economic contribution, especially domestic work; and, gender sensitive data collection; preventing of, and protection against, abuse and exploitation in destination countries: consular facilities to address their needs; and support for the welfare of families left behind – especially children. In 2007, India banned the emigration for women less than 30 years of age going abroad to work as domestic help and care givers based on a recommendation by the National Commission for Women (Khadria, 2009: 81). An NGO report comments on Indian policy on female migration stated as follows: "Restrictive protectionist policies such as the 30-year age limit on emigrating women should be lifted and replaced with those that truly protect women migrants' rights. The policy should, therefore, conceive of female migrants as individuals in their own right, and address the breadth of their migrant experiences utilizing the entire range of international rights instruments".

The Nepal Foreign Employment Law of 2007 also attempted to provide a high level of protection to migrating women workers who constitute less than five per cent of total migrants in Nepal. However, the strict provisions of the new Act on 'safe migration' for women may actually discourage recruitment agencies from promoting women migration.

Moreover, some foreign recruiting countries do not extend their labour laws to the jobs traditionally taken by migrant women.The main examples in this case are Kuwait, UAE, and so on. They have separate migration laws. The low status of women's jobs means lower wages and conditions, and they are susceptible to the additional gender–specific forms of physical and sexual exploitation (ILO, 2004). This can have serious health consequences which in some countries can lead to termination of contract and expulsion of the worker.

In UAE, 'Kafala' sponsorship system places many foreign domestic workers especially females in indentured situations where sponsor holds their papers, secure piece work with several employers and changes the migrant for the sponsorship services. Women are isolated and their movements restricted. Sponsors often allow the women's visas to expire or sell them to other employers in breach of visa conditions. They find themselves outside the law, leading to mental health problems. The recruiting agencies are not monitored by the countries. Many women do not make it back to their home again. For example, ILO has reported on suicides among Sri Lankan female domestic workers as well as Ethopian female migrants in Lebanon, South Africa, Ecuador, Bangladesh, Indonesia, Jamaica, Ghana and many more have introduced very bold reforms and far reaching measures in preparation towards ratification of ILOC 189. South Africa and Indonesia have made progress in extending legal and social protections, including social security coverage and unemployment insurance to migrant domestic workers. Ghana and Zambia have extended labour law coverage to domestic workers, and are working to enact new protective legislations as well as reforms to other policy and legal regimes to make implementation holistic.

Ecuador has recently introduced social security and medical insurance for domestic workers. In addition to stricter enforcement of labour laws, the government provides training and certification to domestic workers, as well as labour attachés and inspectors, law enforcement agents and the judiciary to improve their knowledge of the new provisions and enable speedy resolution of violations. Trinidad and Tobago has recently established a special register for domestic workers, to assist in identifying them and providing support. Ghana has established a task force involving all partners, training institutions and civil society organizations to study the current laws and propose reforms and specific measures to deal with special cultural practices such as child fostering. These initiatives were expected to encourage support for ratification and implementation.

Conclusions and Policy Options

Migration is an essential feature of today's world. Transnational networks, environmental change, growing labour shortages and ageing populations, are among the factors contributing to this reality. Current estimates are that there are over 200 million people who have migrated from their home country to another, and around 740 million who have relocated within their own country. Female migration has been on the rise since 1990. There are several key drivers of these movements. The majority of people move for economic reasons for better employment opportunities, higher wages, or diversification of livelihood, education, or move to be with family members to escape political persecution, or insecurity due to war and conflict; some are forcibly relocated for political reasons. And some are compelled to flee from environmental hazards, such as floods, infertile agricultural land or lack of water resources.

While many developing countries have large stocks of immigrants, very few of them have explicit policies on how to deal with immigration or the capacity to manage their borders effectively. They have only few statistics about migration flows, transit, circular or irregular migration.

More attention needs to be given to female migrants and the gender aspects of migration. International agencies like ILO are of the opinion that there must be the elimination of outright bans or restrictions on emigration of women based on age, occupation and pregnancy; and information on "women-friendly" migration channels. Lower-skilled women migrant workers need special attention, especially domestic workers. Ratification of ILO convention is very important in protecting female migrant workers.

Providing knowledge about the migration process and the language of the destination country will also enhance integration and quicker adjustment of migrants to the new labour market. For instance, the Philippine government organizes orientation courses for migrants prior to leaving; during orientation, migrants learn about destination-country customs and laws, the resources available to them at embassies or consulates, important contacts for any problems that might arise, and financial management.

Registration and documentation of domestic workers by both origin and host countries is considered a useful way of identifying migrants and providing them with assistance.

Despite the vast array of good practice frameworks showcased by many governments to increase the rights of migrant domestic workers; effective enforcement remained a major challenge. Many governments consistently raised the lack of enforcement of existing laws and effective regulation of the recruitment industry in general as a threat to protection that requires urgent attention. Private recruiters charge excessively high fees, sometimes at both ends, which could be very costly for migrants and subject them to bondage; and has the potential to undermine the human rights of migrants. Regulation of recruitment practices in both origin and destination countries was acknowledged as fundamental to the promotion of the rights of domestic workers and the consistent application of a rights-based approach.

Finally, the need for reforms in other policy areas such as visa regimes and immigration laws are necessary. The immigration sponsorship visa which ties the employee to first employer, child fostering systems and lack of regulation for domestic violence have the potential to undermine the prospects of ILOC 189. Zambia's example of introducing anti-human trafficking and anti-domestic violence laws to supplement reforms in domestic work was deemed worthy of emulation. Further, efforts at integrating the standards of the ILOC must be underpinned by effective civil remedy systems to address breaches, strong labour unions and greater access to legal services to migrants.

Countries of origin were urged to ensure that criminal complaints are followed through and resolved. A strong labour rights legislative framework in the country of destination is the key for the prevention of abuses. This includes the possibility for migrant workers to change jobs; use of a standardized employment contract recognized in origin and destination countries; adequate labour protection for all migrant workers, including with regard to occupational safety and health, wages and working hours; and prevention of passport retention.

The following practices must be effectively employed by countries of origin to prevent abuses:

* pre-departure preparation, including language training and information on risks relating to migration;

* registration of job offers, expected wages and/or outgoing workers;

* prevention of unethical recruitment practices through regulation/ licensing of private employment/recruitment agencies and the development of a system of incentives/disincentives; elimination of middlemen; establishment of complaints mechanisms in countries of origin and destination;

* the setting up of self-regulatory bodies; and the use of labour attachés in destination countries to verify employers and employment contracts.

The policies should also recognise that migration is basically a labour market and decent work issue, and, therefore, be based on proper assessment of short term and long term labour market demand for migrant workers.

References

ADB (2003). *Combating Trafficking of Women and Children in South Asia.* Regional synthesis paper for Bangladesh, India and Nepal, Asian Development Bank, Manila, April 2003.

CDS (2009). Policy on International Migration Reforms in India: Summary of Policy Recommendations, Centre for Development Studies, Trivandrum.

CEC and MFA (May 2009). '*Towards a Holistic International Migration Policy: Recommendations from Civil Society',* Centre for Education and Communication (CEC) and Migrant Forum in Asia (MFA), India, Yamini Atmavilas, New Delhi.

Elspeth Graham , Lucy P. Jordan, Brenda S.A. Yeoh (2015). "Parental migration and the mental health of those who stay behind to care for children in South-East Asia", *Social Science & Medicine*, vol.132, May, 225-235.

Human Development Report (2009). *Overcoming Barriers: Human Mobility and Development.* World Bank.

Human Rights Watch (2004). "Bad dreams: Exploitation and abuse of migrant workers in Saudi Arabia", *Human Rights Watch,* July, 16 (5).

Human Rights Watch (2006). Building Towers, Cheating Workers: Exploitation of Migrant Construction Workers in the United Arab Emirates, *Human Rights Watch,* New York.

Human Rights Watch (2008). "As if I am not human: Abuses against Asian Domestic Workers in Saudi Arabia", *Human Rights Watch,* New York, July, 2008.

International Organization for Migration (1999). "*The Beijing Platform for Action and Recent Trends in Female Migration in the Asia Pacific.*" Intergovernmental meeting to review the implementation of the Beijing Platform for Action, 26-29 October, Bangkok. A paper drafted for IOM by Maruja Asis, Scalabrini Migration Center, Philippines, in consultation with IOM officials.

ILO (2003). *Regional Tripartite Meeting on Challenges to Labour Migration Policy and Management in Asia.*
www.ilo.org/asia/info/public/pr/WCMS_BK_PR_58_EN/lang--en/index.htm.

ILO (2004). *Towards a Fair Deal for Migrant Workers in the Global Economy.* Report 92 VI www.ilo.org/global/publications/ilo-bookstore/order-online/...EN/.../index.htm

ILO (2006). "Dispelling the migrant myth", Special issue on Bringing decent work into focus, in " World of Work Magazine No. 57, September 2006, p.23.

ILO (2006a). *The ILO Multilateral Framework on Labour Migration: Non-binding Principles and Guidelines for a Rights-based approach to Labour Migration.* Geneva, International Labour

Office
http://www.ilo.org/public/english/protection/migrant/download/multilat_fwk_en.pdf.

ILO (2007). *Trade Union Declaration on the Rights of Migrant Workers from South Asia.* The ILO-NTUC Sub regional Workshop for the Protection of Migrant Workers through Networking Trade Unions, Kathmandu, Nepal on 26-28 September 2007, International Labour Office.

ILO (2008). *Gulf Forum on Temporary Contractual Labour: Recommendations,* Abu Dhabi, January 23-24, 2008.

ILO (2008b). Summary and directions for action. Regional symposium on deployment of workers overseas: A shared responsibility, Dhaka, Bangladesh, 15-16 July 2008, International Labour Office.

ILO (2008a). *Improved Migration Infrastructure Needed to Better Protect Soaring South Asian Labour Migrants*, Regional symposium on deployment of workers overseas: A shared responsibility, Dhaka, Bangladesh, 15-16 July 2008, Press Release by the International Labour Office dated 14 July 2008 http://www.ilo.org/asia/info/public/pr/lang--en/WCMS_098049/index.htm

ILO (2008b). *Gulf Forum on Temporary Contractual Labour: Recommendations*, Abu Dhabi,January 23- 24, 2008.

ILO (2008c). *Summary and Directions for Action. Regional symposium on Deployment of Workers Overseas: A Shared Responsibility*, Dhaka, Bangladesh, 15-16 July 2008, International Labour Office.

ILO (2009). *Decent Work for Domestic Workers*. Report IV(1), International Labour Conference, 99th Session, 2010, International Labour Office http://www.ilo.org/public/english/protection/condtrav/pdf/dw_eng.pdf

IOM, (2005). *Human Rights in Times of Conflict and Terrorism,* Louise Doswald-Bec, Geneva, International Organization for Migration.

IOM (2008). *World Migration 2008*. Geneva, International Organization of Migration

Khadria, B., (ed.) (2009). *India Migration Report 2009: Past, Present and the Future Outlook*,

International Migration and Diaspora Studies Project, Zakir Husain Centre for Educational Studies, School of Social Sciences, Jawaharlal Nehru University, New Delhi, India.

Kumar, S. K. (2010). "Policy on international migration reforms in India", In: S. Irudaya Rajan (ed.), *Governance and Labour Migration: India Migration Report 2010*. New Delhi, Routledge India, February.

Martin, P. (2007). *The Economic Contribution of Migrant Workers to Thailand: Towards Policy Development*. International Labour Organization, Bangkok.

MEWOE (2006). Overseas Employment Policy. Dhaka, Notification Dated, 7 Kartik 1413/22 October 2006, Ministry of Expatriates' Welfare & Overseas Employment , Government of Bangladesh.

MFEPW (2008).National Labour Migration Policy for Sri Lanka. Colombo, Ministry of Foreign Employment Promotion and Welfare, Government of Sri Lanka, Colombo. http://www.ilo.org/public/english/protection/migrant/download/mpolicy_srilanka_en.pdf

OECD-http://stats.oecd.org/index.aspx, Immigrants by sector in Migration statistics – Population & Demography, 2010.

OECD (2009), *International Migration Outlook*, iwww.oecd.org.

Promoting Regular Emigration and Protecting Emigrants. Islamabad, Policy Planning Cell, Labour and Manpower Division, Ministry of Labour and Manpower.

UN DESA (2008) Trends in Migrant stock, Population Division, U.N, (UN data base, pop/DB/MIG/STOCK/2008)

UNDESA (2012). Population Facts No. 2012/3 June 2012 United Nations Department of Economic and Social Affairs, Population Division www.unpopulation.org.

UNESCAP (2003) (United Nations Economic and Social Commission for Asia and Pacific). *'Promoting the MDG s in Asia and the Pacific- Meeting the challenges of poverty reduction.'* Asia-Pacific Regional MDGs Report 2003.

UNFCCC United Nations Framework Convention on Climate Change (2007). *CLIMATE CHANGE: IMPACTS, VULNERABILITIES AND ADAPTATION IN DEVELOPING COUNTRIES*
https://unfccc.int/resource/docs/publications/impacts.pdf

UNFCCC United Nations Framework Convention on Climate Change (2010). *'Report of the Conference of the Parties on its sixteenth session, held in Cancun from 29 November to 10 December 2010'* FCCC/CP/2010/7/Add.1.

United Nations (2006). *International Migration and Development: Report of the Secretary-General.* New York, Sixtieth session: Agenda item 54 (c)- Globalisation and Interdependence:

International Migration and Development, A/60/871, United Nations.

United Nations Framework Convention on Climate Change (2009). *International Migration Outlook 2009*. OECD, Paris.

United Nations Department of Economic and Social Affairs (UNDESA) (2012). Migrants by origin and destination: The role of South–South migration. *Population Facts,* No. 2012/3, UNDESA Population Division, New York.

World Bank (2005). *Equity and Development ,* World Development Report, 2006.

World Bank (2010). *Migration and Remittances Factbook 2011*, Washington, D.C., The World Bank.

Workpermit.com (2007). 'Time Extended for Illegal Migrants to leave Dubai under Amnesty' *Global Immigration News*, 30 August, 2007.

Zachariah, K. C. and S. Irudaya Rajan (2008). Kerala Migration Survey 2007, Research Unit on International Migration, Centre for Development Studies, Trivandrum and the Department of Non-Resident Keralite Affairs, Government of Kerala, Trivandrum, India.n.org

International instruments:

Universal Declaration of Human Rights, G.A. Res. 217A, U.N. GAOR, 3d Sess., Supp. No. 16, U.N. Doc. A/810 (1948).

Convention relating to the Status of Refugees, *opened for signature* July 28, 1951, 19 U.S.T. 6259, 189 U.N.T.S. 137, and the Protocol relating to the Status of Refugees, *opened for signature* Jan. 31, 1976, 19 U.N.T.S. 6223, 606 U.N.T.S. 267.

Convention on the Elimination of All Forms of Discrimination Against Women, *opened for signature* Dec. 18, 1979, G.A. Res. 34/180, 34 U.N. GAOR, Supp. No. 46, U.N. Doc. A/34/46 (1979), 1249 U.N.T.S. 13 (entered into force Sept. 3, 1981).

Chapter Fourteen

Privatisation of Cyprus Turkish Airlines: Contextualising Some Labour-related Issues, Polemics and Policies

Fatma Güven-Lisaniler

Introduction

Recent decades have given rise to pronounced economic and political transformations for many, including North Cyprus. Since the late 1970s, a new economic and political paradigm — liberalisation, privatisation and globalisation (LPG) — began to impose its market rationality at an increasingly global level. This new paradigm is characterised by reduced expenditures or the privatisation of public services and state owned enterprises, and the expansion and creation of new markets. The general strategy is aimed at establishing a level playing field for the private sector. In many countries, the shift to increasingly market-governed social policies to provide such a level playing field to the private sector, especially privatisation, has led to demonstrations and the political polarisation of the society.

North Cyprus, as a small, politically unrecognised state,[xlix] is no exception in terms of economic and political transformations. Despite the difficulties of integrating into the world economy due to its political non-recognition, liberalisation and privatisation have been especially important in the series of reform measures implemented since the 1980s, as recommended by the donor country (Turkey) as well as by the policy makers and experts on and off the island. However, the implementation of these measures has met with limited and mixed success, and in some cases, complete failure and the decline of the economy. The country continues to face a severe economic crisis and high unemployment. The failure of the LPG policies has provoked opposite reactions from different segments of the society. The main opposition party and most of the unions have argued that this failure is due to the alien character of the reform package. It was prepared and imposed by the donor country and does not respond to the sentiments and the *true* needs of the society and the economy. Thus, while the need for the restructuring of the economy has been acknowledged, the argument has been put forward that the reform program should be devised by the locals and should avoid privatisation. According to the business organisations and most economists, however, the government did not follow the reform package fully and firmly, and the existing measures need strengthening, especially the implementation of privatisation policies.

In recent years, the government's increasing efforts to implement privatisation have provoked opposite reactions and have largely split public opinion. Consequently, this fuelled street demonstrations, mass protests and the political polarisation of the society. The protests have ensued from the criticism that market-governed social policies, especially privatisation, have distinctly varied effects and ramifications on the labour market. Specifically, it creates jobless growth and transforms employment in favour of unregistered enterprises that actually lead to the flexibilization of work and undermining of organised labour power, with serious effects on welfare and working conditions as well as inequalities in distribution. However, the supporters of the reform package have based their support on the well-known merits of liberalisation and privatisation, that is, the efficient allocation of scarce resources and increasing efficiency that leads to higher economic growth, lower unemployment and an increase in the welfare of the society. The two groups have agreed on the need and objective of the reform package and are observing the same evidence, but draw different inferences from the same events. Political polarisation entails risk; political debates get fierce, and may even threaten the very existence of a civil society (Dixita and Weibullc, 2007), reduce the stability of government decisions (Keefer and Knack, 2002) and present a key obstacle to social and political progress and the implementation of policy reforms (Esteban and Schneider, 2008). Reaching a consensus on appropriate policies in a polarised society is difficult (Torenvlied and Klein Haarhuis, 2008).

To assess the possible effects of political polarisation on the implementation of policy reforms, this study proposes to examine the impact of privatisation policies and polemics in North Cyprus. Such an examination offers insight into the impact of privatisation and sources of backlashes against privatisation policies that allow us to analyse the causes and the possible effects of polarisation on policy reforms.

The study is timely and important for three reasons. First, the country is facing a severe economic crisis, and privatisation forms an integral part of the array of reform measures recommended by the policy makers and experts, and, more importantly, is a condition of the donor country (Turkey). Second, although the case used in the study, Cyprus Turkish Airlines (CTA), is not the first privatised state owned enterprise (SOE), it is the largest and the first enterprise to generate massive protests, leading to intensely negative news coverage and political polarisation. Further, unions and opposition parties have seen privatisation as targeting national values which should not be taken over by foreigners.[1] News articles have highlighted popular objections to large-scale layoffs and the welfare losses of the workers. Public opinion also appears to have become increasingly negative over time, leaving grounds for the privative effect of the reform measures on the North Cyprus economy. Third, a large public enterprise in a monopoly position in electricity and public utilities, such as water and telecommunication, is yet to be divested. This research allows us to assess the impact of privatisation on the labour of the first large divested state monopoly and to understand whether increased polarisation is consistent with the perception or reasoning that the polarisation will produce useful policy implications for the privatisation of large SOEs and public utilities in the future.

The next section will provide a brief overview of the debates on privatisation policies and the development and scope of the privatisation policies in North Cyprus. Then the study's investigation into the effects of privatisation on labour will be outlined. Subsequently, the possible reasons for the protest demonstrations, and whether the economic evidence yielded by this study is consistent with the backlash against the privatisation policies and reasoning for polarisation, will be discussed. Lastly, the conclusion will discuss the findings and policy implications.

Privatisation in North Cyprus: Development and Scope

The establishment of SOEs in North Cyprus, which are now being or will soon be privatised, coincides with the economic and socio-spatial restructuring process of the Turkish Cypriot community in 1974. The de-facto division of the island in 1974 resulted in the majority of the Turkish and Greek Cypriot populations residing in the north and south, respectively. The spatial change which this partition brought about to the previously scattered Turkish and Greek Cypriot populations led to some production units once belonging to either Greek or Turkish Cypriots lying idle in both the north and the south of the island.[li]

With the establishment of the Turkish Federated State of Cyprus (TFSC) in 1975, after the division of the island, the Turkish Cypriots entered a phase of reorganisation. Besides setting up their governmental administrative units, they reactivated idle production units in order to maintain and improve their economic existence (Güven, 1984; Keser, 2012). The necessary funding and the technical and administrative know-how to operate these SOEs, which was severely lacking at the time, were provided by Turkey. These shortcomings and the statist economic development approach of the Turkish government of the time were influential in reactivating the idle productive units as SOEs. In the end, 10 different SOEs were established in the manufacturing, transport, trade, electricity and tourism sectors, where the number of people employed within these SOEs amounted to the 5% of overall employment (Güven, 1984). Those SOEs served as a means for Turkish Cypriot economic existence and a symbol of their political existence and independence (Keser, 2012).[lii] For example, CTA (national airline) symbolised[liii] the people's protest against the political non-recognition of their newly established state and the economic embargoes imposed on it.

Since the year after the establishment of the TFSC (1976), under the framework of 'Technical Assistance', the financing of the main investments and public expenditure of North Cyprus has been provided by Turkey (the only country to grant political recognition to North Cyprus) through bilateral economic protocols. Until the 1986 Protocol (İsmail, 2001), the funds and loans provided by Turkey were unconditional and comprised 40–50% of public financing.

Table 14.1 List of Privatised SOEs

	Name of the SOE	Year of Privatisation	Strategy	The New Owner(s)
1	Cyprus Turkish Tourism Enterprises: 17 hotels, 67 apartments, 26 shops, 1 nightclub and 1 beach	1996, 1997	overseas trade sales	foreign
2	Sanayi Holding Ltd.: 46 manufacturing plants	1996, 1998	overseas and private trade sales, liquidation	foreign
3	Cyprus Evkaf Foundation's tourism enterprises: 3 hotels	2007, 2008, 2009	overseas and local leasing (private firms and employees)	foreign + local
4	Eastern Mediterranean Univ.: pre-university education units; primary and high school	2009	overseas leasing	foreign
5	Cyprus Turkish Airlines	2006, 2010	joint venture and liquidation	foreign
6	Cyprus Turkish Petroleum Ltd.	1997, 2010	private trade sales	local
7	Turkish Alcohol and Wine Industry ltd.	2003, 2010	overseas trade sales	foreign
8	Ercan Airport Management Enterprises	2012	overseas leasing	foreign
9	Industry, Trade and Management Enterprises	2012	overseas trade sales	foreign
10	Co-op Dairy	2013	local cooperatives trade sales	local

With the 1986 and 1987 Protocols, the release and the use of the funds and loans were bound to a series of conditions including the liberalisation of the markets and the privatisation of public services and SOEs (İsmail, 2001). This made privatisation a public concern, especially for the trade unions. Privatisation policies became more pronounced in the 1997 Protocol (İsmail, 2001: 15), and they were included for the first time in the Development Programs of North Cyprus (1997) (SPO, 1996: 72, 73). No attempt, however, was made to provide any law governing the privatisation policy included therein. Hereafter, two large SOEs in the tourism and manufacturing sectors were privatised (1996–1998) (Aslan, 2011). In the following years, despite the development programs and economic protocols suggesting privatisation, it was not implemented until the introduction of the protocol covering 2004–2006. By the end of 2012, all of the SOEs, besides those in electricity, seaports and telecommunication services, were privatised, mainly by overseas trade sales and leasing. The Table 14.1 provides the privatisation years and the strategies of the privatised SOEs since the beginning of the privatisation process.Background of Privatisation Polemics

As listed in Table 14.1, the privatisation of SOEs and public services has continued since 1996. The initial objections to privatisation were mainly that it was an alien policy, as the 'privatisation unit' was established as one aspect of the structural adjustment package proposed by the donor country (Turkey-TRNC Economic Protocol, 1987) (İsmail, 2001), and that it had a negative employment effect. However, the government of North Cyprus asserted that privatisation is a homemade policy, and that there would be a positive employment effect of enhanced economic growth. Later, high unemployment and the 2001 banking crisis and ensuing economic crisis, slowed down the implementation of the privatisation program. In addition, the donor country's reluctance to uphold the conditions of the reform package urged the government to postpone the implementation. With this, the privatisation efforts ceased until 2004.

Thus, for six years, from 1998 to 2004, there were no attempts at privatisation. However, with the introduction of the 2004–2006 Economic Protocol, strict measures were implemented to compel the North Cyprus government to comply with the conditions of the reform package, and privatisation policies were reintroduced.

The ideologically Leftist government at the time had concerns about using privatisation explicitly, highlighting the positive effects of reorganising the SOEs on economic growth and the long-term efficiency and employment gains. Taking advantage of the high economic growth through the construction boom triggered by peace negotiations (Mehmet and Yorucu, 2008; Yorucu and Keleş, 2007), the Leftist government attempted to decrease the need for public financing from Turkish funds and aid, and introduced measures to increase the efficiency and profitability of SOEs. This was met with strong resistance from unions, resulting in a standstill. On the part of the unions and opposition parties, the imported nature of the privatisation program and negative effect of the reorganisation on employment in the short term were highlighted. The unions made use of the impact of past privatisation experiences to solidify their objections. They laid claims that in privatised tourism enterprises, registered local workers were being replaced by migrant unregistered or illegal workers, especially from Turkey (Parliamentary Minutes Magazine, 1997). One of the main arguments of the unions against the migrant workers from Turkey was that they 'tend to have lower supply prices as compared to the local Turkish-Cypriot workers. This is demonstrated by the lower wage rates and poorer working conditions that they are willing to accept' (Besim and Jenkins, 2006: 3), as the wages in North Cyprus were more attractive than those in Turkey.

Yet the evaluation of the privatisation program, from the standpoint of the majority of economists within the country, tended to be favourable.[liv] The evaluation criteria of the economists who were in favour of privatisation typically included profitability, labour productivity, firm growth, employment growth and market valuation, as summarised in Megginson and Netter's (2001) comprehensive work on the economic and political merits of government versus private ownership. The counter arguments of the economists against privatisation largely centred on the negative effects of privatisation on employment and asset distribution. Unions and intellectuals, despite having objections to negative labour and consumer effects, based their salient objection on the imported nature of the privatisation program which, according to them, did not respond to the value systems and social norms of their society. This included the objections to transfer public assets, through privatisation, to foreigners. On the part of the society, privatisation was codified as a policy that harms the poor and even the middle class. According to this argument, the effect would be rising prices for public services, moving people out of good jobs into bad ones, or even to unemployment, and giving away national treasures. All this would be to the benefit of the foreign (specifically, Turkish) corporations and investors, and compradors.

It seems that the rejection of the privatisation policies by both unions and intellectuals was not only due to their economic consequences but because people may have felt betrayed when the policies changed certain basic principles of social life (McKenzie et al., 2003: 223; Granovetter, 1985). This included things like the provision of public utilities by private firms instead of the state and the nation. The opponents claimed that allowing private firms, especially foreign private firms, to provide public utilities would allow for the abuse of people and would threaten the economic existence of North Cyprus, and thus its societal existence.

In response to the strong resistance of the unions and intellectuals, the Leftist government resigned and called for early elections. The outcome was the landslide victory of the right-wing party which, ironically, had promised to stop the implementation of the privatisation program and reform package. However, only a year after the election, this new government announced its dedication to the reform package and privatisation. Hence, in 2010, the national airline of North Cyprus (CTA) was liquidated and its employees were laid off. Thus, concern for the welfare impact of privatisation was brought to the fore following the tragedy of 418 CTA workers losing their jobs and suffering monetary and non-monetary losses.

The personal tragedy of the dismissed CTA workers evoked negative opinions about privatisation, accompanied by negative press coverage. Two demonstrations,[lv] called 'The Communal Existence Mass Meetings', organised by the 'Unionist Platform', could be interpreted as an indication of the increasing poor public opinion about privatisation and the reform package. This low opinion was not restricted to the workers of the SOEs that were privatised or would be subject to privatisation in the near future. The diversity and the characteristics of the participants of the two demonstrations, representing all ages, genders and socioeconomic classes, showed that the clear majority disapproved of the privatisation policies.

Another outcome was that some of the economists who had favoured privatisation began to raise awareness of the lack of scope and objectives of the privatisation program, and the importance of including the re-employment and compensation of the welfare losses of the dismissed workers in the law.[lvi] As a result of this disapproval, the Privatisation Law (PL) was enforced in 2012, providing the broad contours of the privatisation program and chapters guaranteeing employment for a certain period and the re-employment of dismissed workers in public administrative units (PL: 3(27-28), 30(17-18))[lvii]. Additionally, the law included a provisional clause (PL: 7(39)) dictating the re-employment of dismissed CTA workers in governmental administrative units, though the CTA had been informally liquidated before the enforcement of the privatisation law.

A year-and-a-half after liquidation, 65% of the dismissed CTA workers (almost 90% of the native workers) were re-employed in public administration units. Yet there was no chapter or article in the PL about compensating the welfare losses of the dismissed workers. On the other hand, the only pronounced objective of the privatisation program was 'decreasing the share of the public sector in the economy' (PL, 2012: 1(3-4)), although the objective of the privatisation, as a means to increase consumers' or workers' welfare, did not appear in explicit terms. Nevertheless, the union demonstrations and strikes continued, and the public opinion became increasingly negative, even though the government provided employment guarantees for a certain period of time (three years) and deferred the employment effect of privatisation.

Impact of Privatisation on Labour: Employment and Welfare Effects

This section analyses the privatisation of CTA as a case study of the employment and workers' welfare effects of privatisation. The employment effect is analysed by examining the re-employment opportunities of former CTA employees, and the effect on the employees' monetary welfare losses is estimated by the changes in monthly earnings, employee benefits and retirement benefits. Non monetary losses are estimated by interviews with ten former CTA workers.

Employment Effect

It is generally believed that privatisation leads to a fall in employment and lower wages, at least in the short run (Gupta et al., 1999). However, in the long run, employment may even increase if privatised firms are tempted to inject new capital as a result of an overall improvement in the economy (Megginson and Netter, 2001; Gupta et al., 1999; Kikeri, 1997; Boubakri and Cosset, 1998). It is also acknowledged that in some cases, restructuring and privatisation may reduce employment permanently, and in case of liquidation, all employees may lose their jobs (Gupta et al., 1999). However, as Rodrik (1993: 357) highlighted, the losers or gainers from the reforms 'cannot be determined *ex ante*'. The uncertainty about the identities of the losers and gainers has the potential to block the implementation of the policy reforms

(Fernandez and Rodrik, 1991, cited in Rodrik, 1993). The CTA privatisation experience is a good example of how uncertainty blocked the adoption of the reorganisation and privatisation policies. Neither during CTA's reorganisation process (2006) nor after its liquidation (2010) did the employees experience job losses. In 2006, CTA's airport services department was privatised, but the employees of the privatised department continued to work in the public–private joint venture company. In 2009, due to CTA defaulting on its debts, all flights were cancelled and the enterprise was informally liquidated. Thus, the rest of the employees (527) lost their jobs. They (95% of the local dismissed CTA workers) were, however, re-employed by the government 18 months after being laid off. Thus, it can be assumed that there were no job losses amongst the North Cyprus-based (North Cyprus citizens) former CTA employees.

We may conclude that the employment effect was not consistent with the backlash against privatisation, since there were no job losses for North Cyprus citizens upon liquidation. However, being re-employed does not mean that there were no welfare losses. Privatisation could have had deteriorating effects on the contractual conditions of the re-employed employees or those who remained employed by the privatised firm (Gupta et al., 1999).

Effect on Contractual Conditions: Monetary and Non-monetary Welfare

The changes in monthly earnings and retirement benefits (pension and gratuity) are used to evaluate the effect on the workers' monetary welfare in a pre- and post-privatisation comparative framework. The study sample consists of 258 workers, amounting to 74% of the total North Cyprus-based dismissed CTA staff, who were re-employed by the government. The data employed for the analysis were provided by the CTA union. They capture tenure (years of employment with CTA), CTA jobs and the individual characteristics of the sample of workers (Table 14.2).

Table 14.2. Individual Characteristics of Employee Sample

Gender	Characteristics	N	Minimum	Maximum	Mean	Std. Deviation
Women	Age	170	24	54	36.2	6.3
	Work experience	170	4	23	10.8	5.6
	Years of schooling	170	6	18	13.0	2.4
	CTA job	N	%			
	Manager	2	1.2			
	Technical personnel	2	1.2			
	Flying personnel	89	52.4			
	Office clerk	66	38.8			
	Worker	11	6.5			
	Total	170	100.0			
Men	Age	88	28.2	53	39.1	5.8
	Work experience	88	14.1	22	12.2	6.1
	Years of schooling	88	6	18	11.7	2.9
	CTA job	N	%			
	Manager	5	5.7			
	Technical personnel	16	18.2			
	Flying personnel	0	0.0			
	Office clerk	46	52.5			
	Worker	21	23.9			
	Total	88	100.0			

Source: CTA union

The majority (about 43%) of the re-employed CTA staff were office clerks. The mean years of schooling of the sampled employees were 12.6 years. The mean years of schooling of the females was about 2.5 years more than the years of schooling (13.0 years) of the males (11.7 years). On the other hand, the tenure of the males was one year more than the females. Managerial, flying and technical personnel payments may be associated with relatively high paid jobs as compared to the office staff. The following section investigates the existence and extent of the changes in the monthly earnings of the dismissed CTA staff upon re-employment.

Effect on Monthly Earnings

The effect on monthly earnings was analysed by calculating the difference between the workers' gross average monthly earnings in CTA and their earnings in state employment. The average monthly earnings for a CTA worker were 4,763 Turkish lira (TL), compared to TL 2,408 in state employment (Table 14.3). Dismissed CTA workers experienced significant losses upon re-employment. On average, state employment monthly earnings were 49.9% less than CTA monthly earnings.

The fall in earnings varied according to gender, former CTA job and individual characteristics. The women's earnings, on average, fell almost 1% less compared to men. In general, the 'better educated' experienced fewer losses (Table 14.4).

Table 14.3 Changes in the gross average monthly earnings of sampled CTA workers

	CTA monthly earnings (2010) (TL)	State monthly earnings* (2012) (TL)	Change	Total Change	Change (%)
Total	4,734.60	2,373.80	−2,360.8	−609,086.4	−49.9
Women	4,763.0	2,408.6	−2,354.4	−400,248.0	−49.4
Men	4,703.50	2,309.60	−2,393.9	−210,663.2	−50.9

Source: Author's own calculations using data provided by the CTA union
*State monthly earnings calculated by the use of TRNC personnel office state salary scale, CTA tenure and education level of the dismissed workers.

For state employment, two measures were used to determine the salaries of the re-employed CTA workers. These were based on education and CTA tenure (PL, 56.1). There were significant differences between the male and female workers with regard to education. While 26% of the female employees held a university degree, this was 15% for the males. Furthermore, 26% of the males were primary school graduates, as compared to 6% of the females (Appendix A). In general, these figures for education reflect the distribution of North Cyprus' labour force. Employed women holding a university degree (32.9%) were almost 10% more than men (20.3%), while primary school graduate women (19%) were almost 10% less than men (30%) (SPO[a], 2010: Table 14.2). The differences benefited women, as they had lower earning losses compared to men, since the primary measure in the determination of the new salary (state employment salary) was the level of education.

In state employment, all workers were employed as office clerks under temporary contracts, and the CTA tenure was confined to 14 years. Thus, sector specific professional skills, such as flight dispatcher, aircraft maintenance and stewardess, and CTA tenure above 14 years were disregarded in the determination of state monthly earnings. Therefore, workers with higher educational attainment, non-sector specific professional skills and CTA tenure under 14 years experienced a lower loss. On the other hand, workers in managerial positions with sector specific professional skills and CTA tenure of more than 14 years experienced higher losses.

Table 14.4 Change in monthly earnings after dismissal as a percentage of CTA earnings*

	Total	Women	Men
Primary school	48.8 (15)	52.0 (6)	46.9 (9)
Middle school	52.8 (17)	55.3 (4)	52.1 (13)
High school	47.5 (153)	47.3 (104)	48.0 (49)
College	56.4 (9)	57.5 (8)	46.0 (1)
University	55.2 (56)	56 (42)	52.7 (14)
Graduate	55.9 (8)	56.2 (6)	54.9 (2)
CTA tenure: 9 years or less	53.9 (112)	54.2 (78)	53.4 (34)
15 or more years	46.2 (78)	47.2 (48)	44.7 (32)
CTA job: manager	36.7 (7)	39.3 (2)	35.8 (5)
technical personnel	50.3 (18)	50.0 (2)	50.4 (16)
flying personnel	53.5 (89)	53.5 (89)	(0)
office clerk	48.0 (112)	46.9 (66)	49.8 (46)
worker	52.9 (32)	58.0 (11)	52.4 (21)

Source: CTA union. *The numbers in parentheses denote the number of workers within each category.

The fall in monthly earnings may also reflect the loss of a good job match or the loss of non-competitive rents associated with CTA employment. In the case of the managers, the fall in earnings (63%) could reflect the loss of a high rank job. For skilled technical personnel and flying personnel, the fall in earnings (50% and 47%, respectively) could reflect the loss of a good job match. The loss of office workers (52%) may reflect the loss of non-competitive rents associated with CTA employment. However, non-competitive rents associated with CTA employment cannot be excluded in either case, be it for managers or skilled workers. The findings are consistent with the backlash against privatisation and also explain the resistance of the unions to the privatisation policies. The unions which opposed the privatisation policies were those of the public sector employees and SOEs. The 16% wage gap (Guven-Lisaniler and Ugural, 2010) between the public and private sectors may indicate one of the reasons for the backlash against privatisation and the continuation of the objections and protests of the unions after the government provided the re-employment guarantee.

Other Aspects of Welfare Losses: Changes in Employee Benefits, Working Conditions and Retirement Benefits

The post-dismissal jobs not only paid lower salaries but were also lower quality in terms of employee and retirement benefits. Social security coverage, work hours and union membership remained the same, but annual leave of 40 days was cut to 30 days. Under CTA employment, all the workers had subsidised lunches and transportation to work, and had maternity, child and marriage grants, and death and funeral benefits. In the post-dismissal jobs, however, besides incomparable child allowances, they received no such benefits. Furthermore, their retirement pension and gratuity payments were lowered due to the decrease in salaries, and the monthly earnings loss also decreased the retirement and pension contributions (see Table 14.5).

Table 14.5. Estimated changes in retirement pension and gratuity of sampled employees

Retirement pension	Average loss	(%)
	Total	14.6
	Women	14.3
	Men	15.2
Retirement gratuity	Average loss	(%)
	Total	49.9
	Women	49.4
	Men	50.7

Source: Author's own calculations

The loss in monthly earnings amounting to almost 50% on average resulted in a 14.6% loss in retirement pensions and a 49.9% loss in gratuity (Table 14.5). Regarding the monthly earnings loss, the men experienced greater gratuity and pension losses than the women. The loss in monthly income and retirement benefits is consistent with the backlash against privatisation.

Changes in Capabilities

Privatisation is a means and not an end in itself. The pronounced positive effects of privatisation are on productivity, profitability, allocative efficiency and economic growth. In turn, this means the development of a country and the welfare of its people.

However, workers' welfare (happiness) does not depend solely on results (level of income, employment). Human interactions (interactions at work) and the processes (processes of re-employment and adaptation to work) carry as much importance. This approach argues that in determining the welfare effect of any policy, the focus should be on the effective beings and performances of people, that is, on their capabilities (Sen, 2004, 2005; Kabaş, 2006).

The non-monetary welfare impact was considered as the welfare loss caused by limitations in the workers' functioning and capabilities. In-depth interviews with 10 dismissed CTA workers (5 women and 5 men) enabled the researcher to gain some understanding of the subjective evaluations of the CTA workers' previous and current levels of welfare. The interviewees were selected using the snowballing technique. The life history method of interviewing provided insight into the multi-dimensional aspects of the individuals, including the critical stages and periods of their lives (Rosie, 1993; Taylor and Tilley, 1998). Further, deprivation theory and Amartya Sen's capability approach[lviii] were employed to assess the interview transcripts. The non-monetary aspect of welfare (workers' happiness) was captured by two questions requiring the workers' subjective evaluations of their pre- and post-dismissal welfare and job satisfaction.

All of the interviewed workers considered their current welfare to be worse than it had been during their tenure with CTA (lower remuneration, low/no job satisfaction, limited social interaction) and would have preferred to go back if they could. This suggests that CTA's attractive salaries and employee benefits were unattainable in the state employment as well as during their period of economic, social and cultural deprivation. Before re-employment, for 18 months, they experienced economic deprivation, in the sense of the restrictions imposed on them for spending on material necessities and on meaningful leisure activities. They also experienced different forms of social and cultural deprivation. Paid work, as the principal source of income, is also the source of an individual's identity and sense of self-worth. The former CTA workers experienced changes in the physical and social conditions of the workplace as well as a sense of undervaluation, due to the lack of promotion opportunities as temporary workers and their unaccounted years in service.

Within the capabilities approach, capabilities primarily represent the freedom to achieve functionings that are of value to the people. According to the theory, if the functionings constitute the well-being of the people, capabilities represent the freedom to achieve that state of well-being (Sen, 2005). The information provided in the interviews demonstrates that the freedom of the re-employed CTA workers to achieve well-being was limited; in other words, their functionings were inhibited.

Besides remuneration, they encountered exclusion in the workplace and a sense of isolation both during and in the aftermath of the liquidation process. This created a sentiment among the workers that the welfare losses they had endured went beyond the aforementioned monetary losses. This was readily identifiable when they were asked to compare their former and current welfare and job satisfaction levels. Even though the workers were offered the possibility of re-employment in the public sector, resolving the matter of their loss of employment and the deprivation associated with the loss of social security and retirement benefits, the workers showed signs of experiencing a welfare loss, as if their monthly earnings had remained the same. This could partly reflect the deprivation of the freedom to achieve the functionings that were of value to them, namely, socialising with co-workers, generating extra income by working overtime or receiving a promotion. In addition, this partly reflects the deprivation of self-esteem. The workers had not been included in any step of the privatisation process, but nonetheless had been held responsible for the liquidation of CTA due to their uncompromising attitudes during the reorganisation process. They had been demeaned before the society, lost their jobs and had been victimised. Although they were eventually offered re-employment, this was not done in a way that indicated that their labour was needed; rather, it was done as if out of charity, as their skills and CTA tenure were ignored upon their re-employment.

Discussion: Policies and Polemics

The findings presented are consistent with the popular perceptions concerning the impact of privatisation on workers' welfare, which are also consistent with the findings of researchers and academics that privatisation leads to a fall in wages in the short term, but inconsistent with the negative employment effect (Birsdall and Nellis, 2002; Khan, 2003; Gupta et al., 1999; Azam, 1994). On the other hand, the findings conflict with the one explicitly pronounced aim of the privatisation program: 'decreasing the share of public sector in the economy'.

In the studied case, there was no employment loss for the dismissed TRNC citizen workers. They were all re-employed either by private sector firms or (mainly) by the government, that is, the public sector, or continued their employment in the privatised department of CTA. However, the dismissed workers did experience significant welfare losses due to contractual deterioration upon re-employment. On the other hand, the share of the public sector in the economy increased, in the sense of the increased employment share of the public sector after privatisation. That could be seen as indicating the failure of the privatisation policy. The findings on the labour impact of privatisation could partly reflect the sample bias or the formulation and/or implementation of the privatisation policy and program. These two possibilities shall be discussed in greater detail as follows.

As already noted, the sample faced limitations. The sample covered only dismissed CTA workers who were re-employed by the government and did not cover the dismissed workers continued to work in the privatised department of CTA or those re-employed by private firms or those who became self-employed. What would the evaluation of the workers' welfare have been if all workers dismissed from CTA or other previously privatised SOEs' dismissed workers had been included in the study? The rest of the workers dismissed from CTA were not included in the sample due to a lack of data. However, the welfare effect would have been comparable, at best, due to the following reasons.

First, although there was a wage gap between the public and private sectors, the gap for the new entrants decreased due to the adoption of a new salary scale in the public sector in 2012 under the public sector reform. The new salary scale for public employment is comparable with prevailing average salaries in formal private sector jobs. The dismissed CTA workers were subject to this new salary scale upon their re-employment. This new salary scale placed the beginning salary for state employment at TL 1,500 and minimum wage at TL 1,415 per month in 2013 (TL 1,237 between 2009 and 2012) (SPO, 2013), which is lower than public employment salaries, making the monthly income loss (welfare loss) larger. Second, the loss of CTA tenure was more probable and would be higher for private sector employment, since there was no local private firm operating in the airline sector that would value their CTA tenure or job specific skills. Third, there was a high probability of remaining unemployed due to high unemployment (11.9%; 8.9% for men and 17.5% for women in 2010) or of being employed in the informal sector, since informal employment made up 35–40% of the total labour force in North Cyprus during the period in question (Besim and Jenkins, 2006). Fourth, the monthly earnings of the CTA workers that continued to work in the privatised department of CTA dropped by 50% on average after the privatisation (interview with one of these workers, 1.10.2012). Lastly, informal sector jobs offered lower wages and no social security.

Thus, in terms of the sample, the study has merit for representing the welfare of the dismissed CTA workers. Nevertheless, future studies would benefit from a larger sample covering workers dismissed upon privatisation, as this could make the findings more accurate and informative in terms of policy formulations.

It can be argued that the public's negative perception of privatisation was not necessarily formed due to the economic consequences in terms of employment or welfare losses but because people felt betrayed when these policies destroyed certain basic principles of social life. One such principle is that public enterprises and utilities should be controlled by the nation to avoid abuses of the local people by foreigner investors. Regardless of whether this concept is misconceived or lacks a theoretical basis, it can become codified in the minds of individuals, who have witnessed a series of events benefiting powerful foreign private interests to the detriment of the unprivileged locals, for instance, by modifying the rules of the game previously defined according to the country's underlying social structure (Granovetter, 1985).

The following examples will clarify this point. When the government announced that the Cyprus Turkish Electricity Authority (CTEA) was going to be privatised, it faced strong resistance from the CTEA union, in the form of demonstrations and power cuts, and harsh criticism from economists and intellectuals. The suggestion was administrative autonomy instead of privatisation. The CTEA union also came up with a proposal detailing the restructuring process and necessary amendments to the law for administrative autonomy. The proposal was prepared by the voluntary contributions of the economists and experts. The main argument against the privatisation of the CTEA was as follows. Due to the lack of domestic capital, the privatisation of the CTEA would end with the formation of a private foreign monopoly. Consequently, the government would be unable to control the monopoly's abuse of power, resulting in increased prices and decreased service quality. This would pose a great threat to the economic existence and independence of the country. The proposal of the union received strong support from the public and economists, including those who were in favour of privatisation. A similar approach was evident in the privatisation of a public high school, which was privatised by transferring operation rights to a private Turkish company. In the privatisation process of this public high school (Eastern Mediterranean College [EMC]), which is a part of a public university (Eastern Mediterranean University [EMU]), the proposal of local businesspersons to undertake the operation rights of the school was supported by most of the teachers unions, economists and the public. The justification of the teachers unions for supporting the proposal was similar to the CTEA case, in that the existence of a foreign education institution threatened Turkish Cypriot society's societal existence.

Consequently, in the above two examples, the real debate was not about the economic or labour impact of privatisation but the fear of possible abuse, and the economic and social domination of foreign investors and the effect of privatisation on the existing value system and individual perceptions of what the socioeconomic life in a country ought to be. That is, it was a historical reflex to protect Turkish Cypriots' traditions and identity. From a socio-cultural standpoint, 'individual motivations, constraints, and cognitive mechanisms of selection are conditioned by ideologies and social interaction' (Castaneda, 2004: 2). We may conclude that the privatisation program did not respond to the value systems, social norms and sentiments of Turkish Cypriot society, and thus social governance was lacking. Social governance is a set of mechanisms that influences individuals' behaviour due to their membership in specific social networks and communities (Durlauf, 1999: 2). The decision to privatise CTA may be an example of a lack of social governance. It did not value the sentiment of the society regarding possessing a national airline, which was, for years, proposed by the politicians and opinion leaders as the symbol of the objection of Turkish Cypriots' to political, economic and cultural isolation due to political non-recognition. CTA was their 'national flag in the sky', representing their economic, political and societal existence in spite of all the countries that denied their independent identity.

The divergence between the aim of the privatisation program declared in the law — decreasing the share of the public sector in the economy — and the consequence of the privatisation program — increasing the share of the public sector in the economy — may reflect the poor conviction of the government with regard to the program. In the end, this was a reform conditioned by the donor country.

Summary and Conclusions

The impact of privatisation on labour is a universal concern. This study principally focused on the welfare impact of privatisation on dismissed workers in North Cyprus. It used CTA, which was liquidated as part of the privatisation program in North Cyprus, as a case study. The welfare impact of privatisation in this study referred to the impact of the privatisation on the workers in terms of their monetary and non-monetary welfare.

Pre- and post-privatisation monthly earnings and retirement benefits were used to evaluate the impact of the privatisation on the workers' monetary welfare. The study sample covered 74% of the North Cyprus-based dismissed CTA workers. The findings revealed that the dismissed workers experienced significant earnings losses upon re-employment, amounting on average to 50% of their CTA earnings. The earnings losses were smaller for women, for the better educated, for less sector-specific skilled workers and for those with a shorter tenure with CTA.

Post-dismissal jobs were not only characterised by lower earnings but were also lower quality in terms of employee and retirement benefits, retirement pensions and gratuity. Some non-monetary attributes of the post-dismissal job were not easily quantifiable; therefore, it was difficult to calculate the true welfare losses on the basis of the more easily observable earnings losses. However, the magnitude of the true welfare (monetary and non-monetary) losses could be inferred from the subjective evaluations provided by the workers themselves. All of the interviewed workers considered their current welfare to be worse than it had been during their CTA employment, and would have preferred to go back if they could. This suggests that the attractive monetary and attributed employee and retirement benefits of CTA employment were unattainable in the state employment, as well as economic deprivation (Han and Phillips, 2008). Furthermore, all of the interviewed workers considered their work environment (social and/or physical) to be worse than it had been during their CTA employment, thus suggesting social deprivation (social exclusion at work) (Brownlee, 2013: 3).

Policy Implications

The backlash against privatisation that led to the political polarisation in North Cyprus is consistent with the welfare losses and deprivations of the dismissed workers. However, it is plausible that the backlash against privatisation could have been due not only to the economic consequences but also to the fact that the privatisation did not coincide with the value system, social norms and sentiments of Turkish Cypriot society, thereby implying a lack of social governance (McKenzie et al., 2003: 220). Alternatively, it could reflect the readiness of the country to absorb SOE reforms (Kaur, 2004: 14) depending on how the privatisation was structured and who the owners would be? (Kikeri et al., 1994; Guriev and Megginson, 2005: 2; McKenzie, 2003: 220).

The findings of this chapter shed light not only on the earnings losses but also on the extent of the welfare losses due to the privatisation-related dismissals. Moreover, they indicate the possible reasons for the backlash against the privatisation which led to political polarisation. The insight into the factors stemming from both the earnings and welfare losses could prove useful to policy makers in designing privatisation programs, re-employment processes or compensation packages for dismissed workers. Furthermore, the analysis provides several observations about the social and political sensitivities involved in the process of privatisation and the potential of these sensitivities to halt all other reforms. It is important for policy makers to develop strategies for dealing with this, such as implementing social governance in the privatisation process which addresses the social values, traditions and sentiments of the society.

Today, there political polarisation or policy segregation is occurring in many parts of the world with regard to economic and social issues, such as discrimination, multiculturalism, religion, immigration, human rights, terrorism, civil war and nuclear armament policies. Perhaps the risk of polarisation may be reduced if, instead of avoiding controversial and pressing issues, more information about the current situation and the possible positive and negative effects of policies on different segments of the society is made available in the public debate.

References

Aslan, H. (2011). "Neo-liberal bakışın tahakkümü altında bir yeniden yapılandırma sürecinden geçen Kıbrıs Türk toplumunun siyasal iktisadına dair bazı tespitler", *Gaile*, 17.07.2011, (http://www.yeniduzen.com/detay.asp?a=32869).

Azam, J.P. (1994). "The unceratin distribution impact of structural adjustment in Sub Saharan Africa", In: R. Van Der Hoeven and F. Van Der Kraaij (eds.), *Structural Adjustment and Beyond in Sub Saharan Africa.* London and Porsmouth, NH: James Currey and Heinmann, 100-114.

Besim, M. and Jenkins, G.P. (2006). "Informal but not ınsignificant: Unregistered workers in North Cyprus", Queen's Economics Department Working Paper, 1058 (http://ssrn.com/abstract=897673).

Birdsall, N. and Nellis, J. (2002). *Winners and Losers: Assessing the Distributional Impacts of Privatization.* Center for Global Development *Working paper* no.6. Washington.

Boubakri, N. and Cosset, Jean-Claude (1998). "The financial and operating performance of newly privatised firms: Evidence from developing countries", *Journal of Finance,* 53:(3), 1081–1110.

Brownlee, K. (2013). "A human right against social deprivation", *The Philosophical Quarterly*, Forthcoming; Warwick School of Law Research Paper No. 2013/02. (http://ssrn.com/abstract=2212037, http://dx.doi.org/10.2139/ssrn.2212037).

Castañeda, G. (2004). *The Barcelonnettes: an Example of Network- Entrepreneurs in XIX Century Mexico. An Explanation Based on a Theory of Bounded Rational Choice with Social Embeddedness.* Vol. 8, in Departamento de Economía Aplicada, Document de treball No. 04/02. Universidad Autonama de Barcelona.

Dixita A.K. and Weibullc J.W. (2007). "Political polarization", *PNAS*, 104(18), 7351–7356.

Durlauf, S.N. (1999). "The Case 'against' social capital", *Focus*, 20(3), 1-5.

Esteban, J. and Schneider, G. (2008). “Polarization and conflict: Theoretical and empirical issues”, *Journal of Peace Research*, 45(2), 131–141.

Han, G.S. and Phillips, H. (2008). “Downsized costs of privatisation in the era of restructuring: Experiences of “voluntary” retirement’, The Australian Sociological Association (TASA) Proceedings.

Granovetter, M. (1985). “Economic action, social structure, and embeddedness”, *American Journal of Sociology*, 91(3), 481–510.

Gupta, S., Schiller, C. and Ma, H. (1999). “Privatization, social impact, and social safety nets”, IMF Working paper WP/99/68. Washington: International Monetary Fund.

Güven, F. (1984). ‘74 Öncesi ve Sonrası Kıbrıs Ekonomisi (Cyprus economy: pre and post-74)’. Master thesis. İstanbul University, Istanbul.

Güven-Lisaniler, F. and Uğural, S. (2010). ‘Public-private wage determinants and wage gap in North Cyprus’, paper presented at the Eurasia Business and Economics Society Annual Istanbul Conference, Istanbul.

İsmail, S. (2001). *TC-KKTC İkili Anlaşma Protokol ve Sözleşmeleri (TR-TRNC Bilateral Protocol and Agreements)*. İstanbul: Aha Publications.

Kabaş, T. (2006). ‘A. Sen’in Kapasite Yaklaşımına Göre Türkiye’de Yoksulluğun Boyutları Extent of poverty in Turkey and Sen’s capability approach)’ *Ekonomik Yaklaşım,* 17(60-61), 77-92.

Keser, U. (2012). ‘Federation of Cypriot Turkish Associations-Nacak Collaboration and its economical development efforts in history Cypriot Turkish Struggle’, *History Studies*, 4/1, 299-333.

Keefer, P. and Knack, S. (2002). ‘Polarization, politics and property rights: Links between inequality and growth*’, Public Choice,* 111, 127–154.

Khan. I.A. (2003). “Impact of privatisation on employment and output in Pakistan”, *The Pakistan Development Review,* 42(4), 513–536.

Kikeri, S. (1997). “Privatization and labor: What happens to workers when governments Divest?”, *World Bank Technical Paper*, 396. Washington DC: The World Bank.

McKenzie, D., Mookherjee, D., Castañeda, G. and Saavedra, J. (2003) ‘The distributive impact of privatization in Latin America: Evidence from four countries, *Economía*, 3(2): 161-233.

Megginson, W.L. and Netter, J.M. (2001). "From state to market: A survey of empirical studies on privatization", *Journal of Economic Literature*, 39(2): 321-389.

Mehmet, Ö. and Yorucu, V. (2008). "Explosive construction in a micro-state: environmental limit and the Bon curve: Evidence from North Cyprus", *Construction Management and Economics*, 26: 79–88.

Parliamentary Minutes Magazine (1997, December 15). TRNC, 3th Congress: 1616-1689.

Privatisation Law (PL) (2012). No. 24/2012 (http://www.mahkemeler.net).

Rodrik, D. (1993). 'The positive economics of policy reform", *The American Economic Review*, 83(2), 356-361.

Rosie, A. (1993). '"He's a liar, I'm afraid": truth and lies in a narrative account', *Sociology* 27(1), 144-152.

Turkish Embassy Nicosia (2009). '2009-2012 Kamunun Etkinliğinin ve Özel Sektörün Rekabet Gücünün Artırılması Programı (Program for increasing Public sector efficiency and Private sector competitiveness)'. (http://www.yhb.gov.tr).

Sen, A. (2004). *Özgürlükle Kalkınma (Development as Freedom)*. 2st edn. İstanbul: Ayrıntı.

Sen, A. (2005). "Development as capability expansion", In: S. Fukuda-Parr and A.K.S. Kumar, (eds.), *Readings in Human Development*. Oxford: Oxford University Press, 3-16.

Taylor, S. and Tilley, N. (1998). "Asking questions in social research: theory and method", in D. Field and S. Taylor (eds.), *Sociological Perspectives on Health, Illness and Health Care*. Oxford: Blackwell Science, 39-57.

TRNC State Planning Organization (SPOa) (2013). Households Employment Survey, 2010 (http://www.devplan.org/Isgucu/2010.pdf).
TRNC State Planning Organization (SPO) (1996). 1997 Development Program (Draft): Third 5 Year Development Plan (1993-1997). Nicosia: SPO.

Torenvlied, R. and Klein, Haarhuis C.M. (2008). 'Polarization and Policy Reform: Anti-Corruption Policymaking in Sub-Saharan Africa', *Journal of Peace Research*, 45(2), 223-240.Yorucu, V. and Keleş, R. (2007). "The construction boom and environmental protection in Northern Cyprus as a consequence of the Annan Plan", *Construction Management and Economics*, 25, 77–86.

Table 14A. Education by Gender

Gender	Education Level	Frequency	Percent
Female	Primary	6	3.5
	Junior high school	4	2.4
	High school	104	61.2
	College	8	4.7
	University	42	24.7
	Graduate	6	3.5
	Total	170	100.0
Male	Primary	9	10.2
	Junior high school	13	14.8
	High school	49	55.7
	College	1	1.1
	University	14	15.9
	Graduate	2	2.3
	Total	88	100.0

Source: CTA Union

Notes

Introduction

[i] The Stolper-Samuelson theorem states that international trade necessarily lowers the real wage of the scarce factor expressed in terms of any good.

[ii] The Heckscher-Ohlin-Samuelson model attempts to explain the composition of trade between countries and the implications of trade for income distribution within the countries. It states that an increase in the relative price of a good increases the real wage of the factor used intensively in producing that good, and lowers the real wage of the other factor.

[iii] The imputed output approach is developed by Lloyd and Schweinberger (1997) as a direct analysis of the link between trade and the household distribution of income.

Chapter 2

[iv]See, for instance, Galbraith (2002), Atkinson and Piketty (2006) and Milanovic (2010).

[v] Countries which have resisted such cuts and have even increased such spending have not experienced increases in inequality.

[vi] It should be noted that the so-called rolling back of the state in fact calls for strong state intervention to push through not only policy reforms but also – as we will argue later – to change institutions in ways that forcibly increase market flexibility. The approach is not quite a laissez-faire on of classical liberalism, but an active reformist state of neoliberalism.

[vii] For instance, when Mario Monti, the Italian Prime Minister, implemented labor market reforms, he declared that "It's a labour market reform for growth and employment" (April 4, 2012), and said that a key aim would be to eliminate the "dualism" of Italy's current labor market. Angela Merkel, the German prime minister, also declared in mid-May 2012 that "to promote growth … [one] … does not necessarily have to spend money", but "to reduce unemployment through structural reform" through measures "to improve labour market flexibility."

[viii]The Indian government has recently expressed support for employment flexibility. Its 2012-13 *Economic Survey* states that "it may be the stringent protection that is afforded by the existing regulations that is responsible for both the paucity of good jobs as well as inadequate protection that most workers have … It is, therefore, imperative that consensus building on labour market reforms should start soon … If indeed rigid labour laws are determined to be the key constraining factor in the creation of productive jobs, win-win reforms are easily available." (Government of India, 2013).

[ix] This law, called "Accord National Interprofessionnel" (ANI) has been adopted by the French Parliament on April 9th, 2013. It reproduces an agreement signed on January 11th, 2013, by an employers' union (MEDEF, representing mostly the firms listed on the French stock market) and three minor employees' unions (CFDT, CFTC and CFE-CGC). It will increase both external numerical flexibility (by allowing employers to fire employees much more easily) and internal flexibility (people will not be allowed to refuse a change in their workplace or employees will be allowed to choose when an employee works and is paid, and does not work and consequently does not get paid). On January 12th, 2013, the minster of industrial relations Michel Sapin has declared that in this agreement "one can find the methods and the tools for employment, fighting unemployment, and invert the unemployment curve".

[x] This form of flexibility can be distinguished from three other forms of it, that is: wage flexibility, functional flexibility, and internal numerical flexibility (see Atkinson, 1984). Wage flexibility (sometimes also called "financial" flexibility) refers to the degree to which wages can adapt to the level of economic activity and the differences between labor supply and labor demand. Functional flexibility (or "organizational" flexibility) refers to how easy it is to transfer employees to various tasks within the firm. Internal numerical flexibility (or "working time" flexibility) consists in adjusting working hours or schedules of employees already hired by firm. While calls for increasing wage flexibility, for instance by reducing the power of unions, is a staple of the free market approach, the other are usually not stressed in the recent discussion on structural reforms of changes in employment protection legislation

[xi]Although there is no consensus on what is precisely meant by the neoclassical approach, several distinct but related definitions are available (see Dutt, 2014). Some define it in epistemological terms, requiring that behavior and outcomes be explained in terms of individual optimization. Others define it in terms of ontology, that individuals are self-interested, materialistic and insatiable (sometimes referred to as the *homo economicus*), and that real economies are comprised of (more or less) smoothly functioning markets which are cleared by variations in prices so that all resources are fully utilized, in which there are no "distortions" such as price setting firms with market power, externalities and asymmetries in information and where the

future is knowable with certainty or in terms of objective probabilities. Some stress that the normative goal of societies is to attain efficient outcomes, in which no individuals can be made better off without making others worse, all according to their reckoning in which other considerations such as fairness and distributive justice are irrelevant. Finally some stress that the appropriate policy for governments to follow is to interfere as little as possible with the functioning of free markets, apart from defending the realm and maintaining law and order. These definitions are not the same, since one can follow the optimizing approach and yet show that markets are inefficient because of a myriad of market failures and government intervention is required not only to overcome such inefficiencies but also for promoting fairness - see Stiglitz (2012) for a recent analysis which follows a neoclassical optimizing approach but stresses importance of market failures and fairness and recommends an activist state. However, there is also a certain consistency between them, since the first three definitions, using the so-called fundamental theorem of welfare economics – according to which, under certain conditions, perfectly competitive decentralized outcomes are efficient – are taken to justify the final definition about the minimalist state. For our purposes we can interpret the neoclassical approach to encompass the first two definitions just mentioned, and consider an economy in which there are no market distortions, in which all agents maximize their utility or profits, and in which there is perfect information about the economy, including the future, apart from random events that have objectively-given probability distributions.

[xii] See Dutt (2015) for a fuller discussion of these issues.

[xiii] Bartlett (1989, p. 30), for instance, presents a rare attempt to use the optimizing approach to explore power in economics using a generalization of the definition in contexts in which there is imperfect information, organizations involving such rules such as the employment relation, and endogenous preferences which can be influenced by others.

[xiv] This is also stressed by Solow (1990) from a neoclassical perspective.

[xv] We should point out that, regarding the possible negative effects of productivity of job security, we do not take EPL to imply that workers cannot be fired under any conditions, but the rapidity at which adjustments can be unilaterally made by firms is restricted. Such restrictions do not prevent workers who perform poorly from being dismissed, but prevent such dismissal on unsubstantiated whims of employers, and allow for a fair review process.

[xvi] The discussion of the model draws on the analysis of Dutt, Charles and Lang (2014).

[xvii] If the relative wage and relative labor requirements are constant it does not matter

which labor costs are taken into account as a basis for price setting. When any of these are allowed to change, however, the relevant labor cost will have an important role to play.

[xviii] This extends the result of Dutt (1984) and Rowthorn (1981) which dealt only with short-term labor to the case of both short- and long-term labor.

[xix] See also Bhattacharjea (2006) for an assessment of these and other empirical studies on employment legislation in India.

Chapter 3

[xx] http://www.bloomberg.com/news/2013-01-14/un-s-figueres-says-self-interest-must-drive-climate-laws.html. [cited May 8, 2013]

[xxi]Cited by Mark Hertsgaard (2011). *Hot: Living Through the Next Fifty on Earth.* Boston: Houghton Mifflin Harcourt, p. 1.

Chapter 5

[xxii]Early documentation of these processes appeared in Thomas (1996).

[xxiii]See Standing (1999), pp. 62-73. 'Globalisation has intensified pressure on governments to scale back on labour rights and welfare, because these are presentable as costs eroding a country's capacity to compete in tradables and encouraging portfolio and direct foreign investment to shift to where such costs and prospective costs are lower' (68).

[xxiv]See, for instance, Charney (1991).

[xxv]See Koivusalo and Ollila (1997).

[xxvi] I give an account with more constraints on public reason than in the account of Habermas (xxxx) but fewer constraints than in the account of Rawls (1999). Fred d'Agostino (xxxx) gives a very useful overview of different approaches to public reason.

xxvii Rawls (1999) says that a state is well-ordered when there is a publicly shared conception of justice to which, it is thought, the structure and functioning of state and society ought to conform (p. 72).

[xxviii] Here I am stressing something that Rawls mentions but does not stress in The Law of Peoples. What Rawls stresses is that officials must believe that a common good conception of justice is at work in such states, and 'this belief must be demonstrated by a willingness to defend publicly the state's injunctions as justified by law' (61).

[xxix] 'It is not the case that the interests of some are arbitrarily privileged, while the interests of others do for naught.' What Rawls stresses about this is the broader point that 'a hierarchical society's system of law [must] must be such as to impose moral duties and obligations on all persons within its territory.' (61)

[xxx] In Roger Paden's (1997) reconstruction of Rawlsian international procedures, the same problem will arise. According to Paden, all societies seek the same good, namely protection of their just institutions. But weak aggregators would invoke jus this end to justify their refusal to reduce workforce segmentation unless they received extensive international support, and rich aggregators would invoke this good as a reason for refusing to provide such support.

[xxxi] Rawls's (1971) second principle is: 'Social and economic inequalities are to be arranged so that (a) they are to be of the greatest benefit of the least-advantaged members of society, consistent with the just savings principle (the difference principle); (b) offices and positions must be open to everyone under conditions of fair equality of opportunity' (p. 302).

Chapter 6

[xxxii] Comments on earlier drafts of this paper by Myron Frankman, B.N. Ghosh, Parvesh K. Chopra, are gratefully acknowledged with the usual disclaimer that the author alone is responsible for all opinions and interpretations.

[xxxiii] In algebraic notations, and following Piketty (2014), $r > g$, where r = rate of return on physical capital and g = growth rate, with the understanding that r increasingly represents speculative capital gains realized on the stock market. For an early analysis and discussion, see Mehmet (1999): 17-32.

[xxxiv] Center-Periphery relationship also applies to the North American Native population. These first peoples have been pushed onto "reserves" as a result of unequal treaties in the 19th century and tribal and indigenous lands and resources have been expropriated by European settlers and their descendents who have become the wealthiest people on earth.

[xxxv] Some labor mobility, of course, is permitted in the global labor market, either as selective migration [e.g. in Canada or the EU] to select the most qualified potential migrants, or, for humanitarian reasons [e.g. refugee or family reunification cases], but these flows are too inadequate.

[xxxvi] Literature on Global Public Goods is growing in tandem with cross-boundary problems such as global warming, international pollution, health and safety, etc., cases where national jurisdictions and private markets fail [cf. Barrett, 2007].

[xxxvii] The idea of taxing currency transactions, as in the Tobin Tax [http://www.bbc.co.uk/news/business-15555812], is a logical step, endorsed by many key actors, but it should be expanded and linked to autonomous international development as proposed in this paper. More recently, Thomas Piketty has raised the issue of global capital taxation, as noted above. At a minimum, or as a first step, funds transferred to tax-havens by the super-rich to avoid home-country taxation might be subjected to international tax.

Chapter 7

[xxxviii] This is a revised paper presented at a Panel: "The Global Impact of the Financial Crisis: Social and Political Impacts", XXII World Congress of Political Science, The International Political Science Association, 8-12 July 2012, Madrid, Spain. The authors would like to thank former Shop Stewart Jens Crumlin and Professor Henning Jørgensen for useful comments.

Chapter 8

[xxxix] The World Bank stated that the first wave of globalisation began in 1870 and ended at the beginning of World War I in 1914. It was characterized by a reduction in trade barriers and improvement in transportation technologies, which resulted in major migration of about 10% of the world's population. The next wave occurred from 1950 to 1980 during which multiple trade agreements occurred between developed nations which left out the developing world. The final (and current) wave of globalisation (beginning 1980) in contrast has been characterized by the willingness of developed nations to remove trade barriers in order to attract foreign capital.

[xl] The original model was based on two countries, and had two commodities that could be produced. Since there are two (homogeneous) factors of production this model is sometimes called the "2×2×2 model", assuming that the only difference between countries was the relative abundances of labor and capital. It has *variable factor proportions* between countries: Highly developed countries have a comparatively high ratio of capital to labor in relation to developing countries. This

makes the developed country capital-abundant relative to the developing nation, and the developing nation labor-abundant in relation to the developed country. With this single difference, Ohlin was able to discuss the new mechanism of comparative advantage, using just two goods and two technologies to produce them. (One technology would be a capital intensive industry, the other a labor intensive business. The model has been extended since the 1930s by many economists. These developments did not change the fundamental role of variable factor proportions in driving international trade, but added to the model various real-world considerations (such as tariffs) in the hopes of increasing the model's predictive power, or as a mathematical way of discussing macroeconomic policy options. Notable contributions came from Paul Samuelson, Ronald Jones, and Jaroslav Vanek, so that variations of the model are sometimes called the Heckscher-Ohlin-Samuelson model or the Heckscher-Ohlin-Vanek model in the neo-classical economics.

[xli] Wassily W. Leontief in 1954 did an econometric test of the H–O model found that the US, despite having a relative abundance of capital, tended to export labor intensive goods and import capital intensive goods. This problem became known as the Leontief paradox.

[xlii] Linder hypothesis was proposed by Staffan Burenstam Linder in 1961 as a solution to Leontief paradox and it outlines the international trade patterns as: the more similar demand structures of countries, the more they trade with one another.

[xliii] This definition excludes the dynamics of income from employment, and the demography and dynamics of workplaces (entrepreneurial job-creating and job-destroying activity).

[xliv] Structural equation modelling is also a multivariate technique combining aspects of multiple regression and factor analysis to estimate simultaneously a series of interrelated dependence relationships. Such models include one or more linear regression equations that describe how the endogenous constructs depend upon the exogenous constructs; their coefficients are called path coefficients. It is a powerful statistical approach in that it combines the measurement model and the structural equation model into a simultaneous statistical analysis. It provides parameters estimates of the direct and indirect association between observed variables and tests how well a model explains covariance in the data.

[xlv] In a structural equation modelling analysis, there are two models called as inner model (structural model) and outer model (measurement model). The inner model describes the relationships between the latent variables of model. The path coefficients of inner model are called as inner coefficients. The outer model illustrates the relationships between the latent variables and their indicators (manifest variables). The path coefficients of outer model are called as outer coefficients (weights and loadings).

[xlvi] An exogenous variable is a variable that is not caused by another variable in the model. Usually this variable causes one or more variables in the model.

[xlvii] An endogenous variable is a variable that is caused by one or more variable in the model. Note that an endogenous variable may also cause another endogenous variable in the model.

[xlviii] Structural parameter or coefficient is a measure of the amount of change in the effect variable expected given a one unit change in the causal variable and no change in any other variable. Although like a regression coefficient this coefficient may not be estimable by multiple regression.

Chapter 14

[xlix] Due to political factors which fall outside the scope of this paper, North Cyprus (Turkish Republic of Northern Cyprus) is not recognised politically by other countries except for Turkey, and is subject to an economic embargo imposed by the internationally recognised Republic of Cyprus controlled by Greek Cypriots.

[l] See “28 Ocak Mitingi” (Mass meeting on 28 January), *Gaile*, 6 February 2012, and K-Pet neden satılıyor? (Why is Cyprus Turkish Petoleum (K-Pet) being sold out?), *Gündem Kıbrıs,* 11 November 2011.

[li] In 1974, there was a military coup against the government of the Republic of Cyprus. Turkey, as a guarantor nation, fearing that the coup would be followed by a declaration of *enosis* and attacks on Turkish Cypriots, intervened. About 40% of the territory of the island had been captured by the time a cease-fire was arranged. *Enosis* had been thwarted, but in order to guarantee the safety of the Greek and Turkish Cypriots, the two sides agreed to population exchanges de facto dividing the island into north and south, where the Greek Cypriots would live in the south and the Turkish Cypriots in the north.

[lii] See also Ahmet Tolgay, “Özelleş tirmenin kısa tarihi…” (A brief history of privatisation…), *Kıbrıs Gazetesi*, 25 November. 2011; “Endüstri mirasımız ‘kepçe’ darbeleriyle çöktü” (Our industrial heritage has been crashed down by a ‘dipper’).

[liii] See KTHY’nin kuruluş yıldönümü: kapatıldığı günü ve kapatanları unutmayacağız” (Anniversary of the establishment of CTA: We never forget the day of liquidation and those responsible for it), *Ada Basını,* 4 December 2012 and “Erken seçim şart oldu” (Early elections became a must)”, *Haberdar,* 20 June 2011.

[liv] See Okan Şafaklı, “Özelleştirmeye karşı olmaya saygı duyarım da, Özelleştirme

Yasası'na karşı olmak..." (I respect being against privatisation but not being against privatisation law...), *Star Kıbrıs*, 19 March 2012 and Vedat Yorucu, "Özelleştirme ama nasıl?" (Privatisation, but how?), *Kıbrıs Son Dakika*, 9 October 2010, Ünal Akifler "Şimdi ufalma ve acı ilaç zamanı" (It is time for contraction and swallowing the bitter pill), *Haber Kıbrıs*, 1 April 2011.

[lv] See "KKTC'de olaylı miting" (Eventful meeting in TRNC), *Milliyet*, 02 March 2011. "KKTC mitinge hazırlanıyor" (TRNC gets ready for mass meeting), *Dünya Bülteni*, 01 March 2011. "Mitinge binlerce kişi katıldı" (Thousands of people attended the meeting), *Akşam*, 02 March 2011.

[lvi] See Vedat Yorucu, "Önce Özelleştirme Yasası sonra uygulama: hükümete çağrı" (First privatisation law, then implementation of the program: an appeal to the government), *Yenidüzen*, 16 October 2010, Ünal Akifler "Şimdi ufalma ve acı ilaç zamanı" (It is time for contraction and to swallow the bitter pill), *Haber Kıbrıs*, 1 April 2011.

[lvii] Privatisation Law – third chapter: rules regarding personnel: Article 27. Redundancy payment rights, Article 28. Incentives for re-employment after privatisation, Article 29. Employment incentives in public sector institutions and organisations as well as in public sector institutions and organisations established under specific laws, Article 30. Re-employment opportunities for other dismissed public personnel and workers due to privatisation.

[lviii] Amartya Sen's capability approach provides the underlying conceptual framework for the World Bank in producing the Human Development Index to rank countries in terms of their development levels. According to this approach, the limitations or enhancements of the individual's 'capabilities' (beings and doings, i.e. the functionings a person is able to achieve) diminish or increase his/her welfare (Sen, 1992: 6 in Kabaş, 2006).

Index

www.ingramcontent.com/pod-product-compliance
Ingram Content Group UK Ltd.
Pitfield, Milton Keynes, MK11 3LW, UK
UKHW020133290926
15471UKWH00003B/468

9 781842 902509